NINETEENTH CENTURY STARS

Edited by
Robert L. Tiemann
and Mark Rucker

For The Society for
American Baseball Research

Nineteenth-Century Stars
Table of Contents

NINETEENTH-CENTURY STARS (ISBN 0-910137-35-8). Published by The Society for American Baseball Research, Inc., P.O. Box 10033, Kansas City, Mo. 64111. Postage paid at Manhattan, KS. Copyright © 1989 Society for American Baseball Research, Inc. All rights reserved. Reproduction in whole or in part without written permission is prohibited. Printed by Ag Press, Manhattan, KS.

Photo Credits

Bruce Foster: 74
Barry Halper: 66
Harper's Weekly: Front cover
Library of Congress: Back cover
Randy Linthurst: 126
Lou Lipset: 14, 22, 26, 27,38, 47, 53, 57, 71, 72, 75, 76, 87, 88, 93, 95, 98, 105, 107, 109, 113, 129, 132, 134, 138
Missouri Historical Society: 86, 120
National Baseball Library: Inside front cover, 8, 13, 18, 19, 23, 31, 33, 34, 36, 37, 39, 40, 46, 48, 49, 58, 59, 61, 63, 64, 65, 67, 70, 73, 79, 80, 89, 90, 91, 94, 96, 99, 108, 114, 115, 116, 117, 118, 119, 123, 125, 131, 133, 137
New York Library: 10, 12, 28, 29, 44, 50, 51, 68, 82, 83, 111, 122
Joseph Overfield: 54
Mark Rucker: Inside back cover, 7, 11, 15, 17, 20, 21, 25, 32, 35, 41, 42, 43, 45, 52, 55, 60, 62, 69, 77, 78, 84, 85, 92, 97, 101, 102, 103, 104, 106, 110, 112, 120, 121, 122, 124, 127, 128, 136, 139, 140, 141, 142
Frank Steele: 9
John Thorn: 16, 24, 30, 56, 100, 130, 135

INTRODUCTION

By Robert L. Tiemann

When baseball evolved in the nineteenth century from a child's game to adult social recreation to professional sport, the very best players emerged into the public consciousness to become America's first sports heroes. More than three dozen of these long-ago stars have been enshrined in baseball's Hall of Fame, but scores of other outstanding pre-1900 players have fallen into obscurity. With this book, the Society for American Baseball Research, through the efforts of its committee on the 19th century, attempts to bring some forgotten stars back into the limelight. By going beyond the published statistics, SABR authors have tried to achieve greater insight into the careers and lives of these men and into the nature of baseball in their time.

You'll find some real characters in these pages. There were "glory boys," fan favorites and boo-targets. There were alcohol abusers, rule-breakers and game-fixers, team jumpers and company men.

And there were innovators. The game these men played was constantly changing — in its rules, its strategies, its tactics. The first known box score from 1845 shows only eight players to a side, but nine were used a year later. Games were initially won when one team reached 21 aces (runs) and led after even innings, nine innings not being adopted until 1857. A batted ball caught on the first bounce put the batter out through 1863, and the "foul bound out" remained on the books until 1885. Pitching resembled horseshoes, soft and underhand, until Jim Creighton took the baseball world by storm with fast underhanded pitching in 1859. Overhand deliveries were not allowed until 1884. Teams relied on one pitcher as much as possible until Chicago's Larry Corcoran and Fred Goldsmith were formed into the first pitching rotation in 1880. Gloves and catcher's masks were unknown until the mid-1870s, and veterans like Bid McPhee disdained the use of a glove until well into the 1890s.

As pitchers like Boston's Jim Whitney and Charlie Buffinton began to dominate and fielders like Cleveland's Fred Dunlap and Jack Glasscock became more expert, scoring fell off dramatically by the mid-'80s. So the pitcher's movements were restricted greatly in 1887, and the pitching distance was increased in 1893, fueling a resurgence in scoring in the '90s. That last decade of the century was dominated by great teams and managers like Frank Selee's Boston Beaneaters and Ned Hanlon's Baltimore Orioles, teams that excelled at aggressive baserunning and offensive teamwork.

The earliest known admission charge (50 cents) for a ballgame was imposed in 1858, and the first enclosed commercial ballpark was built in 1862. The first professional league, awarding the first pennant, was formed in 1871. "Minor" leagues appeared as early as 1877, and two and even three "Major" leagues competed for fans and players in the 1880s. Playing schedules expanded to six games a week, and top salaries rose from below $2000 in 1869 to near $5000 in just over twenty years. The establishment of a monopoly by the National League in 1892 and depression times during that decade led to a significant drop in salaries and a shrinking of the minor leagues. At the turn of the century, one minor league, the Western League, changed its name to the American League and broke the National League's monopoly, leading to new levels of prosperity. At the same time, the adoption of the foul strike rule altered the scoring balance again. All of these changes were played out on the field every day by the players.

This project was conceived by SABR 19th Century committee chairmen Mark Rucker and John Thorn several years ago. Although they have turned the committee chairmanship over to Bob Tiemann, they remained active in this project, along with many others. Biographies have been submitted by thirty-one SABR members with Joseph M. Overfield leading the way with twenty-five biographies. The sketches were reviewed for accuracy by Bob Tiemann, Bob Davids, Vern Luse, and Bob McConnell. Richard Puff, Len Levin and Paul Adomites did the copy-editing. Mark Rucker developed the book design and selected the photographs. Bob Tiemann put together the statistics. Paul Adomites, SABR Publications Director, coordinated this multi-pronged effort.

From the first real shortstop, Dickey Pearce, and the first professional player, Jim Creighton, to turn-of-the-century standouts like George Davis and Fred Tenney, 136 biographical sketches of players and managers are included here. No particular criterion was used in selecting the players included, except that Hall-of-Fame members are excluded, and despite special efforts to get sketches of certain men, many worthy players remain absent from these pages.

Come meet the men who were there at the beginning, as baseball itself was taking shape. The Society for American Baseball Research is pleased to submit to you this work on "Nineteenth Century Stars."

A Note On The Statistics

The statistics have been added to supplement the biographies in the text. However, they are not purported to be complete, official, or definitive. Unlike the biographical section, which was some years in the making, the tables have been put together quickly and suffer from some shortcomings.

Nineteenth-century statistics varied tremendously — from the care and completeness of their compilation, to the statistical methods used in figuring averages, and even to the choice of statistics chosen for publication. In many cases, even the basic statistics given in this section were unavailable. And in many more cases, the numbers published in different sources were different. The figures presented here are taken from wherever they could be found in a brief period of research with little or no effort being made to resolve the conflicts among sources. As a result, the numbers in this section often differ slightly from the statistics quoted by the authors of the individual biographies.

In addition to our panel of authors, several SABR members provided additional information upon request. They included Vern Luse, Ray Nemec, Bob Davids, Bob Hoie, Joel Franks, and John Thorn. Vern Luse and Ray Nemec were especially generous with their time and research. The following source materials were used as well: Baseball guides by DeWitt, Beadle, Spalding, Reach, and *Sporting Life*, *The Baseball Encyclopedia* by Macmillan, *Daguerreotypes* by Paul MacFarlane and *The Sporting News*, the Stagno Collection of National Association box scores and Michael Stagno's National Association batting statistics, *Minor League Stars* Vol. 1 & II by SABR, *Sporting Life*, *The Sporting News*, the New York *Mercury*, the New York *Clipper*, the St. Louis *Globe-Democrat*, and the editor's past baseball research notebooks.

The statistics included are:

G - Games played (if followed by the symbol #, the batting and fielding statistics are incomplete for the season)

R - Runs scored

H - Hits

BA - Batting Average - These have been adjusted for the pre-1877 era to remove bases on balls from the at bats total. However, for 1887 bases on balls are counted as hits in these figures.

SA - Slugging Average - Bases on balls are counted as singles for 1887 only.

POS - Position(s) played - The positions listed are those at which that a player started at least 10% of his games, with a maximum of three positions listed.

E - Fielding Errors - These do not count passed balls, wild pitches, or bases on balls where it was possible to delete those from the published statistics.

FA - Fielding Average - If followed by the symbol #, the errors and fielding average are for only the first position listed, otherwise the fielding statistics are for all positions listed. In some cases, they are for all positions played during the season.

GP - Games Pitched - Includes both starting and relief appearances. If followed by the symbol #, the pitching statistics for the season are incomplete.

W-L, R, H - Games Won and Lost, runs and hits allowed as a pitcher. These figures are only approximate.

NOTE: For some years in the 1860's, the number of outs made by a batter-runner and the number of total bases made on hits are also given in parentheses. In a few cases, these figures are given as averages per game played.

ROBERT EDWARD ADDY
(The Magnet)

Born: 1838, Rochester, N.Y.
Died: April 10, 1910, Pocatello, Idaho
BL TL 5-8, 160

The facts about Robert Addy's birth and death are fuzzy. Both the Turkin/Thompson and the Macmillan encyclopedias indicate he was born in Rochester, N.Y., in 1838 and that he died in Pocatello, Idaho, on April 10, 1910. A 1965 letter from Addy's daughter, Mrs. Hugh Ivey, to the late Lee Allen is in agreement on the place and year of birth (although she calls it "about" 1838), but says he died April 9, not April 10. A letter in the Addy file in Cooperstown quotes an 1874 pamphlet written by George Wright which states that Addy was born in Canada. A brief obituary in the 1911 Spalding *Guide* indicates that he died on April 10, 1910, in his 67th year, which would mean he was born in either 1842 or 1843.

The uncertainties of his vital statistics aside, Addy moved to Chicago when he was quite young and at a young age he became adept at the new sport of baseball. Late in 1865, he joined the Forest City Club of Rockford. The star pitcher of the Forest Cities, who played their first match games in 1866, was future Hall of Famer and sporting goods magnate Albert G. Spalding. The team at first was strictly amateur, but toward the end of the decade it began the practice of divvying up the gate receipts among the players, after expenses, thus becoming semiprofessional. One account (*Spink Sport Stories*, Vol. #3,

pg. 85) says Addy's cut after an 1870 tour of the United States and Canada came to $15.25.

In 1871, Addy and the Rockford nine became members of baseball's first professional league, the National Association. Among his teammates that year was future Hall of Famer Adrian Anson. Addy played second base and shortstop and batted .254, while third baseman Anson batted .352. The season was a disaster for the Forest Cities, and their 6-21 record and last-place finish resulted in the disbanding of the team. In his 1900 autobiography, *A Ballplayers Career*, Anson wrote of Addy: "He was one of the best of the lot, was a good, hard, hustling ballplayer, a good base runner and a hard hitter. He was honest as the day is long. He was an odd sort of genius and quit the game because he thought he could do better at something else."

Addy did, indeed, leave the game in 1872, but it was to be several years before he quit for good. In 1873, he returned to play with Boston and Philadelphia and batted .326, while playing in both the infield and outfield. He switched to the Hartfords in 1874 and batted .264, and then in 1875 — the last year of the Association — he batted .263 for the Philadelphia Athletics. In 1876, the maiden year of the National League, he rejoined his old

teammates of Rockford days, Spalding and Anson, on the Chicago White Sox. The team made a shambles of the first pennant race by finishing first with a 52-14 record. As these were pre-reserve rule times, Addy moved to Cincinnati for the 1877 season and experienced a precipitous drop from first place to the cellar as the Reds posted a pathetic 15-42 record. A quarter of the way through the season, outfielder Addy became captain Addy, succeeding Lip Pike. At the end of the season, in which his managerial record had been 5-19, he was given $100 and his walking papers.

It was published in one Cincinnati newspaper that Addy was fired as much for his imbibing as for his poor record. The Cincinnati *Enquirer* made an oblique reference to this problem in a story about a skating rink venture of Addy's in Chicago saying, "Bob stands up better on ice than he does on land."

After the rink project failed (he had tried to popularize baseball on ice), Addy went to California and became manager of a tin shop. In 1888 or thereabouts, he moved to Evanston, Wyoming, and then in 1890 to Pocatello, Idaho, where he operated a hardware store for 20 years. He died there from heart disease.

— Joseph M. Overfield

			G	R	H	BA	SA	POS	E	FA	GP	W-L	R	H
1866	Forest City of Rockford							2b						
1867	Forest City													
1868	Forest City		15	70	(43 outs)			c						
1869	Forest City		23		124	(205 TB)								
1870	Forest City		55		200	(277 TB)		2b						
1871	Forest City	NA	25	30	32	.274	.325	2b-ss	49	.767				
1873	Phila-Boston	NA	41	49	72	.355	.419	rf-2b	22	.780				
1874	Hartford	NA	50	25	50	.236	.297	2b	71	.797				
1875	Philadelphia	NA	69	59	78	.256	.315	rf	35	.768				
1876	Chicago	NL	33	36	40	.282	.324	of	13	.800				
1877	Cincinnati	NL	57	27	68	.278	.310	of	22	.805				

CHARLES BUSTED BALDWIN
(Lady)

Born: April 10, 1859, Ormel, N.Y.
Died: March 7, 1937, Hastings, Mich.
BL TL 5-11 170

The baseball life of Charles Baldwin is a tale of two seasons and a curious nickname.

With a modest record of 73-41 in six major league seasons (three of which were mere cups of coffee), the left-handed Baldwin probably would not merit inclusion here were it not for his remarkable year with Detroit (NL) in 1886 and his feat of winning 4 games in the post-season series between Detroit and the St. Louis Browns in 1887. And then there was his nickname, "Lady."

Baldwin was born in Ormel, N.Y., a tiny hamlet about 60 miles southeast of Buffalo. When he was 18, his family moved to Hastings, Mich., where he learned the rudiments of the game. He started professionally with Grand Rapids (Northwest League) in 1883 before joining Milwaukee of the same circuit the next season. In 1884, he also appeared in seven games with Milwaukee in the ill-fated Union Association. He was a mature 26 when midway through the 1885 season he joined the Detroit Wolverines (NL) and teamed up with Charley Bennett, who was one of the great catchers of the day. Baldwin's 1885 record was an unprepossessing 11-9, but his ERA was a dazzling 1.86.

The failure of the 1886 Detroits to win the pennant was not the fault of Lady Baldwin. He won 11 of his first 12 starts; he pitched one 1-hitter, five 2-hitters and five 3-hitters, and had 7 shutouts, which was best in the league. He started 56 games and completed 55, hurled 487 innings, struck out 323 and wound up with a 42-13 (.764) record and an ERA of 2.24.

The Wolverines followed their second-place finish in 1886 with a pennant in 1887, but it was a bittersweet year for Baldwin. His arm, overworked in 1886, never was at full strength. Additionally, he had trouble adjusting to the new rule requiring the pitcher to keep one foot on the back line of the box and take only one step in delivering the ball. He was so bad that on July 27 he was sent home without pay. (His salary was a princely $3,200.) Baldwin improved after rejoining the team in August, winning 7 of his last 8 games. In the 15-game challenge series between Detroit and the St. Louis Browns (AA), precursor of the World Series, Baldwin won 4 of 5 starts, including the clinching game, and held the Browns to a feeble .155 batting mark.

As far as major league stardom is concerned, that was it for Baldwin. His arm dead, he pitched a few games for Detroit in 1888 and for Brooklyn (NL) and Buffalo (PL) in 1890 before retiring.

The nickname? The mystery is not how he acquired it, but how he managed to survive in baseball as long as he did while bearing such a handle. He earned the name not because he was effeminate, but because he behaved the way ladies were supposed to behave: he did not smoke, swear or imbibe. In an interview he gave in 1934 when he was 74, he said he had yet to taste alcohol or tobacco.

After retiring from the diamond, Baldwin operated a farm in Hastings, Mich., until 1910 when he sold out and moved into town. In 1919, he started a real estate business at which he enjoyed great success. In 1937, the man they called Lady died in Hastings. He was 77.

— Joseph M. Overfield

			G	R	H	BA	SA	POS	E	FA	GP	W-L	R	H
1884	Milwaukee	NWL	34	21	35	.273	.343	p-of			21	9-10	100	141
	Milwaukee	UA	7	6	6	.222	.333	of-p	2	.818	2	1-1	6	7
1885	Milwaukee	WL	16	13	14	.246	.298	p			16	11-4	60	91
	Detroit	NL	31	12	30	.242	.339	p-of	10	.880	21	11-9	85	137
1886	Detroit	NL	57	25	41	.201	.255	p	4	.969	56	42-13	200	371
1887	Detroit	NL	24	15	33	.347	.368	p	8	.826	24	13-10	138	286
1888	Detroit	NL	6	5	6	.261	.261	p	4	.692	6	3-3	46	76
1890	Brooklyn	NL	2	1	0	.000	.000	p	0	1.00	2	1-0	7	20
	Buffalo	PL	7	4	8	.286	.321	p	0	1.00	7	2-5	72	85
1892	Binghamton	EL	1	1	1	.200	.200	p			1	1-0	6	8
1894	Grand Rapids	WL	2	0	0	.000	.000	p	1	.500	2	1-0	10	16

FRANCIS CARTER
BANCROFT

Born: May 9, 1846, Lancaster, Mass.
Died: March 30, 1921, Cincinnati, Ohio

Frank "Banny" Bancroft was associated with professional baseball as a manager and an executive for more than 40 years.

Never a professional player, he developed a liking for the game playing as an amateur in his hometown of Lancaster, Massachusetts, and later while serving in the Civil War. His service time provided his first managing experience as he organized games between Union Army Regiments.

After the war, Bancroft settled in New Bedford, Massachusetts. He founded the local hotel, the Bancroft House, which prospered. Always a businessman at heart, he owned a theater, opera companies and a minor league baseball team. He managed hockey teams for a number of years.

In 1878 New Bedford entered a team in the International Association, baseball's first minor league. Bancroft was chosen to manage the team. Managerial duties at that time encompassed not just field managing, but management of the business as well. Immediately Bancroft demonstrated that he was an excellent handler of athletes. He also demonstrated an innovative business style. Midway through the season, he pulled his team from the league and went barnstorming. His team played a record 130 games that season and won the championship of New England.

The next year Bancroft accepted an offer to manage the Worcester entry in the same league. His team started slowly. By late May

he was given an ultimatum by the board of directors to make good or be fired. Bancroft began to revamp his roster by bringing in new talent. Two of his most notable acquisitions were Art Irwin and Lee Richmond. Both started their first game as professionals June 2, 1879, in an exhibition game against the Chicago White Stockings. Richmond pitched a no-hitter that day in a game that signaled a change in the fortunes of the Worcester club. By season's end, many acclaimed the Worcesters as the finest team in professional baseball. Bancroft proved to be a shrewd judge of talent. His signing of Richmond may have saved his baseball career.

After the season, the innovative Bancroft, the Charles Finley of his day, led his team on a spring tour of Cuba and the South. This was only the second time that a professional team had played abroad, and was the introduction of professional baseball to the Caribbean. The success of 1879 propelled the Worcesters into the National League for the following season, where an initial rush faded, with the Worcesters finishing a creditable fourth.

Bancroft was an independent sort, strongwilled and resentful of front office involvement in the running of the team. Upset by his board of directors, he quit the team at the end of the 1880 season. He went to manage the Detroit Wolverines, during their first season in the N.L. He took four of the better Worcester players with him. But he stayed in Detroit

only two years. Once again, his dissatisfaction with front office meddling caused him to move. He repeated this scenario, for the same reasons, changing teams six times, a la Billy Martin.

Bancroft still holds the major league record for teams managed with seven. Following two years in Detroit he went to Cleveland for a year and then to Providence for two more. He also managed the minor league Rochester franchise, the Athletics, Indianapolis and Cincinnati. He was out of baseball during 1886, the only year he would miss until his death in 1921.

The 1884 season was the pinnacle of Bancroft's career as a field manager. Behind workhorse Hoss Radbourne's 60 wins, his Providence Grays won the National League pennant by 10½ games. The Grays met the New York Metropolitans in the first World Series, winning three straight.

Bancroft became part of the front office he was so often at odds with during his field managing days. He began the first of his 29 straight seasons as business manager of the Cincinnati Reds in 1892. During this time he made a return exhibition tour of Cuba and another of Hawaii. He also filled in as interim field manager on one occasion.

At the time of his death, Bancroft was one of the most popular men in baseball with acquaintances extending from coast to coast.

— John Richmond Husman

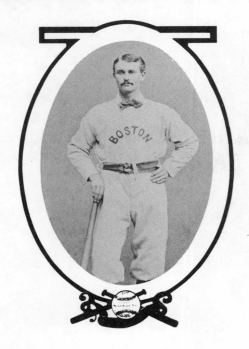

ROSCOE CONKLING BARNES
(Ross)

Born: May 8, 1850, Mt. Morris, N.Y.
Died: February 8, 1915, Chicago, Ill.
BR TR 5-8 ½, 145

Roscoe Conkling Barnes, an extraordinarily talented batsman and second baseman, was the greatest of 19th century players, according to many of his peers. His batting average for his prime years (1871 to 1876) was .389. Henry Chadwick rated him tops as "the model second baseman," superior in all requisite skills: judgement, range, speed, sureness, etc.

Raised in Rockford, Ill., Barnes and Albert Spalding joined the Forest Cities of Rockford in 1866 from the junior Pioneers and remained with the team through 1870. In 1871, manager Harry Wright of the Boston Red Stockings (NA), signed Barnes, Spalding and several former Cincinnati Red Stockings. These players formed the nucleus of the formidable Boston club which won four National Association championships from 1872 through 1875 with an incredible .804 winning percentage. Barnes batted .404 in 1872 and .402 the next year.

Boston's "Big Four" of Barnes, Cal McVey, Spalding and Deacon White jumped to the Chicago White Stockings for 1876 as arranged by Spalding. Chicago dominated that first National League season with a 52-14 record while Barnes led the circuit with 126 runs scored, 138 hits, a .429 batting average (now raised from .403 by subtracting bases on balls from at bats), and a .590 slugging average. No other major league batting champion has exceeded his league batting average by such a wide margin. Many of Barnes' singles were fair foul hits via a technique he thoroughly mastered, although he also hit with power.

His performance declined sharply in 1877, not because fair foul hits had been outlawed, but due to illness which idled him from mid-May to early September and permanently diminished his muscular strength. Barnes played only 22 games, batting and fielding below form. He sued the Chicago club for the salary withheld during his sickness, but lost the suit in the Chicago County Courts.

Personable and nattily dressed off field and a dashing, graceful figure in uniform, Barnes thrilled fans with his mastery as a base runner, "scientific" batter, and fielder of effortless ease. George Wright at short and Barnes at second for Boston formed, perhaps, the first truly great keystone duo. Spalding once called Barnes his "ideal of a ballplayer who could be depended upon to perform with success any play requiring skill and immediate execution to win a game." Barnes was not always so motivated as was attested by Harry Wright's plaint to Chadwick that Barnes "has provoked me time and again by his careless and indifferent play when other players are trying their best."

The rest of Barnes' career was anticlimactic. He captained the Tecumsehs of London, Ontario, (International Association) in 1878; shortstopped for Cincinnati in 1879; stayed out of baseball in 1880; and finished as shortstop for Boston (NL) in 1881. Subsequently, he held various white collar jobs around Chicago and remained a bachelor until his death from heart disease.

— Frank V. Phelps

			G	R	H	BA	SA	POS	E	FA	GP	W-L	R	H
1866	Forest City of Rockford							ss						
1867	Rockford													
1868	Rockford		15	75	-	(35 outs)								
1869	Rockford		23	-	111	(174 TB)								
1870	Rockford		56	-	176	(263 TB)								
1871	Boston	NA	31	66	63	.399	.570	2b-ss	37	.851				
1872	Boston	NA	45	81	97	.424	.576	2b	33	.899				
1873	Boston	NA	60	125	137	.428	.606	2b-3b	62	.864				
1874	Boston	NA	51	72	89	.341	.410	2b	55	.853				
1875	Boston	NA	78	114	142	.360	.429	2b	77	.868				
1876	Chicago	NL	66	126	138	.429	.590	2b	36	.910	1	0-0	8	7
1877	Chicago	NL	22	16	25	.272	.283	2b	23	.838				
1878	Tecumseh	IA	42	25	40	.235	.282	2b	23	.922				
1879	Cincinnati	NL	77	55	86	.266	.316	ss-2b	67	.855				
1881	Boston	NL	69	42	80	.271	.325	ss	53	.854				

ESTEBAN ENRIQUE BELLAN
(Steve)

Born: 1850, Havana, Cuba
Died: August 8, 1932, Havana, Cuba
5-9, 154

Esteban Bellan was the first Latin American to play organized baseball in the United States and was one of the pioneers who introduced the game to his native land of Cuba. Unfortunately, precious little else is known about his life.

Born into a Cuban (as opposed to Spanish) family in La Havana in 1850, Bellan was playing in the U.S. with the Unions of Morrisania in 1868 as the first Cuban war for independence from Spain broke out. In 1869, "Steve" played with the Unions of Lansingburgh (better known as the Troy Haymakers). He stayed with the Haymakers until the club folded in midseason in 1872 and was therefore a member of the first professional league, the National Association of Professional Base Ball Players, which was founded in 1871. Bellan played his last championship game on June 9, 1873.

Bellan was only a fair hitter against North American pitching (hitting in the .250 range) without outstanding extra base power. His best game was probably a 5-for-5 performance with 5 RBIs against Al Spalding and Boston on August 3, 1871. In the field, he primarily played third base, although he occasionally filled in at other infield and outfield positions. In the days before gloves, he was good at stopping hot shots, but his throwing was very erratic and his error totals were fairly high.

Bellan returned to Cuba and was among the first to introduce the game to that country while participating in the first organized game there in 1874. He was also the first player to hit 3 home runs in one game in Cuba, accomplishing the feat for Havana against Matanzas on Dec. 27, 1874. He had never hit a single home run in National Association play back in the U.S.

Championships were started in Cuba in 1878, and Bellan was the player-manager of the Havana team from that time until 1886. He led his squad to championships three times: 1878-79, 1879-80 and 1882-83.

Bellan died in Havana on Aug. 8, 1932.

Emilio Sabourin has generally been considered the father of Cuban baseball, although that title may now have to be shared with Esteban Bellan.

— Robert L. Tiemann and
Jose de Jesus Jimenez Jr., M.D.

			G	R	H	TB	BA	POS	E	FA	GP	W-L	R	H
1868	Union Morrisania		20	78										
1869	Troy		30	-	91	142								
1870	Troy		40	-	91	119		3b						
1871	Troy	NA	29	27	32	41	.248	3b	41	.707				
1872	Troy	NA	23	22	30	33	.254	s-3-o	28	.738				
1873	Mutual	NA	7	4	7	9	.206	3b-2b	16	.556				
Played for Havana in the Cuban league in subsequent years														

CHARLES WESLEY BENNETT

Born: November 21, 1854, New Castle, Pa.
Died: February 24, 1927, Detroit, Mich.
BR TR 5-11, 180

Charlie Bennett was and is acclaimed as the outstanding catcher of his era. He was extremely popular with fans and earned the respect of his teammates as a field leader.

Bennett began his major league career in Milwaukee in 1878. The team's one-year stay in the National League was a dismal one and it folded. He was signed by Frank Bancroft for the 1879 season. He caught and played center-field for Worcester's crack minor league team. He was with them when they attained major league status in 1880, beginning a stint in the National League that would end in tragedy 14 years later.

During the 1880 season, Bennett shared catching duties with Doc Bushong. Their assignment was a challenging one. The team's pitcher was J. Lee Richmond, master of the hard curve. Bennett was behind the plate for Richmond's historic perfect game. Years later, Richmond said of Bennett, ". . . the best backstop that ever lived. He went after everything, he knew no fear and he kept his pitcher from going into the air."

Bennett moved to Detroit with his manager Bancroft for the 1881 season. He would remain with the Wolverines for eight seasons — the entire history of the franchise. His brilliant play behind the plate and his outstanding tactical leadership made him extremely popular. The highlight of his career in Detroit came in 1887 when the Wolverines rolled to the National League pennant. They went on to trounce St. Louis of the AA 10 games to 5 in a traveling "World Series" played in 10 different cities.

Bennett was off to Boston in 1889 to become a part of the super team there. Eventually the Beaneaters would win three consecutive pennants, 1891-1893. While he was there, Bennett caught three Hall of Famers — Kid Nichols, John Clarkson and Hoss Radbourne.

Bennett's career ended suddenly in January 1894. Embarking on a hunting trip, he was running to catch a moving train in Wellsville, Kansas, when he missed his grip and fell beneath the wheel. He lost both legs.

Bennett was quite a contract jumper. The Pittsburgh Alleghenies of the AA sued him for breach of contract. Bennett retaliated in the courts and won. He defected with the Brotherhood in 1890, but was persuaded to rejoin the NL before playing a game.

Bennett's record of continuous service was unusually long, particularly during his era, and especially for a catcher. He caught 16 years with little protective equipment. His vocation was brutal, and he paid the price. *The Sporting News* said of his battered hands ". . . he has not a whole or straight finger in the lot. Every joint is swollen or misshapen."

Bennett was a model of the catcher that is invaluable in spite of a weak bat. In 15 major league seasons he never led his league in any hitting category. Playing his position was a different story. He was the league leader in putouts, total chances per game and double plays on many occasions. Seven times he led all National League catchers in fielding percentage. After baseball he returned to Detroit. Confined to a wheelchair, he opened a store selling tobacco and newspapers. Fans would go out of their way to patronize his business. He was given a "Day" at the ballpark and presented with a wheelbarrow full of silver dollars by his grateful following. Further appreciation was shown by naming Detroit's first American League park for him. The Tigers played at Bennett Park from 1896 until 1911. Charlie Bennett died in Detroit in 1927.

In 1983 Charlie Bennett was recognized by the SABR 19th Century Committee as the best catcher of all 19th century players who are not in the Hall of Fame.

— John Richmond Husman

			G	R	H	BA	SA	POS	E	FA	GP	W-L	R	H
1874-76	Neshannock													
1876	Aetna of Detr.													
1877	Milwaukee		63	47	71	.264		c	59		.879			
1878	Milwaukee	NL	49	16	45	.245	.310	c-of	41	.849				
1879	Worcester	NA	42		-	.327		of-c	-	.839				
1880	Worcester	NL	51	20	44	.228	.306	c	31	.913				
1881	Detroit	NL	76	44	90	.301	.482	c	20	.962				
1882	Detroit	NL	84	43	103	.301	.450	c-3b	39	.939				
1883	Detroit	NL	92	56	113	.305	.474	c-2-o	38	.934				
1884	Detroit	NL	90	37	90	.264	.378	c	63	.903				
1885	Detroit	NL	91	49	94	.269	.447	c-o-3	50	.906				
1886	Detroit	NL	72	37	57	.243	.362	c	24	.955				
1887	Detroit	NL	46	26	69	.363	.495	c	10	.961				
1888	Detroit	NL	74	32	68	.264	.395	c	18	.966				
1889	Boston	NL	82	42	57	.231	.320	c	23	.955				
1890	Boston	NL	85	59	60	.214	.320	c	23	.959				
1891	Boston	NL	75	36	55	.215	.332	c	19	.960				
1892	Boston	NL	35	19	23	.202	.263	c	11	.948				
1893	Boston	NL	60	34	40	.209	.304	c	12	.953				

MARTIN BERGEN

Born: October 25, 1871, North Brookfield, Mass.
Died: January 19, 1900, North Brookfield, Mass.
BR TR 5-10, 170

The dichotomy that was Martin Bergen is best illustrated by a pair of quotes from Boston manager Frank Selee after Bergen committed suicide at the height of his career.

Bergen was, said Selee, "one of the greatest ballplayers who ever went upon the diamond." But, he added, "I knew Bergen was not in his right mind."

His teammates echoed these sentiments. Hugh Duffy called him "perhaps the best baseball catcher I ever saw," noting the speed and accuracy with which he threw. But batterymate Ted Lewis admitted, "I have always been afraid of him." And club president Arthur Soden noted after Bergen's suicide: "I am not surprised. Bergen has shown signs of insanity for two years."

Bergen always was a loner and brooder, frequently fighting with his teammates, but he controlled his emotions enough to serve as regular backstop for Boston's National League pennant winners in 1897 and 1898. However, the death of his young son, Willie, in April 1899 apparently shoved him over the edge. Devastated, he twice left the team on the road and returned to his family in North Brookfield, Mass. His teammates were incensed, feeling his absence was hurting their pennant chances. But the fans were forgiving and he rewarded them by throwing out three basestealers and delivering a game-winning hit in the ninth inning the second time he returned to the lineup.

With Bergen playing in only 72 of 152 games

and slumping from .280 to .258 at the plate, Boston finished second, eight games behind Brooklyn. After the season, Bergen retreated to North Brookfield, fearing his teammates "would murder him." A heavy smoker and chewer, he was treated for "tobacco heart."

Meanwhile, Soden was attempting to trade or sell his troublesome catcher to New York or Cincinnati. A deal with Chicago for Frank Chance also was discussed. But Bergen could not bear another season away from his family. On the morning of January 19, 1900, Bergen killed his wife, his son and his daughter with an ax, then cut his own throat with a razor.

— Bob Richardson

			G	R	H	BA	SA	POS	E	FA	GP	W-L	R	H
1892	Salem	NEng	59	39	63	.247	.365	c	32	.933				
1893	Wilkes-Barre	EL	3	2	1	.100	.100	c-3b	1	.900				
1894	Lewiston	NEng	97	87	136	.321	.450	c	24	.959				
1895	Kansas City	WL	113	118	188	.372	.541	c	27	.956				
1896	Boston	NL	65	39	66	.269	.376	c	24	.921				
1897	Boston	NL	87	47	81	.248	.318	c	16	.963				
1898	Boston	NL	120	65	129	.289	.377	c	24	.961				
1899	Boston	NL	72	32	67	.257	.326	c	16	.955				

LOUIS BIERBAUER

Born: September 28, 1865, Erie, Pa.
Died: January 31, 1926, Erie, Pa.
BR TR 5-8, 140

Louis Bierbauer began his career with the Erie "Jareckis" in 1884. Local star Dell Darling was also on the team. When the Erie Olympics team was organized the following year, Louis joined them. Players were signed such as Count Campau to play first base. In addition to Bierbauer and Darling, later a catcher for Pop Anson's Chicago White Stockings, was Mike Morrison, later with the Metropolitans, Baltimore, Detroit and Cleveland.

The Olympics entered the Interstate League, and suffered one of the first no-hit shutout losses at the hands of the Springfield (Ohio) nine. The league disbanded in early June.

Bierbauer joined Hamilton in the Canadian League. In 1886 he signed with the Philadelphia Athletics. In 1890 he jumped to the Brooklyn PL club. After the Brotherhood disbanded he accepted a lucrative offer from Pittsburgh.

Philadelphia, thinking he would return to them, was shocked when he signed with Pittsburgh and a great howl went up. The Philadelphia papers called the Pittsburgh team a bunch of Pirates. The name has stuck.

Bierbauer played with Pittsburgh from 1891 through 1896. In 1897 he went to the St. Louis Nationals and wound up his career in the Eastern League in 1902. An old leg injury slowed him up, playing a part in this decision.

He returned to Erie and worked as a brass molder until he passed away in 1926.

— Lefty Blasco

			G	R	H	BA	SA	POS	E	FA	GP	W-L	R	H
1884	Erie	Intst												
1885	Hamilton													
1886	Athletic	AA	137	56	127	.244	.308	2b	73	.922	2	0-0		
1887	Athletic	AA	126	74	162	.302	.369	2b	48	.937	1	0-0		
1888	Athletic	AA	134	83	148	.279	.351	2b	68	.916	1	0-0		
1889	Athletic	AA	130	78	170	.313	.429	2b	50	.947				
1890	Brooklyn	PL	133	129	186	.320	.455	2b	38	.956				
1891	Pittsburgh	NL	121	60	103	.206	.262	2b	55	.929				
1892	Pittsburgh	NL	153	82	154	.240	.336	2b	42	.956				
1893	Pittsburgh	NL	128	81	151	.298	.403	2b	33	.959				
1894	Pittsburgh	NL	131	88	159	.302	.412	2b	52	.937				
1895	Pittsburgh	NL	119	55	122	.255	.319	2b	39	.947				
1896	Pittsburgh	NL	59	33	74	.287	.372	2b	12	.966				
1897	St. Louis	NL	12	1	10	.217	.217	2b	5	.921				
1898	St. Louis	NL	4	0	0	.000	.000	2-s-3	4	.765				
1899	Grand Rapids	WL	123	58	139	.284		2b	36	.952				
1900	Clv-Mlw-Buff	AL	128	38	110	.239	.268	2b-ss	41	.943				
1901	Buff-Htfd	EL	109	39	94	.261		2b	25	.954				
1902	Newark	EL	18	0	8	.116		2b						

THOMAS HENRY BOND
(Tommy)

Born: April 2, 1856, Granard, Ireland
Died: January 24, 1941, Boston, Mass.
BR TR 5-7½, 165

Only one major league pitcher since 1876 has won 40 or more games three years in succession. That man is Tommy Bond.

Like most young fireballers, Bond had control problems early in his career, as well as a reputation for "ruining" catchers with his "cannonball" delivery. But after failing a tryout with the Brooklyn Atlantics in 1873, he mastered his wildness by practicing against a door and the next season became the Atlantics' mainstay, posting a 22-32 record for a mediocre team. He defeated the champion Boston Red Stockings in consecutive games in Boston on May 23 and 26, 1874. On September 30 he was the last visiting National Association pitcher to win in Boston. But the next day the Red Stockings got their revenge by beating him 29-0. (Boston won its final six home games in 1874 and all 33 home games in 1875.)

In 1875, Bond followed captain Bob Ferguson to Hartford. For the first two months of the season, he played right field while learning the curveball from teammate Candy Cummings. By July, however, Bond had mastered the pitch and had become the team's top pitcher. In 1876, Cummings sat on the bench while Bond pitched 45 of the team's first 47 National League games. Then Bond publicly accused Ferguson of selling a couple of recent games, but the club's owners backed Ferguson and Bond was suspended for the remainder of the season.

Meanwhile, the Boston Red Stockings — still boasting a nucleus of their four-time National Association champions — were seeking a replacement for ace pitcher Al Spalding. The club signed Bond in September 1876 for the following season.

It was a perfect match. Buoyed by better support, Bond chalked up 40, 40 and 43 victories the next three years to lead Boston to National League pennants in 1877 and 1878, and a second place finish in 1879. He led the league in shutouts three times and in wins, ERA and strikeouts twice each.

Bond's reign as the NL's premier pitcher, however, ended abruptly. Hampered by the absence of a crack catcher as well as a sore arm, Bond dipped to 26-29 in 1880 as the Boston team deteriorated. After an 0-3 start in 1881, he retired.

Bond managed at Worcester (NL) during part of the 1882 season, and later tried a comeback with Boston's Union Association team in 1884, changing his delivery to throw almost from shoulder level as permitted by the new rules. Although he pitched well early in the season, Bond tailed off and finished the season with Indianapolis (AA), where he was 0-5.

After finally leaving the game, Bond entered the leather business, then began a 35-year career (1891 to 1926) in the Boston City Assessor's office. Repaying his debt to Cummings, Bond helped coach at Harvard and tutored aspiring Boston-area hurlers, including a pair of Cambridge youngsters who went on to the Hall of Fame: John Clarkson and Tim Keefe.

— Bob Richardson

			G	R	H	BA	SA	POS	E	FA	GP	W-L	R	H
1874	Atlantic	NA	55	25	54	.219	.255	p	26	.862	55	22-32	441	616
1875	Hartford	NA	72	32	79	.273	.329	p-rf	46	.807	40	19-16	152	302
1876	Hartford	NL	45	18	50	.275	.318	p	15	.887	45	31-13	164	357
1877	Boston	NL	61	32	59	.228	.266	p	9	.937	58	40-17	248	530
1878	Boston	NL	59	22	50	.212	.237	p	9	.941	59	40-19	223	571
1879	Boston	NL	65	35	61	.238	.258	p	8	.959	64	43-19	204	543
1880	Boston	NL	76	27	62	.220	.241	p-of	16	.930	63	26-29	277	559
1881	Boston	NL	3	0	2	.200	.200	p	1	.889	3	0-3	17	40
1882	Worcester	NL	8	1	4	.133	.133	of-p	4	.714	2	0-1	13	12
1884	Boston	UA	37	21	48	.296	.364	p-of	12	.868	23	13-9	120	185
	Indianapolis	AA	7	0	2	.130	.130	p-of	3	.636	5	0-5	51	62
1885	Memphis	SL	3	1	3	.250	.333	p			3	2-1	24	26
1886	Brockton	NwEng	4	2	3	.231	.231	p	6	.700	4	3-1	27	36

JOSEPH EMLEY BORDEN

Born: May 9, 1854, Jacobstown, N.J.
Died: October 14, 1929, Yeadon, Pa.
BR TR 5-9, 140

Joseph Emley Borden's major league career only lasted parts of two seasons, but this small right-handed pitcher is credited with two notable "firsts" in baseball history.

Borden was born on May 9, 1854 into a prominent family in Jacobstown, N.J. When he began his baseball career, he pitched under the pseudonym of Nedrob (Borden spelled backwards) and Joseph E. Josephs, because his parents disapproved of his activity on the diamond.

His initial famous "first" occurred on July 28, 1875 when he pitched the first major league no-hitter. He hurled the gem while pitching for the Philadelphia "Fillies" in a 4-0 victory against the Chicago White Stockings in a National Association game. It was the only no-hitter in the five-year history of the National Association.

Borden pitched in 7 games for Philadelphia in 1875, playing under the name of Joe Josephs and winning only 2 of 6 decisions.

In 1876, the National League was formed and Borden, playing under his real name, signed a three-year contract with the Boston entry. On April 22, Boston and the Athletics played the very first NL game at the A's home grounds at 25th and Jefferson streets. A crowd of 3,000 saw Borden triumph in the inaugural, 6-5, to become the first pitcher to win a National League game. The contest took only two hours and five minutes to complete.

There is some confusion in the encyclopedias and press reports on Borden's pitching record with the Bostons in 1876. Some list it as 12-12 while others have it as 11-12. He appear-

ed in 32 games, 29 as a pitcher and 3 as an outfielder.

Borden's career bizarrely terminated before the end of the 1876 season when he was released and finished the year, according to baseball legend, as the groundskeeper at the Boston ballpark. He received a cash settlement to terminate his contract. Although only 22, Borden never played in another major league game.

On October 14, 1929, the date on which Connie Mack's Athletics clinched the World Series against the Chicago Cubs in Philadelphia, Borden died a few miles away in Yeadon, Pa., at age 75. He is buried in Oakland Cemetery, West Chester, Pa.

— Randy Linthurst

			G	R	H	BA	SA	POS	E	FA	GP	W-L	R	H
1875	Philadelphia	NA	7	3	3	.107	.107	p	15	.500	7	2-4	30	47
1876	Boston	NL	32	19	25	.207	.231	p-o	29	.651	29	12-11	174	257

ASA BRAINARD
(Count)

Born: 1841, Albany, N.Y.
Died: December 29, 1888, Denver, Col.
TR 5-8½, 150

When Harry Wright was assembling his Cincinnati Red Stockings for the 1869 season, he looked to New York for his pitcher and signed 28-year-old Asa Brainard of the Knickerbocker club for $1,100. (Only Wright himself at $1,200 and his brother, George at $1,400 were paid more.) Harry Ellard wrote in his book, *Baseball in Cincinnati*: "Brainard was considered the most graceful and terrific pitcher that had ever gone to the box up to that time." He threw with speed (only Williams of the Olympic Club of Washington was reputed to throw faster) and also imparted a wicked twist to the ball. "In delivering the ball, he would cross his legs, placing the left toe behind his right foot and then take a step forwards," Ellard said of Brainard's pitching style.

When Brainard came to Cincinnati, he boarded with a family named Truman. The late Mr. Truman had been a partner in the printing firm that started the famed "McGuffey Readers" and had been at one time quite affluent. But now, the widowed Mrs. Truman and her two daughters, Mary and Margaret, were forced to take in boarders and to work as seamstresses to make ends meet. Shortly after arriving, Brainard came down with smallpox. While Mary Truman nursed him back to health, a romance developed, and the two were married just as the team was beginning its spring practice.

The 1869 Red Stockings, the first avowed professional team, was undefeated. The only blot on the team's record was a disputed 17-17 game with the Haymakers of Troy, N.Y., on August 27. While they played and defeated all the prominent teams from coast to coast, it is only fair to point out that many of their victories were at the expense of so called "country teams," whose players had little skill and even less experience.

Brainard pitched almost every game of the 65 played in 1869 (one account notes that he pitched every one, but this cannot be verified), and continued his duties into the 1870 season. He was in the box at the Capitoline grounds in New York on June 14, 1870 when the Atlantics of Brooklyn defeated the Red Stockings, 8-7, in 11 innings, and broke their long winning streak in the most famous game of the pre-league years. After the 1870 season, in which the Red Stockings lost five more games, the team disbanded.

During the '69 and '70 seasons, manager Wright and his star pitcher often clashed. David Q. Voigt, in *American Baseball*, citing the Harry Wright papers, says that Brainard was hard to manage and was hypochondriacal, often trying to beg off from a game. On one occasion, the team arrived in Buffalo early in the morning. Most of the men were ready for bed, but not Brainard and Fred Waterman, who wanted to roam the streets seeking action. Voigt also tells of an 1869 game in which a rabbit scurried on the diamond near the pitcher's box. Brainard threw the ball at the rabbit as two runs scored. The chances are the two runs did not mean much, since the Reds Stockings outscored their opponents by an average margin of 41-9, according to figures in Ellard's book.

In 1871, Brainard joined the Olympics of Washington, a charter member of the National Association. After a 13-5 record in 1871, he played for the Middletown Mansfields and the Lord Baltimores, also of the National Association, through the 1874 season, then faded from the scene. His overall NA won-lost mark was 24-56, a far cry from his record with all winning Red Stockings.

Thanks to the late Lee Allen, indefatigable chronicler of the game's early years, a few facts are known about Brainard's personal life. Allen found that Brainard deserted his wife after the 1870 season, leaving her destitute and responsible for raising their infant son, Truman Brainard. In 1882 Brainard was running an archery range on Staten Island and was badly hurt when hit in the hand by an arrow. He later moved west and operated a pool room in Denver, where he died in 1888, the first of the '69 Red Stockings to pass. One story, probably apocryphal, has it that the term "ace," when used to describe a star pitcher, is derived from Brainard's first name. As the story goes, some teams of the 1870s began to call the pitcher "their Asa," after Brainard, which, in due time, became "ace."

— Joseph M. Overfield

			G	R	H	TB	BA	POS	E	FA	GP	W-L	R	H
1860	Excelsior		19	48		(58 outs)								
1861	Excelsior													
1862	Excelsior		(3.2 r/g)			(2 o/g)								
1863	Excelsior		10	28		(22 outs)								
1864	Excelsior		10	24		(31 outs)								
1865	Excelsior		7	25		(20 outs)								
1866	Excelsior		14	35		(46 outs)								
1867	National		6	16		(15 outs)								
1868	Cincinnati		38	137		(111 outs)		p						
1869	Cincinnati		55	-	195	278		p						
1870	Cincinnati		66	-	217	284		p						
1871	Olympic	NA	30	24	30	34	.226	p	7	.870	30	12-16	292	361
1872	Olym-Mansfld	NA	16	10	21	24	.296	p	10	.730	12	2-10	179	182
1873	Baltimore	NA	16	18	18	20	.290	p-rf	6	.750	14	5-7	139	176
1874	Baltimore	NA	47	19	50	52	.250	p-2b	29	.855	29	4-23	330	416

THEODORE BREITENSTEIN
(Ted)

Born: June 1, 1869, St. Louis
Died: May 3, 1935, St. Louis
BL TL 5-9, 165

Although he compiled a losing lifetime record and an earned run average of more than 4.00, Ted Breitenstein was at one time considered the best left-handed pitcher in baseball.

A St. Louis native, young Theodore gained his first fame at age 20 by pitching the Home Comforts team to the local championship in 1889. In 1891 he was given a trial with the big league Browns and then sent to Grand Rapids in the Northwestern League. When that team folded, he was brought back to the Browns, where he warmed the bench until the final day of the season. Given his first start, Breitenstein hurled a brilliant no-hitter, walking one Louisville batter while facing the minimum of 27 men.

With the Browns in the expanded National League in 1892, Ted was erratic, showing plenty of stuff, but little control.

Breitenstein had another losing season in 1893 as the Browns finished in 10th place. Ted was involved in 20 1-run games that year, winning only 8 of them. In 1893, Breitenstein was teamed with Heinie Peitz to form the popular "Pretzel Battery."

Although the Browns were still quite weak in 1894, Breitenstein finally put together a winning season while leading the league in games and innings pitched. Although he wasn't that big (5 feet 9 inches and 165 pounds), Ted was remarkably durable, so much so that owner Chris Von der Ahe abused him upon occasion. After pitching 34 innings in the first eight days of September 1894, Ted pitched a complete game in the opener of a doubleheader on the ninth. Still, when Dad Clarkson was knocked out of the box in the first inning of the nightcap, Von der Ahe called Breitenstein in to pitch again. Ted refused, claiming exhaustion, and was fined $100 and suspended on the spot!

Breitenstein's control became better (though it was never great), and he was rated among the top pitchers in the league. He threw a drop curve, an inshoot, and a good change of pace. But his money pitch was a moving fastball, which he could make rise or ride in on a right-handed hitter. His pitching philosophy was, "when in doubt use speed and plenty of it."

Despite two more losing seasons with St. Louis, Breitenstein was still labeled as a $10,000 pitcher when he was sold to Cincinnati in October 1896, although later reports dropped the price to $7,500 and $5,000. Playing at last for a contending team with some pitching depth, Breitenstein enjoyed his two most successful seasons in 1897 and 1898 with the Reds. On April 22, 1898, in his second start of the season, Ted pitched another no-hitter, beating Pittsburgh 11-0. As in his 1891 masterpiece, he walked only 1 man and faced the minimum number of batters.

His victory totals and workload fell off in 1899 and 1900, and he was released back to St. Louis. After just 3 games with the Cardinals in 1901, he was sent down to St. Paul. After a brief stay there, Ted called it quits.

But his career was revived the next year when he was induced to join his old teammate Charlie Frank, who was managing Memphis in the Southern Association. After two years with Memphis, Breitenstein followed Frank to New Orleans, where Ted stayed through 1911. In 10 years in the Southern Association, Breitenstein amassed a 157-89 record and pitched on four of Charlie Frank's pennant winners.

After retiring as a player, Breitenstein put in nine years as a Southern Association umpire. He finally left the game for good after an umpiring stint in the Texas League in 1921. He returned to St. Louis, where he lived with his wife, Ida, until her death in 1935. Nine days after she passed away, Ted suffered a fatal heart attack.

— Robert L. Tiemann

			G	R	H	BA	SA	POS	E	FA	GP	W-L	R	H
1891	St. Louis	AA	6	2	0	.000	.000	p	0	1.00	6	2-0	11	15
	Grand Rapids	NWL	32	12	21	.176	.261	p-of			21	12-9		
1892	St. Louis	NL	47	16	16	.122	.137	p-of	6	.949	39	9-19	192	280
1893	St. Louis	NL	49	18	26	.177	.211	p	8	.939	48	19-24	197	359
1894	St. Louis	NL	63	27	40	.220	.280	p-of	10	.929	56	28-25	321	497
1895	St. Louis	NL	72	25	42	.193	.202	p-of	22	.880	54	19-30	295	458
1896	St. Louis	NL	51	21	42	.259	.315	p-of	8	.943	44	18-26	236	376
1897	Cincinnati	NL	41	16	33	.266	.395	p	3	.964	40	23-12	174	345
1898	Cincinnati	NL	41	16	26	.215	.248	p		.961	39	20-15	170	313
1899	Cincinnati	NL	33	18	27	.352	.438	p-of	5	.937	26	13-9	107	219
1900	Cincinnati	NL	41	12	24	.190	.262	p-of	7	.929	23	10-10	106	205
1901	St. Louis	NL	3	1	2	.333	.333	p	0	1.00	3	0-3	26	24
	St. Paul	WL	23	-	20	.263	.307	p-of	3	.938	12	5-6	48	81
1902	Memphis	SL	76	27	63	.257		p-of	9	.940	-	19-14		
1903	Memphis	SL	52	17	47	.293		p-of	8	.944	35	17-11		
1904	New Orleans	SL	44	17	26	.191	.265	p-of	11	.909	29	15-8		
1905	New Orleans	SL	46	10	22	.150	.177	p-of	5	.965	28	21-5		
1906	New Orleans	SL	33	7	26	.250	.317	p	7	.940	31	21-7		
1907	New Orleans	SL	68	19	56	.245	.342	of-p	7	.944	14	5-9		
1908	New Orleans	SL	29	4	12	.152	.190	p	1	.991	27	17-6		
1909	New Orleans	SL	34	6	24	.258	.290	p	5	.954	26	13-10		
1910	New Orleans	SL	37	4	14	.141		p	5	.960	37	19-9		
1911	New Orleans	SL	22	4	14	.200	.229	p	4	.942	21	11-10		

LOUIS ROGERS BROWNING
(Pete, The Gladiator)

Born: June 17, 1861, Louisville, Ky.
Died: September 10, 1905, Louisville, Ky.
BR TR 6-0, 180

Pete Browning, the legendary Louisville batsman for whom the first modern barrel shaped baseball bat — the Louisville Slugger — was made, was the best known star produced by the fabled American Association, the National League's heartiest pre-modern-era competitor.

During a spectacular 13-year career from 1882 through 1894, Browning compiled a record of substantial proportions that more than offset his severe defensive limitations. His lifetime batting average of .343 is the 10th highest in the history of the game (exceeding even Babe Ruth's), and ranks third among the game's righthanded batsmen, exceeded only by Hall of Famers Rogers Hornsby and Ed Delahanty.

Born June 17, 1861, Louis Rogers Browning was the youngest of eight children. As a youth, he was a crack athlete and avid sportsman who adroitly avoided schoolwork in favor of spinning tops, playing ball and shooting marbles with his other hookey-playing friends. Amazingly, the one sport he did not enjoy was swimming, despite living just a few blocks from the Ohio River, because it aggravated a painful ear condition which rendered him deaf at a young age.

After breaking in as a pitcher with a local semipro team formed by his friend John Reccius (who with brother Philip were the first set of twins to play professional baseball), Browning turned professional in 1882 when Louisville joined the American Association.

A three-time batting champion, Browning took two crowns with Louisville and another with Cleveland in the Players' League. As a rookie, he led the "Beer and Whiskey League" in 1882 with a .382 average. His inaugural season also included a league leading .521 slugging average and 19 doubles for the neophyte circuit. (The American Association gave professional baseball a host of innovations including Sunday baseball, beer at the ballpark, the popularization of "Ladies Day"

as a standard baseball promotion, league control of umpires, the percentage system of determining pennant winners, and standardized contractual procedures.)

Browning repeated his batting championship in 1885 with a .362 mark that included a league-leading 174 hits. He garnered his last title in 1890 when he headed the Players' League with a .387 average that included a circuit-topping 40 doubles. Along with Ross Barnes and Hall-of-Famer Dan Brouthers, Browning was one of three men to take titles in two separate leagues during the premodern era.

Browning might have taken five batting titles instead of three had it not been for a pair of freak events. In 1886, he batted .340 only to lose to teammate Guy Hecker's .342 mark. Denied a shot at consecutive titles and his third crown in five years, the lone honor afforded Browning was the dubious distinction of being the only player ever to lose a batting title to a pitcher. The next year, Browning posted numerous personal bests, including a .402 average, only to run into Triple Crown winner Tip O'Neill's .435 mark, the second highest average recorded in single season play.

Ironically, Browning's greatest achievement in baseball may have come off the field. Early in the 1884 season, Browning broke his favorite bat. He then was approached by a young apprentice woodmaker and ardent fan, John A. "Bud" Hillerich, who offered to custom-make another bat for him. Following Browning's immediate success with the personalized bat, the shop of J. Frederich Hillerich (Bud's father) was flooded with orders from ballplayers wanting the "new" bat.

Though this story has attained a certain mythical quality during the years in the eyes of some historians, there is substantial evidence to verify this incident, including the word of Bud Hillerich himself, who maintained its accuracy to the end of his life at age 80 in 1946.

Additionally, this accidental meeting led to the establishment of the Hillerich & Bradsby Company, still today the world's No. 1 batmaker.

After playing his first nine seasons in Louisville, Browning spent his last four seasons on a whirlwind tour among five National League clubs. After concluding his career in 1894, Browning enjoyed a peaceful retirement *(continued on page 143)*

(continued on page 143)

			G	R	H	BA	SA	POS	E	FA	GP	W-L	R	H
1881	Eclipse		40	-	57	.333		3b	-	.885				
1882	Louisville	AA	69	67	110	.382	.514	2-s-3	58	.877				
1883	Louisville	AA	84	95	121	.338	.458	o-s-3	43	.832				
1884	Louisville	AA	105	101	155	.341	.476	3-o-1	54	.899	1	0-1	3	2
1885	Louisville	AA	112	98	176	.367	.532	of	27	.897				
1886	Louisville	AA	112	88	159	.339	.450	of	44	.791				
1887	Louisville	AA	134	137	281	.471	.612	of	45	.870				
1888	Louisville	AA	99	58	120	.313	.435	of	23	.894				
1889	Louisville	AA	83	39	82	.253	.352	of	22	.882				
1890	Cleveland	PL	118	114	191	.391	.535	of	27	.907				
1891	Pitts-Cinc	NL	105	64	129	.324	.427	of	19	.919				
1892	Cinc-Louv	NL	104	57	112	.292	.383	of	20	.913				
1893	Louisville	NL	57	37	79	.369	.453	of	15	.887				
1894	Allentown	PaSt	44	49	68	.332	.468	of	6	.932				
	St.Louis-Bkn	NL	3	2	3	.333	.333	of	0	1.00				
1896	Columbus	WL	26	15	34	.333	.471	of	6	.900				

CHARLES G. BUFFINTON

Born: June 14, 1861, Fall River, Mass.
Died: September 23, 1907, Fall River, Mass.
BR TR 6-1, 180

In 1884, Boston pitcher Charley Buffinton won 47 games, lost 16, compiled an ERA of 2.15, completed 63 of 67 starts, pitched 587 innings, walked 76, struck out 417 and pitched 8 shutouts. In addition, he played 13 games in the outfield and 11 at first base and batted .267.

But 1884 was by no means the only good year enjoyed by Buffinton.

A product of the mill town of Fall River, Mass., Buffinton as a young man gained a reputation as a ballplayer of promise. A catcher at first, he soon eschewed that position after taking a few foul tips in the face and turned to pitching with occasional stints at first base and in the outfield.

Buffinton broke in with Boston (NL) early in the 1882 season and compiled a 2-3 record. He then was 24-13 the next year as he and Grasshopper Jim Whitney (37-21) led the Beantowners to a pennant and to a two-games-to-one decision over the New York Metropolitans (AA) in postseason play.

After his career-best 1884 season, in which Old Hoss Radbourn and Providence took the flag, Buffinton slipped to 22-27 in 1885 and 8-10

in 1886 when he developed arm trouble. Boston, feeling he was through, released him. But he came back strongly with Philadelphia (NL) in 1887, 1888 and 1889, winning 21, 28 and 27 games, respectively, while losing 17 each season.

He jumped to the Philadelphia Brotherhood club in 1890 (19-14), and, after that league folded, joined Boston (AA), where in 1891 he compiled an outstanding 28-9 record. With the demise of the Association at the end of the '91 season, he moved to Baltimore (NL). When the Orioles tried to cut his salary in mid-season 1892, he quit and never played another major league game.

Buffinton's final figures for his 11 seasons show a 231-151 record (.605) with an overall ERA of 2.96. One of the best hitting pitchers of his era, he banged out 543 hits, including 7 home runs, and had a lifetime mark of .245.

Buffinton's best pitch was an overhand curveball, referred to in those days as a drop. Some accounts say he invented that particular variation of the curve, but there is no proof of it. It is known, however, that catchers had great difficulty in holding him and batters hit

a lot of ground balls off his deliveries. One of the notable days of Buffinton's career was his August 9, 1884 duel against Radbourne, which was 0-0 after 10 innings. In the 11th, Arthur Irwin of Providence hit a home run that went through a one-foot hole in the right-field fence to seal a 1-0 victory for the Grays. Buffinton never pitched a no-hit, no-run game, but he did hurl two consecutive 1-hitters on August 6 and 9, 1887, while with Philadelphia — a feat accomplished only six other times in major league history.

When his baseball career was over, Buffinton returned to Fall River, where he became a successful and respected businessman dealing in cotton and coal. According to a paper prepared for the Fall River Historical Society by SABR member Philip T. Silvia Jr., Buffinton was Fall River's most famous native son during the 19th century. He died unexpectedly in a Fall River hospital on September 23, 1907, while preparing to undergo surgery. He was only 46.

— Joseph M. Overfield

			G	R	H	BA	SA	POS	E	FA	GP	W-L	R	H
1882	Boston	NL	15	5	13	.260	.380	o-p-1	7	.821	6	2-3	38	55
1883	Boston	NL	86	28	81	.238	.287	of-p	33	.804	43	25-12	191	346
1884	Boston	NL	87	48	94	.267	.344	p-o-1	22	.918	67	47-16	228	506
1885	Boston	NL	82	26	81	.240	.302	p-o-1	27	.922	51	22-27	237	425
1886	Boston	NL	44	27	51	.290	.330	1-p-o	16	.932	18	7-10	132	203
1887	Philadelphia	NL	66	34	83	.296	.357	p-o-1	19	.916	40	21-17	233	471
1888	Philadelphia	NL	46	14	29	.181	.219	p	10	.939	46	28-17	138	324
1889	Philadelphia	NL	47	16	32	.208	.221	p	9	.916	47	28-16	213	390
1890	Philadelphia	PL	42	24	41	.273	.340	p	16	.890	37	19-16	221	312
1891	Boston	AA	58	16	34	.188	.227	p-of	10	.937	48	28-9	154	336
1892	Baltimore	NL	13	7	15	.349	.419	p	3	.917	13	4-8	91	120

THOMAS EVERETT BURNS

Born: March 30, 1857, Honesdale, Pa.
Died: March 19, 1902, Jersey City, N.J.
BL TR 5-9, 165

A popular trivia question is, "Who played third base on the Tinker to Evers to Chance team?" Most will know the answer to that one. Twenty years earlier, however, Chicago had another famous nine, and a more difficult question is, "Who played third for the team?" The answer is Tommy Burns, who was regarded by some as the top man at the position in his day.

Burns' partners in the White Stocking infield were Cap Anson, Fred Pfeffer, and Ned Williamson. From 1880 to 1885 Burns played short and Williamson third; then they switched positions f-2or the next four years. Of Burns, Anson said: "He was a fair to average batter, but was hardly fast enough to be considered a really good shortstop. He was a fair baserunner, using excellent judgment in that respect, and a first-class slider, going into the bases head first . . .; in fact, he was more of a diver than a slider . . . At third base Burns was as good as the best of them, he excelled at the blocking game, which he carried on in a style that was particularly his own and which was calculated to make a baserunner considerable trouble."

As a boy, Burns started playing baseball for amateur teams around New Britain, Conn. At age 19 in 1876, he became a professional with the Providence team, one of his teammates being Ned Hanlon. He quit Providence to play for Auburn, N.Y., and in 1878 was with Hornells(ville) of the International Association. The following year he was a star for Albany, the top club in the National Association, which led to his being signed by Anson for 1880. He then became a member of the White Stockings "stonewall infield," which was noted for outwitting opposing base runners with their trick plays. As stated above, he played short and Williamson third through 1885, after which they switched positions. Anson claims that the latter arrange-

ment brought out the best in both men, but he never explained why he waited so long to make the change. Burns was the only regular other than Anson who didn't defect to the Players League in 1890 and subsequently became regarded as Anson's righthand man.

Burns' greatest day as a hitter was September 6, 1883. The White Stockings slaughtered Detroit 26-6, scoring 18 runs in the seventh inning. Tommy slammed 2 doubles and a homer in that inning and thus holds six records: most extra base hits in an inning (3 — he is the sole possessor of this record; the others are shared), most total bases in an inning (8), most hits in an inning (3), most runs scored in an inning (3), most times facing pitcher in an inning (3), and most doubles in an inning (2). He also made the record books on August 6, 1890, when he and Malachi Kittredge hit grand slams in the same inning.

A fever contracted during spring training in Hot Springs, Ark., in 1892 essentially ended his playing career. He was released to be-

come the manager for Pittsburgh, although he was fired ten weeks later. Burns went on to manage Springfield of the Eastern League, winning a pennant there in 1895. When Anson was eased out at Chicago, Burns was named as his replacement in 1898. The team finished fourth with a respectable 85-65 record that year, but dropped to eighth the following year, and Burns was replaced by Tom Loftus.

Burns returned to his home in Springfield, Mass., and managed the Eastern League team there in 1900, moving to Buffalo with the team the following year. He was to have managed Jersey City in 1902, but was found dead in bed from a heart attack on March 19, 1902 while visiting the home of P. T. Powers, president of the Eastern League.

Burns didn't drink or smoke and was regarded as a very honest man. He was popular as a player and well liked as a manager, although it was said that he was too easy-going to be successful in the latter capacity.

— William McMahon

			G	R	H	BA	SA	POS	E	FA	GP	W-L	R	H
1877	Auburn		71		-	.255		3b	-	.802				
1878	Hrnlsvl-Albany	IA	37	29	40	.261	.327	3b	23	.851				
1879	Albany	NA	49	51	58	.262		3b	-	.894				
1880	Chicago	NL	85	47	103	.309	.378	ss-3b	39	.864				
1881	Chicago	NL	84	41	95	.278	.389	ss	52	.870				
1882	Chicago	NL	84	55	88	.248	.346	2b-ss	65	.873				
1883	Chicago	NL	97	69	119	.294	.430	ss-2b	84	.861				
1884	Chicago	NL	83	54	84	.245	.359	ss	69	.839				
1885	Chicago	NL	111	82	125	.272	.409	ss	96	.844				
1886	Chicago	NL	112	64	123	.276	.375	3b	49	.890				
1887	Chicago	NL	115	57	146	.317	.413	3b	61	.872				
1888	Chicago	NL	134	60	115	.238	.315	3b	49	.905				
1889	Chicago	NL	136	64	135	.257	.349	3b	72	.880				
1890	Chicago	NL	139	86	149	.277	.362	3b	54	.898				
1891	Chicago	NL	59	36	55	.226	.280	3b	24	.892				
1892	Pittsburgh	NL	12	7	8	.205	.205	3b-of	9	.629				
1893	Springfield	EL	65	57	76	.296	.374	2b	33	.916				
1894	Springfield	EL	37	28	51	.336	.447	2b	20	.907				
1896	Springfield	EL	1	0	2	.400	.400	2b	0	1.00				

THOMAS P. BURNS
(Oyster)

Born: September 6, 1864, Philadelphia, Pa.
Died: November 11, 1928, Brooklyn, N.Y.
BR TR 5-8, 183

Tom Burns, a native of Philadelphia, started playing organized baseball in 1880 as an outfielder with the Shibe Club, a strong amateur nine in Philadelphia. After stints with other amateur teams in Atlantic City and Baltimore, where he pitched in addition to playing the outfield, Burns made his professional debut in 1883 as a pitcher with Harrisburg of the Inter-State Association. In 1884 Burns started the season with Wilmington in the Eastern League as the team's shortstop, but also pitched occasionally. In late August, Wilmington, with a 49-12 record and leading the league by about 15 games, joined the outlaw Union Association and Tom Burns was a major leaguer. After only two games in the Union Association, Burns was lured to Baltimore of the rival American Association, where he played both infield and outfield and also pitched two games. He wound up his rookie major league season with a .290 batting mark for 37 games. Tom's average slipped to .231 in 1885 and late in the campaign he was released to Newark of the Eastern League where he helped that team win the pennant in 1886.

Burns was back in the majors to stay with Baltimore in 1887. A natural leader, he was named captain of the Orioles and soon had a reputation as one of the noisiest coaches in baseball. With Tom shouting encouragement from either shortstop or third base, lefty Matt Kilroy won 46 games, "Phenomenal" Smith added 25, and the Orioles jumped from the cellar to third place. Burns batted .341 and emerged as one of the leading power hitters in the majors.

For reasons unknown, Burns was replaced as captain at the start of the 1888 season by veteran "Blondie" Purcell and the team started poorly. The Baltimore *Sun* lobbied for Burns to return as captain, but after the change was finally made in early July there was no improvement. Burns was sold to Brooklyn in early August and Purcell left for

Philadelphia a month later.

By now Tom was a full-time outfielder and he became one of the stars of a fine Brooklyn team for the next seven years. After finishing a close second to the St. Louis Browns in 1888, the Bridegrooms won the American Association pennant in 1889 and, after shifting to the National League, won a second consecutive flag in 1890. Brooklyn lost the 1889 World Series to the New York Giants and in 1890 battled to a three-three draw with Louisville when the Series was called off in late October because of bad weather.

During his years with Brooklyn, Burns batted an even .300, was a strong clutch hitter usually hitting in the middle of the lineup, and also was a good outfielder with a strong arm. In the 1889 World Series against the Giants, Tom drove in the winning runs in both the first and fourth games and led Brooklyn with 11 RBIs in the Series.

Burns moved from Brooklyn to the Giants early in the 1895 season where he ended his

major league career. In 1896 Tom hit .394 with Newark in the Atlantic League, once again playing an important role on a pennant winner. He played his final year of pro ball with Hartford in the same circuit in 1897, batting .333 and stealing 32 bases.

Burns had umpired a few games in the National League in 1895 and in 1899 he started the season as a regular umpire in the League, but for reasons not made known at the time he was dropped before the end of June. Upon leaving baseball he spent most of his remaining years in the employ of the borough of Brooklyn.

Burns has been tagged with the name "Oyster" in baseball registers and encyclopedias of recent years, but during his playing years he generally was called Tom or Tommy, and that is also the way the newspapers labelled him. Even his obituaries, which appeared after his death on November 11, 1928, failed to make use of the nickname.

— Ralph Horton

			G	R	H	BA	SA	POS	E	FA	GP	W-L	R	H
1883	Harrisburg	IntstAs	71	44	65	.220	.281	o-s-p	12	.753#		5-8		
1884	Wilmington	EL	61	107	97	.336	.587	ss-p	35	.862	12	7-2	50	72
	Wilmington	UA	2	0	1	.143	.429	ss	2	.778				
	Baltimore	AA	35	34	39	.298	.542	of-2	13	.865	2	0-0	5	12
1885	Baltimore	AA	78	47	74	.231	.349	of-p	27	.883	15	7-4	72	112
	Newark	EL	12	2	8	.174	.174	3b	2	.943				
1886	Newark	EL	85	77	116	.352	.558	3b-of	16	.923#				
1887	Baltimore	AA	140	120	245	.401	.570	ss-3b	102	.838	3	1-0	22	16
1888	Baltimore-Bkn	AA	131	95	158	.299	.434	of-ss	62	.858	5	0-1	11	12
1889	Brooklyn	AA	131	105	153	.304	.423	of	16	.908				
1890	Brooklyn	NL	119	102	134	.284	.464	of	10	.941				
1891	Brooklyn	NL	123	75	134	.285	.417	of	23	.893				
1892	Brooklyn	NL	141	94	171	.315	.454	of	12	.937				
1893	Brooklyn	NL	109	68	112	.270	.412	of	14	.925				
1894	Brooklyn	NL	126	107	184	.359	.509	of	14	.942				
1895	Bkn-NewYork	NL	53	28	49	.258	.342	of	9	.912				
1896	Newark	AtlL	123	119	171	.378	.621	of-1b	17	.951				
	Grand Rapids	WL	8	8	11	.324	.617	of	2	.913				
1897	Hartford	AtlL	126	80	159	.324	.438	of	12	.938				

ALBERT JOHN BUSHONG
(Doc)

Born: January 10, 1856, Philadelphia, Pa.
Died: August 19, 1908, Brooklyn, N.Y.
BR TR 5-11, 165

Albert Bushong, of French-Irish ancestry, was a lanky, long-armed catcher with an accurate throw, who used off-seasons to study dentistry. His style of receiving pitched balls was so gracefully efficient he suffered relatively little permanent hand or finger damage during his 16 years in baseball, despite playing in the barehanded backstop era. In an effort to preserve his good right hand for dentistry, Bushong pioneered the use of a padded glove and the technique of catching primarily with one hand. A light hitter, he usually occupied the eighth or ninth spot in the lineup.

Before graduating from Philadelphia High School in 1876, he caught one game for the 1875 Atlantics of Brooklyn (NA). The summer immediately following graduation he played with the Brandywines of West Chester, Pa., and had a five-game trial with the Philadelphia Athletics, during which he went 1 for 21. In 1877, he performed for Janesville, Wis., where he caught John Montgomery Ward,

who was also just starting a professional career. Bushong joined Buffalo of the International Association in 1878 as reserve catcher, but soon was shifted at his own request to Utica of the same league so he could play regularly.

For 1879, Bushong joined Worcester of the minor league National Association and was with that club when it entered the National League the next year with Bushong and Charlie Bennett splitting backstop assignments. Bennett later went to Detroit (NL) and Bushong became sole first-string receiver for Worcester in 1881 and 1882. Two seasons with Cleveland (NL) followed, between which Doc spent the 1883-84 winter studying dentistry in Bordeaux, France.

After the Cleveland franchise disbanded, Bushong was sold to St. Louis (AA) where he caught for the champion Browns of 1885, 1886 and 1887. Losing his job as a regular to Jack Boyle, he was released to Brooklyn (AA) where he became the prime catcher in 1888

and a substitute in 1889. After seeing little action with Brooklyn (NL) in 1890, he went to the Eastern Association in 1891, where he played till mid-summer. After a brief term as an Eastern Association umpire, he retired from the diamond.

Bushong had obtained a Doctor of Dental Surgery degree from the University of Pennsylvania in early 1882. Once he retired from baseball in 1891, he began to practice dentistry full time at a large dental house in Hoboken, N.J., where two of his brothers also worked. Eventually he became manager of the establishment. Simultaneously, in south Brooklyn, he "built up a large and flourishing practice," according to baseball historian William Rankin. Three of his sons also became Brooklyn dentists.

Bushong died of cancer on August 19, 1908 at the age of 52.

— Frank V. Phelps

			G	R	H	BA	SA	POS	E	FA	GP	W-L	R	H
1875	Atlantic	NA	1	0	3	.600	1.00	c	1	.800				
1876	Athletic	NL	5	4	1	.048	.048	c	21	.588				
1877	Janesville		42		-	.202		c	-	.861				
	Buffalo							c						
1878	Utica	IA	17	8	18	.273	.288	c	22	.848				
1879	Worcester	NA	46		-	.290		c	-	.802				
1880	Worcester	NL	41	13	25	.171	.192	c	30	.918				
1881	Worcester	NL	76	35	64	.233	.287	c	44	.918				
1882	Worcester	NL	69	20	40	.158	.194	c	47	.897				
	Philadelphia		5	3	3	.177	.177	c	2	.923				
1883	Cleveland	NL	63	15	37	.172	.195	c	46	.909				
1884	Cleveland	NL	62	24	48	.236	.276	c	58	.886				
1885	St. Louis	AA	85	42	80	.266	.342	c	39	.934				
1886	St. Louis	AA	107	56	86	.223	.251	c	51	.939				
1887	St. Louis	AA	53	35	64	.295	.313	c	26	.920				
1888	Brooklyn	AA	69	23	55	.209	.237	c	44	.910				
1889	Brooklyn	AA	25	15	13	.162	.175	c	14	.898				
1890	Brooklyn	NL	16	5	13	.236	.273	c	9	.913				
1891	Syr-Lebanon	EA	30	11	17	.160	.160	c	15	.902				

CHARLES COLUMBUS CAMPAU
(Count)

Born: October 17, 1863, Detroit, Mich.
Died: April 3, 1938, New Orleans, La.
BL TR 5-11, 160

Charles C. "Count" Campau was the most productive minor league player of the 19th century. He was also one of the most interesting and colorful players about whom very little has been written.

When he passed away on April 3, 1938 in his adopted home of New Orleans, he was known primarily for his post-playing career as the clerk of scales and placing judge at local race tracks. But for more than 20 years he was a clever fielder, home run hitter, base stealer, manager and storyteller. Few in New Orleans at that time remembered his spectacular 1887 season in the Southern League or any of his other four seasons in New Orleans, the last of which was 1903.

The Campau family was one of the original founding families of the city of Detroit. Michael Campau was born in Montreal in 1667 and led the Campau clan into Detroit. The Count was one of hundreds of descendants of Michael who grew up in Detroit. More than a dozen of the young Campaus of the mid 1800s attended Notre Dame. It was probably there that the Count first honed his baseball playing skills.

In 1883, Campau played semipro ball in the Detroit area. He showed the baseball establishment his batting power four years later when he batted .393, slugged for a .613 percentage and stole 100 bases for the New Orleans Pelicans. His 18 triples led the Southern League and his 17 homers were good for second place. This swatting attracted the attention of the Kansas City team of the Western Association, for which he played 42 games in 1888 (his first of three stays in K.C.). Before the season was over he had replaced the injured future Hall of Famer Big Sam Thompson in right field for the Detroit Wolverines of the National League. This was the first of his five stops — in three different leagues — in Detroit. Campau had a solid year for Detroit in '89, but by then it was for its International Association entry.

The next year, the Count did something which is unlikely to be duplicated: he led both a major and minor league in homers. After banging 3 home runs for Detroit, which led the International League, he moved up to St. Louis of the American Association and belted 10 more to pace that league. The fortunes of Chris Von der Ahe's Browns did not go well early and Der Boss President changed captains five times. The newly-acquired Count got the first of his nine managerial opportunities in late June. He led the team to a fine 27-14 record before being suddenly demoted in August.

Except for two games with Washington in 1894, that was to be end of his time in the bigs.

He was destined to be a bush leaguer, where his dashing looks and colorful playing style endeared him to fans in 20 different cities. Campau had a big "season" for the Seattle "Babies" in 1896. Playing the full 32 games before the Pacific Northwestern League folded, the Count led the league in runs (55), triples (6), homers (13), total bases (110) and slugging percentage (.887). His .403 average, however, was good for only third place.

Interestingly, in 1898 Campau had a cameo appearance with Minneapolis of the Western League. His paths crossed with Perry Werden, who sat out that year with a broken leg. Werden is called the greatest minor

(continued on page 143)

			G	R	H	BA	SA	POS	E	FA	GP	W-L	R	H
1885	Erie	Intst												
1886	Guelph													
1887	Savannah-NOrl	SL	109	133	198	.393	.613	of	25	.889				
1888	Kansas City	WA	42	36	40	.216	.341	of	11	.851				
	Detroit	NL	70	28	51	.203	.259	of	8	.933				
1889	Detroit	IA	112	111	126	.285	.407	of	27	.879				
1890	Detroit	IA	39	29	49	.310	.468	of-3b	-					
	St. Louis	AA	75	68	101	.322	.516	of	7	.947				
1891	Troy	EA	122	86	111	.236	.335	of	23	.852				
1892	Columbus	WL	65	46	61	.262	.391	of	11	.916				
	New Orleans	SL	40	43	50	.331	.503	of	6	.920				
1893	New Orleans	SL	94	98	121	.337	.521	of-1b	-					
	Wilkes-Barre	EL	20	15	28	.326	.570	of	2	.960				
1894	New Orleans	SL	65	66	73	.299	.512	of						
	Washington	NL	2	1	1	.143	.143	of	0	1.00				
	Milw-Detroit	WL	59	66	97	.367	.667	of	18	.867				
1895	Detroit	WL	118	115	171	.359	.565	of	20	.914				
1896	Seattle	PacNW	32	55	50	.403	.887	of-1b	8	.917				
	Kansas City	WL	88	83	106	.325	.503	of	14	.935				
1897	Grand Rapids	WL	132	109	166	.303	.454	of	25	.926				
1898	Mpls-StP-KC	WL	130	101	143	.265	.377	of	13	.941				
1899	Rochester	EL	113	92	129	.279	.420	of	13	.940				
1900	Rochester	EL	130	70	127	.250	.345	of	26	.919				
1901	Binghamton	NYSt	112	67	128	.305	.376	1b	33	.973				
1902	Binghamton	NYSt	102	46	100	.239	.292	1b	29	.977				
1903	New Orleans	SL	9	4	7	.259	.259	1b						
	Binghamton	NYSt	64	39	73	.315	.414	1b	20	.964				
1904	Binghamton	NYSt	118	43	97	.226	.298	1b	26	.965				
1905	Binghamton	NYSt	57	24	35	.176	.231	of	12	.908				

WARREN WILLIAM CARPENTER
(Old Hickory)

Born: August 16, 1855, Grafton, Mass.
Died: April 18, 1937, San Diego, Calif.
BR TL 5-11, 186

When third baseman Warren Carpenter was released in 1889 after eight seasons with the Cincinnati Reds (AA), the Cincinnati *Enquirer* lamented that it might have had something to do with his nickname: Old Hickory. "It is often that a man's nickname is a detriment to his success. People have called W. W. Carpenter 'Old Hick' for so long that people think he has been around forever." Actually, he was only 34 when the axe fell.

A rarity in baseball, apart from pitchers, is the man who throws left and bats right. Rarer still is the athlete who throws left and plays the infield, first base excepted. Such a player was Hick Carpenter who in 12 years in the majors played 1,059 games at third base, plus a few games at second and short. Lee Allen, in his book *Cincinnati Reds*, called Carpenter "the most skillful of the left-handed infielders of the last century." This might be construed as damning with faint praise because even in the last century left-handed infielders were

not that common. Two others were Jimmy Macullar, who played 425 games in the infield, and Bill Greenwood, who played 565.

Carpenter began his major league career with Syracuse (NL) in 1879, conventionally, as a first baseman; became a third baseman at Cincinnati (NL) in 1880, played a year at Worcester (NL) and then moved to the Cincinnati Reds (AA). From 1882 to 1889, Carpenter helped the Reds to seven first division finishes and one pennant, while gaining recognition as one of the best players at his position.

It is a commentary on the fielding standards of that era that Carpenter, though considered one of the best at third base, totaled 478 errors in eight seasons with the Reds, an average of almost 60 per year. The hot corner was obviously not an easy position to play in the '80s, with many still playing gloveless or with the crudest of hand protection. For example, Jack Gleason of St. Louis (AA) made 83

errors in 1882; John McCormick of Baltimore (AA) booted 84 in 1883 and Arlie Latham miscued 88 times for St. Louis (AA) in 1886. Bid McPhee, who played second base for the Reds each of the eight years that Carpenter played third and a player with close to Hall of Fame credentials, made 443 errors in the same period, though he handled more chances.

With Carpenter's release by the Reds in 1889, his major league career was over, except for one game with St. Louis (NL) in 1892. He did, however, continue in baseball with Kansas City of the Western Association.

After his baseball days were over, Carpenter became a pullman conductor and was at one time a deputy collector of customs. He was 82 when he died in San Diego in 1937, and no place in his obituary was it mentioned that he played almost 1,100 major league games as a left-handed infielder.

— Joseph M. Overfield

			G	R	H	BA	SA	POS	E	FA	GP	W-L	R	H
1875	Taunton		16	22	24			of-2b	19	.791				
1876	Ithaca		64	68	68			2b	61	.853				
1877	Syracuse		101	49	92	.236		3b	63	.850				
1878	Syracuse	IA	39	27	47	.299	.350	3b-1b	24	.815				
1879	Syracuse	NL	65	30	53	.203	.226	1-3-o	42	.917				
1880	Cincinnati	NL	77	32	72	.240	.287	3b-1b	45	.853#				
1881	Worcester	NL	83	40	75	.216	.280	3b	56	.851				
1882	Cincinnati	AA	80	78	125	.354	.433	3b	59	.838				
1883	Cincinnati	AA	95	99	132	.302	.382	3b	48	.870				
1884	Cincinnati	AA	109	80	128	.265	.331	3b	43	.884				
1885	Cincinnati	AA	112	89	138	.291	.363	3b	55	.861				
1886	Cincinnati	AA	111	67	104	.221	.272	3b	60	.854				
1887	Cincinnati	AA	127	70	139	.269	.321	3b	51	.849				
1888	Cincinnati	AA	136	68	147	.267	.327	3b	60	.878				
1889	Cincinnati	AA	123	67	126	.257	.329	3b	62	.853				
1890	Kansas City	WA	111	78	123	.264	.333	3b	52	.871				
1891	Kansas City	WA	121	70	128	.248	.298	3b	67	.867				
1892	Indianapolis	WL	49	18	43	.211	.250	3b	29	.880				
	St. Louis	NL	1	0	1	.333	.333	3b	2	.714				

ROBERT LEE CARUTHERS
(Bob)

Born: January 5, 1864, Memphis, Tenn.
Died: August 5, 1911, Peoria, Ill.
BL TR 5-7, 140

An outstanding pitcher and heavy hitter, Bob Caruthers starred for five pennant-winning teams in six years from 1885 through 1890. Contemporary statistics credited him with more than 200 pitching victories and a batting average above .300. And he was an excellent fielder and good baserunner.

Born in the family of a wealthy Memphis lawyer, Bobby was sickly as a boy, and a doctor recommended outdoor exercise. So the boy took up baseball, over the objections of his mother. The family moved to Chicago when Bob was a teenager, and he made a name for himself playing for local amateur teams.

He began his professional career in 1883 at age 19 by signing with Grand Rapids. He played right field and pitched for Minneapolis the following season. When the Northwestern League collapsed, Caruthers signed with the St. Louis Browns for $250 per month. He made his major league debut on September 7, 1884, beating the Athletics on a 4-hitter, 6-2.

In 1885 he surprised the baseball world by winning 40 of his 53 games for the pennant-winning Browns. A small man (5-7, 140), Caruthers had a muscular physique and good running speed. As a pitcher he had a quick deceptive righthanded delivery with considerable speed. But his greatest asset was said to be his "headwork," i.e., the ability to size up an opposing batter at a glance and exploit his weakness.

After the season ended, the cosmopolitan Caruthers accompanied teammate Doc Bushong to France, whence he engaged in a trans-Atlantic salary dispute that earned Caruthers the nickname "Parisian Bob." He eventually signed for $3,200.

"The steady, careful, unphenomenal, but invariably effective work" (as one newspaper described it) of pitchers Caruthers and Dave Foutz paced St. Louis to another pennant in 1886. The pair also split the rightfield duties

in the latter part of the season. He starred in the World Series versus Chicago. At bat he went 7-for-24 with 2 doubles and 2 triples, and as pitcher he was 2-1 with a 1-hit shutout and a 10-inning victory in the Series clincher.

Despite an attack of malaria, Caruthers had an amazing season in 1887, being credited with a 29-9 pitching record, a .459 batting average (.357 without counting walks as hits) and 59 stolen bases. He was practically the only Brown to do well in the World Series that year, pitching four of the team's five victories in the 15-game tour. But owner Chris Von der Ahe blamed the team's defeat on carousing and card-playing, and Caruthers (an expert billiards and poker player) was among the players put on the market. He was sold to Brooklyn for $8,250 and got a $5,000 salary from his new club, making him the highest-paid player in the American Association. His pitching and outfielding helped the Bridegrooms climb to second place in 1888. In 1889 Caruthers concentrated strictly on pitching. The results were Bob's last big season (40-11) and Brooklyn's first big league pennant. In 1890 Bob had a fine first half (19-8 through July). Then outfield work increased his play-

ing time and reduced his pitching work. He finished 23-11 with a .265 average as Brooklyn won the pennant again, this time in the National League.

After one more fair season with Brooklyn in 1891, Caruthers jumped to St. Louis for 1892. His pitching arm was nearly gone, but his hitting made him a regular outfielder for St. Louis. After brief stints with Chicago and Cincinnati in 1893, Bob slipped to the minors. He finished up with Burlington in the Western Association in 1896.

On August 16, 1886, Caruthers became the first of three hurlers in major league history to collect 4 long hits in a game — 2 homers, a triple and a double. Unfortunately, he allowed 10 runs in the eighth inning and lost the game 11-9 when he was tagged out at home in the ninth trying to stretch his triple into a home run.

He then turned to umpiring around the Midwest. He worked in the American League in 1902 and 1903. He was umpiring in the Three-Eye League in 1911 when he suffered a nervous collapse. He died on August 5.

— Robert L. Tiemann and
L. Robert Davids

			G	R	H	BA	SA	POS	E	FA	GP	W-L	R	H
1883	Grand Rapids	NWL	50	51	63	.288	.349	of	12	.851				
1884	Minneapolis	NWL	51	31	44	.218	.267	p-of	9	.934	35	17-15	144	236
	St. Louis	AA	23	15	22	.262	.357	p-of	5	.833	13	7-2	34	61
1885	St. Louis	AA	60	38	45	.207	.281	p-of	11	.917	53	40-13	196	430
1886	St. Louis	AA	87	91	107	.342	.518	p-of	18	.888	44	30-14	163	323
1887	St. Louis	AA	98	94	195	.459	.605	of-p	11	.903	39	29-9	182	398
1888	Brooklyn	AA	94	59	77	.230	.334	of-p	26	.896	44	29-15	180	341
1889	Brooklyn	AA	59	45	46	.267	.384	p	4	.969	56	40-11	224	444
1890	Brooklyn	NL	71	46	63	.265	.340	of-p	20	.881	37	23-11	159	294
1891	Brooklyn	NL	56	25	48	.281	.380	p-of	10	.907	38	18-14	201	323
1892	St. Louis	NL	143	76	142	.277	.357	of	29	.901	16	2-10	75	131
1893	Chi-Cinc	NL	14	15	14	.269	.365	of	4	.846				
1894	Grand Rapids	WL	133	166	181	.331	.448	1b	38	.969				
1895	Jacksonville	WA	92	100	119	.319		1-2b	27	.967	1	0-0	3	-
1896	Burlington	WA	52	45	56	.292	.401	1b	21	.959				
1898	Burlington	WA	3	1	4	.400	.400	of	1	.800				

ELTON P. CHAMBERLAIN
(Ice Box)

Born: November 5, 1867, Warsaw, N.Y.
Died: September 24, 1929, Baltimore, Md.
BR TR 5-9, 168

If for no other reason, Elton Chamberlain deserves to be remembered for his nickname; for giving up four home runs to one batter in a single game; and for his ability to throw with either arm.

But there are more compelling reasons for remembering Chamberlain. Pitching for six teams in 10 major league seasons, he compiled a laudable 157-120 (.567) record. He won 32 games for St. Louis (AA) in 1889; 25 for Louisville and St. Louis (both AA) in 1888, and 22 for Philadelphia (AA) in 1891. He was also a better than average hitter, totaling 9 major league home runs, including a rare (for a pitcher) grand slam off Frank Foreman of Washington on April 30, 1892.

According to historian Lee Allen, Chamberlain gained his distinctive nickname, "Ice Box," by reason of "his austere calm in the face of all hostility by the enemy." The batter who tagged him for four homers in one game was Bobby Lowe of Boston on May 30, 1894 when Chamberlain was pitching for Cincinnati. He shares this dubious distinction with another pitcher, who also bore a memorable

nickname, William (Adonis) Terry, victimized for four home runs by Ed Delahanty, July 13, 1896. Chamberlain was one of three pitchers (Larry Corcoran and Tony Mullane were the others) known to have pitched ambidextrously in a major league game. He pitched seven innings from his normal right side and two innings left-handed on May 9, 1888 when Louisville (Chamberlain's team) routed Kansas City, 18-6.

Chamberlain was born in Warsaw, N.Y., a hilly community, southeast of Buffalo. He moved to Buffalo as a youngster and soon began to play amateur ball. In 1885, while still a teen-ager, he began his professional career with Hamilton, Ontario, moving thence to Macon (Southern League) and to Louisville (AA) in 1886. After winning 18 games for Louisville in 1887 and 14 games through August 1888, he was shipped to St. Louis (AA), where he finished 11-2 in the final six weeks of the season.

After the 1889 season, in which he won 32 and lost 15 for the Browns, there were rumors Chamberlain was to jump to the Chicago

Brotherhoods and join his 1889 manager, Charley Comiskey, who reportedly had offered him an $800 increase. St. Louis owner, Chris Von der Ahe, was so concerned that he sent his son, Eddie, to Buffalo to negotiate with Chamberlain. "Match Comiskey's offer and I will sign," Chamberlain told the emissary. Eddie then wired his father and got the OK.

The Von der Ahes were to regret their profligacy. By May, Chamberlain was back in Buffalo, where it was said "his face was a familiar sight in the pool rooms and other similar resorts." It was being bandied about that he had been "playing for his release," so that he could join the Brotherhood. Eventually, Von der Ahe sold him to Columbus (AA), where he won 12 of 18 decisions. His later travels took him to Philadelphia (AA) in 1891, Cincinnati (NL), 1892-1894, and finally to Cleveland, where he pitched his last major league game in 1896.

Chamberlain was 61 when he died in Baltimore in 1929.

— Joseph M. Overfield

			G	R	H	BA	SA	POS	E	FA	GP	W-L	R	H
1884	Quincy	NWL	2	0	0	.000	.000	3b	3	.500				
1886	Macon	SL	52	22	35	.188	.204	p-of	19	.865	34	13-20	155	252
	Louisville	AA	6	2	3	.158	.158	p-of	3	.800	4	0-3	43	39
1887	Louisville	AA	37	14	38	.268	.310	p	11	.876	36	18-16	244	457
1888	Louisv-StL	AA	40	17	23	.161	.278	p	3	.962	38	25-11	165	238
1889	St. Louis	AA	54	19	35	.199	.312	p	7	.923	54	34-15	215	376
1890	St.L-Columbus	AA	30	9	17	.213	.250	p	5	.897	30	15-8	110	175
1891	Athletic	AA	54	21	36	.205	.312	p-of	10	.919	49	22-23	267	397
1892	Cincinnati	NL	53	13	36	.225	.294	p	9	.904	52	18-23	237	391
1893	Cincinnati	NL	34	9	19	.196	.258	p	4	.933	34	16-12	160	248
1894	Cincinnati	NL	23	10	22	.314	.486	p			23	10-9	154	220
1895	Warren	Iron-Oil												
1896	Cleveland	NL	2	1	0	.000	.000	p	0	1.00	2	0-2	11	21
1899	Buffalo	WL	1		0	.000	.000	p			1	0-1		

JOHN CURTIS CHAPMAN

Born: May 8, 1843, Brooklyn, N.Y.
Died: June 10, 1916, Brooklyn, N.Y.
TR 5-11, 170

What a gold mine of information would have been preserved for posterity had an oral historian been given the opportunity to record the baseball life of John C. Chapman. Other than Henry Chadwick and Albert G. Spalding, it is doubtful if anyone would have been better qualified to recount the game's early history. As a player and manager, he was deeply involved in the halcyon days of amateur baseball of the 1860s, the formation of the National Association in 1871, the founding of the National League in 1876 and in the mushroom growth of minor league ball in the 1880s and 1890s.

As a young man Chapman played with some of the great amateur teams of the East, including the Atlantics of Brooklyn, the Quaker Cities of Philadelphia and the Eckfords of Brooklyn. His longest association was with the Atlantics, where he played more than 300 games. He was in right field on that historic day, June 14, 1870, when the Atlantics defeated the Red Stockings of Cincinnati, 8-7 in 11 innings to break their season-and-a-half winning streak.

Chapman's professional playing career was limited to two years in the National Association (1874 and 1875) and 17 games with Louisville (NL) in 1876. By then his increasing weight had made it impossible for him to cover his outfield position. As a manager Chapman was peripatetic, to say the least, and his major league log shows stops at Louisville, Milwaukee, Detroit and Buffalo, all in the National League, and at Louisville in the American Association. His career major league managerial record was 351-502, with a single pennant, that in Louisville in 1890. In the minors he managed at Buffalo, Holyoke, Springfield (Mass.), Syracuse, Rochester and Toronto.

Chapman was the Louisville manager in 1877 when Jim Devlin, George Hall, Al Nichols and Bill Craver sold out to gamblers and were barred from baseball for life. Chapman had innocently started the chain of events by hiring Nichols after third baseman Bill Hague had developed a boil.

The tall and courtly Chapman enjoyed an impeccable reputation and was highly regarded by fans and players alike. Affable and courteous though he was, he was not known for his garrulity. Said one observer: "Jack Chapman knew and practiced the virtue of silence."

Many great players were given their first opportunities by Chapman. He gave Hughie Jennings his start in 1892 with Louisville and the next year brought out Jimmy Collins at Buffalo. These men were to go into the Hall of Fame together in 1945. He took a chance and signed Frank Grant for Buffalo in 1886, and this pioneer black player rewarded him with three great years. He signed Billy Hoffer for Buffalo in 1893 and honed him for major league stardom.

Chapman, who never married, became manager of a large commercial house after he left baseball, but kept in close touch with the game and attended many reunions. He died in his Brooklyn home of a heart attack on June 10, 1916 at age of 73.

— Joseph M. Overfield

			G	R	H	TB	BA	POS	E	FA
1860	Putnam		2	1			(7 outs)	of		
1861	Enterprise		10	30			(26 outs)			
1862	Atlantic									
1863	Atlantic		11	19			(35 outs)			
1864	Atlantic		22	88			(68 outs)			
1865	Atlantic		18	67			(54 outs)			
1866	Atlantic		18	69			(46 outs)	of		
1867	Quaker City			(5 r/g)			(2 o/g)			
1868	Atlantic		54	224	218	301	(152 outs)			
1869	Atlantic		48	-	197	313		of		
1870	Atlantic		21	-	86	119		of		
1871	Eckford		26	-	30	-		of		
1874	Atlantic	NA	53	32	64	75	.268	rf	18	.798
1875	St. Louis	NA	43	28	44	55	.223	rf	21	.731
1876	Louisville	NL	17	4	16	17	.239	rf	7	.731

JOHN EDGAR CLAPP

Born: July 17, 1851, Ithaca, N.Y.
Died: December 17, 1904, Ithaca, N.Y.
BR TR 5-7, 175

John Clapp, a sturdily built right-handed catcher with an extremely powerful, accurate throwing arm, was among the first receivers to stand in close behind batters. Cap Anson recalled him as "a cool, quiet, plucky fellow and one of the best catchers." *Sporting Life* once said of him: "John is a cool, easy-going fellow, not easily 'rattled' and not much of a manager. As a player he ranks high." In support of the *Sporting Life's* claim, only his 1879 Buffalo club had a winning record in the four seasons he served as a National League pilot.

Taught a printer's trade in his native Ithaca, N.Y., Clapp played various positions for amateur teams as a teen-ager: the Forest Cities of Ithaca; the junior Mansfields of Middletown, Conn.; and the Athletics of Otsego, N.Y.

In 1871, his ability as catcher and leading hitter of the Clippers of Ilion, N.Y., brought him attention, which propelled him into National Association professional baseball

with the 1872 Mansfields of Middletown, Conn. He spent the next three years with the Philadelphia Athletics (NA) catching the swift deliveries of Dick McBride. He accompanied the Athletics on the 1874 trip to England and Ireland arranged by A. G. Spalding. Following the 1875 season he resigned from the Athletics club because it refused to rescind a $200 fine imposed when Clapp left the club to play in an Ithaca at Binghamton, N.Y., town game. He then conducted a sealed bid contest for his services between Buffalo, Hartford, and St. Louis, won by the latter with a $3,000 salary bid, one of the highest salaries ever paid up to that time.

His two seasons with St. Louis produced his best National League batting averages — .305 and .318 as his right-center field drives fell safely — and he caught the shoots of Grin Bradley and Tricky Nichols. In 1878, he went to Indianapolis as captain-manager and left fielder. Subsequently, he caught for and man-

aged Buffalo (NL) in 1879, Cincinnati (NL) in 1880 and Cleveland (NL) in 1881. At Cleveland he gained the nickname "Honest John" because he refused a $5,000 bribe from Chicago bookmakers to throw an important game.

With the independent Metropolitans of New York in 1882, Clapp batted .248 in 97 games. He remained in New York as second catcher and manager when that city entered the National League the following year, but clearly his playing days were over.

For several years, commencing in 1883, Clapp owned saloons in partnership with Met pitcher Jack Lynch, but they did not prosper. Clapp returned to Ithaca about 1890 when he joined the Ithaca police force. He was on duty the evening a heart attack fatally struck him. Among his survivors was a brother, Aaron Clapp, who played in 36 games for Troy (NL) in 1879.

— Frank V. Phelps

			G	R	H	BA	SA	POS	E	FA	GP	W-L	R	H
1871	Clipper of Ilion		19	-	52			c						
1872	Mansfield	NA	19	30	30	.309	.381	c	13	.873				
1873	Athletic	NA	44	36	62	.304	.392	c	23	.908				
1874	Athletic	NA	39	46	48	.291	.442	c-of	23	.878				
1875	Athletic	NA	60	65	77	.263	.345	c	71	.835				
1876	St. Louis	NL	64	60	91	.305	.322	c	59	.970				
1877	St. Louis	NL	60	47	81	.318	.388	c-of	40	.887#				
1878	Indianapolis	NL	63	42	80	.304	.357	o-l-c	24	.913				
1879	Buffalo	NL	70	47	77	.264	.349	c-of	36	.906#				
1880	Cincinnati	NL	80	33	91	.282	.365	c-of	62	.897#				
1881	Cleveland	NL	68	47	66	.253	.314	c-of	44	.877				
1882	Metropolitan		97	79	109	.248		c	80	.895				
1883	New York	NL	20	6	13	.178	.178	c-of	14	.892				
1884	St. Paul	NWL	16	9	11	.186	.203	of	11	.676				

JOHN T. CLEMENTS

Born: June 24, 1864, Philadelphia, Pa.
Died: May 23, 1941, Philadelphia, Pa.
BL TL 5-8 ½, 204

Although not the first, John Clements certainly was the best left-handed catcher in all baseball history. He spent most of his career with Philadelphia of the National League, though most of his rookie year was with the Philadelphia entry in the ill-fated Union Association in 1884. He was a great gate attraction because of his unorthodox catching and throwing styles.

Clements played in 1,157 games in 17 years, had 1,226 hits in 4,283 at bats, including 226 doubles, 60 triples and 77 homers for 1,803 total bases. He scored 619 runs and batted in an unofficial 673 runs.

During the decade of the 1890s, Clements batted .304 — second among catchers only to Mike Grady's .314. His slugging average for the decade led all catchers with .462. His 17 home runs in 1893 was second only to Ed Delahanty's .19. Overall, Clements batted .300

or more six times, including .346 in 1894 when a broken ankle held him to 45 games, .394 in 1895 followed by .359 in 1896. The .373 for the three years is perhaps unsurpassed by any catcher. Clements had his best year in 1895 when he was third in batting at .394, third in homers with 13 and third in slugging with .612. In 1890 he was third in batting with .315 and second in slugging at .472. In 1891 be batted .310, good enough for fourth.

As early as 1884 Clements appeared on the field with a chest protector that jeering fans and sports writers referred to as a "sheepskin." He was among the first to wear such protection. Charlie Bennett, one of the greatest catchers of the 1880s, claims to have appeared on the field wearing a protector as a member of the Detroit team for which he caught from 1881 through 1888, but the exact year is unknown.

Defensively, Clements held his own with his contemporaries. In 1898, he became the first player to catch in 1,000 games. By the end of his career, he caught in 1,073 games. Only Wilbert Robinson at 1,108 and Deacon McGuire with 1,102 caught more games during the 19th century. During the 1890s, he stacked up with his fellow mittmen. In games caught he ranked fifth. He ranked fourth in putouts, seventh in assists, sixth in errors and fifth in total chances. He was fourth in fielding average at .950.

His playing career ended in 1901 with Worcester in the Eastern League. After retiring, Clements went to work at the A. J. Reach plant in Philadelphia. When that factory closed, he went to a baseball factory in Perkasie, Pa. He died of a heart ailment at age 76.
— Al Glynn

			G	R	H	BA	SA	POS	E	FA	GP	W-L	R	H
1884	Keystone	UA	41	38	50	.282	.418	c-of	31	.858				
	Philadelphia	NL	9	2	7	.233	.300	c	12	.836				
1885	Philadelphia	NL	52	14	32	.191	.298	c-of	30	.891				
1886	Philadelphia	NL	54	15	38	.205	.243	c-of	30	.927				
1887	Philadelphia	NL	66	48	78	.306	.404	c	26	.940				
1888	Philadelphia	NL	86	26	80	.245	.307	c	47	.927				
1889	Philadelphia	NL	78	51	88	.284	.371	c	42	.916				
1890	Philadelphia	NL	97	64	120	.315	.472	c	35	.944				
1891	Philadelphia	NL	107	58	131	.310	.426	c	41	.927				
1892	Philadelphia	NL	109	50	107	.266	.418	c	37	.947				
1893	Philadelphia	NL	94	64	107	.285	.489	c	25	.942				
1894	Philadelphia	NL	47	26	59	.343	.494	c	11	.952				
1895	Philadelphia	NL	88	65	126	.389	.599	c	11	.969				
1896	Philadelphia	NL	57	35	66	.359	.543	c	7	.966				
1897	Philadelphia	NL	55	18	44	.238	.384	c	8	.962				
1898	St. Louis	NL	99	39	87	.260	.373	c	11	.971				
1899	Cleveland	NL	4	1	3	.250	.250	c	1	.923				
1900	Boston	NL	16	6	13	.310	.405	c	3	.938				
	Providence	EL	13	3	12	.324	.351	c	3	.955				
1901	Worcester	EL	61	41	68	.309		c	7	.972				

LAWRENCE J. CORCORAN

Born: August 10, 1959, Brooklyn, N.Y.
Died: October 14, 1891, Newark, N.J.
BL TR

Larry Corcoran appeared on the mound for the Mutual and Chelsea clubs of his native Brooklyn in the early weeks of the 1877 season, transferring to the Geneseo Livingstons in late June. By August, he was a member of the Buffalo pitching staff, as that city entered the ranks of professional baseball for the first time.

All these clubs, like Springfield for which he hurled in 1878 and 1879, were mediocre at best, but future stardom had already been predicted for Corcoran. "He has wonderful speed for his strength, and with it a troublesome curve. He also has more than ordinary command of the ball in delivery for so swift a pitcher. He is a good 'headwork' player in the position, and with such a catcher as Snyder or Flint able to support his great pace, it would be difficult to get a base-hit from his pitching." Those words describing Corcoran appeared in the September 13, 1879 issue of the *New York Clipper*.

The following month it was announced that Corcoran would pitch for Chicago in the 1880 season. A highlight of the 1880 campaign was Corcoran's June 4 16-inning 1-1 tie against Providence and John Montgomery Ward. From June 7 through July 13, he won 13 consecutive games. Corcoran's 1-hit victory on August 10 against Ward was surpassed nine days later when he held Boston hitless in a 6-0 triumph. His 43 victories that year is the third highest in baseball history for a rookie — topped only by the 1876 totals of Al Spalding (47) and George Bradley (45). Corcoran's 1881 games-won total fell to 31, but it was still good enough to tie for the National League lead with Jim Whitney of Boston. His top pitching performance of the year was on August 4, a 2-hit shutout against Buffalo and Jim Galvin. Corcoran's combined victory total of

74 for his first two years has been surpassed in baseball history only by Matt Kilroy's 75 gained for Baltimore in 1886-1887.

In 1882, Corcoran enjoyed two 10-game winning streaks: June 29 through July 29 and September 1 through September 30. The latter streak included a no-hitter against Worcester on Sept. 20. Chicago's support at the plate for Corcoran was superlative; they scored six or more runs in 23 of his 40 games, including 35 runs scored on July 24.

After returning to the 30-victory circle in 1883, Corcoran for awhile considered signing with the Chicago club of the fledgling Union Association for the succeeding season. He was, however, forced to rejoin the White Stockings for a reputed $2,100 after Chicago owner Spalding threatened him with blacklisting. Corcoran's 1884 season featured his third no-hitter (on June 27 against Providence). Corcoran had then reached the 30-victory plateau four times — a total exceeded by only five mound immortals: Kid Nichols (7), Tim Keefe (6), John Clarkson (6), Cy Young (5) and Tony Mullane (5).

At the end of the first four weeks of the 1885

season, Corcoran's won-lost record stood at 5-2. It was then reported that he had so strained the muscles of his shoulder that he couldn't throw. In the next few weeks, he showed no improvement and Chicago gave him his release.

New York signed him in July, but he took the mound only three times for the Giants, winning 2 and losing 1. His 8-3 victory over St. Louis on October 8 was the last game he was to win in the majors. Mickey Welch relieved in the eighth in that game after he sprained his ankle.

Corcoran pitched only four games after 1885 — two each in 1886 and 1887 — and was charged with the loss in three of those games.

He appeared briefly as a player and umpire in the minors during the next few years. In the spring of 1891, however, he was forced to give up all such activity after a severe spell of sickness from which he never recovered. He died on October 14, at the age of 32, a victim of Bright's disease. Corcoran possessed all the attributes of greatness except durability.

— John O'Malley

			G	R	H	BA	SA	POS	E	FA	GP	W-L	R	H
1877	Buffalo							p-of						
1878	Springfield	IA	35	7	19	.144	.165	p	44	.764	35	9-23	149	262
1879	Sprgf-Holyoke	NA	39		-	.274		p						
1880	Chicago	NL	72	41	66	.231	.276	p	7	.957	63	43-14	226	404
1881	Chicago	NL	47	25	42	.222	.275	p	11	.893	45	31-14	203	386
1882	Chicago	NL	40	23	35	.207	.308	p	6	.939	39	27-12	161	281
1883	Chicago	NL	68	40	55	.209	.308	p-of	22	.875	56	32-20	270	483
1884	Chicago	NL	64	43	61	.243	.299	p	24	.882	60	35-23	283	473
1885	Chicago-NY	NL	10	9	11	.306	.355	p	1	.968	10	7-3	50	87
1886	NY-Washington	NL	22	9	15	.176	.224	of-s	20	.722	2	0-1	11	16
1887	Indianapolis	NL	3	2	4	.400	.400	p-of	2	.500	2	0-2	30	23
1888	London	IA	28	17	21	.193		of	9	.743				

JAMES CREIGHTON

Born: April 15, 1841, New York, N.Y.
Died: October 18, 1862, Brooklyn, N.Y.

James Creighton should be remembered as baseball's first superstar. Though he died at a very young age, he single-handedly changed the game, as his feats attracted fans nationwide.

Creighton was born in New York City on April 15, 1841. His family soon moved to Brooklyn, where Jimmy took to the new game of baseball. He helped organize his first club, the Young America BBC, which lasted only one season, 1857. The following year, he and George Flanley founded the Niagara Club, where Creighton played mostly at second and third base.

Later he became a part-time pitcher. It was during a match with the crack junior club, the Stars, that Creighton's career took off. A trade card issued after his demise gives this account: "On the final inning of the game when the Stars were a number of runs ahead, the Niagaras changed pitchers, and Jimmy took that position. Peter O'Brien (Capt. of the Atlantics of Brooklyn) witnessed this game, and when Creighton got to work something new was seen in base ball — the low swift delivery, the ball rising from the ground past the shoulder to the catcher. The Stars soon saw they could not cope with such pitching."

Following the contest, Flanley and Creighton were stolen by the Stars. The pair finished the year with the Stars, but jumped to the Excelsior Club, the champions of America, at the start of the 1859 season. Creighton's pitching revolutionized the old style of pitching, which called for an easy toss to the batter. Accolades came, but so did controversy. Baseball conservatives claimed Creighton's style was illegal. On August 4, 1860, the *Brooklyn Eagle* dispatched a reporter to determine the legality of Jim's delivery. The reporter asked "Whether [Creighton's] pitching was a 'jerk,' an 'underhand throw,' or a 'fair square pitch,' and the conclusion we arrived at was, that it was unquestionably the latter; and now that we have seen it attentively, our wonder is that such experienced batsmen as the Atlantics could ever be mastered by it the way they were." Henry Chadwick lauded Creighton for his "head work," and nearly everyone had praise for his deportment and his remarkable hitting.

Creighton is the only player to complete an entire season without being put out. He hit and pitched the Excelsiors to victory on the first tours of the country by a ball team in 1860 and 1861. Young players began imitating Creighton's style, and some even named their teams after him.

It was during a game that Creighton suffered an accident which was to kill him. The story goes that John Chapman was waiting his turn to hit, as Creighton swung hard and smacked a home run. Upon the swing, Chapman heard a pop. After scoring, Jim told Flanley that he must have snapped his belt. But he had not; an internal organ had been ruptured. Creighton's obituary was run on October 20, 1862, two days after the contest. It read: "After suffering for a few days, he expired on Saturday afternoon last at the residence of his father, 307 Henry Street. The remains were encased in a handsome rosewood coffin, with silver mountings and upon a silver plate was inscribed the name, age, etc., of the deceased . . . James P. Creighton, 21 years, 7 months, and 2 days."

— Mark D. Rucker

		G	R	R/G	OUTS	O/G	POS
1858	Niagara of Brooklyn	-	-	-	-	-	of
1859	Niagara-Star	-	-	-	-	-	of-p
1860	Excelsior	20	47	2.4	56	2.8	p
1861	Excelsior	-	-	-	-	-	p
1862	Excelsior	-	-	4.2	0	0.0	p

WILLIAM FREDERICK DAHLEN
(Bad Bill)

Born: 1871, Nelliston, N.Y.
Died: December 5, 1950, Brooklyn, N.Y.
BR TR 5-9, 180

Known as "Bad Bill" because of his frequent altercations with the umpires, Bill Dahlen was an outstanding shortstop and all-around player in the last decade of the 19th century and the first years of the 20th century. He starred in the National League for Chicago, Brooklyn and New York before ending his playing career with Boston and becoming manager of Brooklyn.

Born in 1871 in Nellistown, N.Y., (not far from Cooperstown) Bill got his start as a professional in the New York State League in 1890. His performance attracted the notice of a friend of Chicago Colts captain Adrian Anson, and Dahlen was invited along on that club's spring tour in 1891. Bill not only made the team, he had an outstanding rookie year. Although he was shifted from third base to left field to shortstop, he was a fixture in the No. 3 spot in the batting order.

Anson continued to move Dahlen around the field until 1895, when he finally made him the permanent shortstop. At least he made sure that Bill's bat was in the lineup. Dahlen generally hit fifth, sixth or seventh in the order after his first two years in the league. His best season with the bat was 1894, when he hit .362 and scored 150 runs. During one stretch that season, from June 20 through September 13, Bill hit safely in 70 out of 71 games, going hitless only on August 6.

Dahlen played the game to the hilt. Bill suffered a severe spike wound on Memorial Day 1897 and was out of action until July 25. But in his very first game back, he made a straight steal of home to win the game 1-0. A righthanded free swinger, Dahlen struck out a fair amount, but he also drew a lot of walks and was adept at getting hit by pitches. He hit to all fields, having as much power to right as to left. He was an aggressive base runner and a fine slider. But the outstanding feature of his game was his fielding. He was very quick with plenty of range and an outstanding arm, which was particularly deadly on relay throws. He still holds the records for career assists and errors.

Dahlen also was famous for his raging temper. High-strung and stubborn, Bill was in many fights and suffered numerous ejections. He seemed to enjoy agitating Captain Anson, and on the Colts last road trip in 1896, Anson had Dahlen put off the train in the middle of nowhere after an argument over a trivial sleeping car pass. Bill had a fondness for betting on the horses and he was constantly in debt and seeking an advance on his salary.

After Anson was fired, Dahlen became Chicago's captain in 1898. But he soon lost favor because of his argumentative nature. In 1899, he was transferred to Brooklyn. Although his batting average declined, he was still a tough man in the clutch and his fielding saved many a game. In 1904, he was traded to New York, where he fit into John McGraw's scheme of things perfectly. Although he batted sixth for the first two-thirds of the 1904 season, he is credited with leading the league in RBIs for the year. By 1907, though, his batting average had slipped to .207 and he was traded to Boston. After spending 1908

and 1909 with the Doves, Dahlen was released.

Charley Ebbets immediately signed Dahlen to manage the Brooklyn club. With the Dodgers unable to approach the first division, Bad Bill's frustrations reached new heights. One famous fight came on April 20, 1912, just one day after the league president had shortened a previous Dahlen suspension. Umpire Cy Rigler called a ninth-inning fly ball down the line fair to send the Dodgers to defeat and Dahlen rushed onto the field immediately. The little manager and the big umpire were soon engaged in a wild fist fight, both principals landing several punches before being separated. Although he was unpopular both with the sportswriters and his own players, Dahlen was a big favorite of Ebbets, and he stayed with Brooklyn for four years, 1910-1913.

After he finally was fired, Dahlen worked on the docks and ran a semipro team in Brooklyn. He also owned a filling station. Later, he got a job as bullpen attendant at Yankee Stadium. He died in Brooklyn in 1950 at age 79.

— Robert L. Tiemann

			G	R	H	BA	SA	POS	E	FA	GP	W-L	R	H
1890	Cobleskill	NYSt	85	88	137	.342	.478	2b	58	.917				
1891	Chicago	NL	135	113	145	.263	.396	3-o-s	63	.882				
1892	Chicago	NL	143	116	173	.295	.417	ss-3b	58	.926				
1893	Chicago	NL	116	113	146	.301	.452	3b-o	70	.897				
1894	Chicago	NL	121	150	184	.362	.569	ss-3b	75	.899				
1895	Chicago	NL	131	107	139	.273	.381	ss	84	.907				
1896	Chicago	NL	125	137	172	.361	.544	ss	75	.912				
1897	Chicago	NL	75	67	85	.296	.480	ss	39	.929				
1898	Chicago	NL	142	96	152	.290	.393	ss	78	.909				
1899	Brooklyn	NL	122	88	121	.283	.395	ss	43	.941				
1900	Brooklyn	NL	134	87	126	.260	.346	ss	51	.942				
1901	Brooklyn	NL	131	69	136	.266	.358	ss	51	.936				
1902	Brooklyn	NL	138	68	139	.264	.353	ss	67	.914				
1903	Brooklyn	NL	138	71	124	.262	.342	ss	42	.948				
1904	New York	NL	145	70	140	.268	.337	ss	61	.930				
1905	New York	NL	148	67	126	.242	.337	ss	45	.948				
1906	New York	NL	143	63	113	.240	.297	ss	49	.938				
1907	New York	NL	143	40	96	.207	.254	ss	45	.941				
1908	Boston	NL	144	50	125	.239	.307	ss	43	.952				
1909	Boston	NL	69	22	46	.234	.305	ss-2b	35	.861				
1910	Brooklyn	NL	3	0	0	.000	.000	ph						
1911	Brooklyn	NL	1	0	0	.000	.000	ss	0	1.00				

HUGH IGNATIUS DAILY
(One Arm)

Born: 1857, Baltimore, Md.
BR TR 6-2, 180

Hugh Daily was surly and uncommunicative and almost universally hated by umpires, whom he badgered unmercifully. His lifetime pitching mark was below .500 (73-89 in six seasons), yet there are good reasons for including him here, apart from the fact that he became a major leaguer, despite the handicap of having only one whole arm and part of another. Among those are:

* On September 13, 1883, while with Cleveland (N.L.), he pitched a no-hit no-run game, defeating Philadelphia, 1-0.

* On July 7, 1884, pitching for Chicago (UA) he fanned 19 Bostons, equaling the record that had been set by Charley Sweeney of Providence (NL), exactly one month earlier. In this game, he allowed just 1 hit — a triple by Cannonball Crane. Three days later, also against Boston, he pitched another 1-hitter, giving up a single to John Scannell, making him the first in major league history to pitch consecutive 1-hitters. Only six times since has this feat been duplicated.

* In 1884, pitching for Chicago, Pittsburgh and Washington (all in the Union Association), he fanned 483 batters, second on the all-time list behind Matt Kilroy, who struck out 505 (*The Sporting News Record Book*) or 513 (Macmillan) for Baltimore (AA) in 1886.

Daily's early baseball activity is obscure. *The Sporting News Record Book*, quoting an 1882 story out of Buffalo, notes that he began to play professionally in 1875, but gives no specific teams. His major league career began in 1882 with Buffalo (NL), where he played with such luminaries as Dan Brouthers, Jim O'Rourke, Deacon White, Jack Rowe, Hardy Richardson and Jim Galvin, and won 15 and lost 14. After winning 23 and losing 19 for Cleveland (NL) in 1883, Daily jumped to the Chicago Unions for the 1884 season and compiled his notable 483 strikeouts. When the "Onions" folded after just one season, Daily found his name among those blacklisted for jumping their contracts. He reportedly was removed from the list when he paid a $500 fine, but for all practical purposes his short but brilliant major league career was over. From 1885 to 1887, he pitched for St. Louis (NL), Washington (NL) and Cleveland (AA), winning just 7 games while losing 26 in the three-year span.

Daily was called "One Arm," but perhaps "One Hand" would have been more accurate.

An 1882 Buffalo newspaper story tells how it happened: "Daily was playing with a companion in the Front St. Theater in Baltimore, where he was employed, when an English flint-lock musket suddenly exploded in the hands of his companion. The charge lodged in Daily's left hand, inflicting a wound which necessitated amputation at the wrist. Finding considerable difficulty in using his stump wrist, he invented an adjustable pad for his wrist, which he fastened at the elbow and the swiftest thrown ball, if it strikes the pad over the stump, does not cause pain. In catching the ball, Daily allows it to hit the pad and before it can rebound, encircles it with his right hand." Despite his handicap, Daily was a fair hitter. He is credited with 88 hits in his six seasons. His best year was 1884 when he had 43 hits and batted .214.

Nothing is known of Daily after his 1887 season with Cleveland. Despite diligent efforts by researchers over many years, the place and date of his death are still unknown.

— Joseph M. Overfield

			G	R	H	BA	SA	POS	E	FA	GP	W-L	R	H
1880	Rochester	NA						p						
	Metropolitan		18	10	18	.286		p	11	.732	17			
1881	Metropolitan		33#	-	10	.086		p	9	.828	37	24-12		
1882	Buffalo	NL	29	10	18	.164	.236	p	4	.879	29	15-14	165	246
1883	Cleveland	NL	45	18	18	.127	.134	p	5	.939	45	23-19	190	360
1884	Chi/Pitt-Nat	UA	60	21	43	.214	.254	p	20	.854	58	28-30	-	446
1885	St. Louis	NL	11	1	3	.086	.086	p	2	.913	11	3-8	72	92
1886	Washington	NL	6	2	2	.125	.125	p	4	.750	6	0-6	60	69
	Milw-St.Paul	NWL	19	7	3	.053	.053	p	7		17	9-8	82	126
1887	Cleveland	AA	16	1	4	.069	.069	p	3	.850	16	4-12	100	181

ABNER DALRYMPLE

Born: Sept. 9, 1857, Warren, Ill.
Died: Jan. 25, 1939, Warren, Ill.
BL TR 5-10 ½, 175

Abner Dalrymple was one of the stars of the great Chicago White Stocking teams of the 1880s. In eight seasons with the Cap Anson-led White Stockings, during which they finished first five times, Dalrymple batted at a .295 rate while playing a solid left field.

Dalrymple began playing baseball at age 14 in 1872 when he joined a town team representing his home town of Warren, Ill. He later played with a team organized by the Illinois Central Railroad for which Dalrymple worked as a brakeman. Dalrymple played with this team for three years.

In the summer of 1876, Dalrymple joined the Milwaukee club in the League Alliance. Milwaukee joined the National League in 1878 with Dalrymple stationed in left field. He led the batting list in the official league statistics with a .356 mark. The left-handed hitting Dalrymple also led the loop in outfield putouts his first season while Milwaukee finished in last place among the six league entrants.

Dalrymple joined the White Stockings in 1879 when Albert Spalding paid a reported $2,500 to Milwaukee to secure his services. Dalrymple later claimed to have been the highest paid player on that team drawing a salary of $300 per month.

Several excellent seasons followed for Dalrymple as he served as the Chicago lead-off hitter: He led the league in base hits with 126 and in runs scored with 91 in 1880; four times he led in at bats; and he led the National League in home runs in 1885 with 11. Dalrymple also teamed with Anson on July 3, 1883 to become the first teammates to each smack 4 doubles in one game.

After his playing days ended, Dalrymple was not shy in admitting his use of various tricks to win ball games. One in particular

saved a game for the White Stockings in 1880 against the Boston Red Stockings while robbing an opponent of a home run. With Chicago leading in the ninth inning, Boston loaded the bases with two out. Ezra Sutton, the Boston third baseman, "caught the ball a furious wallop and it sailed directly toward me in left field," Dalrymple recalled. "I had in the blouse of my uniform an extra ball which I had kept there for an emergency. A smokey haze had settled over the field. The ball soared as it neared me back almost against the fence. I seized the concealed ball, stretched my hand upward and leaped, and came down with the ball in my hand. The umpire called the Boston side out."

Dalrymple was sold to Pittsburgh (NL) in 1887, although he missed a substantial

amount of games that year and the next due to illness. He played in the Western Association with Denver in 1889 and with Milwaukee 1890 and 1891. Dalrymple returned to the majors in 1891 when the Milwaukee franchise entered the American Association in August, compiling a .311 average to finish his major league career with a .288 lifetime batting average.

Dalrymple finished out his playing career with Spokane in 1892, Macon in 1893, Indianapolis in 1894 and Evansville in 1895. Dalrymple returned to his hometown of Warren, Ill., after his career. He worked on the Northern Pacific Railroad as a freight brakeman and passenger conductor for 36 years. He died on January 25, 1939.

— Richard A. Puff

			G	R	H	BA	SA	POS	E	FA	GP	W-L	R	H
1877	Milwaukee		61	48	74	.298		of	15	.807				
1878	Milwaukee	NL	61	52	96	.354	.421	of	28	.832				
1879	Chicago	NL	71	47	97	.291	.372	of	40	.728				
1880	Chicago	NL	86	91	126	.330	.458	of	29	.859				
1881	Chicago	NL	82	72	117	.323	.412	of	31	.835				
1882	Chicago	NL	84	96	117	.295	.421	of	27	.877				
1883	Chicago	NL	80	78	108	.298	.402	of	34	.827				
1884	Chicago	NL	111	111	161	.309	.505	of	26	.882				
1885	Chicago	NL	113	109	135	.274	.445	of	27	.879				
1886	Chicago	NL	82	62	77	.233	.326	of	7	.953				
1887	Pittsburgh	NL	92	45	121	.300	.382	of	22	.900				
1888	Pittsburgh	NL	57	19	50	.220	.282	of	9	.908				
1889	Denver	WA	118	142	173	.331		of	55	.844				
1890	Denver-Milw.	WA	111	116	159	.328		of	32	.875				
1891	Milwaukee	WA	76	73	111	.340	.497	of	14	.918				
	Milwaukee	AA	32	31	42	.311	.459	of	3	.936				
1892	Spokane	PacNW	50	49	75	.306	.449	of	7	.945				
1893	Macon	SL	28	22	32	.242	.288	of						
1894	Indianapolis	WL	75	76	117	.355		of	23	.879				
1895	Evansville	SL	48	47	66	.314		of						

GEORGE STACEY DAVIS

Born: August 23, 1870, Cohoes, N.Y.
Died: October 17, 1940, Philadelphia, Pa.
BB TR 5-9, 180

"How is it possible for a man to play big league baseball for 20 seasons, manage the New York Giants twice, start a war between the National and American Leagues and then utterly vanish, without leaving a trace?"

So asked Lee Allen in his Cooperstown Corner column about shortstop George Davis (*The Sporting News*, August 7, 1968). Upon looking dispassionately at Davis's statistics, one would just assume he is in the Hall of Fame. But he is not, and with the present de-emphasis on players whose careers began in the last century, the chances are he never will. Sad, indeed, for here was a man who played from 1890 to 1909, took part in 2,377 games, had 2,688 hits, 454 doubles, 73 home runs, 615 stolen bases and a lifetime mark of .297 — 30 points higher than Bobby Wallace and 39 points higher than Rabbit Maranville, both Hall shortstops. In addition, Davis hit 6 for 6 on August 15, 1895, and hit 3 triples in one game in 1891 and again 1894 (both extra-inning games). Davis also was one of the greatest switch-hitters. He still holds the season (26) and career records (167) for three-base hits for players hitting from both sides of the plate.

Erratic in the field in his early years, Davis improved greatly in later seasons. He fielded .930 in his first 13 seasons, which were in the National League, and improved to .947 in his final seasons in the American League. Overall, he fielded .937, compared to .940 for Wallace, who was a contemporary, and .956 for Maranville, who played later when gloves were improved.

Born in Cohoes, N.Y., Davis began his professional career a short distance away in Albany in 1889. From 1890 to 1892, he played for Cleveland, (NL), first as an outfielder and then as a third baseman. In March 1893, in one of the biggest trades of the decade, Davis was traded to New York for Buck Ewing, considered by many the greatest catcher of the day. Davis was a sensation with the Giants,

batting .362, .346, .330, .320, .358, .307, .346, .324 and .309 from 1893 through 1901. He also managed the Giants in 1901 and parts of the 1895 and 1900 seasons, but with indifferent success (107-139).

In 1902, Davis jumped to Chicago (AL), but jumped right back to the Giants the following year. Meanwhile, in peace negotiations between the two leagues, Davis was awarded to Chicago. Davis, however, through his lawyer, John Montgomery Ward, fought the decision and prolonged litigation ensued. The Davis case almost destroyed baseball's tenuous peace and caused a bitter enmity between Ward and Ban Johnson that lasted the rest of their lives.

Davis played in only four games in 1903, all for the Giants. He reported in 1904 to Chicago, where he played for six more seasons, including the "Hitless Wonders" championship campaign of 1906. The 1909 season was his 20th and last in the majors, although he did

manage Des Moines (Western League) in 1910. His final connection with baseball was as Amherst College coach from 1913-1918.

Little is known of Davis's activities after 1918. There was a report (see Lee Allen column referred to above) that he went to New York to play bridge for a living. For 15 years, Allen searched fruitlessly for some trace of Davis, but wound up in one blind alley after another until one day in 1968 when a woman, claiming she was Davis's niece, came to the Hall of Fame. She put Allen in touch with a sister of the old ballplayer. She had little hard information, but said she believed he had died in Philadelphia State Hospital in 1934. She was wrong on the date, but right on the place. When Allen secured a copy of the death certificate, it showed that Davis had been confined to the Philadelphia State Hospital in 1934 and had died there on October 17, 1940.

— Joseph M. Overfield

			G	R	H	BA	SA	POS	E	FA	GP	W-L	R	H
1890	Cleveland	NL	136	98	139	.264	.375	of	18	.946				
1891	Cleveland	NL	136	115	167	.292	.412	of-3	32	.919	3	0-1	7	8
1892	Cleveland	NL	144	96	151	.253	.357	3-o-s	36	.919				
1893	New York	NL	133	112	199	.373	.587	3b	58	.896				
1894	New York	NL	124	124	170	.346	.543	3b	40	.910				
1895	New York	NL	99	98	131	.343	.513	3b-1b	46	.920				
1896	New York	NL	124	98	158	.320	.455	3b-ss	43	.926				
1897	New York	NL	131	114	188	.358	.501	ss	57	.932				
1898	New York	NL	121	80	148	.306	.384	ss	57	.931				
1899	New York	NL	111	69	144	.349	.436	ss	39	.950				
1900	New York	NL	114	69	136	.319	.406	ss	45	.942				
1901	New York	NL	130	69	153	.309	.418	ss-3	44	.946				
1902	Chicago	AL	132	76	145	.299	.402	ss	40	.947				
1903	New York	NL	4	2	4	.267	.267	ss	3	.875				
1904	Chicago	AL	152	74	143	.256	.357	ss	59	.936				
1905	Chicago	AL	157	74	153	.278	.340	ss	46	.948				
1906	Chicago	AL	133	63	134	.277	.355	ss	42	.944				
1907	Chicago	AL	132	59	111	.238	.288	ss	38	.949				
1908	Chicago	AL	128	41	91	.217	.255	2b-ss	32	.951				
1909	Chicago	AL	28	5	9	.132	.147	1b	3	.986				
1910	Des Moines	WL	32	14	19	.192	.192	2b-ss	10	.925				

EUGENE NAPOLEON DE MONTREVILLE

Born: March 26, 1874, St. Paul, Minn.
Died: February 18, 1935, Memphis, Tenn.
BR TR 5-8 165

Eugene Napoleon DeMontreville was not the dashing hero of a French novel set in the days of Louis XIV, as might be surmised from his name. He was, instead, a professional ballplayer of some reputation.

His name, which often was shortened to DeMont, was one to stir the imagination. Shirley Povich in *Washington Senators* called him "the handsome mustachioed French-Canadian from St. Paul." (Pictures that have survived show him as handsome, but clean-shaven.) Legend has it that James Thurber was so struck by the name that he used it in modified form (Pearl DuMonville) and attached it to the midget-hero of his whimsical short story, "You Could Look It Up." In the story, Pearl goes to bat at a crucial spot with instructions to "wait the pitcher out," but instead swings away at the 3-0 pitch with disastrous results. It has been written that it was Thurber's story that inspired the Bill Veeck-Eddie Gaedel caper of 1951. In his book, *Veeck As In Wreck*, Veeck denies this saying it was Eddie Morrow, hump-backed mascot of the New York Giants, who gave him the idea. John McGraw often said he would put Morrow in a game some day, but he never did.

Born in St. Paul, DeMontreville moved to Washington, D.C. as a youth, where he took up the game. He began his long baseball odyssey as a shortstop-second baseman with Binghamton (Eastern League) in 1894. He also played that same year with Buffalo (Eastern League) and Pittsburgh (NL). It was to be his lot never to stay too long in one place. He became a full-time major leaguer with Washington (NL) in 1896, batting a robust .343, followed by .348 in 1897. His fielding, however, left something to be desired. He led the league in boots both years, with 87 and 78, respectively.

At the end of the 1897 season, DeMontreville was packaged with pitcher Jim Mc-James and first baseman Dan McGann and shipped to Baltimore for catcher Jack Doyle, second baseman Heinie Reitz and pitcher Doc Amole. Harold Seymour, in *Baseball: The Early Years*, writes that one of the Wagner brothers, who owned the Washington club, later bragged that he had talked the official scorer into adding 40 hits to DeMontreville's batting record, to increase his market value. There is a strong suspicion that this was something of a fish story, since DeMontreville had batted .343 in 1896 and was to bat .320 his first year with the Orioles. And making the deal even more palatable to the Birds, in case there had been skullduggery, was the fact the DeMontreville improved his fielding average by an astronomical 58 points.

Despite his outstanding 1898 season, De-Montreville was traded to the Cubs for Bill Dahlen. In August 1899, the Birds got him back; but the franchise in Baltimore was then at the end of its tether and the players were transferred to Brooklyn at the end of the sea-son. Subsequently, he made stops at Boston (NL), in 1901 and 1902; Washington (AL), in 1903; and then briefly in St. Louis (AL) in 1904. He was to go on for several more years in the minors as a player and manager, before hanging up his spikes. His lifetime major league marks are imposing: he batted .306 in 922 games and had 130 doubles, 35 triples and 17 home runs. He also was a top-notch base runner particularly adept at the delayed steal.

On February 18, 1935, while running to investigate a minor fire at the Mid-South Fairgrounds in Memphis, where he was concessions manager, he was fatally stricken. It was ironic that Gene DeMontreville, who was only 61, should die while running. All his life he had run to catch trains, having played or managed in 17 different cities all the way from Montreal to Meridian, Miss.

— Joseph M. Overfield

			G	R	H	BA	SA	POS	E	FA	GP	W-L	R	H
1894	Bnghmtn-Buff	EL	36	31	45	.308	.514	ss	21	.898				
	Pittsburgh	NL	2	0	2	.250	.250	ss	1	.875				
1895	Toronto	EL	112	92	144	.315	.428	ss	76	.892				
	Washington	NL	12	7	10	.217	.370	ss	5	.936				
1896	Washington	NL	133	94	183	.343	.452	ss	97	.890				
1897	Washington	NL	133	92	193	.341	.433	ss-2b	89	.900				
1898	Baltimore	NL	151	93	186	.328	.369	2b-ss	51	.944				
1899	Chicago-Balt	NL	142	83	154	.280	.345	ss-2b	69	.926				
1900	Brooklyn	NL	69	34	57	.244	.286	2-s-3	25	.931				
1901	Boston	NL	140	83	174	.305	.374	2b-3b	39	.946				
1902	Boston	NL	124	51	125	.300	.364	2b	42	.929				
1903	Washington	AL	12	0	12	.273	.318	2b	3	.948				
1904	St. Louis	AL	4	0	1	.111	.111	2b	0	1.00				
	Atlanta	SL	120	68	119	.288	.416	2b-ss	46	.935				
1905	Toledo	AA	152	93	171	.290	.392	2b	46	.950				
1906	Toledo	AA	133	67	148	.282	.373	ss-o	43	.914				
1907	Toledo	AA	28	10	20	.187	.243	2b	16	.900				
	Birmingham	SL	107	65	105	.262		ss	35	.938				
1908	Birmingham	SL	69	28	53	.222		ss	24	.933				
1909	New Orleans	SL	109	33	86	.229		2b-s	21	.966				
1910	New Orleans	SL	107	29	64	.189		2b-s	32	.945				

JEREMIAH DENNIS DENNY

Born: March 16, 1859, New York, N.Y.
Died: August 16, 1927, Houston, Texas
BR TR 5-11 ½, 180

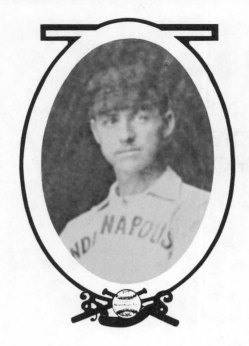

Wide-ranging Jerry Denny snared batted balls equally well with both hands and, although he seldom used a fielder's glove, he ranks among baseball's most sure-handed third basemen. Of major leaguers with 1,000 or more games at third base, he is the all-time per-game leader in both total chances and putouts. He was, however, prone to throwing the ball away once he had fielded it and holds the National League career record for errors at third base. Nevertheless, in half of his 10 full seasons he ranked first or second in fielding average and among the top three third basemen in assists.

Born in New York City, Denny grew to adulthood in orphanages in California, where his Irish immigrant parents had died shortly after moving west. After four years of playing ball in San Francisco — in left field for the Eagles (1877-79) and at third base for the Athletics (1880) — Denny traveled east to play for Providence in the National League. For five years he was the Grays third baseman, until the club's demise following the 1885 season. In 1886, playing for the St. Louis Maroons (NL), Denny enjoyed his finest season as a fielder, leading league third basemen in putouts, assists and double plays, and finishing a close second in fielding average. The Maroons were sold to Indianapolis in 1887. In his three years with the Hoosiers he did the best hitting of his major league career, reaching personal highs in every offensive category, including his only .300-plus season (1887) and 18 home runs in 1889, second best in the league.

But Indianapolis folded, and Denny once again moved on, this time to the New York Giants, where in 1890 he played his last full major league season. In 1891, he played less than half the time for three different clubs. In the off-seasons Denny would return to California to play winter ball. In 1892, he remain-

ed there through the summer as well playing third base for San Jose in the California League.

When San Jose manager George Stallings moved on in 1893 to manage Augusta, Ga., in the Southern League, Denny went with him. Denny returned to the National League in July to complete the season as shortstop for Louisville. He began 1894 as the Colonels third baseman, but was released in midseason, ending his major league career. Denny played many memorable games. On August 17, 1882, he accepted 16 chances in 18 innings, still a record for third basemen in a single game. On May 4, 1889, he became the seventh National Leaguer to hit 6 for 6 (includ-

ing a grand slam home run off Jim Galvin). And in 1890, he tied two league records for third basemen in nine-inning games with 13 chances accepted on May 19 and with 11 assists 10 days later.

Denny is remembered best for hitting the first World Series home run. On October 24, 1884, playing for the National League champion Providence Grays, he homered off Tim Keefe of New York's Metropolitans, AA champs, to win both the game and the series for Providence.

After retiring from baseball, Denny settled in Connecticut, where he operated hotels in Derby and Bridgeport.

— Frederick Ivor-Campbell

Year	Team	League	G	R	H	BA	SA	POS	E	FA	GP	W-L	R	H
1878	SF Eagles	Pac	10			.195		of-1b		.741				
1879	SF Stars	Pac												
1880	SF Athletics	Pac												
1881	Providence	NL	85	38	77	.241	.313	3b	62	.840				
1882	Providence	NL	84	54	81	.246	.350	3b	55	.861				
1883	Providence	NL	98	73	108	.275	.438	3b	52	.876				
1884	Providence	NL	110	57	109	.248	.380	3b	46	.899				
1885	Providence	NL	83	40	71	.223	.324	3b	43	.869				
1886	St. Louis	NL	119	58	122	.257	.356	3b	54	.895				
1887	Indianapolis	NL	112	86	178	.340	.509	3b	58	.889				
1888	Indianapolis	NL	126	92	137	.261	.420	3b-s	56	.904	1	0-0	4	5
1889	Indianapolis	NL	133	96	163	.282	.410	3b	45	.913				
1890	New York	NL	114	50	93	.213	.307	3b	47	.889				
1891	NY-Clv-Phil	NL	59	22	58	.256	.308	3-1-o	26	.916				
1892	San Jose	Cal	172	92	174	.262	.367	3b	71	.901				
1893	Augusta	SL	86	82	96	.279	.485	3b	40	.906				
	Louisville	NL	44	22	43	.246	.337	ss	20	.920				
1894	Louisville	NL	60	26	61	.275	.392	3b	32	.867				
1896	Shelton-Drby	NaugV	-											
1897	Derby	ConSt												
1898	Waterbury	ConSt	85	62	92	.257		ss-2b						
1899	Derby	ConSt	91	70	103	.273	.377	1b						
1900	Derby	ConSt	97	48	101	.280	.368	2b	34	.933				
1901	Drby-Norwch	ConSt	103	79	135	.311		1b						
1902	Brdgpt-Nrwh	ConSt	21	5	16	.195	.280	2b	8	.943				

JAMES ALEXANDER DEVLIN

Born: 1849, Philadelphia, Pa.
Died: October 10, 1883, Philadelphia, Pa.
BR TR 5-11, 175

By midseason 1877, Jim Devlin — after 71 victories in only three seasons as a pitcher — stood on the verge of stardom. He had pitched Louisville into first place in the National League and seemed capable of continuing to bring them the pennant. But after a disastrous late-season road trip, he was accused by his club of helping to throw games. Admitting his involvement, he was expelled from the club and, along with three of his teammates, was banned by the league from professional baseball for life. The players' corruption cost Louisville the pennant and their expulsion from baseball contributed to the demise not only of the Louisville club, but also of St. Louis, where Devlin had planned to pitch in 1878.

For the next six years, through letters and personal pleas, Devlin sought reinstatement. Even the directors of his former Louisville club appealed to the National League in his behalf in 1883, but before the league could consider the appeal, Devlin died of consumption.

Devlin did not begin as a pitcher. In 1872, he played third base for Easton, Pa., moving up the next year to the Philadelphias of the National Association, where he tried out several positions. In 1874, he joined the Chicago White Stockings, playing chiefly at first base and in the outfield. The next year he played the majority of Chicago's games at first base, but also became a pitcher at last, compiling an unimpressive 6-16 won-lost record in 26 games.

When the National League was organized in 1876, Devlin moved on to the Louisville Colonels, where during his two years with the club he pitched nearly all Louisville's games, accounting for all of the team's victories and all but one of its losses. In both seasons he led the league in complete games and innings pitched. Although he also led the league both years in losses, he finished among league leaders in earned run average. In 1877, despite his deliberate losses, Devlin finished second in the league in both wins and winning percentage.

Uneducated and semiliterate, Devlin was left destitute by his expulsion from professional baseball. He eventually found employment as a policeman in his native Philadelphia — and esteem among his new colleagues for his "kind and genial disposition." But his death came too soon after he joined the force for him to lift his family out of the poverty his expulsion from baseball had plunged them into.

The National League's firmness brought suffering to Devlin and his family. But by its repeated refusal to reinstate the "Louisville quartet," the league restored public confidence in the game's integrity and established a precedent for unyielding opposition to corrupt play that has helped keep gambling's influence on baseball to an impressive minimum for more than a century.

— Frederick Ivor-Campbell

			G	R	H	BA	SA	POS	E	FA	GP	W-L	R	H
1873	Philadelphia	NA	23	18	25	.253	.374	1-3-s	32	.835				
1874	Chicago	NA	45	26	59	.288	.312	1b-rf	37	.884				
1875	Chicago	NA	69	60	92	.291	.370	1b-p	52	.918	27	7-16	179	256
1876	Louisville	NL	68	38	94	.315	.369	p	9	.941	68	30-35	309	566
1877	Louisville	NL	61	38	72	.269	.325	p	10	.933	61	35-25	288	617

FREDERICK C. DUNLAP

Born: May 21, 1859, Philadelphia, Pa.
Died: December 1, 1902, Philadelphia, Pa.
BR TB 5-8, 165

The nicknames "Sure Shot Fred" and "King Fred" reflected Fred Dunlap's stature as one of the best players of the 1880s. Many contemporary players and writers believed that he was the greatest player of baseball's first "Golden Age." As late as 1910, Al Spink would state unequivocally that "Fred Dunlap was far and away the greatest second baseman that ever lived."

Dunlap came from a humble beginning. He was born in Philadelphia in 1859 and was orphaned before he was 10 years old. A middle-aged couple took him in but had little regard for his education or well-being. Luckily for the boy, Philadelphia was a baseball city. To escape his otherwise dreary family existence, he constantly played on the fields around the city. In doing so, he made himself a ballplayer.

He first starred with the Gloucester Club of New Jersey in 1874. The next year he played shortstop with the Cregar Club of Camden, New Jersey, followed by play with the Kleinz Club of Philadelphia in 1876. His first professional engagement was with Auburn, N.Y. in 1876. In 1877, when Fred was 18, he was with the Philadelphia Acmes. In 1878 he played with the Hornells of Hornellsville, N.Y., and following their disbandment in August, with Albany, champions of the minor league National Association.

In 1880, Dunlap joined the Cleveland Nationals, beginning a major-league career that lasted until 1891, and included stints with St. Louis, Detroit, Pittsburgh and Washington, as well. He played second base almost exclusively.

At Cleveland, Fred was a member of one of the best 19th century infields, then known as the "Stonewall Infield." Its anchors were Dunlap and "Pebbly Jack" Glasscock, a marvelous fielding shortstop. After four seasons with Cleveland, Dunlap jumped to the St. Louis "Onions" of the short-lived Union Association, becoming the highest-paid player of

his time, with a $3,400 salary. He and the St. Louis team, whom he field-managed, dominated the league. The team entered the National League in 1885.

In 1886, Dunlap was sold to Detroit, an up-and-coming team in the league. The Wolverines won the pennant and World Series in 1887, although Fred was sidelined for 10 weeks after suffering a leg injury in a collision with right fielder Sam Thompson. In November 1887, his contract was sold to Pittsburgh, much to Dunlap's chagrin. He held out for a portion of the purchase price and eventually received over $6,000 in salary and bonus for the season, a staggering sum at the time.

He managed the Alleghenies briefly in 1889 but was soon supplanted by Ned Hanlon, with whom he did not get along. Dunlap's hitting had fallen off and his once-legendary fielding range was gone by the time Pittsburgh finally released him on May 15, 1890. After a one-game trial with the New York Brotherhood team, he sat out of the rest of the season. He began the 1891 campaign with Washington, but on April 20 suffered a career-ending broken leg while sliding.

Dunlap was regarded as the game's premier second baseman throughout the 1880s. After his death, one newspaper described him this way: "The baseball world will perhaps never again see his equal. He never wore a glove and his hands were as small as a woman's, but he could handle any sort of throw or hit, running at the ball from either right or left and never halting at a bad throw or difficult ground hit. Dunlap was ambidextrous. In covering second, he would run and catch a badly thrown ball as well with his left hand as with his right hand. Great as a fielder, he was even greater as a thrower. His aim was as accurate as the best rifle shot."

Fred was also an aggressive slider and fast baserunner. He was a good (though not great) batter, who excelled in the clutch. He batted with some power, although his league-leading 13 home runs in 1884 were greatly aided by the tiny St. Louis ballpark.

Baseball was Dunlap's life. Although he left the game a rich man, he died in poverty in his native Philadelphia in 1902.

— Dennis Goldstein and
Richard A. Puff

			G	R	H	BA	SA	POS	E	FA	GP	W-L	R	H
1877	Auburn		68		-	.266		2b		.849				
1878	Hornellsville	IA	38	26	45	.273	.345	2b	26	.869				
1879	Albany	NA	51	53	61	.259		2b	17	.920				
1880	Cleveland	NL	85	61	103	.276	.429	2b	53	.911				
1881	Cleveland	NL	80	60	114	.325	.444	2b	51	.909				
1882	Cleveland	NL	84	68	102	.280	.354	2b	63	.900				
1883	Cleveland	NL	93	81	129	.326	.452	2b	58	.911				
1884	St. Louis	UA	101	160	185	.412	.621	2b	51	.926	1	0-0	0	2
1885	St. Louis	NL	106	70	114	.270	.333	2b	49	.934				
1886	StL-Detroit	NL	122	83	137	.284	.381	2b	55	.931				
1887	Detroit	NL	65	60	97	.327	.485	2b	24	.948	1	0-0	2	4
1888	Pittsburgh	NL	82	41	84	.262	.333	2b	33	.940				
1889	Pittsburgh	NL	121	59	106	.235	.295	2b	39	.950				
1890	Pittsburgh	NL	17	9	11	.172	.219	2b	13	.873				
	New York	PL	1	1	2	.500	.500	2b	0	1.00				
1891	Washington	AA	8	4	5	.200	.320	2b	6	.818				

CHARLES ANDREW FARRELL
(Duke)

Born: August 31, 1866, Oakdale, Mass.
Died: February 15, 1925, Marlborough, Mass.
BB TR 6-1, 208

Soon after Charley Farrell's birth his family moved to Marlborough, Mass. As a teen-ager Charley worked at a local shoe store and caught for the town team. They were good enough to trump several pro clubs and Farrell was signed by Salem of the New England League. Young Charles attracted the notice of Cap Anson and in 1888 he broke into the National League.

Farrell replaced Silver Flint and shared the catching chores with Tom Daly. He played some at third and when Daly was traded Farrell took over behind the plate full time. His arm was like a whip; he was tall, thin and agile. In 1890 he joined the rebellion, with Chicago; afterward he hooked up with the Boston (AA) entry.

In Boston Farrell became a star. The Beantown "Reds" won the pennant and Charley led the Association in home runs with 12. Before an exhibition game at Rocky Point, Harry Stevens, the famous concessionaire, was introducing the players. "Now batting," he bellowed, "The Duke of Marlborough." The name stuck forever. The Duke was the pride and joy of Marlborough. When he first came home from Chicago all the factories were shut for a great banquet and the 22-year-old received a gold watch, flowers and other gifts. He married a local lass, Julia Bradley, and lived there all his life.

When the American Association collapsed, Pittsburgh picked him up and installed him at third. He hit .215. Back behind the plate he spent a couple of years in New York and Washington. He hit cleanup in Washington and split the catching with old Deacon McGuire. On May 11, 1897, he set an all-time record. Winnie Mercer, a junkball twirler, was pitching and the Baltimore Orioles wanted to run. They tried. Joe Corbett stole a base but eight other men were shot down by Farrell's trusty arm. In spite of his heroics, Washington lost, but it is unlikely that the Duke's feat will be surpassed.

The *Boston Globe* called him a "brainy player" and Ned Hanlon acquired both Deacon and the Duke to handle his hurlers in Brooklyn. They copped two flags there. Duke was spiked in 1901 and missed many days due to blood poisoning. He was sick again in 1902. "Had Farrell been in shape to do duty behind the bat the Superbas would have won all five games with Boston," wrote Tim Murnane. Hanlon withheld his pay. Despite coming back to throw out 12 men in 6 games, Farrell was released; he was out of shape. Harry Stevens had added to his nickname; now he was also "the champion clam eater."

The Boston Americans needed a catcher and they took Duke. He lost 19 pounds the first week of spring training and shaved off his handlebar mustache to look younger. As the only local player on the Boston club, Duke was a popular addition. There was another banquet and he got a 4½ carat diamond on Opening Day. He also threw out five baserunners. He was batting .503 when he tried to steal second in Washington. He slid, caught

his spikes and broke his small leg bone. They carried him off and he stayed with some old Washington pals. During the convalescence he put on more weight and reinjured his leg when he returned. The Americans won the flag, Duke got one World Series at bat, and *Sporting Life* suggested he lose 60 pounds over the winter.

He didn't. "Get an automobile!" a fan yelled as he lumbered toward first. He caught Jesse Tannehill's no-hitter. And he "had the whiskers of his left hand little finger shaved" by a Jack Powell pitch. "No scar left," he dropped his bat, shook his wrist, the ump was skeptical but "Farrell's apparent agony on his face settled it." He was smiling as he ambled down to first while the catcher raged. Good cheer, a smile and a handshake was his trademark and while he tried other careers (he was briefly a U.S. Marshall), baseball was his life. When he died in 1925, he was a coach for the Boston Braves.

— Rich Eldred

			G	R	H	BA	SA	POS	E	FA	GP	W-L	R	H
1887	Lawr-Salem	NEng	47	53	80	.376	.488	c-of	18	.910				
1888	Chicago	NL	64	34	56	.232	.332	c-of	39	.875				
1889	Chicago	NL	101	66	107	.263	.423	c-of	53	.908				
1890	Chicago	PL	117	78	133	.296	.407	c-1b	48	.938				
1891	Boston	AA	122	108	143	.302	.474	3-c-o	44	.917				
1892	Pittsburgh	NL	152	96	136	.231	.331	3b-o	69	.882				
1893	Washington	NL	124	84	143	.280	.380	c-3b	68	.899				
1894	New York	NL	114	50	114	.282	.433	c	41	.937				
1895	New York	NL	90	38	90	.288	.407	c-3b	30	.932				
1896	NY-Washington	NL	95	41	93	.290	.389	c-3-s	39	.896				
1897	Washington	NL	78	41	84	.322	.391	c	16	.951				
1898	Washington	NL	99	47	106	.314	.393	c-1b	28	.950				
1899	Wash-Brooklyn	NL	85	42	80	.301	.417	c	19	.952				
1900	Brooklyn	NL	76	33	75	.275	.352	c	20	.944				
1901	Brooklyn	NL	80	38	84	.296	.384	c-1b	12	.978				
1902	Brooklyn	NL	74	14	64	.242	.277	c-1b	12	.979				
1903	Boston	AL	17	5	21	.404	.538	c	4	.958				
1904	Boston	AL	68	11	42	.212	.278	c	13	.958				
1905	Boston	AL	7	2	6	.286	.333	c	0	1.00				

CHARLES J. FERGUSON
(Fergy)

Born: April 7, 1863, Charlottesville Va.
Died: April 29, 1888, Philadelphia, Pa.
BL TR 5-10 ¾, 165

Charlie Ferguson was one of the first tragic figures in Major League history — a graceful natural athlete who might have become the all-time greatest ball player. Instead, typhoid fever cut him down at age 25, making his bride of two years a widow and causing probably the saddest day in Philadelphia baseball, as teammates, Princeton players he coached during off-season, stunned fans, and the whole baseball fraternity mourned his passing.

In four years as a major leaguer, with Philadelphia (NL) from 1884 through 1887 as a right-handed hurler, he earned a .607 winning percentage (99-64) for an otherwise losing team. As a normally left-handed hitter, he posted a .288 batting average, .362 on base percentage, and .372 slugging average, well above league and Philly averages for that time. And, as a skillful baserunner and fielder at all positions, he was the player without a weakness.

A Charlottesville native, Charley played there in 1882 for the University of Virginia, although not an enrolled student (a practice prevalent among contemporary colleges). In 1883, he pitched and caught for the independent Richmond (Va.) Club, once shutting out Boston (NL) with four singles. After agreeing to rejoin Richmond, he accepted an offer from A. J. Reach of Philadelphia. Richmond protested in vain.

On Opening Day 1884, he bested Detroit, 13-2, and hit 2 singles and a triple, for a prophetic start. During his four seasons, he garnered 21, 26, 30, and 22 wins, with low ERAs and a 2½ to 1 strikeout to walk ratio. He had all the tools: an overwhelming fastball, mastery of assorted breaking pitches, pinpoint control, iron nerve and poise, fielding expertise, and the intelligence to use the tools effectively. In successive starts in August 1885, he blanked Providence with 3 hits followed by a no-hitter. He closed out 1886, his finest pitching season, by winning 11 straight without a loss, culminating with 5-1 and 6-1 victories in a doubleheader versus the pennant-contending Detroits. By opening 1887 with 5 more triumphs before losing, he accomplished a two-season streak of 16 victories.

Each succeeding season Ferguson appeared more frequently in other positions; first in the outfield where manager Harry Wright considered him an outstanding center fielder with a strong, accurate arm, sure hands, ball hawk instincts, and range. His long strides disguised his true speed. Once he beat Boston National League's fastest runner in time trials around the bases. In 1887 Ferguson played some infield. During the final eight weeks, he played second base every day when not pitching and soon was regarded as the best second sacker in the league after Fritz Pfeffer. For the season, he batted .337 (officially, .412, with walks counting as hits) and slugged .470.

But, perhaps Fergy's last days in a baseball uniform produced his greatest sustained performances. In the Phillies' final 17 games of the 1887 season, the club won 16 and tied one to gain second place, the squad's highest spot. Ferguson played in all 17 games, hitting .361, fielding .963 at second (a uniquely superlative average in that era) and compiling a 7-0 pitching record with a 1.75 ERA, which, with one prior win, gave him an 8-game winning streak at season's end. What a way to go out!

— Frank V. Phelps and Jim Sumner

			G	R	H	BA	SA	POS	E	FA	GP	W-L	R	H
1884	Philadelphia	NL	52	26	50	.246	.305	p	13	.887	50	21-25	302	443
1885	Philadelphia	NL	61	42	72	.306	.379	p-o	16	.890	48	26-19	213	345
1886	Philadelphia	NL	72	56	66	.253	.318	p-o	14	.925	48	30-9	147	317
1887	Philadelphia	NL	72	67	123	.413	.540	p-2b	22	.910	37	22-10	166	348

ROBERT V. FERGUSON
(Old Fergy)

Born: January 31, 1845, Brooklyn, N.Y.
Died: May 3, 1894, Brooklyn, N.Y.
BB TR 5-9 ½, 149

Robert Ferguson lasted from 1864 to 1891 as a player, captain, manager, umpire, and, uniquely, as league president (National Association, 1872-1875) while active as a player. His peers characterized him as competitive, authoritative, intelligent, rule-wise, short-tempered, tactless, and, off-field, thrifty and financially acute. A wiry, muscular, right-handed fielder and switch hitter, he hit and ran bases expertly. Because of his sure hand-edness and quick release, he was the pre-mier third baseman of the late 1860s and early 1870s, according to Henry Chadwick. Also an above-average second baseman, he played elsewhere when needed and was one of the first catchers to stay close behind the plate.

After breaking in with the junior Frontiers of Brooklyn in 1864, Ferguson pitched for the senior Enterprise Club in 1865. He then starred during 1866-1874 for the famous Atlantics of Brooklyn, except in 1871 when he represented the Mutuals of New York. From 1869 forward he captained and managed almost every team on which he played. When the Atlantics snapped the two-year winning streak of the Cincinnati Red Stockings in 11 innings on June 14, 1870, Captain Bob, batting lefthanded to avoid the range of shortstop great George Wright, pulled a single to right to drive across the tying run. He later scored the winning tally.

Subsequently, Ferguson played and captained-managed Hartford (NA and NL) 1875-1877; Chicago (NL) 1878; Springfield (NA) 1879; Troy (NL) 1879-1882; Philadelphia (NL) 1883; Baltimore (Eastern League) 1884; New York (NL) (without participating); and Pitts-burgh (AA) 1884.

He bench-managed New York (AA) in 1886 and early 1887. During 16 years as captain-manager, his only team to finish as high as third was Hartford (1875-1877). At Phila-delphia, the team rejected his tyrannical leadership so strongly he was relieved of on-field authority, continuing, however, as sec-ond baseman and manager. In the latter ca-pacity he handled business affairs so effec-tively that the hapless 17-81 Phillies actually made money. In 1884, when he signed with New York (NL), several veterans who had played under his control in Troy objected strenuously and he was forced to leave.

Bob umpired in the National League in 1885; in the American Association from 1887 through 1889, and in 1891; and in the Players' League in 1890 until infirmities prompted his retirement. Fearlessness, impartiality, quick perceptions and decisive calls made him an excellent official, the prototype of the dic-tatorial, no-nonsense type of arbiter. His un-derstanding and interpretation of the baseball code was so logical and clear-cut that many of his decisions later were actually written into the rules.

Having always saved his money and in-vested it prudently, unlike many of his con-temporaries, he was financially well-off at the time of his death of apoplexy in 1894.

— Frank V. Phelps

			G	R	H	BA	SA	POS	E	FA	GP	W-L	R	H
1865	Enterprise		5	16	(14 outs)									
1866	Atlantic		18	44	(64 outs)									
1867	Atlantic		24	82	(67 outs)									
1868	Atlantic		54	212	194	(163")	(312TB)	3b						
1869	Atlantic		47	-	167		(274")	c-3b						
1870	Atlantic		21	-	81		(104")	c						
1871	Mutual	NA	33	30	38	.241	.291	3b-2b	41	.794	1	0-0	9	8
1872	Atlantic	NA	35	32	43	.277	.310	3b	48	.832				
1873	Atlantic	NA	51	36	60	.260	.317	3b	88	.779	4	0-1	29	38
1874	Atlantic	NA	56	34	63	.256	.264	3b	71	.782	1	0-1	10	12
1875	Hartford	NA	85	66	88	.240	.301	3b	74	.816	1	0-0	7	9
1876	Hartford	NL	69	48	83	.264	.322	3b	54	.826				
1877	Hartford	NL	58	40	65	.256	.299	3b	51	.841	3	1-1	15	38
1878	Chicago	NL	61	44	91	.351	.405	ss	48	.872				
1879	Springfield	NA	15	-		.275								
	Troy	NL	30	18	31	.252	.325	3b-2b	26	.800				
1880	Troy	NL	82	55	87	.262	.289	2b	58	.904				
1881	Troy	NL	85	56	96	.283	.360	2b	55	.904				
1882	Troy	NL	81	44	82	.257	.317	2b	44	.914				
1883	Philadelphia	NL	86	39	85	.258	.298	2b	88	.862	1	0-0	2	2
1884	Pittsburgh	AA	10	2	6	.150	.150	o-1-3	7	.857				

WESTON DICKSON FISLER

Born: July 18, 1841, Camden, N.J.
Died: December 25, 1922, Philadelphia, Pa.
5-6, 137

His name, Weston Dickson Fisler, had a patrician ring to it. And in this case, the man did fit the name. He was the son of Lorenzo Fisler, long-time mayor of Camden, N.J. "West," as he was called, was educated in private schools where he learned the rudiments of baseball. Befitting his genteel upbringing, West always dressed immaculately. In later years, he told an interviewer that he would not think of going out on the diamond without white cuffs, a collar and a necktie.

Fisler began to play baseball competitively in 1860 when, as an 18-year-old, he joined the Equity Club of Philadelphia. Before he retired from baseball in 1877, his career was to span baseball's years as a simon-pure gentleman's sport, the entire life of the National Association (1871-1875) and the founding of the National League in 1876. In addition to the Equity Club, Fisler played for various other Philadelphia nines, the Camden Club and the Eckfords of Brooklyn. In 1866, he joined the Philadelphia Athletics for the first of what was to be 11 seasons with the club. In 1868, he was one of nine players awarded a gold medal by the *New York Clip-*

per for excellence in hitting. He hit consistently in all five of his National Association seasons, averaging .293, .327, .313, .383 and .276. In 1876, his one National League year, he batted .288.

Actually, Fisler was better known as a fielder than as a hitter. Despite his small stature (5 feet 6 inches and 137 pounds), he was a first baseman for most of his career and was recognized as one of the smoothest at that position. "At first base, Fisler, it is claimed, never had a superior and few equals," said the *New York Clipper* in a biographical sketch. Adrian Anson characterized him as "a fine, all-around ball player, remarkable for his coolness and nerve . . . He was a quiet sort of fellow, . . . was thoroughly honest and always played the best he knew how."

A highlight of Fisler's baseball life was his participation in the tour of England by the Philadelphia and Boston clubs in 1874. The teams played 14 games on the tour with the Boston club gaining the edge eight games to six. What is sometimes forgotten is that the Americans, some of whom like Harry Wright had played cricket before they played baseball, played six matches against prominent

British cricket clubs and one in Dublin against an all-Irish club and won six times and were leading in the seventh when rain intervened. But there was a catch to this surprising result: the Americans played with 18 men, while the home towners used 12.

In 1877, after leaving the Athletics, Fisler opened a haberdashery in Philadelphia. Later, he worked as a clerk for various Philadelphia law firms. A Philadelphia Athletic to the core, he was almost a daily spectator at that team's games. He also enjoyed billiards and was a familiar figure at a Market Street billiard club. His favorite opponent was a certain young man whom he much admired "because he could always take good naturedly a licking from an old fellow."

The shy, unassuming, almost reclusive Fisler was 81 when he died of pneumonia on Christmas Day 1922 in Philadelphia. Of those who were with him on the English tour of 1874, only Al Reach and George Wright survived him. The one Fisler obituary at hand fails to state if he ever married or who his survivors were.

— Joseph M. Overfield

			G	R	H	BA	SA	POS	E	FA	GP	W-L	R	H
1866	Athletic		16	85	(45 outs)			cf						
1867	Athletic		43	229	(117 outs)			3b						
1868	Athletic		47	231	(111 outs)			1b						
1869	Athletic		39	-	171		(299TB)	1b						
1870	Athletic		36	-	85		(139TB)	1b						
1871	Athletic	NA	28	43	41	.279	.361	1b	8	.969				
1872	Athletic	NA	47	50	84	.346	.428	2b	33	.885				
1873	Athletic	NA	44	45	75	.347	.454	2b-1b	38	.882				
1874	Athletic	NA	37	26	59	.330	.408	1b-2b	19	.945				
1875	Athletic	NA	58	55	74	.276	.340	1-o-2	25	.951				
1876	Athletic	NL	59	42	80	.288	.360	o-2-1	30	.910				
1877	Athletic		96	83	129			1b-2b						

FRANK SYLVESTER FLINT
(Silver)

*Born: August 3, 1855, Philadelphia, Pa.
Died: January 14, 1892, Chicago, Ill.
BR TR 5-10, 170*

Frank Sylvester Flint began life on August 3, 1855 in Philadelphia, Pa. His family moved to St. Louis, Mo., while he was still young. His ballplaying skills attracted the attention of local teams, and he took the field first with the amateur Elephant Base Ball Club in 1874. By 1875, his catching skills were needed by St. Louis professionals. Flint's first game behind the plate for the St. Louis Red Sox came on May 11 against the Chicago club losing in a close one, 1-0. Flint's work behind the plate was largely responsible for the surprisingly close contest, called "one of the most remarkable on record."

Flint, known as "Silver" for his light blond hair, was hired by the Star Base Ball Club of Covington, Ky., to begin their 1876 campaign, which was short-lived. The Stars disbanded in midseason, at which time Flint was picked up by the Indianapolis club. He began catching for them on July 11 for the inaugural game of Indy's new stadium. He stayed in the Hoosier capital for another two years, and in 1878 the team entered the National League.

Flint had already made a name for himself as one of the finest backstops in the country. The Chicago White Stockings wanted his talent and signed him to begin the 1879 season, during which he caught 78 of the 79 games he appeared in. He had the best fielding average for the year, and accompanied the club on their tour of California. Flint was to stay with Chicago for the remainder of his career, being the most reliable receiver captain A-drian Anson could find. He was lauded for his great defense, yet Frank had a number of excellent years with the bat, hitting .284 in 1879 and .310 in 1880.

Flint was a prime example of the old-time hard-nosed ballplayer. He began playing in the days when no gloves or masks were available and continued to field barehanded throughout his career. It was reported that during his tenure, he broke every bone in both hands and in his face. The *New York Clipper* reported that "he has few equals and no superiors as a hard-working and effective catcher, facing pluckily the swiftest and wildest pitching, being an accurate thrower to all bases."

He ended his playing career in 1889 catching 15 games for Chicago. He stayed in the Windy City after retiring until he died on January 14, 1892, only 36 years of age.

— Mark D. Rucker

			G	R	H	BA	SA	POS	E	FA	GP	W-L	R	H
1875	St. Louis Reds	NA	17	4	5	.082	.082	c	36	.727				
1876	Covington Stars-							c						
	Indianapolis		31	23	29	.216		c	29	.885				
1877	Indianapolis	LgAl	120	59	113	.220		c	162	.865				
1878	Indianapolis	NL	63	23	57	.224	.252	c	39	.908				
1879	Chicago	NL	79	46	92	.284	.398	c	42	.915				
1880	Chicago	NL	74	30	46	.162	.225	c	37	.932				
1881	Chicago	NL	80	46	95	.310	.379	c	27	.938				
1882	Chicago	NL	81	48	83	.251	.390	c	37	.935				
1883	Chicago	NL	85	57	88	.265	.358	c	57	.877				
1884	Chicago	NL	73	35	57	.204	.333	c	61	.884				
1885	Chicago	NL	68	27	52	.209	.269	c	36	.927				
1886	Chicago	NL	54	30	35	.202	.272	c	47	.893				
1887	Chicago	NL	49	22	54	.283	.435	c	26	.927				
1888	Chicago	NL	22	6	14	.182	.221	c	11	.926				
1889	Chicago	NL	15	6	13	.232	.304	c	9	.903				

DAVID W. FORCE

Born: July 27, 1849, New York, N.Y.
Died: June 21, 1918, Englewood, N.J.
BR TR 5-4, 130

Shortstop Davey Force was a ranking player for 15 seasons, first in the National Association and then in the National League. But his role in baseball history was fixed by something he did off the field, not on it. Most baseball historians agree that his double contract signing in 1874 played a significant part in the demise of the National Association and the emergence of the National League in 1876.

Force had batted .302 and starred in the field for the Chicago White Stockings (NA) in 1874. In September, before the season was over, he signed an 1875 Chicago contract. Later in the year, he received a better offer from the Athletic club of Philadelphia and signed a second contract, which was not an unusual practice in those pre-reserve clause days. The White Stockings management protested and was upheld by the league's judiciary committee. Subsequently, the committee overruled the earlier decision, asserting the Chicago contract had been signed before the season was over and was, therefore, invalid according to the league's by-laws. William A. Hulbert of the Chicago club was so infuriated that he resolved to bring the Association to its knees. In another year, the Association was dead and Hulbert had fathered the National League.

Force learned baseball as a youngster in New York City, first gaining attention as a catcher for the Unknowns of Harlem. When he was 18, A. G. Mills persuaded him to come to Washington, D.C. to join the Olympic Club. The Olympics were ostensibly an amateur nine, but the suspicion is strong that sub rosa payments were made to its players. Force played for the Olympics from 1867 to 1871, the last year being the maiden season of the National Association.

In the Association's five seasons, Force played for Troy, Baltimore, Chicago and the Athletics in addition to the Olympics. His .412 average in 1872 for Troy and Baltimore led the

league, and his overall Association mark was a healthy .326. He was never to hit that well in the National League, where he played in 1876 (Philadelphia and New York) and 1877 (St. Louis), before joining Buffalo of the International Association in '78, lured by a $1,200 salary offer. Force batted .302 for the Bisons, led the league shortstops in fielding and was chosen by the *New York Clipper* for its all-star team.

When Buffalo moved up to the National League in 1879, it was against the advice of shortstop Force, who wrote to the Buffalo president: "I have heard we are going to join the league. I hope and pray not, for if we do we are gone financially."

Eventually, the Buffalo owners did come to grief, but not until 1885, by which time Force had played seven brilliant seasons for the Bisons. After the Buffalo club disbanded, Force was awarded to Washington, where he played in '86, his last major league campaign. He then played for Memphis (Southern League), Des Moines (Northwestern League) and was player-manager for Memphis in 1888. He umpired in the Western Association in 1889, but then left baseball to take a job with the Otis Elevator Company, his boss there being A. G. Mills, who had signed him for the Olympic Club 22 years earlier.

How good a player was Force? Francis Richter said he was sure-handed on grounders and flies, had a strong throwing arm and was the best shortstop of his era, George Wright excepted. According to Richter, Force, with his bow-legs and muscular frame, was a vest-pocket version of Honus Wagner and possessed "the same awkward grace." Once, in a 12-inning game (Buffalo at Worcester, September 15, 1881), Force, playing second base, handled 11 putouts and 7 assists with but a single error, had 2 unassisted double plays and participated in a triple play. Six days later at Troy, he handled 13 chances without an error.

There is some confusion about Force's size. All sources agree he was 5 feet 4 inches tall, short even for that era. Macmillan gives his weight as 130, but earlier accounts describe him as "a stocky 160 pounds." Lee Allen, in *National League Story*, wrote: "He was built close to the ground, but had the body of a large man." A picture of the 1878 Buffalo club shows Force to be short with a slender build, much slighter than the 165-pound Dave Eggler who is sitting next to him. It is the guess here that the 130-pound figure is closer to the mark.

Force, a pensioner of the Otis Elevator Company, died in Englewood, N.J., on June 21, 1918, just a few weeks short of his 69th birthday.

— Joseph M. Overfield

			G	R	H	BA	SA	POS	E	FA	GP	W-L	R	H
1867	Olympic		14	60		(22 outs)								
1868	Olympic		20	65	63	(56 outs)								
1869	Olympic		26	-	80	(121TB)								
1870	Olympic		27	-	65	(96TB)								
1871	Olympic	NA	32	45	45	.278	.389	ss	39	.845				
1872	Troy-Balt	NA	44	69	93	.406	.454	3b-s	37	.846				
1873	Baltimore	NA	49	77	85	.362	.421	3b-ss	42	.842	3	1-1	20	28
1874	Chicago	NA	59	61	93	.313	.337	3b-ss	62	.826	1	0-0	24	22
1875	Athletic	NA	77	78	120	.309	.366	ss	50	.886				
1876	Athletic-Mut	NL	61	48	66	.230	.251	ss	42	.895				
1877	St. Louis	NL	58	24	59	.262	.311	ss-3b	24	.916				
1878	Buffalo	IA	40	19	44	.265	.289	ss	13	.932				
1879	Buffalo	NL	79	36	66	.209	.237	ss	26	.929				
1880	Buffalo	NL	81	22	49	.169	.203	2b-ss	43	.920				
1881	Buffalo	NL	75	21	50	.180	.219	2b-ss	32	.939				
1882	Buffalo	NL	73	39	67	.241	.295	ss-3b	32	.908				
1883	Buffalo	NL	96	40	82	.217	.262	ss-3b	48	.883				
1884	Buffalo	NL	106	47	83	.206	.253	ss	48	.898				
1885	Buffalo	NL	71	20	57	.225	.257	2b-ss	46	.887				
1886	Washington	NL	68	26	44	.182	.211	ss-2b	37	.897				
1887	Memphis	SL	59	79	123	.432	.516	ss	25	.910				
	Des Moines	NWL	42	41	69	.356	.402	ss	14	.932				
1888	Memphis	SL	45	19	31	.167	.199	ss	16	.904				
	Sioux City	WA	66	31	51	.210	.255	ss	34	.899				

DAVID LUTHER
FOUTZ

Born: September 7, 1956, Carroll County, Md.
Died: March 5, 1897, Waverly, Md.
BR TR 6-2, 165

Dave Foutz started out as a pitching star in the mid-1880s and then made a successful transition to become a first baseman, outfielder and manager in the 1890s.

Born in Maryland in 1856, he went to Colorado in 1879, reputedly to seek his fortune as a gold miner. Instead, he gained fame as a pitcher, racking up a 40-1 record for the Leadville Blues in 1882. His first professional engagement was with Bay City in the Northwestern League in 1883, and, when that club folded in July 1884, he was considered the top pitcher in the minor leagues. The St. Louis Browns outbid several other clubs and bought his contract for $2,000, then a record price. They also paid Foutz $1,600 for the remainder of the 1884 season.

Dave was an immediate success in the big leagues, striking out 13 batters in 13 innings in winning his debut on July 29, 1884. In his first three weeks with St. Louis, he won 7 games and lost 2, both defeats coming in extra innings. A malarial fever laid him up for the next three weeks, but he managed to finish the American Association season with a 15-6 record. His newfound wealth suffered, however, when he bet heavily on loser James G. Blaine in the presidential election that fall.

Signing a big contract for 1885 (rumors put his salary as high as $5,000), Foutz teamed with Bob Caruthers to pitch the Browns to their first pennant. Basically a sidearmer, Foutz was affected very little by a midseason rule change allowing Association pitchers to throw overhand. Foutz relied on what one St. Louis newspaper described as "a curious combination of curve, speed, and strategy." Foutz's beanpole physique (6 feet 2 inches, 165 pounds) inspired nicknames such as "Scissors" and "His Needles." But his calm demeanor and take-charge attitude inspired confidence among his teammates. And his strong hitting and good fielding and base

running contributed to many victories.

In 1886, Foutz enjoyed his best season as a pitcher (41-16). He also became a semi-regular outfielder, sharing the right field duties with Caruthers. In 1887, the year of four strikes, his batting average jumped to .393 (.357 not counting walks). He enjoyed his biggest day at the plate on the Fourth of July by hitting a home run in the morning game and going 5-for-6 with 2 homers and 9 runs batted in in the afternoon. His pitching record stood at 23-8 when he suffered a broken thumb on August 14. When he came back, he could not break his curveball off properly, and his subsequent record was just 2-4, followed by an 0-3 World Series.

Foutz was sold to Brooklyn in November 1887 for a reported $6,000. He was inserted into the pitching rotation late in the 1888 season, but his pitching days were basically over. However, his hitting kept him in the middle of the lineup. A straightforward man who was popular with his teammates, Dave also served as captain late in the season.

Batting third or fourth in the order in 1889,

Foutz played a key role as Brooklyn rallied to overtake St. Louis and win its first major league pennant. The Bridegrooms moved to the National League in 1890 and won the pennant there, too, with Foutz playing first base and batting fourth. Dave's averages were not outstanding, but he was at his best with men on base. His batting slipped in 1891 and he was pushed back to seventh in the order. In 1892, Foutz lost his first base job to Dan Brouthers, although he did get some pitching work during the first half of the season. He also saw action filling in in center field and at first base.

Foutz was appointed Brooklyn's manager in 1893 and he got himself into every game that year, playing left field and first base. During the next two seasons, his health deteriorated and he played less and less. In 1896, he made only two token playing appearances as the team finished in a tie for ninth place after which Foutz was dismissed as manager.

Foutz died somewhat unexpectedly of a respiratory ailment the following spring.

— Robert L. Tiemann

			G	R	H	BA	SA	POS	E	FA	GP	W-L	R	H
1879	Denver		5				.200							
1882	Leadville							p			41	40-1		
1883	Bay City	NWL	61	39	67	.251	.300	p-o	41	.891	43			
1884	Bay City	NWL	39	33	58	.333	.466	p-if			23	18-4	68	128
	St. Louis	AA	33	17	28	.233	.267	p-o	6	.922	25	15-6	96	167
1885	St. Louis	AA	65	42	59	.250	.309	p-l	20	.936	47	33-14	200	351
1886	St. Louis	AA	102	66	116	.280	.389	p-o-l	19	.940	59	41-16	218	418
1887	St. Louis	AA	103	79	176	.393	.536	o-p-l	23	.938	41	25-12	250	459
1888	Brooklyn	AA	140	91	159	.283	.399	o-l-p	23	.963	23	12-7	78	146
1889	Brooklyn	AA	138	121	153	.286	.389	1b	35	.976	12	3-0	53	70
1890	Brooklyn	NL	129	106	154	.303	.432	1b	28	.978	5	1-1	10	29
1891	Brooklyn	NL	130	87	134	.256	.356	1b	31	.976	6	3-2	24	51
1892	Brooklyn	NL	61	33	44	.199	.271	of-p	14	.890	27	13-8	106	210
1893	Brooklyn	NL	130	91	144	.273	.398	of-lb	32	.972	6	0-0	-	28
1894	Brooklyn	NL	73	41	92	.311	.426	1b	15	.979	1	0-0	2	4
1895	Brooklyn	NL	31	14	34	.296	.348	of-lb	9	.928				
1896	Brooklyn	NL	2	0	2	.250	.375	lb-of						

JOHN FOWLER
(Bud)

Born: March 16, 1858, Fort Plain, N.Y.
Died: February 26, 1913, Frankfort, N.Y.
BR TR 5-7, 155

John (Bud) Fowler was the first black to play in Organized Baseball in the 19th century. He also played the longest, 10 years, and appeared in the most games, 465. As one of the best black players of that era, he was able to pave the way for some 70 additional members of his race to play in the minor leagues before unwritten restrictions forced them out at the close of the century.

Fowler was born John W. Jackson in Fort Plain, N.Y., on March 16, 1858. The next year, his family moved to Cooperstown, where his father served as a barber for more than 15 years. No information is available on when the youngster began his baseball career and when and where he took the name Fowler. It is known that the nickname "Bud" resulted from his inclination to call most others by that name.

The first documented mention of Fowler as a player was in April 1878 when he pitched for the Chelsea team in Massachusetts. On April 24 he hurled an exhibition game victory over the Boston National League champions, defeating Tommy Bond 2-1. In May he pitched three league games for the Lynn Live Oaks of the International Association, the first minor league. However, because of his color, opportunities for regulation play were very limited. He played several years in other parts of the U.S. and in Canada before returning to minor league play in 1884 with the Stillwater, Minn., club in the Northwestern League. He was still primarily a pitcher at the time, but was not well supported by his white teammates and began to play more at other positions.

In the next 10 years, Fowler played for 17 different clubs in nine leagues from Montpelier, Vt., to Santa Fe in the New Mexico Territory. He was a good player, very versatile, a fast runner, and a slick fielder at second base, which became his primary position. People came to see him play as he usually was the only black player on a white team. He was not docile when threatened and

had several confrontations with other players and management in the course of his career. It is accurate to say he was a contributing factor in the collapse of several clubs and even the disruption of leagues, but he continued to play with white teams as long as he could.

Fowler helped win a Western League pennant for Topeka in 1886, leading the circuit in triples. The next year he batted .350 for Binghamton in the International League before being cut loose when his teammates refused take the field with him. In 1892, he led the Nebraska State League in stolen bases prior to its breakup in July. He often received favorable mention in the white press of his day, one time being referred to as "one of the best pitchers on the continent of America." Still, he was never given the opportunity to play in the majors.

By the early 1890s it became more and more difficult for blacks to play in the minors. When Fowler could not catch on with an organized league team, he would play with an independent team in Findlay, Ohio. He would go on barnstorming tours in the fall and in the off-season would support himself as a barber, his father's trade. In early 1895 he orga-

nized a strong black team, sponsored by a wire fence company, called the Page Fence Giants. Based in Adrian, Mich., the team toured through the Midwest in its own railroad car playing against a wide range of minor league and independent teams. Ironically, Fowler left the team, his own creation, in midsummer to play in the Michigan State League.

From then on Fowler played mostly with black teams, which he organized and managed himself. In 1904-05 he tried to organized a national colored baseball league, but could not find the necessary financial backing.

A few years later, his health failed and the man described in Sol White's 1907 *History of Colored Baseball* as "the celebrated promoter of colored baseball clubs and the sage of baseball" soon faded into near obscurity. He died at his sister's home in Frankfort, N.Y., on February 26, 1913, and was buried there in an unmarked grave. On July 25, 1987, the Society for American Baseball Research dedicated a memorial stone at the site to commemorate the notable achievements of this 19th century black baseball pioneer.

— L. Robert Davids

			G	R	H	BA	SA	POS	E	FA	GP	W-L	R	H
1878	Lynn	IA	3	1	2	.153	.153	p			3	1-2	18	24
	Worcester	NEng	1	3	0	.000	.000	p			1	0-1	6	5
1884	Stillwater	NWL	48	28	57	.320	.355	o-p-2-c			20	7-8	94	133
1885	Keokuk	WL	8	5	8	.222	.278	2b						
	Pueblo	Colo	5	2	4	.222	.333	o-3-c-p			1	0-1	5	7
1886	Topeka	WL	58	62	77	.309	.506	2b-of			2	0-0	2	3
1887	Binghamton	IL	34	42	55	.350	.478	2b	26	.901	2	0-0	9	16
	Montpelier	NEast	8	10	15	.429	.486	2b-p			1	0-0	3	3
1888	Crwfdv-TrHt	CIntst	53	48	70	.294	.391	2b			1	0-0	2	4
	Santa Fe	NMx	22	29	32	.343	.452	2b			2	0-2	16	23
1889	Greenville	MichSt	92	93	129	.302	.394	2b			2	0-0	9	14
1890	Galesburg	CIntst	27	23	38	.322	.475	of-2b	15	.840				
	Strlg-Glbg-Brln	IlIa	36	18	48	.314	.412	2b						
1892	Lncln-Kearny	NebSt	39	44	47	.273	.343	2b						
1895	Adrian-Lnsg	MichSt	31	40	46	.331	.424	2b-3b						

CHARLES JOHN FULMER
(Chick)

Born: February 12, 1851, Philadelphia, Pa.
Died: February 15, 1940, Philadelphia, Pa.
BR TR 6-0, 158

If ever there was an all-American baseball player, it was Chick Fulmer. Born on Lincoln's Birthday in Philadelphia, the home of the Liberty Bell, he was a descendant of early American settlers. Great-grandfather Michael Fulmer served in the French and Indian Wars; grandfather John Fulmer fought in the Revolution, and his father Michael Fulmer served in the Civil War, rising to the rank of major. Chick enlisted as a drummer boy in the Civil War with the Southwark Guards, but was turned back before his unit saw action because he was only 14.

In the pre-professional days, Fulmer played with the Olympics and the Athletics of Philadelphia and then became a professional with the Forest Cities of Cleveland in 1870. He was with the Forest Cities of Rockford, Ill., in 1871, the first year of the National Association; joined the New York Mutuals in 1872, and then played with hometown Phila-

delphia from 1873 through 1875. He played for Louisville in 1876, the National League's inaugural year; the Alleghenies of Pittsburgh the following year, the first year of the International Association; and then became captain and second baseman of Buffalo of the same circuit in 1878. It was Fulmer who sent a famous telegram back to Buffalo after his team had dropped its opening game to the London Tecumsehs: "Galvin pitched very fine. Umpire very bad. Change umpires tomorrow."

When Buffalo moved up to the National League in 1879, Fulmer stayed on. After taking a year off to manage a traveling troupe that was playing "Uncle Tom's Cabin," he joined Cincinnati of the newly formed American Association as captain and shortstop in 1882. He led his team to the pennant and had his career-high batting year (.281). He played for the Reds in 1883 and then wound it up in

1884 with the Reds and St. Louis (AA).

Never an outstanding hitter, Fulmer's forte was his fielding. Playing mostly at shortstop, he was sure-handed and possessed a strong and accurate arm. He always claimed to have negotiated the game's first unassisted triple play. According to Fulmer, it happened in a game between Philadelphia and Troy in 1873. The Haymakers filled the bases with no one out. The next batter hit a line drive which Fulmer speared with one hand. He then tagged the man who had been on second and ran down the man who had been on first.

At one time, Fulmer served as magistrate in Philadelphia, apparently a position not requiring a legal degree. His last job was as a doorman for the Curtis Publishing Company. He died in his native city on February 15, 1940, three days after his 89th birthday. Annie, his wife of 65 years, survived.

— Joseph M. Overfield

			G	R	H	BA	SA	POS	E	FA	GP	W-L	R	H
1869	Keystone		11	-	23	-	(29 TB)							
1870	ForCtyCleve		8	-	12	-	(15 TB)	rf						
1871	ForCtyRckfrd	NA	16	11	17	.270	.281	ss	28	.786				
1872	Mutual	NA	36	28	51	.305	.347	3b-ss	37	.808				
1873	Philadelphia	NA	49	42	65	.274	.354	ss	69	.815				
1874	Philadelphia	NA	57	49	72	.278	.305	ss-3b	69	.797				
1875	Philadelphia	NA	66	49	64	.218	.239	ss-3b	67	.815				
1876	Louisville	NL	66	28	73	.273	.356	ss	47	.861				
1877	Allegheny	IA	54			.225		2b						
1878	Buffalo	IA	45	24	45	.256	.284	2b	25	.918				
1879	Buffalo	NL	76	30	82	.268	.337	2b	60	.905				
1880	Buffalo	NL	11	3	7	.159	.159	2b						
1881	Athletic	EA						2b						
1882	Cincinnati	AA	79	54	90	.277	.342	ss	45	.895				
1883	Cincinnati	AA	92	52	94	.260	.365	ss	60	.866				
1884	Cincnti-StL	AA	32	13	20	.168	.202	ss	25	.788				
1885	Portland	ENwEg	52	15	40	.196		2b	34	.906				

CHARLES H. GETZIEN

Born: February 14, 1864, Germany
Died: June 19, 1932, Chicago
BR TR 5-10, 172

Charlie Getzien achieved his greatest fame as the right-handed pitching star of the powerful Detroit Wolverines, the 1887 world champions. A native of Germany, Getzien grew up in Chicago and had a nine-year career in the National League from 1884 through 1892.

Getzien's name was usually misspelled as Getzein in the newspapers, and the original German spelling was actually Goetzien. His family immigrated to the United States when he was a young boy, and he took to baseball quickly. After rising high in the Chicago amateur ranks, he began his professional career in 1883 at age 19 when he signed with Grand Rapids in the Northwestern League. He remained with that team until it folded (despite a .754 winning percentage) in August 1884. He was then among five players sold to last-place Detroit in the National League. Charlie lost his big league debut, 1-0, to Cleveland's John Henry, a former Grand Rapids teammate who also was making his debut. Getzien lost eight in a row before posting his first victory, but he finished 5-12 with a 6-inning no-hitter and a 9-inning 1-hitter.

The Wolverines were weak again in 1885 and Getzien was 3-15 through June 24. That day, the club bought out the minor league Indianapolis franchise and imported seven new players. Getzien won his first four games with this new lineup behind him and finished the season 12-25.

Detroit continued to purchase talent, bringing in the famous Big Four from Buffalo, and in 1886 the team was a strong pennant contender. Detroit led Chicago for most of the first four months of the campaign in a tight and exciting race. Getzien pitched 8 no-hit innings against the White Stockings on June 21 before settling for a 4-1, 1-hit victory. The

very next day he beat them again, this time 5-4. But Chicago beat him twice in a July series. Chicago passed Detroit in late August as Getzien slumped in the late going and was fined $300 by manager Watkins for "insolence."

In 1887, Getzien started slowly, but the Wolverines grabbed the lead early in the race and held it. As the other pitchers tailed off during the summer, however, Getzien came on strong. Chicago pulled into a tie for first on August 15, but the next day Getzien stopped them, 5-3, to put Detroit back into the undisputed lead. Charlie won three of Detroit's next five games as well and the Wolverines were never threatened again.

After winning the pennant, Detroit faced the St. Louis Browns in a 15-game touring World Series. Getzien pitched the opener and lost, 6-1, but came back with the most dramatic victory of the series in Game No. 3, a 2-1 victory in 13 innings. He followed this with a 9-0 shutout and finished the series with 4 wins and 2 losses as the Wolverines rolled over the Browns, 10 games to 5.

Getzien had a pronounced straight-armed backswing and a characteristic little skip in

his delivery. He was called the "Pretzel Twirler" because of his peculiar curves. He also had plenty of speed and a fine drop ball and he excelled at mixing speeds.

Charlie slipped below .500 in 1888 as the Wolverines nosedived in the second half of the season. The club folded and Getzien was sold to Indianapolis for 1889. He pitched creditably for the Hoosiers before arm trouble limited his work in the last six weeks of the season. In 1890, he signed with the Boston Beaneaters and once again had a winning record, thanks largely to a 10-game winning streak in July.

In 1891, Getzien lost his spot in the rotation to Harry Staley and was released in July. He failed in a one-game trial with Cleveland in August and was cut again. He caught on with St. Louis in June 1892, hitting a home run and winning his first game, 3-2 in 10 innings. But he had no speed left and he was given his final release in July.

Getzien returned to Chicago where he got a job with the *Tribune* as a typesetter and as a pitcher with the company baseball team. He died of a heart attack in 1932 at age 68.

— Robert L. Tiemann

			G	R	H	BA	SA	POS	E	FA	GP	W-L	R	H
1883	Grand Rapids	NWL	37	21	30	.216	.245	p	39	.861	28#	14-12	153	230
1884	Grand Rapids	NWL	35	30	33	.239	.297	p-o			31	27-4	87	167
1884	Detroit	NL	17	4	6	.109	.109	p	4	.889	17	5-12	70	120
1885	Detroit	NL	40	9	29	.212	.234	p	9	.902	37	12-25	222	361
1886	Detroit	NL	43	14	29	.176	.242	p	1	.988	43	30-11	205	388
1887	Detroit	NL	43	19	40	.241	.313	p	3	.964	43	29-13	228	479
1888	Detroit	NL	46	14	41	.246	.299	p	16	.861	46	19-25	219	411
1889	Indianapolis	NL	45	20	25	.180	.266	p	8	.918	45	18-22	258	395
1890	Boston	NL	41	27	34	.231	.361	p	19	.802	40	23-17	184	342
1891	Boston-Clev	NL	15	4	7	.156	.311	p-of	2	.931	12	4-6	68	124
1892	St. Louis	NL	13	3	9	.200	.267	p	2	.126	13	5-8	87	159

JOHN WESLEY GLASSCOCK
(Jack)

Born: June 22, 1859, Wheeling, W. Va.
Died: February 24, 1947, Wheeling, W. Va.
BR TR 5-8, 160

John Wesley Glasscock, known to all as Jack, was among the greatest shortstops of the 19th century. Playing without a glove until late in his career, he led National League shortstops in fielding percentage six times and was described by Al Spink as "one of the greatest players from a fielding standpoint (that) the game has ever known." Added to his defensive prowess was a lifetime batting average in the .290s, including one NL batting championship.

A lifelong resident of Wheeling, W. Va., Jack was born in 1859 and first went away to play ball in 1877, when he joined the Champion City club of Springfield, Ohio. The following season, he began with the Allegheny club in the International Association and then moved on to the Forest Cities of Cleveland after the Alleghenies folded. In 1879, Cleveland obtained a National League franchise and Glasscock began a 17-year career in the NL.

Primarily a third baseman during that first season, he shifted to shortstop in 1880 when he first teamed with Fred Dunlap to anchor one of the strongest infields in the game. Glasscock was nicknamed "Pebbly Jack" because of his penchant for picking up pebbles in the infield and tossing them aside to try to minimize bad hops. He also had a well-known ritual of pounding his bat on the plate as he stood in the batter's box. He was famed for his wide fielding range and his acrobatic throwing from any posture. His hitting was lackluster in his earlier years, but improved greatly with experience. Although not notably rowdy for the times, Jack was not above locking horns with the umpires on the field nor above imbibing intoxicants after the game. Every winter he returned to Wheeling to work as a carpenter.

His salary from Cleveland rose from $800 in 1879 to $1,800 in 1884, when he jumped the club to sign with the outlaw Union Association, saying that "I have played long enough

for glory, now it is a matter of dollars and cents." He received $2,500 from the Cincinnati Unions for the last nine weeks of the season. When the U.A. folded, Jack had to pay a $1,000 fine to be reinstated in the N.L. He signed with the St. Louis Maroons for $2,200 in 1885.

In 1886, his batting average went over .300 for the first time and in 1889 he reached career highs in average (.352) and hits (205). After two years in St. Louis, the franchise was sold to Indianapolis, where Jack spent three more seasons. Having served as captain in both cities, he reluctantly took over as manager of the Hoosiers in July 1889. He later served as

captain in St. Louis, Pittsburgh and Louisville, but he did not have strong managerial ambitions.

After the 1889 season, Glasscock joined most of the other NL players in pledging to join the new Players' League. But in November, he backed out of his ambiguous PL contract and signed with Indianapolis, thereby becoming the first "double jumper" and earning the lasting animosity of many Brotherhood loyalists. When Indianapolis lost its franchise, Glasscock and several others were transferred to New York, where Jack won the

(continued on page 143)

			G	R	H	BA	SA	POS	E	FA	GP	W-L	R	H
1876	Standard of Whlg.		24		41	.369								
1877	Champion City		9			.333			-	.900				
1878	Allegheny	IA	26	9	20	.204	.224	3b	16	.873				
	For.City Clev		46		54	.295	.366	3b	21	.909				
1879	Cleveland	NL	80	31	68	.209	.255	2b-3b	43	.916				
1880	Cleveland	NL	77	37	72	.243	.307	ss	44	.891				
1881	Cleveland	NL	85	49	86	.257	.313	ss	37	.911				
1882	Cleveland	NL	84	66	104	.291	.450	ss	47	.900				
1883	Cleveland	NL	96	67	110	.287	.368	ss	38	.922				
1884	Cleveland	NL	72	45	70	.249	.302	ss	46	.893	2	0-0	6	8
	Cincinnati	UA	38	48	72	.419	.564	ss	19	.889				
1885	St. Louis	NL	111	66	125	.280	.341	ss	50	.919				
1886	St. Louis	NL	121	96	158	.325	.432	ss	57	.906				
1887	Indianapolis	NL	122	91	183	.349	.414	ss	73	.906	1	0-0	0	0
1888	Indianapolis	NL	113	63	119	.269	.328	ss	59	.903	1	0-0	2	1
1889	Indianapolis	NL	134	128	209	.359	.414	ss	67	.915	1	0-0	4	3
1890	New York	NL	124	91	172	.336	.445	ss	69	.909				
1891	New York	NL	97	46	90	.243	.317	ss	50	.897				
1892	St. Louis	NL	139	84	154	.273	.353	ss	67	.918				
1893	St.L-Pitts	NL	114	81	156	.320	.412	ss	53	.923				
1894	Pittsburgh	NL	86	47	94	.283	.367	ss	35	.934				
1895	Louv-Wash	NL	43	29	52	.292	.343	ss-1b	28	.915				
	Wheeling	Intst						1b						
1896	St. Paul	WL	135	172	263	.431	.539	1b-2b	20	.985				
1897	St. Paul	WL	131	132	192	.345	.441	1b-2b	26	.981				
1898	St. Paul	WL	120	70	125	.263	.307	1b	36	.970				
1899	Fort Wayne	Intst	137	96	179	.325	.423	1b	22	.984				
1900	Fort Wayne	Intst	13	5	12	.261	.304	1b	1	.992				
	Sioux City	WL	65	30	63	.255	.296	1b	12	.983				
1901	Minneapolis	WL	6	1	2	.083	.125	1b	0	1.00				

WILLIAM G. GLEASON

Born: November 12, 1858, St. Louis, Mo.
Died: July 21, 1932, St. Louis, Mo.
BR TR 5-8, 170

A rough and tumble ball player, but an upstanding citizen off the field, Bill Gleason was popular with the local fans, yet detested by opposing players during his years as shortstop of the St. Louis Browns.

A St. Louis native, Bill followed his older brother, Jack, to Peoria and Dubuque to play professional baseball in 1878 and 1879. They returned home in 1880 and joined the semipro St. Louis Reds. The following year they shifted to the Browns, the top team in town. When the Browns gained a franchise in the American Association for 1882, the Gleason brothers moved into the big leagues. Jack, who was considered a harder hitter, played third base and batted leadoff. Bill played shortstop and hit second in the order. Jack lasted only until the early part of the 1883 season. But "Brother Bill," as he was often called in the newspapers, took over the leadoff slot and remained a fixture with the Browns through 1887.

The brothers worked for the local fire department in the off-season. Bill bought a $5,000 house in 1884, although his baseball salary was just $1,800. By the end of the next season, thrifty Bill had built two more houses on the same block near Sportsman's Park.

Bill's personality on the field was anything but staid. He superstitiously straddled the foul line whenever he entered the playing field at the beginning of a game. And once play started, he was like a man obsessed. Like teammates Arlie Latham and Charlie Comiskey, Gleason was famous for his base coaching, especially his penchant for running onto the infield to urge a teammate around the circuit. When he himself was a runner, he thought nothing of colliding with opposing fielders, although "breaking up the double play" was not an accepted part of the game in that era.

As a fielder, Gleason was also liable to give a runner a knee or hip when one came past second base. This sort of thing made him warmly disliked by opponents. As *Sporting Life* put it in 1885, "If he should some day break a limb or his neck, not a ball player in the American Association would feel the slightest regret."

Yet for all his scrapes, Gleason missed only two weeks of action in six years with the Browns. By 1886, Gleason had been supplanted by Latham in the leadoff spot in the Browns batting order. But he contributed nicely elsewhere. Batting fourth, he got 2 two-run singles in the fourth game of the World Series, both coming immediately after Chicago had walked Tip O'Neill with first base open. But Bill was best suited to bat first or second. He was a punch hitter with little extra-base power, but was good at reaching base, especially by being hit by pitches. Though he stole relatively few bases, his speed and fearless style made him a formidable baserunner. As a shortstop he was considered well above average.

On April 30, 1887, Gleason enjoyed a rare 7-for-7 day, although 4 of his "hits" were actu-ally bases on balls. In the World Series that fall, however, his poor fielding contributed to St. Louis' humiliating defeat. The one bright spot for Bill came in the 10th game, when he snared a line drive to start a triple play. After the season, Gleason was traded to the Athletics for Chippy McGarr and Fred Mann.

Gleason opened the 1888 season in the No. 3 spot in the Athletic batting order, but poor hitting soon earned him a demotion to No. 8. When the club bought Frank Fennelly near the end of the season, Bill was benched for the first time in his career. Reduced to substitute status at age 30 and faced with a proposed salary reduction from $2,800 to $2,100, he quit. He made a brief comeback with lowly Louisville in June 1889, but quit again after being benched.

After spending a couple of years in the minors, Gleason returned to St. Louis and joined the fire department full time. In the next 42 years, he rose from pipeman to the captaincy of an engine company, and was still on the active rolls when he died in 1932.

— Robert L. Tiemann

			G	R	H	BA	SA	POS	E	FA	GP	W-L	R	H
1876	St. Louis Reds		34	36	36	.267		cf	8	.852				
1877	Minneapolis							cf						
1878	Peoria		26		-	.216		ss	-	.866				
1879	Dubuque	NWL	24	11	25	.243	.301	ss	-	.826				
1880	St. Louis Reds							ss						
1881	St. Louis Browns							ss						
1882	St. Louis	AA	79	63	100	.286	.360	ss	88	.833				
1883	St. Louis	AA	98	81	122	.285	.390	ss	57	.871				
1884	St. Louis	AA	110	97	128	.269	.349	ss	66	.868				
1885	St. Louis	AA	112	79	118	.253	.313	ss	55	.882				
1886	St. Louis	AA	126	97	141	.267	.320	ss	82	.853				
1887	St. Louis	AA	135	135	214	.336	.369	ss	74	.887				
1888	Athletic	AA	123	55	112	.224	.253	ss	76	.865				
1889	Louisville	AA	16	6	14	.241	.276	ss	19	.819				
1890	Washington	AtlAs	79	63	80	.260	.313	ss	51	.868				
1891	Rockford	Ill-Ia	69	68	99	.330		1b	32	.959				

GEORGE F. GORE

Born: May 3, 1857, Saccarappa, Me.
Died: September 16, 1933, Utica, N.Y.
BL TR 5-11, 195

George Gore, center fielder for the White Stockings, was a talented hitter with speed, whose off-the-field habits ultimately led Cap Anson to get rid of him. He arrived in the majors in 1879 and stayed until 1892, playing in 1,310 games and batting 5,357 times, including participation in four of the original World Series. His nickname was the descriptive "Piano Legs."

Anson said that Gore "came here from New Bedford, Mass., being brought out by Mr. Hulbert . . . He was an all-around ball player of the first class, a hard hitter and a fine thrower and fielder, and had it not been for his bad habits he might have still been playing ball today. Women and wine brought about his downfall, however, and the last time that I saw him in New York he was broken down, both in heart and pocket, and willing to work at anything that would yield him the bare necessities of life."

Existing records don't indicate what Gore did before his late 20s, but he evidently got his start in baseball in the Fall River-New Bedford area, where he played under Jim Mutrie. In 1879, Chicago offered him $1,200 to play for them, but he held out for $2,500, before he settled for $1,900.

In his second year in the majors he won the batting title with a mark of .360. In the first game of the 1885 World Series he batted second behind Abner Dalrymple, but then he was suspended for drunkenness and replaced by Billy Sunday. In the next year's Series he batted leadoff, got the only two Chicago hits in the second game, and hit a home run in the third game. He was released to New York afterward as part of the team housecleaning. It was rumored that the White Stockings were to receive Jim O'Rourke in exchange, but that never materialized.

With New York Gore played in the World Series of 1888 and 1889, hitting .455 in the former and .333 in the latter. He jumped to the New York PL team for 1890, but returned to the Giants the following year. By 1892, age was finally catching up to him and, after splitting the season with New York and St. Louis, he retired. He played briefly in 1894 for Binghamton of the Eastern League. In his later years he lived in Nutley, N.J. He died at age 76 in the Masonic Home in Utica, N.Y., so he somehow survived his earlier dissipation.

Gore's records include: 5 assists in a game, 6 hits in 6 at bats in a game, 5 consecutive extra base hits in a game (3 doubles and 2 triples), and 7 stolen bases in a game (later equalled by Billy Hamilton). Stolen base records for his first eight years are not available, but he was one of the best in baseball. His hitting stats are impressive by any standards. The .360 average in 1880 was 115 points above the league average. His batting averaged 63 points above the league average for his first eight years and 49 points above it overall. His slugging average is above .400, very good for that time, and he averaged 124 runs scored and 178 runs produced per 500 at bats (this tops most of the major hitters of the 1920s and 1930s).

That Gore can be regarded as one of the great leadoff men is demonstrated by his discipline as a hitter. His strikeout ratio is one per every 16 at bats, his base on balls ratio one per every 7.5 at bats. The walks should be put in context: he led the league in that category three times, although, when he started, it took nine balls for a walk and the present four-ball rule was only in effect for his last four seasons. When George drew 102 bases on balls in 1886, it took seven balls to get a walk! John Thorn and Pete Palmer rate Gore 14th among the offensive players of his era, and most of those above him are in the Hall of Fame.

— William McMahon

			G	R	H	BA	SA	POS	E	FA	GP	W-L	R	H
1877	Fall River		33	28	45	.319	.440	of	12	.807				
1878	Hartford	IA	3	1	1	.077	.077	of	1	.857				
	New Bedford		105	100	157	.324	.525	of	47	.797				
1879	Chicago	NL	63	43	70	.263	.357	of-1b	15	.872#				
1880	Chicago	NL	77	70	116	.360	.463	of	21	.871				
1881	Chicago	NL	73	86	92	.298	.424	of	24	.874				
1882	Chicago	NL	84	99	117	.319	.420	of	33	.842				
1883	Chicago	NL	92	105	131	.334	.457	of	34	.868				
1884	Chicago	NL	103	104	134	.318	.415	of	32	.868				
1885	Chicago	NL	108	115	138	.313	.456	of	29	.884				
1886	Chicago	NL	118	150	135	.304	.435	of	29	.876				
1887	New York	NL	111	95	174	.348	.402	of	30	.889				
1888	New York	NL	64	37	56	.220	.283	of	18	.836				
1889	New York	NL	120	132	149	.305	.426	of	41	.864				
1890	New York	PL	93	131	134	.335	.510	of	20	.890				
1891	New York	NL	130	104	150	.285	.363	of	28	.898				
1892	NY-St.Louis	NL	73	56	63	.240	.278	of	14	.912				
1894	Binghamton	EL	48	46	61	.319	.435	of	5	.959				

FRANK GRANT

Born: c. 1865, Pittsfield, Mass.
Died: May 27, 1937, New York, N.Y.
BR TR 5-7 ½, 155

Frank Grant was the greatest Negro baseball player of the 19th century. Born near Pittsfield, Massachusetts, Grant entered organized baseball in 1886, playing for Meriden, Connecticut, of the Eastern League. Midway through the season, Grant signed with Buffalo of the International League. He would remain in Buffalo through the 1888 season, becoming the only black player of the century to play three consecutive seasons for the same white team.

Grant had surprising power for a small-built second baseman. During his career in the prestigious International League, one-fourth of his hits (90 of 348) were for extra bases, and he led the team, and/or league in a variety of offensive categories, including batting average, stolen bases, total bases and home runs. During the 1887 season, he hit for the cycle in one game and stole home twice in another.

As a fielder Grant was known as the "Black Dunlap," in reference to Fred Dunlap, the premier second sacker of the time. Grant's use of his extraordinary range and rifle arm was occasionally derided by the press in opposing cities as a "circus act," but his spectacular fielding was an effective drawing card, both at home and on the road.

Sol White, the pioneer historian of Negro baseball, and Grant's contemporary, said of Grant: "His playing was a revelation to his fellow teammates, as well as the spectators. In hitting he ranked with the best and his fielding bordered on the impossible." So complete were Grant's skills that the Buffalo correspondent to *Sporting Life* declared him the best all-round player that Buffalo ever had, which is no small encomium coming from a city where future Hall of Famers Jim Galvin,

Dan Brouthers, Jim O'Rourke and Hoss Radbourn, as well as Deacon White and Hardie Richardson had already played.

Yet Grant's undeniable talent could not stem the rising tide of racial discrimination both on the field and off. A quiet, modest man, Grant was subjected to racial epithets hurled by opposing fans. Grant and his fellow Negro second baseman Bud Fowler were forced to fashion primitive shinguards to protect themselves from opposing players' spikes, a practice so common in 1887 that Grant was moved to the outfield the following season to prevent injury. The skulls of black players often served as targets for hostile pitchers who objected to playing with blacks. It was said, too, that Grant's teammates refused to sit for team portraits in 1886 and 1888 since they would have included a Negro. By the end of the 1888 season, the International League effectively banished the black player and Grant was forced to wander down the increasingly restricted paths open to him.

As late as 1890 Grant was able to play a full season in organized baseball. He began the year in Harrisburg of the Eastern League. In July, Harrisburg jumped to the Atlantic Association, only with the stipulation that Grant be allowed to play. The following season,

Grant joined the all-Negro Cuban Giants, then called the Big Gorhams, who represented Ansonia, Connecticut in the Connecticut State League. But the league quickly disbanded, and the three games Grant played there were his last in organized baseball. The Gorhams went on to compile a very successful season as an independent team, a team Sol White regarded as one of the best all-Negro teams of the 19th century.

Grant's career faded into obscurity throughout the 1890s. He resurfaced in 1902, playing for the Philadelphia Giants, one of the best Negro teams of the time. He ended his career the following season with the Giants, losing to the Cuban-X Giants and their star pitcher Rube Foster in the 1903 "colored championship series." His name last appeared in the black press in 1909 when he agreed to play in a charity game (which was never played) to benefit the ailing Bud Fowler.

For the remainder of his life, Frank Grant worked as a waiter for a catering service in New York City. He died on May 27, 1937, and is buried in Ridgelawn Cemetery in Clifton, New Jersey. He left no descendants other than his long-forgotten legacy as the greatest black player of the 19th century.

— Jerry Malloy

			G	R	H	BA	SA	POS	E	FA	GP	W-L	R	H
1886	Meriden	EL	44	23	56	.316	.441	2b	16	.933				
	Buffalo	IL	49	38	66	.344	.531	2b	31	.908				
1887	Buffalo	IL	105	81	162	.353	.525	2b	74	.911				
1888	Buffalo	IA	84	95	120	.346	.522	2b-o	50	.888				
1889	Trenton	MidSt	67	72	79	.313	.425	2-3-c						
1890	Harrisburg	ElInst	59	66	84	.333	.488	3-o-2						
	Harrisburg	AtlAs	47	33	62	.332	.444	ss	24	.901				
1891	Ansonia	ConnSt	3	2	5	.385	.462	2b						

MICHAEL JOSEPH GRIFFIN

Born: March 20, 1865, Utica, N.Y.
Died: April 10, 1908, Utica, N.Y.
BL TR 5-7, 160

Michael Joseph Griffin was considered by most to be the best center fielder in the game during his major league career, which spanned from 1887 until 1898. He led his position in fielding for five years during the 1890s and combined his outstanding defensive skills with speed and a good bat.

Griffin was born in Utica, N.Y., on March 20, 1865. The son of a cigarmaker and later a cigarmaker himself, Griffin first played on amateur teams in Utica, including several seasons with the Nine Spots from East Utica. In 1885, Griffin joined the Utica franchise in the recently formed New York State League. Griffin, a left-handed batter, also was part of the Utica franchise when the team joined the new International League in 1886 and won the pennant with Mike playing a strong left field.

Griffin's play in the International League earned him the chance to play with Baltimore of the American Association in 1887 after he was signed out of Utica by Billie Barnie, the Oriole manager that season. A case of mistaken identity actually helped Griffin to the major leagues. When Barnie came to Utica, he was there to see the play of "Sandy" Griffin, another local prospect. Barnie saw Mike Griffin, thinking he was Sandy, and was suitably impressed by his play to sign him.

Griffin is perhaps the first player to hit a home run during his first major league at bat. The home run came during the first inning of a game on April 16, 1887 and was the first of 3 extra base hits he pounded out that day.

When the players' revolt of 1890 came, Griffin joined the Philadelphia team of the Brotherhood League. Griffin manned center field and led the league outfielders with 10 double plays.

Griffin's best seasons came while playing with Brooklyn from 1891 until 1898. For five of those eight seasons, Griffin led all National

League outfielders in fielding percentage and three times led in putouts. He also excelled at the plate as he compiled a .308 batting average during those years and, in 1891, led the National League in doubles with 36. Griffin failed to score 100 runs in only two of his 12 major league seasons. In 1889, he led the American Association with 152 runs scored. Although he had been used throughout the batting order at various stages of his career, Griffin had settled in as the Brooklyn leadoff man by the mid-1890s.

Griffin knocked out 1,776 hits for a lifetime batting average of .299. Five times he batted better than .300 in a season. But, despite these achievements, Griffin never played on a championship team.

From 1895 through the 1898 seasons, Griffin served as captain of the Brooklyn club. In 1898, he replaced Barnie — his first major league manager — as the skipper of the club. Griffin quit as manager after just four games, however, and Charles Ebbets, who had just become club president, took over as the field leader.

The 1898 season would be Griffin's last one

in baseball. He had signed a contract with Brooklyn for $3,500 to serve as center fielder, captain and manager for 1899. But before the season opened, the Baltimore and Brooklyn clubs combined and Griffin found himself offered a new contract for $3,800, although without the privilege of managing. Griffin rejected the offer and refused to report to the Brooklyn club, citing his original contract. He subsequently was released to Cleveland and later to St. Louis, but, when neither club would grant him a contract for $3,500 for the 1899 season, Griffin decided to quit baseball and return to Utica to enter the world of business. Griffin later sued the Brooklyn club for failing to honor his contract and was awarded $2,250 by the New York State Court of Appeals.

Griffin returned to his native Utica where he became a part owner and vice president of the Consumers Brewery Company. He later served as an agent for the Gulf Brewing Company in Utica. Griffin died in Utica on April 10, 1908 of pneumonia.

— Richard A. Puff and
Mark D. Rucker

			G	R	H	BA	SA	POS	E	FA	GP	W-L	R	H
1885	Utica	NYSt	75	52	80	.279		of	16	.892				
1886	Utica	IL	96	86	116	.286		of	17	.923				
1887	Baltimore	AA	136	142	214	.368	.485	of	20	.931				
1888	Baltimore	AA	137	103	139	.256	.336	of	19	.942				
1889	Baltimore	AA	137	152	149	.280	.402	of-ss	45	.890				
1890	Philadelphia	PL	115	127	143	.291	.404	of	12	.961				
1891	Brooklyn	NL	134	106	141	.271	.392	of	16	.960				
1892	Brooklyn	NL	129	103	127	.277	.373	of	9	.969				
1893	Brooklyn	NL	95	85	103	.285	.423	of	8	.965				
1894	Brooklyn	NL	106	123	148	.365	.516	of	12	.963				
1895	Brooklyn	NL	132	139	175	.335	.464	of	11	.972				
1896	Brooklyn	NL	122	102	155	.315	.421	of	13	.961				
1897	Brooklyn	NL	134	137	170	.321	.428	of	17	.955				
1898	Brooklyn	NL	134	92	161	.296	.369	of	7	.980				

GEORGE WILLIAM HALL

Born: June 22, 1849, England
Died: June 11, 1923, Brooklyn, N.Y. (Ridgewood)
BL 5-7, 142

George Hall continues to strike the researcher as an elusive and shadowy figure. Clear enough are his identity as the NL's first home run king, his overall abilities as a batter (.301 in five NA seasons, .345 in two additional NL campaigns), and his status as a player good enough to be desirable to the Boston Red Stockings at their 1874 peak. Beyond these facts, however, the picture becomes hazy.

Most intriguing is his role as a central figure in baseball's biggest scandal of the 19th century, the conspiracy to throw ballgames with three other Louisville Grays, which resulted in their banishment from organized ball in 1877. Following this, he slipped into obscurity in a way which left his birth and death dates a puzzle until recent years. (The Macmillan *Encyclopedia*'s confusion of Hall's death date with that of George *Hale* didn't help.) Finally, there is the matter of those century-old photographs: whatever the setting, Hall never seems willing to look directly at the camera. His demeanor deflects the inquirer's gaze. The notable exception is an 1875 shot at the Boston Grounds, in which, leaning cockily on his bat, he engages the photographer — joined by George Bechtel and William Craver, both of whom were banned for crooked play within two seasons.

Hall came to America in childhood, and developed his skills in the Brooklyn area during the baseball boom which followed the Civil War. Amateur clubs and town teams held the field, but as competition for the prestige and profit of a winner increased, under-the-table payoffs and betting increased as well. Into this atmosphere stepped the immigrant teen-ager.

After an 1868 season with the Excelsior Juniors of Brooklyn, he caught on as first baseman for the Cambridge (N.Y.) Stars, one of the best teams in the East. In 1870, he returned to Brooklyn as centerfielder of the Atlantics. When they decided to reorganize as an amateur club in 1871, however, Hall moved down the coast to play center for the Washington Olympics of the new National Association. He batted only .260, but impressed with the speed and strength of his wiry frame.

In 1872, the Olympics dropped back to "co-operative" status in the league, indicating an economy operation with players paid from gate receipts without guarantee. Hall responded by moving to Baltimore to wear the silk of the Canaries for two strong seasons. That operation, however, folded under the expense of the large twelve-player roster, and Hall joined Cal McVey in moving to Boston and the prestigious Red Stockings for 1874.

In Boston, though called a substitute in deference to the legendary but aging Harry Wright, Hall played the latter's traditional centerfield position in most of the league games, hitting .329, and in several exhibitions. In July of that year, he joined the team's exhibition tour to his native England. For his season's labors, however, he was paid only about half of the $1,000 he had earned in Baltimore. The following season he signed with the Philadelphia Athletics.

The atmosphere in Philadelphia was significantly different from what he had known in Boston. "Baseball pools" were openly played at the ballpark and rowdies controlled much of the action. Moreover, Hall was drawn into the shadows (fatal to the NA) by being reunited with his former teammate and manager in Baltimore, Bill Craver. Once a catcher, this tough, moody figure had developed skills as a second baseman and a crook. He even made the 1875 Brooklyn *Eagle*'s "starting lineup of rogues." It was a fateful relationship.

On April 22, 1876, Hall was stationed in left field for the reorganized Athletics as they engaged Boston in the first NL game. Despite his two hits, the visiting Red Stockings won 6-5, suggesting a season-long pattern. Hall enjoyed his best campaign ever, batting .366 as home run king (5), while the A's slid to 14-45 and were expelled at the league meetings in December for failing to play out their schedule. Without a team, Hall signed with Louisville for 1877, his last season.

The Grays were a strong team, led by holdover Jim Devlin who that year became the only man in major league history to hurl every inning of his team's games. League leaders and favorites late in the campaign, the squad began dropping road games in suspicious ways. Spurred by press accusations and informed by betting patterns, club vice president Charles E. Chase initiated an investigation which led to confessions by Hall, Devlin and Al (73 errors in '76) Nichols.

(continued on page 143)

			G	R	H	BA	SA	POS	E	FA	GP	W-L	R	H
1868	Star		7	16	17		(26TB)							
1869	Star		22	-	71		(113TB)							
1870	Atlantic		21	-	67		(99TB)	cf						
1871	Olympic	NA	32	31	40	.294	.404	cf	9	.914				
1872	Baltimore	NA	53	69	82	.324	.439	cf	17	.844				
1873	Baltimore	NA	35	45	59	.351	.446	cf	12	.882				
1874	Boston	NA	47	58	64	.287	.448	of	19	.819				
1875	Athletic	NA	77	71	107	.297	.419	lf	26	.873				
1876	Athletic	NL	60	45	98	.366	.545	lf	39	.801				
1877	Louisville	NL	61	26	87	.323	.439	lf	11	.900				

EDWARD HUGH HANLON
(Ned)

Born: August 22, 1857, Montville, Conn.
Died: April 14, 1937, Baltimore, Md.
BL TR 5-9 ½, 170

Best known as the man who managed five National League pennant winners from 1894 through 1900, Edward Hugh "Ned" Hanlon served successfully in baseball capacities ranging from player to club president during his long career. He was the slick-fielding center fielder and captain of the World Champion Detroit Wolverines of 1887, assembled and developed the legendary Baltimore Orioles champions of the 1890s, and launched the managerial careers of John McGraw and Hugh Jennings.

Born in Montville in southeastern Connecticut in 1857, Ned began his professional career in 1876 with the independent Rhode Island club of Providence. In the following two seasons, he played for Fall River, Rochester and Albany, doing most of his duty as a third baseman and pitcher. In 1879, however, he shifted permanently to the outfield as his Albany team won the minor league National Association pennant.

Hanlon moved into the National League with Cleveland in 1880, beginning a major league connection that would last until 1907. In 1881 Ned joined the new Detroit club in the NL where he remained through the franchise's eight years in the league. Ned was best known as a player for his aggressive base running and his superb defensive abilities, especially the amount of ground he covered in the outfield. His leadership ability was recognized early and he served his first stint as team captain in 1882 when he was just 24 years old. When Detroit dropped out of the league after the 1888 season, Hanlon was sold to Pittsburgh, where he became manager on August 13, 1889. In 1890 he jumped to Pittsburgh's Players' League franchise, serving not only as center fielder, captain, and manager, but as stockholder and member of the board of directors as well. In 1891 he was back with the National League club and was fired as manager in July because of the discontent caused by his attempts to discipline his hard-drinking teammates.

Hanlon was ready to start the 1892 season as Pittsburgh captain under manager Al Buckenberger, but a severe injury suffered in spring training laid him up. While he was recuperating, he accepted an offer to manage the lowly Baltimore Orioles, a club with a long tradition of losing. A canny judge of young talent, Hanlon negotiated some masterly trades getting Joe Kelley and $2,500 for George Van Haltren; Hugh Jennings for Tim O'Rourke; and Willie Keeler and Dan Brouthers for Billy Shindle and George Treadway. He also made some bargain purchases obtaining Steve Brodie for $800, and suddenly had himself the most powerful team in the league. They won three consecutive pennants from 1894 through 1896. Through his patient instruction and attention to detail, Hanlon's men became the acknowledged masters of the unexpected and daring, especially on offense. They also had the most reliable defense in the league. While the Orioles never had a true pitching ace, Hanlon somehow always came up with a new young star hurler when he needed one.

In 1899 the Baltimore and Brooklyn clubs in the National League merged and Hanlon received 10 percent of the stock in each. He was appointed president of the Baltimore club and manager of the Brooklyn club under the new arrangement and he took most of the Oriole stars to Brooklyn. One man left behind was John McGraw, whom Hanlon made manager of the Orioles. "Hanlon's Superbas," as the new Brooklyn powerhouse was called, was a veteran team that knew how to win and quickly became famous for its late-inning rallies. The Superbas won the 1899 pennant and when the Baltimore club was dropped from the league in 1900, Brooklyn got most of its best players (though not McGraw) and repeated as champions.

During the next five years, however, the Superbas dropped steadily in the standings as the American League raided the team for players and Hanlon engaged in a power struggle with club president Charles Ebbets. Early in 1903, Hanlon purchased the Baltimore ball park and gained an Eastern League franchise to play in it. Hiring first
(continued on page 143)

			G	R	H	BA	SA	POS	E	FA	GP	W-L	R	H
1876	Rhode Island		72	58	81			s-3-p	96	-				
1877	Fall River		87	72	103	.285	.382	p-3b	78	.822				
1878	Rochester	IA	43	21	46	.259	.274	3b-p	29	.804#				
1879	Albany	NA	47			.316		of	-	.800				
1880	Cleveland	NL	73	30	69	.246	.304	of	35	.804				
1881	Detroit	NL	76	63	85	.279	.393	of	18	.897				
1882	Detroit	NL	82	68	80	.231	.360	of	27	.888				
1883	Detroit	NL	100	65	100	.242	.291	of-2	42	.873				
1884	Detroit	NL	114	86	119	.264	.364	of	39	.874				
1885	Detroit	NL	105	93	128	.302	.377	of	40	.858				
1886	Detroit	NL	126	105	116	.235	.298	of	17	.929				
1887	Detroit	NL	118	79	158	.316	.388	of	30	.904				
1888	Detroit	NL	109	64	122	.266	.342	of	21	.919				
1889	Pittsburgh	NL	116	81	110	.231	.321	of	26	.919				
1890	Pittsburgh	PL	119	107	136	.286	.353	of	29	.913				
1891	Pittsburgh	NL	119	87	121	.266	.327	of	33	.881				
1892	Baltimore	NL	11	3	7	.163	.233	of	5	.682				

EMERSON P. HAWLEY
(Pink)

Born: December 5, 1872, Beaver Dam, Wisc.
Died: September 19, 1938, Beaver Dam, Wisc.
BL TR 5-10, 185

When the Hawley twins were born, a nurse, in order to tell which was which, tied a blue ribbon on one and a pink ribbon on the other. Thus did Emerson Hawley, the recipient of the pink ribbon, acquire his unusual nickname. When the boys played ball around Beaver Dam, Emerson pitched and his brother caught and they were known all over the Badger State as the "Pink and Blue Battery." Sadly, this colorful combination did not make it to the majors, but only because Blue, who was just as good a player as Pink, died of pneumonia in 1891.

Pink Hawley became a semipro at Fort Smith, Ark., in 1891 or 1892 (the records are conflicting). While there he faced Krebs, Indian Territory (now Oklahoma), in a classic game. According to an account in the *Utica Globe*, Hawley struck out 21 and did not allow a hit, yet lost the game, 1-0, on a catcher's error. The winning pitcher that day for Krebs was future Hall of Famer Joe McGinnity.

Hawley was only 19 when he made his major league debut with St. Louis (NL) in 1892. The young pitcher, plagued by wildness, struggled to a 30-57 record in three seasons

with St. Louis, and found himself only after being traded to Pittsburgh. In 1895 he was 32-21 for Connie Mack's team, leading the league in shutouts (4), games (56) and innings pitched (444). After winning 22 and then 18 games the next two seasons, he was traded to Cincinnati. Hawley won his first 9 games of the 1898 season for the Reds and finished the year at 27-11. After tapering off to 14-17 in 1899, he was sold to the New York Giants. In 1901 he jumped to Milwaukee (AL), where he closed out his major league career at 7-14. He played a year in 1902 with Buffalo of the Eastern League, and managed LaCrosse of the Wisconsin State League to the championship in the league's inaugural year, 1905. For a critical series that year, the LaCrosse fans "bought" an umpire. LaCrosse swept the series, the umpire was fired and blacklisted, but the results stood. Hawley also pitched, a successful 19-9 record, that year.

Hawley, who pitched right-handed but batted left, was a strong hitter who had 11 major league home runs and hit .308 for Pittsburgh in 1895. A mild, retiring person off the field, he was a terror on the mound. He threw hard and

was wild. He holds the National League record for hitting batters — 195 (in nine seasons). On July 4, 1894, while with St. Louis, he hit the first three batters in the first inning and on May 9, 1896 at Pittsburgh he earned two more niches in the record book by hitting three men in a row in the seventh inning and five in the entire game. Many of his contemporaries thought he should be called "Plunk" and not "Pink."

In his book, *Hot Stove League*, Lee Allen tells of the time Hawley strolled into the cigar store operated by Chief Zimmer. Said Hawley, out of the blue (no pun intended): "Chief, will you forgive me?" (Presumably for hitting him with a pitch the previous season.) "Of course I will," replied the Chief. Next season Zimmer came to bat against Hawley in a one-sided game. Asked Hawley, "How's your batting average, Chief?" "About .214," was the reply. "Let's boost it a bit," Hawley said as he put the next pitch right down the middle. Zimmer connected for a home run and the game wound up 12-1. Hawley had lost his shutout, but had repaid Zimmer for his forgiveness.

— Joseph M. Overfield

			G	R	H	BA	SA	POS	E	FA	GP	W-L	R	H
1892	St. Louis	NL	20	3	12	.169	.225	p	4	.886	20	6-14	116	160
1893	St. Louis	NL	31	12	26	.286	.440	p	9	.820	31	5-17	184	249
1894	St. Louis	NL	53	16	44	.270	.417	p	12	.898	53	19-26	306	481
1895	Pittsburgh	NL	57	33	60	.324	.508	p	13	.906	56	32-21	240	419
1896	Pittsburgh	NL	50	19	39	.239	.362	p	10	.923	49	22-21	202	382
1897	Pittsburgh	NL	40	10	30	.231	.269	p	-	.905	40	18-18	208	362
1898	Cincinnati	NL	43	17	24	.183	.252	p	-	.851	43	27-11	165	357
1899	Cincinnati	NL	34	11	22	.218	.277	p	5	.924	34	14-17	162	289
1900	New York	NL	41	9	25	.203	.252	p	5	.950	41	18-18	198	377
1901	Milwaukee	AL	30	2	19	.260	.315	p	2	.966	26	7-14	136	228
1902	Buffalo	EL	15	7	12	.273		p	4	.911	15	6-8		
1905	LaCrosse	WisSt	29	10	17	.203	.238	p	2	.967	29	17-8	49	145
1906	LaCrosse	WisSt	17	2	15	.374		p	2	.944	17	7-4	21	69
1907	LaCrosse	WisIll						p						
1908	LaCrosse	WisIll	13	3	4	.117		p	1	.951	13			
1909	LaCrosse	WisIll						p						

GUY JACKSON HECKER

Born: April 3, 1856, Youngsville, Pa.
Died: December 3, 1938, Wooster, Ohio
BR TR 6-0, 190

Guy Hecker was that rarest of baseball commodities: a great hitting pitcher. He won 177 games in his nine-year major league career with a .292 batting average. He led the American Association in hitting in 1886 with a .342 average.

Hecker was born in Youngsville, Pa., in 1856. His family soon migrated 40 miles down the Allegheny River to Oil City where Hecker began to play amateur ball. In 1877 he joined his first professional club in Springfield, Ohio, staying only one season before returning to Oil City to be married. He worked for a business house in the western Pennsylvania town and played with local clubs through 1881.

A teammate of his on the 1879 Oil City team was Tony Mullane, who opened the 1882 season with the Louisville Club in the new American Association. At Mullane's urging, Louisville signed Hecker before Opening Day on his reputation as a slugging, good-fielding first baseman and change pitcher. He batted .278 that season and won six games as a backup to Mullane. The highlight of his season came on September 19 when he tossed a no-hitter against the Allegheny Club of Pittsburgh.

In 1883 Mullane moved to St. Louis and Hecker became Lousville's chief hurler. While he won 28 games that season, no one predicted the remarkable pitching year he would post in 1884. In that year he set the American Association single season record with a total of 52 wins. He also set the Association records for complete games (72) and innings pitched (671). For good measure, he also hit .296 and led the club in home runs. He posted 30 wins in 480 innings the following season.

Hecker detested pitching in cool weather and constantly attempted to avoid spring training. He felt light gymnasium work and a few tune-up games immediately before the season were sufficient.

His theories were seriously questioned as he started slowly in 1886. Apparently the 1,151 innings of the previous two seasons had taken their toll on his right arm. He was 2-3 in mid-May and had given way to Toad Ramsey as Louisville's prime pitcher. But he was batting almost .310. He missed most of the next two weeks with a sore arm. People thought his days as a pitcher were over. But with rest and electric treatments on his arm, he returned in mid-June and re-established himself as one of the game's star pitchers. No longer a power pitcher, he successfully converted to a finesse style and chalked up 27 wins.

But the incredible part of the season was that he finished with a .342 batting average to lead the league. In one stretch in August Hecker pitched 7 games in 15 days, won 6 and batted .657 (23 for 35). The big day in that run was the second game of a doubleheader with Baltimore. Hecker went 6-for-7 with 3 home-runs, 2 doubles and 7 runs scored. He had become the first major league pitcher to hit three home runs in a game (tied by Jim Tobin in 1942). His 7 runs scored is still the major league record. He also threw a 4-hitter that day just to show Baltimore he wasn't a one-dimensional player.

The 1887 season marked the beginning of Hecker's decline. The new pitching rules introduced that year limited the hurler to just one forward step. Hecker had used a sort of running start in earlier times, so his delivery was affected greatly. And his previous arm troubles had cut down on his once effective overhand drop pitch. While he batted .319, he won only 19 games. In October he became the first player to play an entire game at first base without a fielding chance.

During the 1889 season he was released by Louisville and accepted a position as an American Association umpire for the remainder of the year.

1890 was the height of the Brotherhood War and the only season of the Players' League. When Ned Hanlon jumped from playing manager of the Pittsburgh NL team to the Players' League Pittsburgh entry, the NL team's management hired western Pennsylvania native Hecker to be player-manager. Pittsburgh finished dead last, 23-113. Hecker pitched (2-12) and played first base, batting .226 in his final major league fling.

He was player-manager for Fort Wayne in the Western League in 1891 and for Jacksonville in the Illinois-Indiana League the following year. He led Oil City to a state amateur championship in 1894 and managed the city's entry in the Iron and Oil League in 1895 and 1898.

After his baseball career he entered the oil business. Later he opened a grocery store in Wooster, Ohio. He was involved in an automobile accident in 1931 which left him with only partial use of his once-mighty right arm. Guy Jackson Hecker died on December 3, 1938 in Wooster, at the age of 82.

— Bob Bailey

			G	R	H	BA	SA	POS	E	FA	GP	W-L	R	H
1877	Champion City		28	18	28	.233		1b	28	.913				
1882	Louisville	AA	78	64	97	.278	.367	1b-p	32	.962	13	6-6	52	75
1883	Louisville	AA	81	59	90	.269	.335	p-o-1	22	.927	51	26-23	280	507
1884	Louisville	AA	79	53	95	.296	.430	p	10	.951	75	52-20	232	525
1885	Louisville	AA	72	45	82	.274	.338	p-1b	15	.949	53	30-23	264	454
1886	Louisville	AA	84	76	118	.342	.443	p-1-o	35	.912	49	26-23	268	394
1887	Louisville	AA	91	89	153	.374	.487	1-p-o	29	.946	34	18-12	211	376
1888	Louisville	AA	56	32	53	.251	.313	1b-p	25	.935	26	8-17	155	255
1889	Louisville	AA	82	42	91	.277	.365	1b-p	23	.967	19	5-13	154	215
1890	Pittsburgh	NL	86	43	77	.226	.318	1b-p	29	.959	14	2-11	102	160
1891	Fort Wayne	NWL	55	42	66	.319	.464	1b	3	0-2	3	0-2		
1892	Jacksonville	Ill-Ind	38	23	40	.274		1b	12	.967				
1894	Oil City	(Indep)	67	87	107	.424	.651	1b						
1895	Oil City	IronOil						1b						

PAUL A. HINES

Born: March 1, 1852, Washington D.C.
Died: July 10, 1935, Hyattsville, Md.
BR TR 5-9 ½, 173

Never one to dodge publicity, outfielder and Washington, D.C. native Paul Hines attempted — in the winter of 1884-1885 — to become the first person to catch a baseball dropped from the top of the newly completed Washington Monument. But when he saw how deeply the dropped ball embedded itself in the hard winter ground, he abandoned the honor to another ballplayer (Phil Baker later caught the ball, but broke two knuckles).

Hines also was willing to accept credit for being the first to perform an unassisted triple play, although some eyewitness accounts of the game (Providence vs. Boston, May 8, 1878) describe his contribution to the admittedly remarkable play as 2 putouts and an assist, not 3 putouts. (After a spectacular running catch of a short fly, center fielder Hines continued on to third to double up one — or both — of the two baserunners who had passed the base on their way home, then threw to second to double up the other runner, or simply "to make assurance doubly sure," as one account put it.)

But Hines could take unchallengeable pride in his 146 hits in 1879. Not only did he earn the prized McKay medal as the National League leader in hits, he also became the first National Leaguer to break the 140-hit barrier — and the only player to have a 140-hit year in the league's first seven seasons. More significant to stat-lovers (although Hines himself couldn't appreciate the honor since contemporary sources gave the batting championship to Abner Dalrymple), Hines is now credited with winning baseball's first triple crown in 1878, leading the National League with a .358 batting average, 50 RBIs and 4 home runs.

Although he led his league in batting only that one time, Hines hit above .300 11 times and nine times led his club to fashion a career batting average during 20 major-league seasons of .301. As a fielder, he was famed for his range in center field and for his often

spectacular barehanded catches. His partial deafness sometimes proved a hindrance in the field and on the base paths, but it also helped spur umpires to develop their now-familiar hand signals.

Hines began his long major-league career in 1872 — after a year or two playing for junior clubs in Washington — with Washington in the National Association. Of the eight major league teams he played for, he achieved his greatest fame with the NL Providence Grays, where he was the only person to play all eight seasons of that club's brief history (1878-1885). His hitting and slugging led the Grays offense in their two pennant-winning seasons, 1879 and 1884. After his big league career ended in 1891, Hines managed and played

minor league ball for five seasons in Mobile, Ala., and in Burlington, Iowa.

Returning home to Washington after leaving baseball, Hines' predilection for making friends with baseball-loving congressmen led him in 1897 to a new career when one long-time friend — former congressman and newly-inaugurated President William McKinley — provided him with what became a long tenure as postmaster in the Department of Agriculture.

Hines lived out his final years in retirement at the Sacred Heart Home in nearby Hyattsville, Md., where, deaf and blind. he died at the age of 83.

— Frederick Ivor-Campbell

			G	R	H	BA	SA	POS	E	FA	GP	W-L	R	H
1870	National													
1871	National													
1872	National	NA	11	10	14	.286	.327	1b-3b	7	.914				
1873	Washington	NA	39	33	60	.333	.411	of	18	.867				
1874	Chicago	NA	59	47	81	.298	.342	of-2b	33	.861				
1875	Chicago	NA	68	45	97	.315	.370	of-2b	49	.856				
1876	Chicago	NL	64	62	101	.330	.438	of	15	.918				
1877	Chicago	NL	60	44	73	.280	.375	of-2b	36	.794				
1878	Providence	NL	62	42	92	.358	.486	of	25	.838				
1879	Providence	NL	85	81	146	.357	.482	of	26	.867				
1880	Providence	NL	85	64	115	.307	.396	of	13	.927				
1881	Providence	NL	80	65	103	.285	.404	of	22	.897				
1882	Providence	NL	84	73	117	.309	.467	of	27	.861				
1883	Providence	NL	97	94	132	.299	.416	of-1b	24	.925				
1884	Providence	NL	114	94	148	.302	.435	of	26	.895	1	0-0		
1885	Providence	NL	98	63	111	.270	.343	of	38	.876				
1886	Washington	NL	121	80	152	.312	.446	o-3-1	47	.885				
1887	Washington	NL	123	83	195	.371	.502	of	25	.886				
1888	Indianapolis	NL	133	84	144	.281	.363	of	26	.912				
1889	Indianapolis	NL	121	77	148	.305	.409	1b	43	.964				
1890	Pitts-Boston	NL	100	52	93	.237	.288	of-1b	25	.932				
1891	Washington	AA	54	25	58	.282	.364	of-1b	15	.909				
1893	Nashville	SL	2	1	1	.143	.429	of	0	1.00				
1895	Burlington	IaSt						1b						
	Burlington	WA	21	16	27	.310		1b	19	.929				
1896	Burlington	WA	26#	23	35	.324	.454	1b	12	.953				
	Mobile	SL	29	17	32	.264	.347	1b	17	.952				

WILLIAM LEOPOLD HOFFER

Born: November 8, 1870, Cedar Rapids, Iowa
Died: July 21, 1959, Cedar Rapids, Iowa
BR TR 5-9, 155

Billy Hoffer, sometimes called Willie, Chick or the Wizard, was a slender, almost frail, right-handed pitcher who relied mainly on his fastball and was described by one of his contemporaries as "a horse for work." It was this latter characteristic that probably led to his short (though brilliant) career.

A Hawkeye all the way, he was born in Cedar Rapids, Iowa, started and ended his professional career there and died there in 1959 at the age of 88. After his Cedar Rapids start in 1891, he moved the next season to Grand Island, Nebraska, Toledo, Ohio, and to Marinette, Wisconsin, the moves not resulting from Hoffer's poor play, but from clubs disbanding. His bad luck continued in 1893 when the Nashville club folded late in the season. But the luck turned from bad to good when he was picked up by John C. Chapman, astute manager of the Buffalo Eastern League club. His late '93 record with the Bisons was a modest 3-4, but Chapman liked what he had seen.

In 1894 Hoffer won 27, lost 19, and in 76 games, some of them as an outfielder, he batted .322 and hit 10 home runs, earning a promotion to Ned Hanlon's famed Baltimore Orioles.

Few comets have flashed across the baseball sky with the brilliance of Billy Hoffer. In his first three seasons (1895-1897), he won 30, 25 and 22 games while losing only 7, 7, and 11, respectively, for a percentage of .755. He started 106 games, finished 93 and worked 926 innings. He pitched in two Temple Cup series, going 0-2 in 1895 and 2-0 in 1896, beating Cy Young of Cleveland in the first game of the latter series.

But Hoffer was fated to fade as quickly as he had burst onto the scene. Troubled by a sore arm in 1898, he was released to Pittsburgh, where his record was 11-10 in a season and a half. In 1900 he surfaced with Cleveland in the still minor American League, where he won 17 and lost 10. On April 21, 1901, Hoffer became a footnote to baseball history when he became the first losing pitcher in American League (major) history, dropping an 8-2 decision, including 7 runs on 6 walks in the first two innings, to Chicago in a game played a day ahead of the other teams.

His major league career over after the 1901 season, Hoffer continued in the game for a few years, managing and occasionally playing for Des Moines and Cedar Rapids. He then took a job with the interurban transit line which ran between Cedar Rapids and Iowa City, serving as a conductor and engineer. An artist of some ability, he designed Christmas cards and drew sports cartoons as a hobby. His one venture into oils was a still life of his 1896 Baltimore uniform, framed by the wood split from the bat he had used to hit .304 for the Orioles that year. He called it "After the Ball is Over."

— Joseph M. Overfield

			G	R	H	BA	SA	POS	E	FA	GP	W-L	R	H
1890	Cedar Rapids	IllIa												
1891	Cedar Rapids	IllIa	40	23	35	.228		p-of			25#	13-11		
1892	Joliet	IllInd	14	7	11	.208		p-of						
	Grand Island	NebSt						p						
	Toledo	WL	1	1	1	.250	.500	p	0	1.00	1	1-0	4	6
	Marinette	WisSt						p						
1893	Nashville	SL	57	27	55	.291	.392	p-of			36	14-17	190	295
	Buffalo	EL	9	7	4	.154	.154	p	0	1.00	9	3-4	47	72
1894	Buffalo	EL	76	63	91	.322		p-of	11	.942	51	28-17	307	516
1895	Baltimore	NL	41	22	27	.216	.256	p	-	.933	41	31-7	142	296
1896	Baltimore	NL	35	23	38	.302	.413	p	-	.878	35	25-7	140	317
1897	Baltimore	NL	42	20	34	.238	.329	p	-	.868	38	22-11	194	350
1898	Balt-Pitts	NL	12	2	6	.171	.257	p-of	1	.958	8	3-4	51	88
1899	Pittsburgh	NL	33	12	18	.198	.220	p-of	7	.909	23	8-11	102	169
1900	Cleveland	AL	43	19	24	.190	.238	p-of	8	.938	30	16-12	104	272
1901	Cleveland	AL	17	3	6	.136	.227	p	3	.930	16	3-7	73	113
	Sacramento	Cal	49	25	42	.245		of-p	6	.936	12	2-10		115
1902	Des Moines	WL	77	26	63	.255	.308	of-p	-	.956	29			
1903	Des Moines	WL	67	37	70	.281	.330	of						
1904	Des Moines	WL	32	16	20	.220	.286	p		.881	31	17-14		
1907	Quincy	Iowa	20	3	13	.203		of	2	.905				
1908	Oklahoma City	WA	22	3	6	.105	.140	p	3	.977	22	10-7		
1909	Cedar Rapids	III	9					p			9	3-6		

MICHAEL JOSEPH HORNUNG
(Ubbo Ubbo)

Born: June 12, 1857, Carthage, N.Y.
Died: October 30, 1931, Howard Beach, N.Y.
BR TR 5-8 ½, 164

"No siree, give me old-timers. They were the boys who would take their medicine, stand the gaff and look for more." So spoke Joe Hornung, a prototype old-time ballplayer if ever there was one. Tough and hard-bitten with hands that were callused, sinewy and strong, he disdained the glove, which he called "sissy," until very late in his career. His curious nickname, "Ubbo Ubbo," came from his calling out those words every time he made a hit or a good fielding play.

Hornung learned to play on the mud-flat diamonds along the Mohawk River in Utica, N.Y. In 1876 when Joe was 19, fellow Utican Juice Latham took him north of the border to join the London (Ontario) Tecumsehs, probably the best of the early Canadian teams. Joe played with London in 1876, in 1877 when the Tecs won the International Association pennant, and midway through the 1878 season when the team folded. He then joined Buffalo in time to celebrate another International As-

sociation pennant. Hornung remained with the Bisons, which had joined the National League, through the 1880 season. His next stop was Boston (NL) 1881 to 1888, then Baltimore (AA) in 1889 and finally New York (NL) in 1890, where he wound up his 12-year major league career. Four more years in the minors with Buffalo, Providence and Worcester (where he broke his leg) spelled the finish to his 19 years as a ballplayer.

Never an outstanding hitter (.257 major league lifetime), Hornung was best known as a fielder. Usually playing left field, he four times led the league in fielding (London and Buffalo, 1878 and Boston, 1881-1883). According to his obituary in the 1932 *Spalding Guide*, Hornung did not muff a fly ball the entire 1884 season, a rare feat in those gloveless days. His arm was strong and accurate and base runners took few liberties with it. A durable player, he once had a string of 464 consecutive games played with Boston, end-

ing September 13, 1884. When Charley Sweeney of Providence fanned 19 on June 7, 1884, Hornung contributed to the record, fanning 3 times.

Among his peers, Joe had a reputation as being somewhat of a crab. On occasion there was an uncharacteristic light moment, such as the time in Cincinnati when he took to the stage in a song and dance act, not knowing his teammates were there en masse. Their barrage of vegetables put a quick end to his stage career.

His playing career over in 1895, Joe took to umpiring and wore the blue in the National, Eastern and Connecticut State leagues until 1902. His last baseball job was as a special policeman at the Polo Grounds, where he would regale fans with tales of the good old days when "men were men and not pampered and spoiled like modern ballplayers."

— Joseph M. Overfield

			G	R	H	BA	SA	POS	E	FA	GP	W-L	R	H
1877	Tecumseh	IA	20	12	21	.236	.303	of		.911				
1878	Tec-Buffalo	IA	45	37	47	.241	.292	of	3	.972				
1879	Buffalo	NL	78	46	85	.266	.389	of	26	.844				
1880	Buffalo	NL	85	47	91	.266	.363	of-1b	20	.874#	1	0-0	2	2
1881	Boston	NL	83	40	78	.241	.343	of	12	.948				
1882	Boston	NL	85	67	117	.302	.402	of	15	.932				
1883	Boston	NL	98	106	124	.278	.446	of	13	.936				
1884	Boston	NL	115	119	139	.268	.400	of	20	.922				
1885	Boston	NL	25	14	22	.202	.294	of	3	.919				
1886	Boston	NL	94	67	109	.257	.307	of	11	.948				
1887	Boston	NL	98	85	135	.297	.379	of	15	.935				
1888	Boston	NL	107	61	103	.239	.311	of	9	.947				
1889	Baltimore	AA	135	73	122	.227	.288	of	26	.915				
1890	New York	NL	120	62	122	.238	.293	of-1b	18	.965				
1891	Buffalo	EA	121	117	139	.277	.389	of	14	.946				
1892	Buff-Prov	EL	97	63	103	.289	.374	of	6	.968				
1893	Providence	EL	55	56	65	.283	.383	of	13	.895				
1894	Worcester	NEng	60	57	66	.260	.295	of	19	.860				
1895	Atlanta	SL	92	64	87	.233		of	8	.960				

PETER JAMES HOTALING
(Monkey)

Born: December 16, 1856, Mohawk, N.Y.
Died: July 3, 1928, Cleveland, Ohio
BL TR 5-7, 160

Peter James Hotaling of Mohawk and Ilion, N.Y., excelled for the Syracuse Stars in 1877 and 1878. His elevation to the major leagues began with Cincinnati in 1879, where there was great optimism for a championship season. Although the team did have a winning year, the Cincinnatis finished fifth in the eight-team National League.

The 22-year-old Pete Hotaling began the season as a heralded rookie center fielder. He was just 5 feet 7 inches tall and weighed 160 pounds, but this is the way the Cincinnati *Enquirer* described him Sunday morning, April 6, 1879: "Hotaling, the new center-fielder, will prove a taking card. He is a broad-shouldered, heavily-built, handsome young fellow, who does everything with a manner that bespeaks confidence. He hits left-handed, and hits hard and beautifully. He astonished everyone this week by the tremendous manner in which he sent the ball spinning in to center-field clean to the railing."

Pete led off the first inning of the first regulation game by beating out an infield grounder. He moved to second on a passed ball, and scored the first run of the year on a double by Ross Barnes. Final score: Cincinnati 7, Troy City 5. Thus, a new major league baseball career was launched with great spirit and success.

That career lasted exactly 10 years, and one has to conclude that it was a very good career, although Pete was one of the first "journeyman" players. In addition to his first year with Cincinnati, he also played one year with Worcester, Boston, and Brooklyn, in the National League, plus one adventuresome year in 1886 in the South playing and managing with Savannah. Before that "experiment," he played three years with Cleveland (NL). He was with Cleveland in 1887 and 1888 when that team was in the American Association before finishing up with St. Joseph of the Western Association in 1889.

Pete Hotaling was a speedy runner and good fielder. His primary position was center field, but he also was an infielder and catcher. The latter position was probably responsible for his nickname: Monkey. His Cleveland *News* obituary, which appeared on July 4, 1928, describes him as a star player who "wore the first mask ever used in baseball. It was made by the Remington Arms Company of Ilion, N.Y., and was a great innovation in those days." This challenges the common understanding that the catcher's mask originated at Harvard with Thayer and Tyng. It is known that Hotaling, as Syracuse's catcher in 1877, wore the first mask ever seen in many of the cities the Stars visited.

With an average of more than 100 hits per year, Pete stroked many doubles and triples, but just 9 homers. He compiled a lifetime batting average of .267. On June 6, 1888, in his final year with Cleveland, he had 6 hits in a 9-inning game against Louisville. This was a rare feat, to be sure.

1888 was also the year when he appeared on three different baseball cards — the first ones to be made by New York's Goodwin and Co., which promoted its Old Judge cigarettes. One pose shows him in a batting stance (lefthanded), one shows him throwing (righthanded), and one shows him hitching up his pants (both-handed!).

Pete completed all baseball connections with a stint managing in Atlanta. Then, having earlier attended Eastman Business College in Poughkeepsie, N.Y., he returned to Cleveland to live out his vocational life in business. He worked as a grocer and finally as a machinist with the White Motor Company. He died of pneumonia at age 71 in 1928 and is buried in Cleveland's Lake View Cemetery.
— Dan Hotaling

			G	R	H	BA	SA	POS	E	FA	GP	W-L	R	H
1876	Ilion							c						
	Poughkeepsie		3	6	6	.400		c	2	.929				
1877	Syracuse		93	66	97	.241	.271	c	139	.764				
1878	Syracuse	IA	39	26	50	.273	.344	c-of	18	.809				
1879	Cincinnati	NL	81	64	103	.279	.390	of	25	.843				
1880	Cleveland	NL	78	40	78	.240	.342	of	15	.896				
1881	Worcester	NL	77	51	98	.309	.385	of	26	.862				
1882	Boston	NL	84	64	98	.259	.328	of	26	.865				
1883	Cleveland	NL	100	54	108	.259	.345	of	42	.829				
1884	Cleveland	NL	102	69	99	.243	.333	of	35	.849				
1885	Brooklyn	AA	94	73	95	.257	.316	of	21	.893				
1886	Savannah	SL	89	79	89	.270	.397	of						
1887	Cleveland	AA	127	103	204	.367	.480	of	33	.898				
1888	Cleveland	AA	98	67	101	.251	·.298	of	25	.878				
1889	St. Joseph	WA	50	20	54	.281		of	9	.908				

WILLIAM ELLSWORTH HOY
(Dummy)

Born: May 23, 1862, Houckstown, Ohio
Died: December 15, 1961, Cincinnati, Ohio
BL TR 5-4, 148

At the third game of the World Series, New York at Cincinnati, October 7, 1961, the first ball was thrown out by an elderly, fragile, white-haired man, who had to be assisted to his seat. Sixty-nine days later, the old man, William (Dummy) Hoy, was dead. His life had spanned 99 years, 5 months and 8 days, which was longer than any other major league ballplayer had lived. Hoy's record was later broken by Ralph Miller, former Brooklyn and Baltimore pitcher, who was a month and 8 days past 100 years when he died in Cincinnati (as had Hoy) on May 8, 1973.

Miller, whose major league career was brief (just 28 games), is remembered only for his longevity; Hoy is remembered not only for his longevity, but for a brilliant baseball career of 18 seasons, 14 of them in the majors.

Overcoming the triple handicaps of deafness (he lost his hearing at age 3 following an attack of meningitis), muteness and small size (5 feet 4 inches), Hoy amassed a record of Hall-of-Fame quality. In 1,798 major league games, he totaled 2,054 hits, 249 doubles, 121 triples and 40 home runs. He scored 1,426 runs, stole 597 bases and walked 1,004 times, while compiling a career batting mark of .288.

Playing center field, where his speed was an asset, Hoy was always rated as one of the best at his position. Thomas Longergan, a writer of that day, said of Hoy: "He was the smartest player I have ever seen, swift as a panther and very fast at getting balls in from the outfield." Hoy is one of three outfielders in major league history to have three assists — outfielder to catcher — in one game (Washington at Indianapolis, June 19, 1889). Jim Jones of the Giants and John McCarthy of the Cubs were the other two.

Hoy was 24 when Frank Selee, later to gain fame as a major league manager, gave him his first chance at Oshkosh (Northwestern League) in 1886. The tiny outfielder struggled the first year, but Selee stood behind him and it paid off. Hoy did so well in 1887 that he was sold to Washington (NL), where he led the league in steals his very first season. In addition to Washington, Hoy played at Buffalo (PL), St. Louis (AA), Cincinnati (NL) and Chicago (AL), making him one of only 29 players to compete in four major leagues. He wound up his career in 1903 with Los Angeles (Pacific Coast League), where at age 42 he played every one of his team's 211 games, had 210 base hits, and stole 46 bases — four more than his age.

It has been written, though possibly apocryphal, that Hoy was responsible for hand signals by umpires. Lee Allen, in *Hot Stove League*, wrote that Cy Rigler started this practice. Rigler did not come into the majors until 1905, two years after Hoy had retired.

The Hall of Fame for Hoy? Not likely at this late date; nonetheless, he was one of the greats of his era with accomplishments that loom even larger considering he could neither hear nor speak.

— Joseph M. Overfield

			G	R	H	BA	SA	POS	E	FA	GP	W-L	R	H
1886	Oshkosh	NWL	71	69	76	.328		of	21	.846				
1887	Oshkosh	NWL	116	108	195	.367	.504	of	31	.888				
1888	Washington	NL	136	77	138	.274	.340	of	27	.897				
1889	Washington	NL	127	98	143	.282	.325	of	35	.890				
1890	Buffalo	PL	122	107	148	.300	.360	of	28	.917				
1891	St. Louis	AA	141	136	165	.291	.360	of	28	.909				
1892	Washington	NL	152	108	166	.280	.354	of	40	.877				
1893	Washington	NL	130	106	138	.259	.310	of	37	.893				
1894	Cincinnati	NL	128	118	158	.312	.476	of	41	.898				
1895	Cincinnati	NL	107	93	119	.277	.403	of	37	.892				
1896	Cincinnati	NL	121	120	133	.296	.423	of	17	.950				
1897	Cincinnati	NL	128	88	144	.292	.375	of	24	.938				
1898	Louisville	NL	148	102	184	.318	.432	of	18	.953				
1899	Louisville	NL	155	113	197	.306	.392	of	24	.936				
1900	Chicago	AL	137	115	139	.254	.311	of	9	.977				
1901	Chicago	AL	132	113	157	.293	.394	of	13	.958				
1902	Cincinnati	NL	72	48	82	.294	.387	of	11	.934				
1903	Los Angeles	PCL	211	156	210	.261		of	23	.950				

WILLIAM A. HULBERT

Born: October 23, 1832, Burlington Flats, N.Y.
Died: April 10, 1882, Chicago, Ill.

Hulbert was president of the Chicago White Stockings from 1875-1882, founder of the National League in 1876, and league president from 1876 to 1882.

Raised in Chicago, where his parents moved when he was 2 years old, he developed a successful wholesale grocery and coal business and became a member of the Chicago Board of Trade. A large, robust man — 6 feet, 215 pounds — he acquired a reputation as an energetic and honest businessman and an optimistic and enthusiastic civic booster.

Although he never played baseball, he supported the Chicago professional team as a stockholder, director, and beginning in 1875 as its president. He vowed to bring Chicago a champion, but the club was an also-ran in the National Association. Before the 1875 season ended he secretly signed top players from other clubs to contracts for 1876 — in clear violation of the Association rules.

Hulbert had acquired the players necessary to win a championship but faced the loss of the players or expulsion from the league for his illegal deeds. He boldly proposed to form a new league before the old one could move against him. Hulbert stressed the shortcomings of the NA: rumors of game fixing, rowdiness on the field and in the stands, mounting debts and competitive imbalance. He secured support from the western cities of St. Louis, Louisville, and Cincinnati before arranging a meeting in New York in February 1876 to propose his new league. Legend has it that he locked the meeting room door and pocketed the key until the owners agreed to his proposals.

Hulbert believed that the long-term stability and profitability of baseball depended on the owners gaining firm control of the sport from the players and on the game gaining respectability in the public eye. The league constitution assured owner domination. To gain public acceptance, Hulbert opposed Sunday games, betting on games, and the sale of alcohol in league parks. When he believed that their actions threatened the game's integrity, he expelled the New York, Philadelphia and Cincinnati teams even though these actions reduced the short-term profitability of the sport. In 1877, he banned for life four Louisville players accused of throwing games, and also banned others for alcoholism.

Hulbert's own Chicago club, which he ran while serving as league president, won championships in 1876, 1880 and 1881.

After a long illness, he died of a heart attack in Chicago at the age of 50.

— William E. Akin

WILLIAM FORREST HUTCHISON

Born: December 17, 1859, New Haven, Conn.
Died: March 19, 1926, Kansas City, Mo.
BR TR 5-9, 175

William F. Hutchison was one of the premier right-handed pitchers of the early 1890s and the mainstay of the Chicago (NL) teams of that era.

Hutchison was born in New Haven, Conn., in 1859 and received a private and prep school education. He attended Yale University and starred for the college baseball team as a shortstop and batsman. Spurning numerous professional baseball offers after graduating in 1880, Hutchison spent a year in postgraduate school and pitched Yale to the eastern collegiate championship. He then went to Kansas City, Missouri, to pursue a career in business.

For seven seasons Hutchison refused all full-time professional offers and, except for brief appearances with Springfield (Northwestern League) in 1883 and Kansas City (UA) in 1884, played only amateur baseball. He engaged during this time in the railroad and lumber businesses and by 1886 was located in Cedar Rapids, Iowa, where he was involved in railroad speculation.

Finally in 1887, Hutchison agreed to pitch for Des Moines (Northwest League), even then bypassing several more lucrative major league offers in order to stay closer to home. He commanded a salary of $3,800 for Des Moines, reportedly the highest in the minor leagues at that time. Hutchison joined Des Moines on May 24, pitched a 6-hit complete game in his first start and compiled a 26-10 record for the season. In 1888 Hutchison didn't join Des Moines until July 4, but still went 23-10, leading Des Moines (Western Association) to the championship by one game over Kansas City.

Business reverses and his decided successes with Des Moines finally convinced Hutchison to make a full-time career out of baseball. For the 1889 season he was sold to

Chicago (NL), owned still by Al Spalding and managed still by Cap Anson. The transition to the National League was unexpectedly difficult for the almost 30-year-old rookie and he was close to release on several occasions. He managed only a 16-17 record, far below the expectations of the Chicago management.

Hutchison's next three seasons were his best and among the best three consecutive seasons ever put together by one pitcher. Successive 42-25, 43-19 and 37-34 records in 1890-1892 gave him 122 victories in just three years. He led the National League in games, games started and complete games those three years. In 1892 he pitched a phenomenal 627 innings (the eighth best total of all time) and struck out 316.

Hutchison had an overpowering fastball, but command of no other pitches until very late in his career when he added a curveball. He was also plagued by poor control, thus his nickname "Wild Bill." He allowed as many as

199 bases on balls in a season and amassed almost as many walks as strikeouts in his career.

The pitching distance was extended to 60 feet 6 inches for the 1893 season. Hutchison, by now almost 34, was unable to adjust and his record dipped to 16-23. Most dramatically, his strikeouts fell from 316 in 1892 to 80 in 1893.

"Wild Bill" was out of the majors by the end of 1895 except for a brief stay with St. Louis (NL) in 1897. He found success with Minneapolis (Western League) through 1899, but retired to Kansas City after that season. He pitched semipro baseball in the Kansas City area until at least 1909 when he was almost 50 years old. He was employed by the Kansas City Southern Railroad for many years after his retirement from baseball.

Hutchison died in Kansas City, Missouri, in 1926.

— Harold L. Dellinger

			G	R	H	BA	SA	POS	E	FA	GP	W-L	R	H
1879	Yale University		24			.308		ss	-	.844				
1880	Yale University		17			.324	.441	ss	-	.730				
1881	Yale University		10	12	—	.286	.429	ss-p	6	.933	5	5-0	24	23
1883	Springfield	NWL						p						
1884	Kansas City	UA	2	1	2	.250	.250	p	0	1.00	2	1-1	11	14
1887	Des Moines	NWL	45	36	58	.335	.486	p	3	.988	40	26-10	199	413
1888	Des Moines	WA	38	22	33	.231		p	7	.977	36	23-10		
1889	Chicago	NL	37	14	21	.158	.195	p	5	.952	37	16-17	205	306
1890	Chicago	NL	71	28	53	.203	.268	p	14	.925	71	42-25	315	505
1891	Chicago	NL	67	27	45	.185	.243	p	13	.906	66	44-19	289	508
1892	Chicago	NL	77	23	58	.225	.314	p	13	.966	75	37-34	319	572
1893	Chicago	NL	46	14	41	.253	.346	p	7	.915	44	16-25	268	420
1894	Chicago	NL	39	30	43	.316	.471	p	5	.917	36	14-20	224	373
1895	Chicago	NL	38	12	25	.198	.278	p			38	13-21	216	371
1896	Minneapolis	WL	55	25	46	.237	.335	p	8	.938	55	38-14	283	471
1897	St. Louis	NL	6	1	5	.278	.389	p	1	.875	6	1-4	41	55
	Minneapolis	WL	44	19	30	.224	.299	p	7	.920	42	16-20	286	413
1899	Minneapolis	WL	27	7	11	.135	.135	p	3	.962	27	14-9		

ARTHUR IRWIN

Born: February 14, 1858, Toronto, Ont., Can.
Died: July 16, 1921, at sea.
BL TR 5-8 ½, 158

Irwin is rated the finest Canadian-born shortstop to play the game. A steady if unspectacular (.241 lifetime) hitter, he was a reliable fielder, and good baserunner who played more than 1,000 games during 13 major league seasons.

While a youngster, he moved with his family to South Boston where at 15 he began playing with strong amateur teams: Aetna (1873-1874) and the Amateurs of Boston (1875-1879). In 1879 he joined the independent professional team in Worcester and was the club's shortstop when it gained an NL franchise the next year.

After three seasons at Worcester, Irwin moved to Providence where he had his finest seasons. He achieved a career-high .286 average in 1883. As the Grays rolled to the pennant the following year, *Sporting Life* reported that Irwin's "daring and almost reckless baserunning" made him "a favorite of the Providence people." His .300 average

helped the Grays sweep the Mets (AA) in the first "World Championship Series." He remained a regular through 1890, playing for Philadelphia (NL), Washington (NL) and Boston (PL).

Irwin is credited by some with introducing the modern fielder's glove in 1885. Catchers and first basemen already wore mitts and some fielders wore skintight gloves, but to protect a broken finger, Irwin devised a padded glove. After his finger healed, he continued to use the glove, and other infielders gradually adopted his style.

He moved into managing as a midseason replacement while playing for Washington in 1889. In his first full season as manager, he led Boston to the 1891 AA pennant. During the 1890s he managed Washington, Philadelphia, New York, and Washington again. Only his 1894 and 1895 Phillies finished above .500. While managing in Philadelphia he wrote a boys' book, *Practical Ball Playing*

(1895) and coached in the first short-lived professional football league. During eight seasons he compiled a 416-427 managerial record.

Irwin remained in baseball until his death in 1921, when, at age 63, he was reported to be the oldest active baseball man. He owned, operated and managed a string of minor league clubs, including teams at Toronto, where he won the International League pennant in 1902, Rochester, Kansas City, Altoona, Lewiston and Hartford. He also scouted for New York (AL) from 1908 to 1912.

While a passenger on a ship between New York and Boston, he either fell, jumped, or was pushed overboard and drowned. After his death, it was discovered that for 30 years he had lived a dual life with wives and children in both Boston and New York.

— William E. Akin

			G	R	H	BA	SA	POS	E	FA	GP	W-L	R	H
1879	Worcester	NA	32	-		.271		ss	-	.849				
1880	Worcester	NL	85	53	91	.259	.344	ss	54	.886				
1881	Worcester	NL	50	27	55	.267	.350	ss	36	.851				
1882	Worcester	NL	84	30	73	.219	.276	3b-ss	78	.835				
1883	Providence	NL	98	67	116	.286	.369	ss	63	.856				
1884	Providence	NL	102	73	97	.240	.302	ss	55	.881	1	0-0		
1885	Providence	NL	59	16	39	.179	.197	ss	41	.873				
1886	Philadelphia	NL	101	51	87	.233	.279	ss	56	.891				
1887	Philadelphia	NL	100	65	143	.339	.424	ss	58	.892				
1888	Philadelphia	NL	125	51	98	.219	.257	ss	64	.900				
1889	Phil-Wash	NL	103	58	89	.231	.301	ss	62	.892	1	0-0		
1890	Boston	PL	96	61	94	.265	.318	ss	59	.888				
1891	Boston	AA	6	1	2	.118	.118	ss	4	.790				
1894	Philadelphia	NL	1	0	0	--	--	ss						

CHARLES WESLEY JONES

Born: April 3, 1850, North Carolina
Died: Unknown
BR TR 6-0, 200

Charlie Jones was born Benjamin Wesley Rippy on April 3, 1850 in Alamance County, North Carolina. He was the third of six children of Abel Rippy, a yeoman farmer, and Delilah Rippy. Sometime after 1860, possibly of the death of his parents, he moved to Princeton, Indiana, where he was raised by Reuben Jones, who was either his grandfather or his uncle. Whatever the relationship, Rippy took Jones' surname.

Charlie Jones began his baseball career in Evansville, Indiana. After several unsuccessful attempts to catch on with the National Association, he finally made the 1875 Keokuk Westerners, one of the poorer teams of that league. The financially and artistically unsuccessful Westerners folded in midseason. Jones played in only 12 games, batting .250. The next year the National Association was replaced by the National League. On Opening Day Jones was the starting center fielder for the Cincinnati Reds. Jones was one of the few bright spots for Cincinnati in a disastrous last place season. He batted .286 with 4 home runs and 38 runs batted in. He was second in the league in homers.

Jones was one of only a handful of Cincinnati players asked to return for the 1877 season, although he did move to left field. This Reds team wasn't much better than the dismal 1876 team. After a 3-14 opening it was announced that the team would disband. Jones then signed with Chicago, for which he played two games before the Cincinnati team was reorganized. Jones was then returned back to the Queen City, where he finished the season with a .313 average, 2 home runs, and 38 RBIs. Jones remained in Cincinnati in 1878 as a resurgent Reds team finished second. He batted .310, with 3 homers and 39 RBIs.

Jones was acquired by the Boston Red Stockings for the 1879 season, where he proceeded to have a career season. He led the league with 9 home runs, 85 runs scored, 62 runs batted in, and 29 bases on balls. He batted .315, and slugged .510, the latter the second best figure in the league. The 1879 season was to be the high point of his career, however. In 1880 Jones finished his National League tenure under controversial and suspicious circumstances. Late in the season he became involved in a salary dispute with club president, Arthur H. Soden. The club, claiming that his play had been "unsatisfactory to the management and his conduct in Boston aggravating beyond the patience of most people," refused to pay Jones his August salary. When Jones protested, he was suspended, fined $100 for "poor play and insubordination," and then expelled from the league. Up to this point Jones was having a fine season, however. He had batted .300 with 5 home runs and 37 RBIs in 66 games. On June 10 he had become the first player in major league history to hit two home runs in one inning. Although there is some indication that Jones' fondness for alcohol was a contributing factor in his feud with the front-office, he was also not the only player involved in a salary dispute with the Boston club that year.

Jones would never play again in the National League. He made several appeals to the league hierarchy, which highhanded officials refused to hear. Although his grievances were eventually upheld by the courts, Jones remained blacklisted by the National League. He operated a laundry in Cincinnati, and in November 1881 signed to play for the Cincinnati team of the American Association for the 1882 season. When the AA attained major league status in 1882, it decided to honor the National League blacklist and Jones was never asked to report. He sued Cincinnati for his 1882 salary but lost in a bitter trial in which Jones' alleged alcohol problem was an issue. Jones did play minor league ball for Portsmouth in 1882.

In 1883 Jones was finally allowed in the American Association for Cincinnati after the NL voted to reinstate most of its blacklisted players. The long layoff had not appreciably eroded his skills. In 1883 Jones was second in the league with 11 home runs and batted .294. He followed with batting averages of .314 in 1884 and .322 in 1885. Time began to catch up with Jones in 1886, when his average dropped to .270. He was traded from Cincinnati to New York in 1887 and finished up his big-league career with a brief appearance in Kansas City in 1888. His career average of .299 included 55 home runs, 170 doubles and 55 triples.

Jones was a colorful, hard-hitting slugger and outfielder. Despite his fondness for John Barleycorn he had a reputation as a gamer and was popular with the fans. Something of a dandy, his extensive wardrobe led to such colorful nicknames as "The Knight of the Limitless Linen." After his baseball career he moved to New York City where he was an inspector of elections. It is not known when or where he died.

— Jim Sumner

			G	R	H	BA	SA	POS		E	FA	GP	W-L	R	H
1875	Keokuk-Hrtfd	NA	13	5	13	.255	.412	lf		4	.750				
	Cincinnati		7	5	8			cf							
1876	Cincinnati	NL	64	40	79	.286	.420	of		27	.857				
1877	Cinc-Chi-Cinc	NL	57	53	75	.313	.471	of-1b		35	.863				
1878	Cincinnati	NL	61	50	80	.307	.452	of		15	.895				
1879	Boston	NL	83	85	112	.315	.510	of		13	.933				
1880	Boston	NL	66	44	84	.300	.429	of		25	.826				
1881-1882							(Blacklisted - did not play)								
1883	Cincinnati	AA	90	84	116	.297	.471	of		24	.884				
1884	Cincinnati	AA	113	117	153	.322	.493	of		28	.889				
1885	Cincinnati	AA	112	109	161	.327	.459	of		37	.869				
1886	Cincinnati	AA	127	87	136	.274	.399	of		35	.874				
1887	Cinc-Met	AA	104	58	140	.331	.437	of		21	.910				
1888	Kansas City	AA	6	2	6	.250	.333	of		4	.667				

WILLIAM MICHAEL JOYCE

Born: September 21, 1865, St. Louis, Mo.
Died: May 8, 1941, St. Louis, Mo.
BL TR 5-11, 185

William M. Joyce was a power-hitting third baseman for several major league teams of the 1890s.

Joyce was born in St. Louis about 1865. He first played professional baseball in 1887 with Leavenworth (Western League) and Kansas City (Western League). In 1888 he played for Ft. Worth and New Orleans in the inaugural season of the Texas League. In 1889 with Houston (Texas League) and Toledo (International League), Joyce first showed the power that served him so well. He hit at least 18 home runs for the "Babies" of Houston (including 3 in one game against Austin) plus 5 more for Toledo (including 3 in a game versus Toronto). His total of 23 home runs was virtually unprecedented at that time in both major and minor leagues.

The 1890 baseball wars allowed Joyce his first major league opportunity. He played third base on the Brooklyn (PL) club put together and managed by Monte Ward. In 133 games Joyce had only 123 hits for a .252 batting average, but also gathered 123 bases on balls, 43 stolen bases, and 121 runs scored.

In 1891 Joyce was with the pennant-winning Boston (AA) club, but suffered a broken leg on July 2. After an 1892 season with Brooklyn

(NL), when he played less than full time, Joyce was traded to the Washington (NL) club, which promptly announced plans to cut his salary from $2,800 per year to $1,800. The salary cut was proposed not because of the performance of Joyce, but as part of an industry-wide cutback on player salaries. Joyce refused to sign and ended up holding out the entire 1893 season.

In 1894 Joyce did join Washington and had perhaps his best overall season hitting .355 with 17 home runs, 21 steals, and 103 runs scored in 99 games. The 1895 campaign also was good for Joyce as he again belted 17 home runs. The multitalented Joyce, however, did more than just hit for power. He also hit for average, was speedy and smart on the bases, and he played good defense. T. P. Sullivan said of Joyce, "Of the many brainy and aggressive batters I ever saw he was my ideal, he knew what to do at a critical stage of the game." Joyce's way of playing baseball earned him the nickname of "Scrappy Bill."

During the 1896 season, Joyce was traded to New York (NL), where he became player-manager. He is considered to be the first Texas Leaguer to manage in the major leagues. He helped his own cause greatly in

1896 by hitting .333 and leading the National League in home runs with 14. The club finished strong under Joyce's direction, winning 26 of 40 games.

The 1897 NL season featured one of the best pennant races in history. Boston finally won out in the last week of the season over Baltimore with Joyce's New York Giants finishing a strong third in the 12-club league with an 83-48 record. Joyce hit .306 and scored 110 runs in 110 games. On May 18, 1897 Joyce had a record-tying 4 triples in one game — the last time the feat was accomplished.

Joyce continued as New York player-manager through mid-1898, when he was replaced by Cap Anson as bench manager. Anson lasted only 22 games and then was replaced anew by Joyce. Joyce left the majors after the 1898 season with a career batting average of .294, 264 stolen bases and 821 runs scored in just 905 games. Despite playing only eight years of the decade, Joyce was the No. 7 home run hitter of the 1890s with 71.

Joyce was later a long-time scout for the St. Louis Browns. He died at St. Louis in 1941.

— Harold L. Dellinger

			G	R	H	BA	SA	POS	E	FA	GP	W-L	R	H
1887	Lvnwth-KC	WL	7	3	10	.323	.452	3b-of						
1888	Fort Worth	Tx	47	38	40	.226	.288	3b			2	0-1	16	15
	New Orleans	Sou-Tx	7	2	6	.231	.231	3b						
1889	Houston	Tx	85	-	73	.235		3b-2b	51	.889				
	Toledo	IA	30	27	18	.163		3b	22	.816				
1890	Brooklyn	PL	133	120	130	.269	.391	3b	104	.818				
1891	Boston	AA	65	76	75	.309	.506	3b	41	.849				
1892	Brooklyn	NL	97	89	93	.249	.389	3b	52	.855				
1894	Washington	NL	99	103	126	.355	.648	3b	52	.866				
1895	Washington	NL	128	111	147	.309	.529	3b	73	.852				
1896	Wash-New York	NL	130	121	158	.333	.524	3b-2b	62	.890				
1897	New York	NL	110	110	121	.306	.412	3b	60	.859				
1898	New York	NL	145	91	131	.258	.392	1b	48	.967				

FRANK BISSELL KILLEN

Born: November 30, 1870, Pittsburgh, Pa.
Died: December 4, 1939, Pittsburgh, Pa.
BL TL 6-1, 200

Although injuries ruined two seasons at the very height of his career, Frank Killen was one of the top pitchers in baseball in the mid-1890s. The hard-throwing lefthander led the National League in wins in 1893 and was his team's Opening Day hurler seven times in his 10 years in the majors.

Killen started out as a catcher and had gained some local fame around his native Pittsburgh even before switching to pitching at age 18. Within a year, his pitching had gained him a professional berth in the Michigan League in 1890. That circuit folded early in the season, however, and Killen moved up through the Interstate League, which also folded, and finished the season as a member of the Minneapolis club in the Western Association.

In 1891 he was one of the Millers' top pitchers. When the Milwaukee club jumped the Western Association to join the major league American Association in August, the Minneapolis franchise closed up shop. Killen was signed by Milwaukee and was in the majors before his 21st birthday. He won 7 of his 11 decisions in the AA, including a 1-hit shutout of the powerful Boston Reds.

Milwaukee lost its franchise in the merger of the National League and the AA, and Killen was snapped up by the Washington Senators, whose pitching staff he dominated in 1892. His 29-26 record gave him the only winning mark on the team and he was the only pitcher to win more than eight games. For this yeoman service, Washington offered Killen a paltry $1,800 for the following season. Frank held out through spring training and finally was traded to Pittsburgh for Charley Farrell, who was also a holdout. Playing in his home town, Killen nearly pitched the Pirates to the 1893 pennant, winning 34 and losing only 10. Frank had a tentative foot-tapping start to his delivery that reminded one sportswriter of a man whose shoes were too tight. But once he launched into his mo-

tion, the batter had to look out for one of the best fastballs of the day. Killen was not shy about intimidating hitters with high, hard stuff, and he was known to follow his brush-backs with a few wisecracks about the batter's manhood. If a fight ensued, Frank was likely to be found in the middle of it.

Killen slumped in mid-1894, going 6 starts without a victory before winning on July 23. Three days later, Frank's season was ended when his arm was broken by a line drive off the bat of Cleveland's Patsy Tebeau.

He was slowly regaining his form in 1895 when he was spiked at home plate by New York's Parke Wilson on June 8. Enraged by what he felt was an intentional attempt to injure him, Killen slugged Wilson and was ejected from the game. There was some talk of suspending him, but Killen went out and beat the champion Orioles four days later. Then he became seriously ill from blood poisoning resulting from the spike wound and was through for the season.

Frank rebounded with a fine season in 1896.

He was leading the league in wins with 29 through Labor Day, but then lost his last 5 starts. He won his first 5 games in 1897, however, finished only 17-23. The Pirates released him outright on August 1, 1898, apparently to reduce the team's payroll. Killen was quickly signed by Washington in August 1898, but the Senators released him in April 1899. He caught on with Boston in May only to be cut again in July.

Killen was given a six-game trial by the Chicago Colts in 1900, five of his games being against his old Pittsburgh team. But he was dropped in June and was unsuccessful in one game with the White Sox. The next three seasons were spent in the minors with Wheeling, Indianapolis, and Atlanta. He had a brief fling as an umpire in 1906, but then retired from the game.

Back in Pittsburgh he operated a saloon and had real estate investments. He died of an apparent heart attack at age 69 in 1939.

— Robert L. Tiemann

			G	R	H	BA	SA	POS	E	FA	GP	W-L	R	H
1890	Manistee	MichSt						p			10	10-0	40	
	Grand Rapids	IL	4	3	2	.154	.154	p	2	.833	4	3-1	16	22
	Minneapolis	WA	24	12	24	.315		p	7	.794	24	17-7	110	151
1891	Minneapolis	WA	38	30	26	.208	.408	p			38	21-15	-	330
	Milwaukee	AA	11	8	8	.229	.314	p	2	.943	11	7-4	43	73
1892	Washington	NL	65	27	37	.199	.328	p	22	.865	60	29-26	279	448
1893	Pittsburgh	NL	55	35	47	.275	.450	p	14	.895	55	35-13	214	401
1894	Pittsburgh	NL	28	14	21	.256	.317	p		.909	28	14-9	160	261
1895	Pittsburgh	NL	14	7	13	.342	.395	p			13	5-5	69	113
1896	Pittsburgh	NL	55	29	40	.231	.347	p	10	.929	52	29-15	236	476
1897	Pittsburgh	NL	42	16	34	.258	.318	p		.818	42	18-22	240	417
1898	Pitts-Wash	NL	45	16	32	.267	.292	p		.857	40	16-20	194	350
1899	Wash-Boston	NL	14	3	8	.174	.196	p	4	.886	14	7-7	77	126
1900	Chicago	NL	6	0	3	.150	.150	p	3	.888	6	3-3	31	65
	Chicago	AL	1	0	0	.000	.000	p	0	1.00	1	0-1	6	12
1901	Wheeling	WA	25	-	23	.225	.353	p	4	.942	25	13-8	-	107
1902	Indianapolis	AA	30	16	24	.296	.407	p-o-l	2	.963	24	16-6	86	187
1903	Indianapolis	AA	5	3	6	.428	.500	p	0	1.00	3	2-1	21	38
	Atlanta	SL	23	5	18	.296		p	7	.893	23	6-14	-	165

MATTHEW ALOYSIUS KILROY

Born: June 21, 1866, Philadelphia, Pa.
Died: March 2, 1940, Philadelphia, Pa.
BL TL 5-9, 175

Matthew Kilroy began his professional pitching career in 1885 with Augusta in the Southern League. A highlight of that season was his 10-inning 2-hitter on July 6 against Atlanta.

Manager Billy Barnie of the American Association Baltimore Orioles signed Kilroy to a contract after the 1885 campaign. Kilroy appeared on the mound in 68 games in 1886, 66 of which he completed. In 21 of those games, he allowed less than 6 hits. They included 1-hitters on April 26, August 20 and September 21. On October 6, against Pittsburgh's Ed Morris, he hurled a no-hitter, winning 6-0.

With a tail-end team that finished last in runs scored and batting average, Kilroy compiled a 29-34 won-lost record. The rest of the Baltimore staff won 19, while losing 49. It is for strikeouts, however, that Kilroy's 1886 season will forever be celebrated. He struck out 10 or more batters 21 times during the year. Early record books show Kilroy's season total as 505; more recently, the total of 513 has been given. In either case, it remains the nonpareil

of strikeout records, challenged only by Louisville's Tom Ramsey who fanned more than 490 batters that same year.

In reaction to fears of pitching domination of the game, rulesmakers instituted the four-strike rule in 1887. Under that aberration, Kilroy's strikeouts fell to 217 for that season. Kilroy's games won total, however, including doubleheader victories on July 26 and October 1, soared to 46 — still the record for a lefthander. Kilroy's combined total of 75 victories for his first two seasons remains the record for all major league pitchers. Baltimore rewarded Kilroy for his 1887 performance with a $2,600 contract for the 1888 season.

Although Kilroy suffered from a sore shoulder in 1887 as a result of a collision at third base with Arlie Latham, it was not until 1888 that he had serious arm problems. He was out of action most of early May and late July as he fell below 20 victories for the first time.

Kilroy came back strongly in 1889. His 29 victories included a 1-hitter against Col-

umbus on July 18. Eleven days later, in a game called at the end of seven innings because of darkness, Kilroy held St. Louis hitless in a 0-0 struggle against Jack Stivetts.

That was Kilroy's last year with Baltimore. He signed with the Boston club of the Players League for 1890, but that year, his arm problems turned acute. He made but five pitching appearances after July 31. Kilroy's major league career lasted another five years, but he amassed only an 11-19 record after 1890. Always a fair hitter and a fast runner, Kilroy finished his career as a leadoff hitter and rightfielder for Chicago and Hartford.

A lifelong Philadelphian, Kilroy operated a restaurant near Shibe Park for many years after his retirement as a player. In the earlier of those years, he often took time out from his business to coach the members of Connie Mack's pitching staff. He was not without competence for the task.

— John J. O'Malley

			G	R	H	BA	SA	POS	E	FA	GP	W-L	R	H
1885	Augusta	SL	62	41	55	.228	.245	p	19	.964	52	29-22	193	304
1886	Baltimore	AA	68	33	39	.178	.201	p	28	.841	68	29-34	364	476
1887	Baltimore	AA	72	46	87	.323	.387	p	20	.911	69	46-20	324	742
1888	Baltimore	AA	43	13	24	.167	.229	p	6	.928	40	17-22	221	347
1889	Baltimore	AA	65	33	60	.290	.386	p-of	18	.904	59	29-25	291	476
1890	Boston	PL	31	11	20	.213	.277	p	7	.935	30	11-15	166	268
1891	Cincinnati	AA	8	2	3	.150	.150	p-of	2	.895	7	1-4	44	51
1892	Washington	NL	4	0	2	.200	.200	p	3	.786	4	1-1	11	20
	Athletic	EL	2	0	0	.000	.000	p-of			2	0-1	14	12
1893	Louisville	NL	5	4	7	.438	.625	p	0	1.00	5	3-2	41	57
1894	Louisville	NL	8	2	2	.118	.118	p	4	.778	8	0-5	42	46
	Syracuse	EL	30	22	33	.336		p	10	.883	28	18-9	159	290
1895	Syracuse	EL	55	40	79	.373		p-of	9	.927	31	14-9	164	287
1898	Chicago	NL	26	20	22	.239	.272	of-p	5	.914	13	6-6	67	119
1899	Hartford	EL	50	34	48	.246	.262	of	7	.885				

CHARLES FREDERICK KING
(Silver)

Born: January 11, 1868, St. Louis, Mo.
Died: May 19, 1938, St. Louis, Mo.
BR TR 6-0, 170

A strong and talented pitcher, Charley "Silver" King enjoyed great success early in his career, but he quit baseball while still in his 20s rather than accept the low salaries available in the 1890s.

He was born Charles Frederick Koenig in the heavily German city of St. Louis in 1868, but sportswriters translated his name to King early on. The nickname "Silver" came from his white, white hair. Charley started his professional career with St. Joseph of the Western League in 1886.

King was given a trial by Kansas City of the National League in the last two weeks of the season, during which he pitched in five games. The club then folded and Charley had trouble collecting the $200 salary that he had been promised. It was the first of his many pay disputes.

He signed with his hometown team, the champion St. Louis Browns, for the 1887 season. He won his first 7 games with the Browns and compiled an outstanding 34-11 record for the season. King thereupon demanded a 100 percent salary increase to $3,600 for 1888. Despite his professed intention of quitting baseball to work for his father as a bricklayer, he signed for less. His top salary in St. Louis was $3,200.

As the Browns' most reliable pitcher, King performed spectacularly in 1888. Only 20 years old, he pitched 586 innings in the regular season and had a 45-21 record. Against arch-rival Brooklyn, he finished 8-4 with one 1-hitter, two 2-hitters, and a 1-0 loss in a 3-hitter. In the World Series versus the New York Giants, King opened with a 3-hitter and had a 5-hitter the next time out, but St. Louis lost both games. Charley wound up 1-3 in the series.

A powerfully built man with a barrel chest, long arms, and huge hands, King's durability was not surprising to those who saw him. A righthander, he possessed great speed and good control. He had a crossfire sort of motion, starting in the back left corner of the pitcher's box and stepping across to the right side while releasing the ball "over his left shoulder." His sideways movement was so extreme that opponents constantly complained that he was out of the box when he delivered the ball. He was a poor hitter and fairly slow on the base paths, but was a good fielder. And his quick delivery made him very difficult to steal bases against.

In 1889 he was 33-17 with "only" 440 innings pitched, thanks largely to the presence of another top pitcher, Elton Chamberlain, on the St. Louis staff. King pitched another 1-hitter against Brooklyn on June 2. In 1890 King jumped to the Chicago PL club and had another fine season (32-22). On June 21 of that year he pitched a no-hitter, but he lost the game 1-0 thanks to a two-base error by shortstop Dell Darling.

After the demise of the Brotherhood, King negotiated a jump to the Pittsburgh Pirates in 1891, where he earned his top salary of $5,000. After a disappointing season (14-29), New York took over his salary for 1892. When the Giants management cut his pay by $1000 in mid-season, he jumped the team briefly.

Charley pitched poorly in 1893, although he still had good speed. This may have been due to the introduction of the pitching rubber, which curtailed King's movement. He was released by New York in May and signed by Cincinnati a month later. Faced with another drastic reduction in salary, King quit pitching and joined his father's business in 1894. After sitting out for two years, he made a lackluster comeback with Washington (NL) in 1896 and 1897. Somewhat embittered, he returned to St. Louis, where he was successful enough as a brick contractor to retire at age 57. He died 13 years later on May 19, 1938.

— Robert L. Tiemann

			G	R	H	BA	SA	POS	E	FA	GP	W-L	R	H
1886	St. Joseph	WL	-	21	24	.147		p	18	.941				
	Kansas City	NL	7	0	1	.045	.045	p-of	2	.846	5	1-3	35	43
1887	St. Louis	AA	62	28	69	.280	.313	p-of	15	.879	46	32-12	235	525
1888	St. Louis	AA	66	25	43	.208	.300	p	12	.926	66	45-21	216	451
1889	St. Louis	AA	56	37	43	.288	.296	p	5	.957	56	34-16	262	462
1890	Chicago	PL	58	25	31	.168	.238	p	6	.952	56	30-22	237	434
1891	Pittsburgh	NL	49	12	25	.169	.223	p	10	.896	48	14-29	242	385
1892	New York	NL	52	27	38	.228	.329	p	11	.904	52	20-24	259	397
1893	NY-Cincinnati	NL	24	13	9	.167	.304	p	4	.915	24	8-10	124	187
1896	Washington	NL	22	9	16	.276	.379	p	-	.827	22	10-7	108	179
1897	Washington	NL	24	8	11	.193	.228	p	-	.884	23	8-9	120	196

FREDERICK AUGUSTUS KLOBEDANZ

Born: June 13, 1871, Waterbury, Conn.
Died: April 12, 1940, Waterbury, Conn.
BL TL 5-11, 190

When old-timers like Fred Tenney were asked late in life to name the top players of the 19th century, one of the names they often mentioned was Fred Klobedanz. That is not so much a tribute to Klobedanz as it is an indication of the dearth of lefthanded pitchers prior to 1900. Not that Klobedanz wasn't effective, but he had only two full seasons in the majors.

After chalking up 28-9 and 26-6 records at Fall River (New England League), Klobedanz was sold to Boston (National League) for $1,200 in August 1896. He helped Boston to first place finishes the following two seasons, winning 26 games in 1897 and 19 games in 1898. His southpaw curveballs made him an effective starter behind right-handed 20-game winners Kid Nichols, Ted Lewis and Vic Willis.

Klobedanz yielded more than a hit an inning and walked nearly twice as many as he struck out, but these handicaps were offset by his fancy fielding teammates. However, he was clumsy afield; his slow delivery made him easy prey for base stealers and tighter enforcement of the balk rule cramped his style. Thus, when he started slowly (1-4) in 1899, he was sold to Worcester (Eastern League).

Klobedanz was taunted by Eastern League fans when reports surfaced that he had served as a strikebreaker by moving scenery at a Boston theatre during the winter. This reputation may have prompted Boston to discard Klobedanz, but reports did not mention the rumors at the time of his release.

Klobedanz was effectively finished as a major leaguer (he pitched one game for Boston in 1902), but he still had enough to sparkle in the minors for another decade, finishing a 17-year career in 1908 with 287 wins (234 of them in the minors). Throughout his minor league career, Klobedanz saw frequent duty at first base and in the outfield when he wasn't pitching, and he was one of the top home run threats of his day. Home run records are not available for most of his minor league seasons, but he hit 7 in 89 games with Boston and compiled a .281 career average. Curiously, his batting average declined steadily in each league, starting in the high .300s and winding up below .200 when he retired.

— Bob Richardson

			G	R	H	BA	SA	POS	E	FA	GP	W-L	R	H
1892	Portland	NEng	57	28	54	.260		p-of	8	.924	31	19-10		
1893	Ptld-Lwstn-Dov	NEng	49	37	53	.306		p-of	10	.900	28	10-14		
1894	Fall River	NEng	74	66	88	.313	-	p-of			22	13-6		
1895	Fall River	NEng	59	-	81	.377	.726	p	6	.949	42	28-11		
1896	Fall River	NEng	51	45	69	.357		p	12	.928	34	25-6		
	Boston	NL	11	4	13	.317	.488	p	2	.905	10	6-4	41	69
1897	Boston	NL	48	29	48	.324	.466	p	-	.828	38	26-7	193	344
1898	Boston	NL	43	12	27	.213	.315	p-1b	8	.934	35	19-10	170	281
1899	Boston	NL	5	3	2	.182	.455	p	0	1.00	5	1-4	23	39
	Worcester	EL	37	17	27	.243	.432	p	15	.921	32	16-8		
1900	Worcester	EL	50	13	31	.196		p	12	.906	41	21-20		
1901	Worcester	EL	43	19	26	.188		p	6	.932	43	19-16		
1902	Lawrence	NEng	49	17	46	.349	.508	p	3	.974	42	25-10		
	Boston	NL	1	0	1	.500	1.00	p	0	1.00	1	1-0	1	9
1903	Lawrence	NEng	42	14	34	.295	.378	p	4	.940	25	11-13		
1904	Lawr-NwBdfd	NEng	65	18	51	.251	.320	p	7	.937	-	18-21		
1905	New Bedford	NEng	21	5	10	.167		p			21	10-8		
1906	New Bedford	NEng	46	12	33	.241	.380	p	9	.900	33	17-10		
1907	New Bedford	NEng	3	0	2	.222	.222	p	0	1.00	3	1-1	12	23
1908	Brockton	NEng	6	1	0	.000	.000	p	0	1.00	3	0-3	16	27

WILLIAM ALEXANDER LANGE

Born: June 6, 1871, San Francisco, Ca.
Died: July 23, 1950, San Francisco, Ca.
BR TR 6-1 ½, 190

Bill Lange was born in the Presidio district of San Francisco and resided in the Bay Area until his death. Like most boys in the 1880s, he left the classroom before finishing high school. At age 18 he began his professional baseball career in the Pacific Northwest as a catcher and second baseman with Port Townsend, Washington. After batting over .300 in 1889 and 1890, he moved up to Seattle of the Northwest League where he hit .329 in 1892.

In 1893 he joined Chicago where he remained the regular center fielder for the rest of the decade. During his seven-year major league career, Lange was among the game's most colorful, popular and talented players, although his star has faded over time. He did not capture a batting title, did not hit .400, and because he walked away from the game at the peak of his career his chances of Hall-of-Fame election are slim. In truth, however, Lange may have been the best all-around outfielder of the 1890s. Contemporaries rated him the equal of baseball's greatest. No less than Al Spink, founding editor of The Sporting News, remembered Lange as "Ty Cobb enlarged, fully as great in speed, batting skill and baserunning." Clark Griffith concurred that Lange was "Ty's equal."

Lange had all the skills: he hit for average and power, possessed great speed on the bases, owned a strong arm and was among the game's top fielders. After a mediocre rookie season, he hit over .300 for the next six years, compiling a .330 career average. His 1895 .389 average has not been surpassed by a Cub since. He also holds the club stolen base record of 84 (1896) as well as career thefts, 399. As for his fielding, old-timers for a generation told the apocryphal story of his running through a fence to catch a sure home run, and Bernard Malamud borrowed the idea for The Natural.

The Chicago Tribune called him "the most popular man who ever wore a Chicago uniform." The fans referred to him as "Big Bill" and "Little Eva." Although he was one of the game's largest players, he walked with a distinctive strut. His personality mirrored the spirit of the "Gay Nineties." Fun-loving and carefree, he had a fondness for practical jokes, women and night life (which made Anson's final years as a manager frustrating ones). His aggressive and flamboyant play made him a crowd favorite.

At the top of his career, he shocked the baseball world by announcing his retirement. The father of his hometown girlfriend refused to approve his daughter's marriage to a professional ballplayer. So Lange quit the game. Despite huge salary offers, especially from clubs in the new American League, he never returned to professional play. He did serve later as West Coast scout for Cincinnati and coach at Stanford University, but his income was derived from his insurance and real estate agency. The marriage, however, ended in divorce.

— William E. Akin

			G	R	H	BA	SA	POS	E	FA	GP	W-L	R	H
1891	Seattle	PacNW	36	17	39	.305	.461	c-p	9	.949	11	4-7	52	82
1892	Seattle	PacNW	57	54	67	.303	.407	of-c	19	.920				
	Oakland	Cal	53	42	57	.277	.403	of	12	.918				
1893	Chicago	NL	117	92	132	.288	.415	2b-of	48	.899				
1894	Chicago	NL	112	87	145	.324	.445	of	33	.903				
1895	Chicago	NL	123	120	186	.388	.578	of	29	.919				
1896	Chicago	NL	122	114	156	.333	.467	of	25	.928				
1897	Chicago	NL	118	119	170	.353	.488	of	14	.952				
1898	Chicago	NL	113	79	141	.335	.441	of	25	.919				
1899	Chicago	NL	107	81	135	.325	.416	of-1b	9	.978				

HENRY E. LARKIN

Born: January 12, 1860, Reading, Pa.
Died: January 31, 1942, Reading, Pa.
BR TR 5-10, 170

Henry E. Larkin was a hard-hitting first baseman-outfielder who played in three major leagues during a 10-year career. He also managed for a brief period in 1890 in the ill-fated Players' League.

Larkin was born in Reading, Pa., in 1860. He hit the big leagues in 1884 as an outfielder for the Philadelphia Athletics of the American Association. After a .276 rookie season, Larkin hit .329, .319 and .310 in consecutive seasons. In 1885 and 1886 he led the Association in doubles with 37 and 36 and hit at least 12 triples in each of his years in that league.

After slumping to .269 in 1888, Larkin rebounded to hit .318 in 1889. Although not serious contenders, the Athletics did finish third in the latter two years.

Larkin was one of the disgruntled National League and Association players who formed the rebel Players' League in 1890. Larkin played first base for the Cleveland team, batting .332 and finishing fifth in the league with 112 runs batted in. He also managed the team through July, compiling a 34-45 record. Larkin ended up back in the Association in 1891, as a first baseman for the Athletics, where he bat-

ted .279 with a career high 10 home runs. The Association went under after the 1891 season. Larkin finished his career with the Washington Senators, one of four Association teams absorbed into the National League after the demise of the former league. He batted .280 in 1892 and .317 in 1893, his last season.

Larkin finished his career with some impressive statistics, including a .303 average, 1,430 hits, 259 doubles, 114 triples, and 97 stolen bases. He died in 1942 in Reading, Pa., the town of his birth.

— Jim Sumner

			G	R	H	BA	SA	POS	E	FA	GP	W-L	R	H
1883	Reading	Intst	62	58	83	.355	.487	of	-	.877				
1884	Athletic	AA	87	61	97	.296	.445	of	16	.884				
1885	Athletic	AA	108	114	154	.338	.530	of	30	.918				
1886	Athletic	AA	139	136	184	.327	.458	of	37	.881				
1887	Athletic	AA	126	105	202	.371	.477	of-1b	28	.933				
1888	Athletic	AA	135	97	154	.283	.403	1b	36	.972				
1889	Athletic	AA	133	108	167	.324	.428	1b	33	.975				
1890	Cleveland	PL	125	93	166	.327	.477	1b	32	.976				
1891	Athletic	AA	133	94	147	.279	.441	1b-of	26	.975				
1892	Washington	AA	119	76	130	.280	.390	1b	38	.969				
1893	Washington	NL	81	54	101	.323	.444	1b	30	.964				
	Reading	PaSt	16	14	24	.338	.408	1b						
1894	Altwn-Altna	PaSt	60	58	92	.339	.469	1b						
1895	Altwn-Rdg	PaSt	66	68	102	.358		1b	11	.987				

WALTER ARLINGTON LATHAM
(Arlie)

Born: March 15, 1860, W. Lebanon, N.H.
Died: November 29, 1952, Garden City, N.Y.
BR TR 5-8, 150

The baseball career of Arlie Latham spanned an incredible 76 years. Renowned as a free spirit during his playing days, he was also an umpire, manager, coach, executive and press box attendant. Known as "The Freshest Man on Earth," from a song written for him, he was one of baseball's truly unique personalities.

Latham began his professional career playing for the semipro Stoneham, Mass., team in 1875 when he was 15 years old. It would be eight years before he would become the regular third baseman for the American Association St. Louis Browns. Along the way he played at Pittsfield, Worcester, Philadelphia, and briefly for Buffalo.

Although not often a statistical leader, Latham led baseball in enthusiasm. He was a fierce competitor, a cheerleader for fans, and a merciless heckler. He would badger opposing players and encourage his fans to do the same. Latham often roamed the coaching lines to steal signs. Crowds loved him; he was a clown and a prankster, and was an accomplished tumbler who incorporated acrobatics into a game on more than one occasion.

Running and throwing were Latham's strong suits. He stole 129 bases in 1887. Additionally, he possessed one of the strongest arms in baseball and was proud of it. Many times Arlie accepted the challenge of a throwing contest, and usually for a wager, which he most always won. One such contest, however, caused him injury from which he never recovered. Oddly enough, Latham's manager at St. Louis, Charles Comiskey, was involved. Comiskey put up $100 to settle an argument between Arlie and Doc Bushong, the Browns catcher, as to who had the stronger arm. Latham won the prize in his first throw, although, he so severely damaged his unwarmed arm that he would never field his position as he had previously done. He carried his misshapen arm to the grave.

Latham was the spark plug of Chris Von der Ahe's highly successful Browns teams of the 1880s that won four consecutive pennants. He played in four "World Series," the most memorable of which came in a losing effort to Detroit in the 15-game traveling series of 1887. In the series, he batted .333, stole 12 bases and was the pivotman for the first triple play recorded in postseason competition.

After part of a season with Chicago (PL) in 1890, Latham moved to Cincinnati of the National League. Five seasons there and his playing days essentially were over. He made several token appearances later, the last for John McGraw's Giants in 1909. He also managed three games in 1896.

Latham's popularity carried over to the theater. He played to audiences during a short stage career that began while he was still in baseball. Arlie was in demand by promoters everywhere as he toured during winter months demonstrating his baseball skills. These included such tricks as cutting short the base paths when the umpire's attention was elsewhere. Latham also was invited to accompany Al Spalding on his "round-the-world" baseball tour in 1889, but couldn't make the trip as he was already booked to appear in the Broadway play, "Fashions."

Following his career as an active player, Latham umpired for three seasons in the National League. From there, he went to coaching. In 1909 he became baseball's first full-time coach. His assignment was to coach third base and teach the art of baserunning to the New York Giants. He got into four games himself that season and on August 18 became

(continued on page 143)

			G	R	H	BA	SA	POS	E	FA	GP	W-L	R	H
1879	Stoneham		37		-	.283			-	.811				
1880	Buffalo	NL	22	9	10	.127	.190	ss-of	-					
1881	Philadelphia	EA						3b						
1882	Philadelphia	-	127		-	.284		3b	-	.863				
1883	St. Louis	AA	98	86	100	.246	.310	3b	52	.876				
1884	St. Louis	AA	110	115	123	.276	.375	3b	65	.869				
1885	St. Louis	AA	110	84	102	.213	.264	3b	47	.877				
1886	St. Louis	AA	134	152	175	.303	.382	3b	80	.843				
1887	St. Louis	AA	136	163	243	.362	.452	3b	65	.878				
1888	St. Louis	AA	133	119	150	.264	.326	3b	62	.882				
1889	St. Louis	AA	118	108	130	.254	.326	3b	57	.887				
1890	Chicago	PL	52	47	51	.242	.332	3b	29	.865				
	Cincinnati	NL	41	35	41	.250	.280	3b	27	.853				
1891	Cincinnati	NL	135	117	145	.271	.383	3b	61	.902				
1892	Cincinnati	NL	152	111	148	.238	.283	3b	65	.887				
1893	Cincinnati	NL	127	101	150	.282	.350	3b	55	.892				
1894	Cincinnati	NL	130	132	167	.314	.438	3b	64	.867				
1895	Cincinnati	NL	112	93	143	.311	.403	3b	52	.861				
1896	St. Louis	NL	8	3	7	.200	.200	3b	10	.744				
	Scranton	EL	44	49	46	.257	.285	3b	19	.873				
	Columbus	WL	59	58	62	.257	.320	3b	29	.873				
1897	Mansfield	Intst	91	115	117	.305		1b	47	.953				
1898	Hartford	AtlnL	67	-	69	.260		1b	22	.970				
1899	Washington	NL	6	1	1	.167	.167	2b-of	0	1.00				
1909	New York	NL	4	1	0	.000	.000	2b	0	1.00				

ANDREW JACKSON LEONARD

Born: June 1, 1846, County Cavan, Ireland
Died: August 22, 1903, Roxbury, Mass.
BR TR 5-7, 155

Major league baseball can be said to have had several beginnings. Andrew Leonard was present at them all. He was a member of the famous 1869 Cincinnati Reds, the first openly all-professional team, a charter member of the National Association of Professional Baseball Players, the first professional league, and a charter member of the National League, the dominant major league of the 19th century.

Andrew Leonard was born June 1, 1846 in County Cavan, Ireland. Raised in Newark, New Jersey, Andy played for nearby Jersey clubs, including the strong Irvington nine, and for the Buckeyes of Cincinnati. He was recruited by Harry Wright for the Cincinnati Red Stockings in 1869 for a salary of $800. A hatter by trade, he was an integral part of the mighty Red Stockings, being a strong-armed leftfielder and hard-working team player.

When the professional National Association was formed in 1871, he signed with the Washington Olympics. On July 7 he scored 3 runs in the sixth inning during the Olympics' 18-run rally against the Kekiongas. He joined Wright in Boston the following season and helped the Red Stockings to four straight championships. With Boston he generally batted in the third, fourth or fifth position in the order until 1876 (when the National League began) when he moved up to the second spot. He played for pennant winners there in 1877 and 1878.

Leonard wound up in Rochester in 1879 and attempted to revive his fading skills with Cincinnati in 1880 before failing vision forced his retirement from the game. In his final game, on July 3, 1880, his errors allowed Providence four runs in a 6-4 Cincinnati loss.

Throughout his career Leonard was overshadowed by more illustrious teammates. However, no less an authority than Cap Anson praised Leonard as "a splendid judge of high balls, a sure catch . . . a swift and accurate long-distance thrower . . . . a good batsman and a splendid base runner."

Leonard worked for the water department in Newark until 1895, then returned to Boston where he worked for George Wright's sporting goods firm, Wright and Ditson, until his death.

— Bob Richardson and Jim Sumner

			G	R	H	BA	SA	POS	E	FA	GP	W-L	R	H
1864	Hudson River		5	8	(17 outs)									
1865	Hudson River		7	19	(28 outs)									
1866	Hudson River		5	6	(17 outs)									
	Irvington		16	59	(40 outs)			3b						
1867	Irvington		21	61	(64 outs)			cf						
	Americus		5	6	(17 outs)									
1868	Irvington													
1869	Cincinnati		54	-	211	(358 TB)		lf						
1870	Cincinnati		74	-	269	(419 TB)		lf						
1871	Olympic	NA	31	32	43	.291	.378	2b-lf	27	.827				
1872	Boston	NA	46	59	84	.346	.407	lf-3b	16	.842				
1873	Boston	NA	58	81	95	.312	.395	lf-2b	28	.859				
1874	Boston	NA	71	68	109	.320	.390	o-2-s	45	.814				
1875	Boston	NA	80	87	127	.322	.381	lf	44	.793				
1876	Boston	NL	64	53	85	.281	.327	lf-2b	36	.871				
1877	Boston	NL	58	46	78	.287	.305	lf-ss	25	.870				
1878	Boston	NL	60	41	68	.260	.328	lf	21	.777				
1879	Rochester	NA	20		-	.302		ss						
1880	Cincinnati	NL	33	15	28	.211	.256	ss-3b	21	.832				

EDWARD MORGAN LEWIS
(Parson)

Born: December 25, 1872, Machynlleth, Wales
Died: May 24, 1936, Durham, N.H.
BR TR 5-10 ½, 158

Machynlleth, Wales' sole contribution to professional baseball is Edward Morgan Lewis, who was born there on Christmas Day in 1872. Ted's family moved to Utica, N.Y., when he was 8, where he lived by the Erie Canal. He left school early to work as a bundleboy, but for four years he studied borrowed books at night. By earning $12 a week as a surveyor's helper, Lewis managed to put aside $50 to enter Marietta College. There he worked as a letter carrier, hotel clerk and janitor and learned to played baseball. He later transferred to Williams College and defeated the college nines of Yale, Harvard and Princeton with some slick pitching. After he graduated in 1896, he signed with Boston (NL).

In 1897 Lewis became part of Boston's rotation. "Lewis gives promise of being a good pitcher. He has fine curves and fair command when not working on his sidehand delivery; a delivery he uses mostly for bases on balls," wrote sportswriter Tim Murnane. Control was always a problem for Ted.

He spun his first shutout shortly after arriving in Boston and ex-Boston outfielder Tommy McCarthy predicted that Lewis would be a star before the year was done. He was.

"When at concert pitch there are few better than Lewis," Murnane wrote. Lewis finished 21-12 in 1897 as Kid Nichols (30-11) and Fred Klobedanz (26-7) led Boston to the championship. The following season Lewis (26-8), Nichols (29-12), Vic Willis (24-13) and Klobedanz (19-10) brought Boston the pennant

again. The team slipped just a tad the next two years and after a 13-12 season Lewis was in a quandary. He had continued his education by adding a master's degree from Williams in 1899 and he was an ordained minister. Baseball wasn't a proper profession for a gentlemen of his sort. Lewis was wrapping up classes on the vocal expression of literature (he loved poetry from childhood on, especially Browning and Whitman) at Curry College in the spring of 1901 when he made his decision: "I am going to go in for serious life work in the fall and do not care to expose myself to the telling strain of playing baseball. If I have the misfortune to pitch in a losing game it takes me days to get over it."

In 1901, Lewis welcomed the new American League, saying any National League player who ignored his option clause was justified morally and legally. In his debut he twirled an 18-hitter and won with ease. The Philadelphia A's were really low on pitchers and after three innings Boston led 21-4 so Lewis coasted home to a 23-12 victory. They all weren't that easy: he pitched the first Red Sox shutout through snow and sleet in Cleveland on May 25. "Teddy Lewis will pitch good ball for the Boston Americans no matter how many others may croak," said Orioles catcher Wilbert Robinson.

Lewis was "steady as a minister should be . . . Chicago's heaviest hitters went down before his speedy delivery like corn stalks before a gale," wrote the *Herald*'s Jake Morse

of one game. He later pitched 6-hit relief for 11 innings in another, but lost to Nixey Callahan in the 13th when, on a Fred Hartman bunt, he flung the ball into the stands. On September 9, he announced his retirement. "Parson Lewis is closing his career in a blaze of glory," said the *Globe* as he edged Callahan with a 2-hitter in his final game.

He was just 29 when he quit to teach English at Columbia University. He'd coached at Harvard for four years and wished to do the same at Columbia, but the faculty members objected to an educator stooping to such a task, so his direct involvement with baseball ended.

In 1904 Lewis left Columbia for Williams and later shifted to the University of Massachusetts. He ran for the U.S. House of Representatives from Massachusetts in 1910 and 1914, but lost both times. In 1926 Lewis became president of UMass, but the politics there bothered him so he left to take over the presidency of the University of New Hampshire one year later. He guided U.N.H. until his death in 1936. In Durham, N.H., he played catch in his yard with Robert Frost and they discussed the great poems. Frost also read at his memorial service (Tennyson and Whitman) and today baseball at U.N.H. is played at Lewis Field.

— Rich Eldred

			G	R	H	BA	SA	POS	E	FA	GP	W-L	R	H
1896	Boston	NL	6	1	2	.111	.167	p	0	1.00	6	1-4	32	37
	Providence	EL	9	3	6	.194	.258	p	1	.941	9	5-2	46	65
1897	Boston	NL	38	15	28	.248	.265	p	-	.806	38	21-12	188	316
1898	Boston	NL	42	17	37	.282	.328	p	-	.841	41	26-8	134	267
1899	Boston	NL	29	9	25	.260	.292	p	-	.861	29	17-11	119	245
1900	Boston	NL	30	10	10	.137	.137	p	5	.903	30	13-12	115	215
1901	Boston	AL	39	14	21	.174	.207	p	6	.931	39	16-18	169	299

HERMAN C. LONG

Born: April 13, 1866, Chicago, Ill.
Died: September 17, 1909, Denver, Co.
BL TR 5-8 ½, 160

Herman Long was one of the better short-stops of the 1890s and a consistent offensive threat for Boston and other clubs from 1889 to 1904.

Long was born in Chicago about 1866. Although little is known of his early life, he spoke German fluently so it seems likely his parents were German immigrants.

Long first played professional baseball in 1887 with Arkansas City (Kansas State League) and Emporia (Western League). He advanced to the strong Western Association in 1888, playing first for Chicago and then Kansas City. The minor league Kansas City (Western Association) team Long joined in July was one of two clubs in the "Kawsmouth Metropolis" that season, the second being the major league Kansas City (AA) club. The minor league club, fortified by Long, was by far the better of the two clubs and finished second by only one game to a great Des Moines club.

The two Kansas City clubs of 1888 were merged into one major league entry for 1889 and Long began his major league career as the regular shortstop for the "Cowboys." He fielded brilliantly, although often erratically. He covered more ground than anyone ever had imagined possible and made more errors than was usual even in an era of frequent misplays. Long made some 108 errors, but also hit .279 with 89 stolen bases and 137 runs scored in 136 games.

Kansas City fans were indifferent when, after the 1889 season, the owners pulled the Cowboys out of the AA and rejoined the Western Association. The fans were indifferent, that is, until they learned Long would have to be sold to a major league team. After conversations with several covetous major league clubs, Long was ultimately sold to Boston (NL) for a reported $6,500.

Also joining Boston in 1890 was right-handed pitcher Kid Nichols, who would aver-

age more than 30 wins a year during the 1890s while en route to the Hall of Fame. Boston won pennants in 1891, 1892, 1893, 1897 and 1898. Long batted as high as .339 and .327, scored as many as 149 runs, and hit as many as 12 home runs in a season. RBI totals were not officially compiled during his time, but modern research indicates two 100-RBI seasons. Long was a great baserunner and earned the nickname of "The Flying Dutchman" several years before the title was appropriated for Honus Wagner. A memorable home plate collision in 1893 incapacitated Long for three weeks and shattered Pittsburgh catcher Connie Mack's ankle and leg.

Long played with Boston through 1902 and also briefly with New York (AL), Detroit (AL) and Philadelphia (NL). He was later a minor league player manager with Toledo (AA), Des Moines (Western League) and Omaha (West-ern League).

Long's career major league batting average is calculated at .279 for his 16 seasons, with more than 2,100 hits, 1,450 runs and some 534 stolen bases, plus 92 home runs and 1,050 RBIs. All are among the better totals in history for shortstops.

Long's career fielding totals are interesting. He made more than 1,000 errors in his major league career, plus 150 or more in the minors. As such, Long probably made more errors than any other shortship in the history of professional baseball. He made as many as 108 errors in a season, but totals in excess of 100 were by no means unknown. Although Long led the NL in errors during two seasons, he also led the league in fielding percentage during two other campaigns.

Long died in Denver, Colorado, in 1909.

— Harold L. Dellinger

			G	R	H	BA	SA	POS	E	FA	GP	W-L	R	H
1887	Arkansas City	KanSt	-					ss						
	Emporia	WL		-	24	.277		ss	6	.915				
1888	Chicago-KC	WA	120	115	131	.247		ss-of	51	.897				
1889	Kansas City	AA	136	137	160	.280	.368	ss	108	.883				
1890	Boston	NL	101	95	108	.251	.343	ss	66	.898				
1891	Boston	NL	139	130	166	.288	.411	ss	85	.902				
1892	Boston	NL	151	114	185	.286	.386	ss	102	.889				
1893	Boston	NL	128	149	159	.294	.391	ss	95	.887				
1894	Boston	NL	104	137	154	.324	.505	ss	71	.893				
1895	Boston	NL	124	110	172	.319	.441	ss	80	.898				
1896	Boston	NL	120	105	172	.343	.463	ss	83	.897				
1897	Boston	NL	107	89	145	.322	.444	ss	66	.905				
1898	Boston	NL	144	98	161	.275	.372	ss	67	.927				
1899	Boston	NL	145	90	148	.257	.362	ss	60	.928				
1900	Boston	NL	125	80	127	.261	.391	ss	48	.937				
1901	Boston	NL	138	55	118	.228	.305	ss	43	.946				
1902	Boston	NL	120	41	98	.227	.262	ss-2b	43	.944				
1903	NY-Detroit	AL	91	27	70	.220	.267	ss-2b	47	.906				
1904	Toledo	AA	39	13	36	.242	.289	ss	15	.918				
	Philadelphia	NL	1	0	1	.250	.250	2b	1	.889				
1905	Des Moines	WL	118	78	146	.307	.366	ss	43	.936				
1906	Omaha	WL	69	16	54	.213	.237	ss	31	.914				

ROBERT LINCOLN LOWE

Born: July 10, 1868, Pittsburgh, Pa.
Died: December 8, 1951, Detroit, Mich.
BR TR 5-10, 160

It seems incongruous today that a player with a career total of 70 home runs is best remembered for a power-hitting display. However, Bobby Lowe etched his name forever into the record books when he became the first player to hit four homers in a game.

Lowe's big day came on May 30, 1894, at Boston's Congress Street Grounds, temporarily pressed into service after fire destroyed the South End Grounds two weeks earlier. After going 0 for 6 in the morning game of the Memorial Day doubleheader and making an out his first time up in the afternoon contest, Lowe clubbed four straight home runs off Cincinnati's Elton (Ice Box) Chamberlain. He then added a single for 17 total bases, a major league record that stood for more than 60 years. Although the left-field fence was only 250 feet distant, the Boston

Globe reported that all of Lowe's belts were "line drives far over the fence . . . good for four bases on open prairie."

Lowe, while batting leadoff in the Boston lineup, opened the third inning with his first home run and connected with one man on later the same inning. He had a solo homer in the fifth, a three-run shot in the sixth and a single in the eighth.

The barrage highlighted Lowe's best season in the majors. He batted .346 with 17 homers (one behind teammate and league-leader Hugh Duffy) and 115 RBIs. Lowe had hit 13 home runs in 1893, but didn't reach double figures again in 18 major league seasons. Although he never led the league in percentage, Lowe was considered a crack fielder and was an accomplished base runner as well, stealing 43 bases in 1891 and finishing with

302 career thefts.

Lowe began his major league career as a utilityman in 1890 after Boston purchased his contract from Milwaukee (Western Association). He continued as a handyman, but emerged as the regular leftfielder for Boston's National League champions in 1891 and 1892. The following season, manager Frank Selee shifted Lowe to second base and he quickly became a fixture in one of baseball's best infields ever, playing a key role on Boston's pennant winners in 1893, 1897 and 1898. Although his hitting declined after 1897, Lowe remained in the majors until 1907, finishing his 18-year career in Detroit (AL), where he remained the rest of his life. He scouted for the Tigers for a while, then went to work for the Detroit Department of Public Works.

— Bob Richardson

			G	R	H	BA	SA	POS	E	FA	GP	W-L	R	H
1887	Eau Claire	NWL	108	100	174	.369	.508	of-3b	18	.888				
1888	Milwaukee	WA	114	81	116	.246	.356	of	24	.900				
1889	Milwaukee	WA	97	72	127	.315	.422	of-ss	21	.916				
1890	Boston	NL	52	35	58	.280	.391	s-o-3	11	.944				
1891	Boston	NL	125	92	129	.260	.356	of-2	19	.935	1	0-0	1	3
1892	Boston	NL	124	83	116	.245	.319	of-if	39	.903				
1893	Boston	NL	126	130	157	.298	.428	2b	49	.936				
1894	Boston	NL	133	158	210	.341	.525	2b	59	.927				
1895	Boston	NL	99	102	125	.301	.422	2b	27	.957				
1896	Boston	NL	73	59	99	.320	.382	2b	16	.967				
1897	Boston	NL	123	87	154	.309	.419	2b	34	.952				
1898	Boston	NL	149	69	154	.272	.338	2b	37	.958				
1899	Boston	NL	152	81	152	.272	.335	2b	39	.954				
1900	Boston	NL	127	65	132	.278	.342	2b	34	.951				
1901	Boston	NL	129	47	125	.255	.299	3b	33	.912				
1902	Chicago	NL	119	41	116	.246	.286	2b	33	.957				
1903	Chicago	NL	32	14	28	.267	.371	2b-1	11	.940				
1904	Pittsburgh	NL	1	0	0	.000	.000	Ph						
	Detroit	AL	140	47	105	.208	.259	2b	27	.964				
1905	Detroit	AL	60	17	35	.193	.254	o-3-2	4	.974				
1906	Detroit	AL	41	11	30	.207	.248	s-2-3	16	.939				
1907	Detroit	AL	17	2	9	.243	.297	3-o-s	3	.889				
1908	Grand Rapids	Cen	119	46	103	.235		3b	32	.919				

No Photo Available

HENRY VAN NOYE LUCAS

Born: September 5, 1857, St. Louis, Mo.
Died: November 15, 1910, St. Louis, Mo.

Henry Lucas came to the baseball world with a substantial fortune and desiring a baseball club. He not only got his wish, but also was handed the presidency of a fledgling league. However, within a short time, he not only lost his league, but also his team and most of his fortune.

Henry Van Noye Lucas was born into wealth on September 5, 1857 in St. Louis. Henry's father, James H. Lucas, was a lawyer, one of the founders of the Missouri Pacific Railroad, and had established a bank in St. Louis, which continued to expand the Lucas family fortune.

Henry Lucas was a baseball enthusiast from the very start. As a teen-ager he organized games at the family estate in Normandy, a suburb of St. Louis. When Henry was 17, his older brother, John B. C. Lucas, was instrumental in St. Louis joining the National Association, the predecessor of the National League. John served as president of the St. Louis club for three years, including the Browns' first two years in the National League.

Henry attended St. Louis University and Seton Hall College. He married Louise Espenschied in 1880, but they were later separated.

By 1883 Henry Lucas, in his mid-20s and president of the Mound City Transportation Company, was anxious to get into major league baseball. St. Louis was represented in the new American Association by the St. Louis Browns and Lucas was not interested in the National League because of its higher admission prices and its ban on Sunday games. Thus he turned toward the Union Association which was being organized as a third major league. At the Union meeting in Philadelphia on December 18, 1883, the other owners were so impressed by Lucas' knowledge of baseball and the great wealth he could bring to the league, that they elected him president by acclamation.

Lucas was the guiding force behind the Union Association, assembling a strong team for St. Louis and giving financial assistance to a number of other clubs. The St. Louis Maroons won their first 20 games in 1884 and went on to win the pennant by 21 games. Their 91-16 (.850) record was the best ever in major league baseball, but the one-sided pennant race quickly led to a lack of interest, even in St. Louis. The death of the Unions was apparent before the season ended and Lucas began a campaign, eventually successful, to get his team into the National League.

Picked to finish second in 1885, the Maroons got off to a slow start and came in last. Although they moved up to sixth in 1886, Lucas became disenchanted with his continuing losses and quit the team in August. St. Louis brewer Adolphus Busch was among the new owners, but the franchise was sold to Indianapolis during the winter.

Although Henry Lucas is listed as manager of St. Louis for the years 1884 through 1886 by some sources, such was not the case, according to newspaper accounts of the day. Newspapers give the title to Ted Sullivan and Fred Dunlap in 1884, Dunlap and Alex McKinnon in 1885, and Gus Schmelz in 1886.

Estimates of Lucas's baseball losses ranged as high as $500,000 — a sizable amount for that day — and he also was suffering other business losses. Several of his river barges sank in 1885 and, because of his baseball losses, he was unable to replace them. He also incurred heavy real estate setbacks. By 1889 his fortune was dissipated and he became a railway clerk at a small salary. A few years later the sports bug bit him again and, building an expensive indoor bicycle track, he assembled many famous riders and staged a national indoor bicycle race. However, this venture proved to be another financial disaster.

Henry Lucas tried other endeavors, including the insurance business, but without success. The last three years of his life were spent working as an inspector with the City of St. Louis Street Department. His death at the home of his niece on November 15, 1910, resulted from blood poisoning, apparently brought on by an ankle injury several years earlier. Heart disease may have also contributed to his death.

In reporting the death of Henry Lucas, *The Sporting News* reported that "he possessed many fine traits and deserved more consideration and better care than was afforded him in his declining days by relatives and former friends with sufficient means to have secured for him comfort and attention that his depleted purse could not provide."

— Ralph Horton

DENNY LYONS

Born: March 12, 1866, Cincinnati, Ohio
Died: January 2, 1929, West Covington, Ky.
BR TR 5-10, 185

Denny Lyons started his career in 1885 with Columbus, Ga., of the Southern League by batting .230 and fielding .874 before moving up to Providence (NL) for four games. He was back in the Southern League again in 1886, but this time with Atlanta, where he batted .316 and fielded .912 before being sold to the Athletics of the American Association. He was in the "Bigs" until 1898 when he moved to the Western League with Omaha and St. Joseph. He played in the Interstate League with Wheeling, West Virginia in 1899 and 1900 and wound up his career with Beaumont of the South Texas League in 1903, where he led the league in fielding at first base with a .982 average.

Lyons was one of the better hitters at the hot corner during his career. He batted .310 during 13 years, including seven years above .300. His tops was .367 in his first full year with the Athletics. He also had seasons of

.329 in 1889, .354 in 1890, .315 in 1891 and .306 and .323 in 1893 and 1894, respectively. He slipped to .295 in 1895, but was limited to 33 games because of a knee injury. He rebounded to .307 in 1896 and wound up his career in the majors batting .206 with Pittsburgh in 1897, where he played mostly at first base.

Lyons' best season was in 1887. Not only was his .367 the fourth highest in the league, he was fourth in slugging at .523, third in total bases (298), third in hits (209), and second in doubles with 43. He was second in batting in 1890 with his .354 mark. His .329 in 1889 was good enough for third.

Defensively during the decade of the 1890s, he ranked near the middle of the pack with a fielding average of .895. Only two third sackers fielded over .900 during that decade: Lave Cross at .938 and Billy Nash at .903.

Two or three achievements by Lyons gener-

ally overlooked were his 1.5 putouts per game, second only to Jerry Denny among third basemen, and his four chances per game, which is tied for third place. He also holds the record for putouts for a season (255 in 1887). On September 3, 1887 he had 5 doubles in a doubleheader against Cincinnati.

Lyons was a traveler during his career in the majors. His first five years were spent with the Athletics (AA). He then spent one year at St. Louis in the same circuit, followed by one year with the Giants, two with Pittsburgh, another one at St. Louis (NL) and two more at Pittsburgh. Clubs wanted his heavy hitting in the middle of the batting order, but his frequent lushing tried management's patience and led to numerous suspensions and premature releases.

— Al Glynn

			G	R	H	BA	SA	POS	E	FA	GP	W-L	R	H
1885	Columbus	SL	94	50	81	.227	.325	3b	46	.873				
	Providence	NL	4	3	2	.125	.188	3b	3	.833				
1886	Atlanta	SL	79	72	103	.327	.470	3b	33	.883				
	Athletic	AA	32	22	28	.226	.282	3b	16	.861				
1887	Athletic	AA	137	128	284	.469	.623	3b	53	.897				
1888	Athletic	AA	111	98	145	.325	.435	3b	44	.889				
1889	Athletic	AA	131	131	171	.337	.479	3b	81	.858				
1890	Athletic	AA	88	79	116	.355	.538	3b	34	.908				
1891	St. Louis	AA	120	124	142	.315	.455	3b	59	.871				
1892	New York	NL	108	71	102	.261	.396	3b	55	.865				
1893	Pittsburgh	NL	131	103	147	.318	.444	3b	51	.909				
1894	Pittsburgh	NL	72	51	79	.311	.445	3b	30	.903				
1895	St. Louis	NL	33	23	38	.290	.389	3b	16	.877				
1896	Pittsburgh	NL	118	77	134	.307	.420	3b	46	.889				
1897	Pittsburgh	NL	37	22	27	.206	.359	1b	5	.986				
1898	Omaha/St.Joe	WL	62	35	65	.291	.363	1b	22	.969				
1899	Wheeling	Intst	113	73	133	.311	.443	1b-3b	46	.934				
1900	Wheeling	Intst	135	73	126	.242	.329	3b	41	.937				
1903	Beaumont	SoTx	85	50	188	.274		1b	17	.982				

ROBERT T. MATHEWS
(Bobby)

Born: November 21, 1851, Baltimore, Md.
Died: April 17, 1898, Baltimore, Md.
BR TR 5-5, 145

Bobby Mathews stands as one of the finest pitchers of the 19th century. At his retirement in 1887, he had won more games (298) than any other major league pitcher. Today he has more victories than anyone not in the Hall of Fame.

Mathews was a fierce competitor and he made the most of his modest physical equipment. With Candy Cummings, he was one of the very first to throw the curveball, and was reputed to have originated the spitter. Early in his career, he is said to have pitched 37 games in as many days. He was a very quick and nimble fielder, and occasionally played the outfield when not pitching. However, his hitting was lackluster.

At age 16 (1868), Bobby began his career with the Maryland Juniors. During the following two season he toiled for the parent Marylands.

For the 1871 season he and his catcher, Bill Lennon, moved to the newly formed National Association and the Kekiongas of Fort Wayne. There he won the first NA game, 2-0, over the Forest Cities of Cleveland. He yielded only five hits (Deacon White had three) to a team which later beat a local nine 132-1. Mathews' classic May 4 shutout was the lowest scoring game in the first four NA seasons. Unfortunately his own Kekiongas were the feeblest-hitting team in the circuit.

In 1872, with the formation of the hometown Lord Baltimores, he posted the first of many winning seasons. Most of his NA fame grew out of his three campaigns (1873-75) with the New York Mutuals. Games such as his 2-hit, 38-1 victory over Chicago on June 18, 1874, buoyed his reputation. All told, his 132 NA wins placed him behind only Al Spalding and cricketeer Dick McBride. His success was again in spite of a weak offense; the Mutuals were the Association's weakest attack.

When the Mutes entered the National League in 1876, Mathews remained their hard-luck pitching mainstay. He was the

pitcher as New York played Louisville to a 15-inning, 5-5 stalemate on July 8, then added 16 innings on July 10 before his team took an 8-5 victory. The "Green Stockings," however, failed to play out their schedule in '76, and with the team's demise, Mathews and his longtime catcher, Nat Hicks, were unattached.

In 1877, both had the misfortune to play for the woeful Cincinnati aggregate, and responded with mediocrity before the team folded in June. Mathews then pitched briefly for the Buckeyes of Columbus.

For the third straight season, in 1878, Mathews pitched for an unstable team. The Live Oaks of Lynn moved in toto to Worcester at mid-year. On August 15, he threw a 2-hit shutout of the Boston champions which attracted George Wright's attention. When the latter moved to Providence in 1879 as manager, he immediately hired Mathews as a change pitcher (behind Monte Ward) and substitute. The classic photograph of the champion 1879 Grays at Messer Park shows the two veterans reclining side-by-side.

The departure of Wright, and the League's

new austerity measures (such as reserve lists and salary caps) led Mathews and others (including Cal McVey) to play ball on the West Coast in 1880. The diminutive pitcher caught on with the independent Star team of San Francisco. His first turn in the box, on May 2, Mathews delivered a 12-strikeout performance.

The 1881 season saw Mathews return to Providence (behind Ward and Hoss Radbourn) and a final victorious appearance for Boston and the departing Harry Wright. He remained in Boston throughout the following season, pitching in tandem with Long Jim Whitney and taking occasional turns in the outfield.

It was Mathews' move to the Philadelphia Athletics in 1883 which began the happiest chapter of his career. The the A's owners had erected a new park at 26th and Jefferson, brought Harry Stovey over from Worcester, and looked to the veteran Mathews as their pitching mainstay. He did not disappoint, winning 30 games for the first of three consec-

(continued on page 144)

			G	R	H	BA	SA	POS	E	FA	GP	W-L	R	H
1871	Kekionga	NA	19	15	23	.258	.315	p	8	.833	19	6-11	243	271
1872	Baltimore	NA	49	34	49	.200	.208	p-of	23	.760	48	25-18	347	461
1873	Mutual	NA	52	40	43	.192	.232	p	20	.825	52	29-22	354	490
1874	Mutual	NA	65	47	70	.235	.262	p	35	.783	65	42-22	373	635
1875	Mutual	NA	70	23	47	.177	.207	p	35	.819	70	29-38	412	681
1876	Mutual	NL	56	21	44	.197	.224	p	28	.810	56	21-34	395	693
1877	Cincinnati	NL	15	5	10	.169	.169	p	14	.658	15	3-12	132	208
	Buckeye	IA	4	0	1	.063		of-p			1	0-1	7	10
1878	Lynn	IA	20	12	17	.212	.253	p	47	.726	20	8-12	120	195
1879	Providence	NL	43	25	35	.202	.231	p-of	39	.878	27	13-6	92	194
1880	Star of S.F.	Pac						p						
1881	Prov-Boston	NL	35	8	23	.180	.203	of-p	11	.744	19	5-8	90	143
1882	Boston	NL	45	17	38	.225	.260	p-of	9	.836	34	19-15	144	278
1883	Athletic	AA	45	15	30	.176	.188	p	11	.889	44	30-13	225	396
1884	Athletic	AA	49	26	33	.177	.215	p	27	.800	49	30-18	233	401
1885	Athletic	AA	48	22	30	.162	.178	p	10	.881	48	30-17	241	394
1886	Athletic	AA	24	16	23	.261	.295	p	8	.884	24	13-9	150	226
1887	Athletic	AA	7	5	9	.310	.310	p	2	.923	7	3-4	64	100

JAMES ROBERT McALEER

Born: July 10, 1864, Youngstown, Ohio
Died: April 29, 1931, Youngstown, Ohio
BB TR 6-0, 180

Jimmy McAleer devoted 30 years to baseball as a player, manager and club owner. When Ban Johnson was moving the American League to major league status in 1901, McAleer was probably his most successful recruiter, luring many National Leaguers into the Johnson fold. But a dozen years later, when McAleer was president of the Boston Red Sox, a dispute turned the two old friends into bitter enemies, and the breach was never repaired, although to Johnson's credit, it should be said he offered the olive branch on many occasions.

McAleer was a center fielder of rare talent, but a mediocre hitter. A career .255 hitter, he never reached the .300 mark in 13 major league seasons, except for 1902, when he played only 2 games. Henry P. Edwards, a Cleveland writer, said, "He was the best centerfielder there ever was." Billy Evans, the American League umpire and writer, said that McAleer was the first outfielder to take his eyes off the ball and then run right to the spot where it was to land.

McAleer never was associated with a major league pennant winner until he became owner of the Boston Red Sox in 1912. It was this pennant and the World Series victory over the Giants that followed which led to his break with Johnson and to his eventual withdrawal from baseball.

McAleer made his professional debut with hometown Youngstown, Ohio, in 1882 or 1884 (accounts differ) and then played with Charleston, South Carolina (Southern), Memphis (Southern) and Milwaukee (Western Association) before making it to the majors with Cleveland (NL) in 1889. He jumped to the Cleveland (PL) in 1890 but returned to the National League club after the Brotherhood folded, remaining there until 1898. He managed Youngstown (Interstate) in 1899 and for Cleveland in the still minor American League in 1900. In 1901, the year the American League claimed major status, McAleer was Cleve-

land's manager, thus gaining him the distinction of playing for Cleveland in four different leagues — National, Players', American (minor) and American (major).

After the 1901 season, McAleer, at the request of Ban Johnson, took over the club just transferred from Milwaukee to St. Louis. He did a great job of recruiting National League players and guided the Browns to second place. He remained at St. Louis through 1909, but with little success. His only other first-division finish was a fourth place in 1908. He concluded his managerial career with Washington (American) in 1910 and 1911, each year winding up seventh. Overall, his managerial log shows 736 wins and 889 losses (.453).

In the fall of 1911, under the imprimatur of Johnson, who was probably a secret investor, McAleer and Robert McRoy, who had been Johnson's secretary, acquired controlling interest in the Boston Red Sox, with McAleer as president. According to an interview McAleer gave to Frank B. Ward of the Youngstown Vindicator, one of the Red Sox investors was a Chicago banker to whom Johnson was beholden and who was also the father-in-law of Boston manager Garland (Jake) Stahl.

McAleer and Stahl were both aggressive and outspoken and, inevitably, sparks flew. The Sox won the pennant in 1912, and in the World Series, in which Boston defeated New York, 4 games to 3, a serious confrontation occurred when McAleer tried to tell Stahl whom to pitch in the sixth game. The hostility between the two men deepened in 1913, culminating in the firing of Stahl. In all the bitter wrangling, Johnson, because of his obligations to the Chicago banker (McAleer's version), refused to back McAleer. McAleer never forgave him. At the end of the season, McAleer sold his stock in the Red Sox to Joseph Lannin and retired to Youngstown.

On April 28, 1931, McAleer, who was suffering from cancer, was listening to a ball game on the radio with friends when attacks associated with his illness caused him to leave the room several times. Finally, he stood before his bathroom mirror and shot himself. Death came 10 hours later on the 29th. It was one month and one day after the death of his longtime friend and then enemy, Byron Bancroft Johnson.

— Joseph M. Overfield

			G	R	H	BA	SA	POS	E	FA	GP	W-L	R	H
1884	Youngstown	IrOil						of						
1885	Youngstown	Intst						of						
1886	Charleston	SL	64	28	48	.205	.239	of	9	.930				
1887	Memphis	SL	94	98	151	.346	.415	of	23	.884				
1888	Memphis	SL	45	43	62	.330	.436	of	11	.896				
	Milwaukee	WA	86	65	99	.284	.362	of	14	.932				
1889	Cleveland	NL	110	66	105	.235	.282	of	13	.955				
1890	Cleveland	PL	86	58	93	.272	.342	of	16	.942				
1891	Cleveland	NL	136	97	134	.237	.312	of	20	.938				
1892	Cleveland	NL	150	92	138	.241	.343	of	16	.960				
1893	Cleveland	NL	91	63	87	.253	.282	of	16	.937				
1894	Cleveland	NL	64	36	75	.299	.394	of	9	.953				
1895	Cleveland	NL	132	82	154	.290	.352	of	16	.958				
1896	Cleveland	NL	116	76	131	.289	.344	of	15	.951				
1897	Cleveland	NL	24	6	20	.220	.242	of	3	.947				
1898	Cleveland	NL	106	47	87	.238	.246	of	10	.962				
1900	Cleveland	AL	20	7	18	.234	.234	of	1	.982				
1901	Cleveland	AL	3	0	1	.143	.143	o-3-p	0	1.00	1	0-0	5	2
1902	St. Louis	AL	2	0	2	.667	.667	of	0	1.00				
1907	St. Louis	AL	2	0	0	-	-	Pr	-	-				

JAMES McCORMICK

Born: 1856, Glasgow, Scotland
Died: March 10, 1918, Paterson, New Jersey
BR TR 5-10 ½, 226

Portly, mustachioed Jim McCormick hardly looked like a baseball player. Yet he won at least 263 major league games (some authorities credit him with 264 or 265), and Cap Anson, for whom he pitched in 1885 and 1886, called him "one of the best men . . . that ever sent a ball whizzing across the plate. He was a great big fellow with a florid complexion and blue eyes, and was utterly devoid of fear, nothing that came in his direction being too hot for him to handle."

Not much is known of McCormick's early days, nor do the records contain his exact birth date. He pitched for the Columbus Buckeyes of the newly formed International Association in 1877. He first appeared in the majors with the new Indianapolis team in 1878. That team folded, and next year he joined another new team in Cleveland as player and captain (at age 23). He was originally listed as the "change pitcher" behind Bobby Mitchell, but McCormick ended up pitching three-quarters of the team's games, including the opening series with Providence, in which after losing the first 2 games, he shut out the Grays 4-0 in the third game.

Neither Jim nor his team was very effective in 1879, but next year he posted 45 of the team's 47 victories as it finished third. Cleveland slipped to seventh in 1881, and McCormick was replaced as captain early in 1882. He continued to pitch for Cleveland until 1884. In August of that year McCormick, shortstop Jack Glasscock, and catcher Fatty Briody jumped to Cincinnati of the Union Association for a reported $1,000 apiece. The indignant Cleveland *Plain Dealer* said that McCormick, believing he was no longer effective in the National League, requested his release so that he could pitch against hitters who didn't know him. The Cleveland man-

agement offered to sell him the release for $100 but refused a Cincinnati offer to buy the players, and so the players just left for more money. McCormick went on to a 21-3 record for Cincinnati, winning his last 14 games, so his two-team record for 1884 was 40-25.

In 1885 McCormick started with Providence but was picked up by Anson's White Stockings and teamed with John Clarkson to pitch Chicago to a pennant. He was hardly washed up in the National League; by the end of the season he was the clutch pitcher for Chicago. The White Stockings came into New York for a four-game series, leading by two. McCormick won his two starts 7-4 and 8-3, allowing no earned runs. Shortly thereafter he won the clincher against Philadelphia, again allowing no earned runs. In the World Series against the St. Louis Browns, McCormick won 2 games and lost 2, the Series ending with 3 victories for both teams plus a tie. McCormick's ERA for the series was 1.55.

1886 was another strong year for McCormick, as he won his first 16 games through July 1 and finished with a 29-11 record. He pitched the second game of the World Series

against St. Louis and was bombed by the Browns, 12-0, as Tip O'Neill tagged him for 2 home runs. He had a sore arm and didn't pitch again in the Series. A holdout the next season, he was traded. His last year in the majors was 1887, when he was 13-23 for a weak Pittsburgh team. He quit at age 32 when Pittsburgh proposed to cut his monthly pay. Because the club kept him on its reserve list for several years, he never attempted a comeback.

In evaluating McCormick's career one should note conflicts in the records; e.g., his W-L record is given as 263-214 in the Macmillan *Encyclopedia*, 264-214 in the *Encyclopedia of Sports*, and 265-215 in *Daguerreotypes*. It is difficult to evaluate pitchers from this era, as the standards are so different from today, but in a typical year, his earned run average would be about 0.50 below the league average. He was the leader in ERA (an honorary category, as the records were not kept then) twice and in shutouts once.

— William McMahon

			G	R	H	BA	SA	POS	E	FA	GP	W-L	R	H
1877	Buckeye	IA	16	3	8	.133	.133	p-of			14	6-6	58	95
	Indianapolis	LgAl	13	5	13	.274		p-of	11	.605	46	65		
1878	Indianapolis	NL	15	5	8	.143	.161	p	19	.800	14	5-8	59	129
1879	Cleveland	NL	75	35	62	.220	.270	p-of	13	.933	62	20-40	275	581
1880	Cleveland	NL	78	34	71	.246	.284	p	22	.886	74	45-28	382	588
1881	Cleveland	NL	70	45	79	.256	.320	p-of	13	.898#	59	29-30	273	493
1882	Cleveland	NL	70	35	57	.218	.290	p	13	.917	68	36-29	256	549
1883	Cleveland	NL	43	21	37	.236	.274	p	14	.895	42	27-12	147	316
1884	Cleveland	NL	49	15	50	.263	.332	p-of	2	.979	42	19-22	208	357
	Cincinnati	UA	27	12	27	.245	.291	p-of	10	.932	24	21-3	61	151
1885	Prov-Chicago	NL	29	15	27	.227	.311	p	6	.937	28	21-7	124	225
1886	Chicago	NL	42	17	41	.236	.316	p	6	.941	42	31-11	157	337
1887	Pittsburgh	NL	36	9	35	.254	.304	p	8	.927	36	13-23	217	446

GEORGE WASHINGTON McGINNIS
(Jumbo)

Born: February 22, 1864, Alton, Illinois
Died: May 18, 1934, St. Louis, Missouri
TR 5-10, 197

George W. McGinnis, known as "Jumbo" because of his big belly, was the young pitching star of the St. Louis Browns in the first years of the American Association. Although his career ended at age 23, he posted more than 100 pitching victories in the Association.

George was a top pitching prospect by his middle teens. At the behest of Charlie Houtz, McGinnis was brought to St. Louis in 1879 to pitch for the Browns, which at the time was the best semipro club in town. Pitching against weak local opposition, McGinnis was undefeated at home and successful on the team's only road trip even though he was only 15 years old. He continued to pitch for the Browns through 1881, except for a brief jump to the Dubuque Reds in August 1880.

When St. Louis was awarded a franchise in the fledgling American Association for 1882, McGinnis joined four other semipro Browns in signing with the new professional Browns. Still only 18, George was one of the team's top stars, being a fine pitcher and a moderately good hitter. In the opening game, he knocked out 2 doubles while pitching a 9-7 victory. And in one game in August, he drove in 5 runs in a 7-6 triumph. Unfortunately, he was the team's only reliable pitcher, and when he sprained an ankle in July, the Browns fell to the second division.

In 1883, he was joined by Tony Mullane, and the Browns nearly won the pennant. McGinnis had 28 wins and 6 shutouts, but his record against the Athletics was just 2-4, as the A's edged the Browns for the pennant by one game.

Mullane was gone in 1884, and McGinnis was once again ace of the staff. He hurled back-to-back one-hit shutouts against Brooklyn on July 13 and 15, running up a string of 17 hitless innings between the 2 hits. But he slumped in the later going and was displaced by rookie pitchers Dave Foutz and Bob Caruthers.

In 1885 McGinnis rode the bench as the Browns got off to a 23-5 start. When he finally got a chance to pitch, on June 2, he lost to snap a 17-game team winning streak. He was used sparingly after that, compiling a 6-6 record for the season. On July 3 he pitched a 1-hitter against Baltimore, missing a no-hitter when he was slow covering first base on a ground ball to the right side.

McGinnis was never much of a runner or fielder, owing to his round physique. His build was attributed to his off-season occu-

pation as a glass blower and not to overeating. An underhand speed pitcher, he was rated as especially tough on lefthanded batters. He was an even-tempered chap who was always courteous with the fans, making him quite popular in St. Louis.

Although he lost a lot of weight during the winter, he lost his No. 3 spot on the Browns' pitching staff in 1886. On July 8 he was showcased against Baltimore, winning 10-0, and was sold to the Orioles that night. He beat St. Louis four times before the end of the season but finished with a mediocre 16-18 overall record. In 1887 he started with Cincinnati, but was dropped in June because of shoulder troubles.

He returned to St. Louis as a glass blower and also did some umpiring. Failing eyesight ended his days as an ump, and eventually he went blind. A St. Louis newspaper got wind of his condition and raised a subscription to pay the cost of corrective surgery, which restored McGinnis's eyesight. George continued to live in modest comfort in St. Louis until his death in 1934, at age 70.

— Robert L. Tiemann

			G	R	H	BA	SA	POS	E	FA	GP	W-L	R	H
1879-81	St. Louis Browns		-					p						
1882	St. Louis	AA	51	17	46	.226	.294	p-of	15	.889	44	25-17	238	376
1883	St. Louis	AA	45	20	34	.233	.308	p	21	.857	45	28-16	170	325
1884	St. Louis	AA	40	16	11	.224	.224	p	15	.875	40	24-16	194	331
1885	St. Louis	AA	13	3	11	.220	.220	p	5	.912	13	6-6	59	98
1886	StL-Baltimore	AA	36	11	23	.187	.268	p	11	.853	36	16-18	214	342
1887	Cincinnati	AA	8	8	7	.219	.355	p	4	.810	8	3-5	68	128
	Milwaukee	NWL	2	1	2	.286	.571	p	0	1.00	2	0-1	10	15

JAMES THOMAS McGUIRE
(Deacon)

Born: November 2, 1865, Youngstown, Ohio
Died: October 31, 1936, Albion, Michigan
BR TR 6-1, 185

In 1881 Hastings, Michigan, boasted a young left-handed pitcher with a dynamite fastball and a puzzling curve no local catcher could handle. In Albion, Michigan, there was a rawboned young catcher with powerful hands and a frame that was tougher than pine knots. Albionites said he could hold any pitcher. Word spread and the gentlemanly battery of Charles (Lady) Baldwin and James (Deacon) McGuire was formed.

Both pitcher and catcher became major league players. Baldwin achieved stardom first, in 1886 and 1887 with the Detroit Nationals, but soon faded from the game, his arm shot. McGuire was a different story. He lasted 26 major league seasons, longer than any other player in the game's history. His 1,781 games were spread among 12 teams.

McGuire was born in Youngstown, Ohio, but moved to Albion, where he apprenticed as an iron molder while still a teen-ager. After gaining his reputation in the amateur ranks of southern Michigan, he became a professional with Terre Haute in 1883. He advanced to Toledo (American Association) in 1884, batting a feeble .185 in 45 games. The unimpressive start was not indicative of what lay ahead. He was to wind up his long career with a .278 lifetime mark and not play his last game until May 18, 1912.

Like James (Deacon) White, with whom he played briefly in 1888, McGuire gained his nickname by dint of "his quiet demeanor and splendid habits." It has been said he was never fined and never put out of a game. Once when asked about some questionable decisions, he replied: "Even if the umpiring had been bad, I would not have said a word."

McGuire's best years were spent with one of the worst teams in baseball history — the 1894-1898 Washington Senators. In that span the hapless Senators finished eleventh twice, tenth, ninth and sixth in the 12-club National League, with a 258-417 (.382) mark. Meanwhile, McGuire, catching almost every game, batted an overall .314, with 677 hits, 108 doubles, 27 triples, 23 home runs and 355 RBIs, and found the energy to steal 58 bases. He caught in every game for the Senators in 1895, a baseball first.

He took over as manager of the Senators June 24, 1898, but was replaced by Arthur Irwin in September after a 21-47 record. Two other managerial opportunities also ended in failure. He was below .500 with Boston (AL) in 1907 and 1908 before being fired. In 1909 he succeeded Nap Lajoie at Cleveland, but never could get the team going and was let go early in the 1911 season. He then joined Detroit as an assistant to Hughie Jennings. On May 18, 1912, he was pressed into action after the Detroit players struck in protest over Ty Cobb's suspension following an altercation with a fan. At the age of 46, he did not disgrace himself, coming up with a hit, a run, 3 putouts, 3 assists and 2 errors. McGuire remained with the Tigers as a coach and scout until 1926, when he became baseball coach at Albion College.

McGuire's hands were unusually large and strong. Nonetheless, the hazards of catching took their toll. Over the years, every one of his fingers was broken at least once. His gnarled fingers became famous and were often photographed. It has been said he was the first major leaguer to put a raw steak inside his glove to protect his hands in the pre-mitt days.

McGuire died in Albion (some accounts say it was Duck Creek) on October 31, 1936, two days short of his 71st birthday.

— Joseph M. Overfield

			G	R	H	BA	SA	POS	E	FA	GP	W-L	R	H
1883	Terre Haute													
1884	Toledo	AA	45	12	28	.184	.250	c	29	.906				
1885	Indianapolis	WL	16	11	15	.246	.344	c	11	.925				
	Detroit	NL	34	11	23	.190	.256	c	26	.921				
1886	Philadelphia	NL	50	25	33	.198	.287	c	39	.899				
1887	Philadelphia	NL	41	22	57	.354	.478	c	35	.884				
1888	Phil-Detr	NL	15	7	17	.266	.391	c	15	.837				
	Cleveland	AA	26	15	24	.255	.362	c-1b	17	.907				
1889	Toronto	IA	99	72	100	.282	.455	c	49	.926				
1890	Rochester	AA	87	46	99	.299	.408	c-1b	36	.946	1	0-0		
1891	Washington	AA	114	55	125	.303	.426	c-of	55	.913				
1892	Washington	NL	97	46	75	.241	.350	c	30	.925				
1893	Washington	NL	63	29	62	.262	.359	c-1b	31	.912				
1894	Washington	NL	104	67	130	.304	.412	c	39	.912				
1895	Washington	NL	133	91	178	.330	.479	c	38	.939				
1896	Washington	NL	108	60	125	.321	.416	c	30	.936				
1897	Washington	NL	93	52	111	.338	.463	c	19	.952				
1898	Washington	NL	131	60	132	.273	.329	c-1b	24	.972				
1899	Wash-Brooklyn	NL	105	47	106	.305	.385	c	16	.967				
1900	Brooklyn	NL	71	20	69	.286	.365	c	15	.952				
1901	Brooklyn	NL	85	28	89	.296	.375	c	16	.970				
1902	Detroit	AL	73	27	52	.227	.323	c	14	.952				
1903	Detroit	AL	72	15	62	.250	.306	c	16	.933				
1904	New York	AL	101	17	67	.208	.258	c	20	.970				
1905	New York	AL	72	9	50	.219	.268	c	11	.975				
1906	New York	AL	51	11	43	.299	.333	c	10	.962				
1907	NY-Boston	AL	7	1	3	.600	1.20	c	0	1.00				
1908	Bos-Cleveland	AL	2	0	1	.200	.400	1b	0	1.00				
1910	Cleveland	AL	1	0	1	.333	.333	c	0	1.00				
1912	Detroit	AL	1	1	1	.500	.500	c	2	.714				

EDWARD JOHN McKEAN

Born: June 6, 1864, Grafton, Ohio
Died: August 16, 1919, Cleveland, Ohio
BR TR 5-9, 160

Ed McKean compiled a .302 career batting average during a 13-year major league career, all but the last with Cleveland. He was the captain and hustling, umpire-baiting shortstop of the Cleveland Spiders when they challenged Baltimore and Boston for NL supremacy in the 1890s.

He grew up in Cleveland before starting his professional career in 1884 with Youngstown in the Iron and Oil Association. After three minor league seasons he was ready for the majors, but because he had already signed with Rochester of the International League when he inked a contract with Cleveland, he faced a long wrangle before the National Commission approved his joining his hometown club.

McKean remained Cleveland's regular shortstop for 12 seasons. In his first five years, Cleveland fielded lackluster teams. McKean provided a solid bat (.318 in 1889) and gained a

reputation for aggressive base running, hustle, and "coaching." But his defense left much to be desired as he committed 102 errors his rookie season, then followed it with two years of league-leading misplays.

Cleveland became one of the dominant teams in the 12-team NL. In 1891, McKean was appointed field captain, Patsy Tebeau became manager, Cy Young emerged as a 20-game winner, Jesse Burkett joined the team, and "Cupid" Childs became McKean's keystone partner. In 1892, the Spiders captured the second-half championship of the League's only scheduled split season. Boston, easy first-half winners, swept the post-season playoff.

McKean put together his best seasons between 1893 and 1896. For four consecutive years he hit over .300 (.310, .357, .342, .338), scored more than 100 runs, and drove in more than 100. With McKean and Burkett at the top

of the batting order batting .300 and .500, the second-place Spiders upset the Orioles in the 1895 Temple Cup series. The two clubs met for the Cup again the following year, but the Orioles reached the peak of their fame by sweeping the series.

Cleveland and McKean both slipped after 1896. His weight, which had been a trim 160 pounds when he entered the majors, ballooned to a chunky 180, further reducing his never-vast range. By his final season, 1899, when he was shifted to St. Louis, he was only a part-time player.

After his major league career, he managed in the minors at Rochester in the International League and Springfield and Dayton in the Central League. He died at age 55, leaving his wife Belle and four children.

— William E. Akin

			G	R	H	BA	SA	POS	E	FA	GP	W-L	R	H
1884	Youngstown	IronOil	-					2b						
1885	Nashville	SL	6	4	5	.185	.185	2b	4	.886				
1886	Providence	EL	20	11	19	.221	.256	ss	19	.859				
	Rochester	IL	76	62	97	.305	.343	ss	14	.872				
1887	Cleveland	AA	132	95	216	.364	.445	ss	102	.852				
1888	Cleveland	AA	131	94	164	.299	.425	ss-of	50	.893				
1889	Cleveland	NL	123	86	159	.318	.430	ss	62	.907				
1890	Cleveland	NL	136	95	157	.296	.417	ss	75	.903				
1891	Cleveland	NL	141	114	169	.281	.377	ss	86	.893				
1892	Cleveland	NL	128	75	141	.270	.333	ss	84	.872				
1893	Cleveland	NL	125	103	169	.310	.473	ss	74	.902				
1894	Cleveland	NL	130	115	199	.355	.501	ss	66	.911				
1895	Cleveland	NL	132	131	197	.344	.494	ss	67	.911				
1896	Cleveland	NL	133	100	190	.335	.453	ss	58	.914				
1897	Cleveland	NL	127	86	144	.273	.381	ss	50	.924				
1898	Cleveland	NL	151	89	172	.285	.376	ss	56	.929				
1899	St. Louis	NL	67	40	76	.281	.352	s-1-2	34	.923				

ALEXANDER J. McKINNON
(Mac)

Born: August 14, 1856, Boston, Mass.
Died: July 24, 1887, Charlestown, Mass.
BR TR 5-11 ½

Al McKinnon played his final game of baseball on July 4, 1887. Having appeared that morning in Philadelphia as Pittsburgh's regular first baseman, that evening he complained of not feeling well and the following day was reluctantly compelled to interrupt his banner season (.365) for a journey home to Boston. He had typhoid fever. Before his departure he told a friend, "I feel pretty sick. I can't sweat. I don't believe I tried harder in my life to break a sweat than I did this morning, but it was no go." Though nursed tenderly by his wife and mother at home, his condition sank. He died on July 24, aged 30.

In his 12-year career, "Mac" had experienced most of what it meant to be a ballplayer in the 19th century.

His career began in 1875, when he was a first baseman for the amateur "Stars" of his native city, Boston. He was a familiar sight on the Commons.

Several of his friends and teammates went on to greater fame. Lew Brown was a big-league catcher, 1876-1884; John Morrill was a fine infielder 1876-1890; and tough John L. Sullivan became the bare-knuckle heavyweight champion of the world.

Mac began his professional career in 1876 with an independent team, the Syracuse Stars. It was one of the best, and he built a regional reputation as a first-rate batter and fielder, during three seasons. He was in the field for the classic 15-inning scoreless tie of May 1877, between the Stars and the NL St. Louis Browns.

His first taste of high-caliber competition came as the Stars joined the International Association in 1878. They could have tied for the pennant by winning one remaining game with Rochester, but the club disbanded before it could be done (six of thirteen clubs finished).

In 1879, amid shifting franchises and eligibility hassles Mac was caught in a paper vise. When Syracuse had (with Buffalo) join-ed the NL, Al decided to play elsewhere and signed on with the Capitol City Club of Albany of the National Association (lacking Canadian clubs, no longer *International*!) The club folded in mid-May, with most of the players ending up in Rochester, where they were used to form a club to be sponsored by a patent medicine firm known as the "Hop Bitters." Meanwhile, with the change, Troy of the NL had snapped up McKinnon, signing him to a five-month contract with $75 up front. Then it became clear that he belonged to two teams and expulsion was threatened by both the NL and National Association. An honest man (as illustrated by his refusal in Syracuse to throw a game for gamblers) he returned the advance, (was barred by the League) and went to Rochester.

This struggle for custody was largely pointless, for Mac had fallen prey to another perennial enemy, illness, and missed most of the 1879 season. It appears that, for a time, he suffered from paralysis of his left side, which left a lingering stiffness thereafter, affecting his agility and running speed.

With this season-long nightmare, McKinnon left the ball field and for several years pursued business in the West. During his travels home, he met the young woman he married on November 27, 1882. There were no children.

At a special meeting of the NL on March 5, 1883, he was reinstated and joined the Philadelphia club. Sickness, however, led him to request and receive his release, in May.

Finally, in 1884, he began his four-season NL career, during which he hit .296. His first year, in New York, his presence forced the move of Roger Connor to *second base*. In 1885-86, Mac played first base for Henry Lucas' St. Louis Maroons, next to Fred Dunlap and Jack Glasscock. It was a great infield, as McKinnon paced the league with .978 fielding in 1885. When that team folded, he moved to Pittsburgh for its initial NL season (as "Zulus," "Potato Bugs," and "Smoked Italians") where he became an exemplary leader. Each year he improved — raising his average, reducing his strikeouts, bettering his fielding. He had hit safely in 15 straight games. Then came the fever . . .

In death, Al McKinnon was the first player to be honored by Monte Ward and the Ballplayers' Brotherhood, yet to flex its muscle. His funeral occasioned an unprecedented outpouring of love and respect from those in baseball and his fellow citizens of Boston. His gravesite in Lowell was completely covered with floral offerings. A 5-by-7-foot piece came from the Pittsburgh club, others from Boston, Indianapolis (6-foot crescent), Philadelphia and Detroit, still others from friends Ned Williamson, Jimmy Manning, John Morrill and some two dozen more. Al's obituary rang true: "The many beautiful floral tributes from the professionals testify to the high regard in which 'Al' was held by those with whom he was brought daily into contact. He was a man of whom everybody spoke well. In fact, he had no enemies. It was impossible to harbor any ill-will toward 'Mac.' He would not stoop to do a mean act and was one of the most quiet fellows I ever met in the baseball business."

— James D. Smith, III

			G	R	H	BA	SA	POS	E	FA	GP	W-L	R	H
1875	Lowell of Boston		32		46	.331		1b	33					
1876	Syracuse		62	71	83	.306	.387	1b	29	.949				
1877	Syracuse		103	51	131	.293	.335	1b	45	.955				
1878	Syracuse	IA	31	17	37	.277	.316	1b	16	.949				
1879	CapCty-Roch	NA	22		-	.316		1b						
1884	New York	NL	116	66	128	.272	.394	1b	53	.955				
1885	St. Louis	NL	100	42	121	.294	.370	1b	25	.978				
1886	St. Louis	NL	122	75	148	.301	.385	1b	47	.963				
1887	Pittsburgh	NL	48	25	76	.365	.510	1b	12	.977				

JOHN J. McMAHON
(Sadie)

Born: September 19, 1867, Wilmington, Delaware
Died: February 20, 1954, Delaware City, Delaware
BR TR 5-9, 185

Despite his unathletic build and his reputation as a carouser, John J. "Sadie" McMahon was a hard-working right-handed pitching star. He was the ace of the pitching staffs of the Athletics and Orioles in the early 1890s, before a shoulder injury ended his career at the age of 30.

In his youth, McMahon pitched on a variety of local amateur and professional clubs in northern Delaware and southeastern Pennsylvania. His work with the Norristown team in 1889 finally got him noticed by the big leagues, and he was signed by the Athletics of Philadelphia in midseason. He won his American Association debut on July 5, beating lowly Louisville 9-1, but then lost his next 4 games. But he adjusted to faster company soon enough and won 7 straight decisions in September to finish with a 16-12 record. This penchant for streaks (both winning and losing) would continue throughout his career.

In 1890, he was far and away the Athletics best pitcher. He ran his record to 20-7 by the Fourth of July, as the Athletics led the AA race. But the team was losing money and eventually went bankrupt in September, so McMahon was sold to Baltimore along with Wilbert Robinson and Curt Welch. Still, McMahon led the Association in wins, games and innings pitched and strikeouts. With the Orioles in 1891, McMahon was again the workhorse of the AA, leading in wins, innings and shutouts.

McMahon was usually teamed with catcher Robinson in what was dubbed "the Dumpling Battery" because of the plumpness of both men. Sadie had wonderful control and never appeared to get rattled on the mound. He was even reputed to intentionally fall behind on the count to hitters in order to make them overconfident. His best pitches were a good, high fastball and an effective overhand drop ball. He was an excellent fielder on the mound, and on grounders to first he could beat even the swiftest runners to the bag, pot belly or no.

Sadie was also something of a hell-raiser, especially on the road. In 1892, his drinking got him suspended for the final month of the season after he missed a game and then cussed out manager Hanlon and owner Von der Horst in an argument about the subsequent fine.

McMahon was back performing well in 1893, although the Orioles continued to languish in the second division. When the team suddenly became a pennant contender in 1894, McMahon's record improved dramatically. He was 25-8 when a shoulder injury sidelined him at the end of August. The Orioles were able to win the pennant anyway, but they were struggling to stay in the race the following summer. Baltimore slipped from first place to third during a July road trip. When they returned home on August 3, McMahon came off the injured list to pitch his first game of the year. He won a dramatic, 1-0 victory and ran off an 8-game winning streak as the Orioles surged back into first place. Hanlon spotted Sadie carefully (6 of his 15 starts came in failing light in the second games of doubleheaders), and McMahon's 10-3 record was crucial to the team's successful pennant drive.

Although he pitched Opening Day for the Orioles in 1896, Sadie struggled to regain his form. He was only 10-9 with a strong team when "stomach trouble" sidelined him during a July road trip. When he tried to return to action, his shoulder injury flared up again, limiting his usefulness. He was released over the winter and was 0-5 in a trial with Brooklyn in 1897.

McMahon returned to Delaware City and pitched in the local leagues. One day in 1903 he showed up in Baltimore to visit old teammates Hugh Jennings and Wilbert Robinson, who were running the Eastern League Orioles. Sadie volunteered to pitch a game, beating Newark on August 15, but then he returned to Delaware.

He was on John McGraw's payroll as a scout from 1911 to 1925. He died in Delaware City in 1954 at the age of 86.

— Robert L. Tiemann

			G	R	H	BA	SA	POS		E	FA	GP	W-L	R	H
1889	Athletic	AA	30	9	15	.143	.143	p		6	.919	30	15-13	169	265
1890	Athletic-Balt	AA	61	34	45	.212	.274	p		9	.963	60	36-21	285	513
1891	Baltimore	AA	61	31	43	.205	.267	p		11	.934	61	35-24	261	493
1892	Baltimore	NL	49	11	25	.140	.157	p		12	.895	48	20-25	254	430
1893	Baltimore	NL	43	13	36	.243	.264	p		18	.835	43	24-17	264	378
1894	Baltimore	NL	35	17	37	.287	.357	p		-	.869	35	25-8	173	317
1895	Baltimore	NL	15	5	16	.302	.321	p		-	.771	15	10-4	54	110
1896	Baltimore	NL	22	6	9	.123	.151	p		-	.850	22	12-9	100	195
1897	Brooklyn	NL	9	2	5	.200	.200	p		1	.958	9	0-5	53	75
1903	Baltimore	EL	1		1	.250	.250	p		0	1.00	1	1-0	5	12

JOHN ALEXANDER McPHEE
(Bid)

Born: November 1, 1859, Massena, N.Y.
Died: January 3, 1943, San Diego, Cal.
BR TR 5-8, 152

For 18 years, Cincinnati's "Bid" McPhee was the finest second baseman in the game. Disdaining the use of a glove for a decade after it came into general use and remaining barehanded until late in his career, he compiled fielding statistics that are still remarkable a century later. He is currently credited with having led his league in double plays in 11 seasons and in fielding average in nine seasons. He is the only second baseman ever to top 500 putouts in a season (525 or 529 in 1886), and his average of .982 in 1896 was recognized as the major league record for second basemen until 1925. Only Eddie Collins had more career putouts and total chances, and only Frank Frisch more chances in a single season. The accolade "King Bid" was well-earned.

McPhee was born in the Canadian border town of Massena, New York, in 1859, but grew up in the Mississippi River town of Keithsburg, Illinois. He left home for Davenport, Iowa, in 1877 to play ball and work for a shipping firm. Although at one point he quit playing ball to work full time as a commission agent, he resumed his playing career by joining the independent Akron club in 1880. In 1882 he joined the newly-minted American Association Cincinnati Reds and played on his first and only pennant-winning team, leading the Association's second sackers in putouts, double plays and fielding average.

A righthander who was fast enough to hit in the leadoff spot occasionally, McPhee was consistent and effective, though not spectacular, as a batsman. He rapped out nearly 2,300 base hits and walked close to 1,000 times to achieve a career on-base percentage of at least .390. He scored more than 100 runs in a season 10 times and ranks in the top 25 in career runs scored.

Although not a big man, he could hit the long ball. He led the Association in home runs in 1886, which helped him earn a $2,300 salary for 1887. And he had a real knack for triples, reaching double figures nine times. He had 3 three-base hits in one game against New York's Amos Rusie in 1890, the year the Reds switched to the National League.

The 60½-foot pitching distance was introduced in 1893, and the following season McPhee hit over .300 for the first time (not counting 1887, when walks were counted as hits). But his fielding had fallen below league-leading levels in the '90s, since all his contemporaries were using gloves. For his part, Bid insisted that he could do just as well barehanded, and every spring he worked diligently to toughen his hands for the season ahead. When he opened the 1896 season with a sore finger, however, he finally broke down and put on a glove. The result was amazing, as he was officially listed with a .982 average for the season, fully 16 points above the recognized record at the time. Bid's mark was not exceeded until Sparky Adams posted a .983 in 1925.

In a rowdy era, Bid was one of the game's gentlemen. He performed spectacularly but was personally sober and sedate, always in prime physical condition and quietly proud of never having been ejected from a game. An 1897 ankle injury, which laid him up for three months, was his only serious injury. When it threatened to cut his career short, the Cincinnati fans and sportswriters staged a special benefit that netted McPhee $3,500.

Bid recovered, however, and did not retire until after the 1899 season. He returned to manage the Reds in 1901, finishing last, and then quit on July 11, 1902 amid rumors that Joe Kelley was about to jump from the American League to take over the team. McPhee retired to Los Angeles and did some scouting for the Reds. He severed all connections with baseball in 1909 and died in San Diego 34 years later.

— A.D. Suehsdorf

			G	R	H	BA	SA	POS	E	FA	GP	W-L	R	H
1878	Davenport		39		65	.333		2b-of	44	.799				
1879	Davenport	NWL	20	8	19	.229	.241	of-2b	-	.858				
1880	Akron							2b						
1881	Akron							2b						
1882	Cincinnati	AA	78	44	70	.218	.296	2b	42	.921				
1883	Cincinnati	AA	96	61	87	.243	.344	2b	52	.919				
1884	Cincinnati	AA	113	106	135	.292	.377	2b	64	.925				
1885	Cincinnati	AA	110	77	121	.275	.330	2b	51	.923				
1886	Cincinnati	AA	140	139	153	.272	.397	2b	58	.944				
1887	Cincinnati	AA	129	132	210	.354	.460	2b	40	.927				
1888	Cincinnati	AA	111	88	110	.240	.336	2b	48	.938				
1889	Cincinnati	AA	135	110	146	.269	.365	2b	39	.958				
1890	Cincinnati	NL	132	125	135	.256	.386	2b	51	.942				
1891	Cincinnati	NL	138	108	143	.258	.364	2b	36	.960				
1892	Cincinnati	NL	144	110	169	.295	.391	2b	45	.954				
1893	Cincinnati	NL	127	102	138	.281	.379	2b	41	.954				
1894	Cincinnati	NL	128	113	154	.320	.478	2b	53	.941				
1895	Cincinnati	NL	115	107	129	.299	.417	2b	38	.950				
1896	Cincinnati	NL	117	81	132	.305	.386	2b	12	.982				
1897	Cincinnati	NL	81	45	85	.301	.408	2b	17	.966				
1898	Cincinnati	NL	133	72	121	.249	.346	2b	32	.956				
1899	Cincinnati	NL	111	60	104	.279	.370	2b	26	.955				

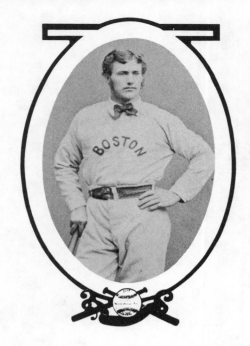

CALVIN ALEXANDER McVEY

Born: August 30, 1850, Montrose, Iowa
Died: August 20, 1926, San Francisco, Ca.
BR TR 5-9, 170

Cal McVey began his professional career at age 18 with the famous Cincinnati Red Stockings of 1869, and quickly became one of the brightest lights in the game's first decade of openly professional play. A recreational boxer who some believed could have succeeded as a prize fighter, McVey not only proved himself a sharp hitter, but also demonstrated a powerful right throwing arm and a defensive versatility that led him in time to every position in the field, including 36 games as pitcher.

Born in rural Iowa, McVey discovered baseball after moving to Indianapolis at the age of 11. He became so good at the game that when he was only 16 he was invited to play for a local university team, and soon was playing for the Westerns and the Actives, two of Indianapolis' leading clubs.

Cincinnati manager Harry Wright was impressed with McVey's play against his club in 1868, and when the Red Stockings turned fully professional the next year, Wright hired him (at $700) to play right field. The only teenager on the club, McVey (as one contemporary account put it) "was in a measure an experiment, but turned out a splendid player."

When Cincinnati abandoned its professional status after 1870, McVey joined manager Wright and two other teammates as the nucleus of Boston's Red Stockings in the New National Association, baseball's first professional league. His .362 batting average during the NA's five seasons was second only to the .379 of sometime teammate Ross Barnes.

After two seasons in Boston as Al Spalding's catcher, McVey departed for Baltimore where — though still only 22 years old — he managed the Lord Baltimores through two-thirds of the season while dividing his playing time between catcher and several other positions. The club, 23-14 under his management, finished third. The next year, though, he returned to Boston and (as Deacon White had become the club's catcher) to right field. His 131 hits and 90 runs scored led the league, and Boston won its third consecutive pennant. A year later, after Boston (with McVey now chiefly at first base) had helped sink the unbalanced and ill-organized National Association with a lopsided 71-8 won-lost record and a fourth pennant, McVey jumped with Barnes, Spalding and White to Chicago.

With McVey usually batting third, the "Big Four" led the White Stockings to the first National League pennant. Cal also acted as change pitcher and contributed 4 complete-game victories over second-place Hartford. But the next year, with White back in Boston and Spalding virtually retired from pitching, not even McVey's sparkling .368 BA could prevent Chicago from falling into fifth place.

McVey left Chicago in 1878 to manage and play third base for Cincinnati, a club that had finished last in the first two National League seasons. He led the team into second place, only 4 games behind Boston. But after a fifth-place finish the next year, McVey, at age 29, left major league ball for California, which he had first visited during Cincinnati's pioneering cross-country tour in 1869.

For a decade McVey organized, managed and played for clubs in California before retiring from baseball. But he never lost touch with the game, and more than once baseball friends throughout the country rallied to assist him through such personal crises as the loss of his home in the great San Francisco earthquake and fire of 1906 and a 30-foot fall into a Nevada mine in 1913. In his later years — well into his 70s — McVey worked to support himself as a special policeman and night watchman.

In 1968, his native state honored his achievement as one of professional baseball's first superstars with election to the Iowa Sports Hall of Fame.

— Frederick Ivor-Campbell

Year	Team	League	G	R	H	BA	SA	POS	E	FA	GP	W-L	R	H
1869	Cincinnati		57	-	217	(348 TB)		rf						
1870	Cincinnati		72	-	262	(389 TB)		rf						
1871	Boston	NA	29	43	66	.431	.556	c-rf	19	.863				
1872	Boston	NA	46	59	84	.346	.407	c-o	32	.853				
1873	Baltimore	NA	38	49	73	.382	.508	c-o-s	27	.861				
1874	Boston	NA	70	91	124	.364	.457	of-c	40	.789				
1875	Boston	NA	82	88	137	.352	.494	l-o-c	63	.913	3	1-0	9	15
1876	Chicago	NL	63	62	107	.347	.406	c-p	26	.954	11	5-2	21	57
1877	Chicago	NL	60	58	98	.368	.455	c-p-3	45	.850	17	4-8	84	129
1878	Cincinnati	NL	61	43	83	.306	.395	3b	42	.814				
1879	Cincinnati	NL	81	64	105	.297	.381	lb	42	.946	3	0-2	25	34
1880	BayCty-Athl	Pac												
1885	S.F.Pioneers	Cal												

JOUETT MEEKIN

Born: February 21, 1867, New Albany, Indiana
Died: December 14, 1944, New Albany, Indiana
BR TR 6-1, 180

Jouett Meekin was a highly successful National League pitcher in the 1890s. He was best known, however, for one extraordinary season early in his career and one major controversy late in his career.

Meekin was a Hoosier, born in New Albany, Indiana, in 1867. The tall righthander hit the big leagues in 1891, pitching for the Louisville Colonels of the American Association. He won 10 and lost 16 in an undistinguished debut. He pitched the next season for Louisville and Washington in the National League and stayed with Washington for the 1893 season. He compiled a 10-20 record in 1892 and a 10-15 season in 1893, the year the pitching distance was increased from 55 feet 6 inches to its present 60 feet 6 inches. Meekin's 4.96 ERA in 1893 indicates some period of adjustment on his part. It should be noted that the first three teams Meekin pitched for were quite poor.

Nonetheless nothing in Meekin's first three seasons prepared baseball fans for the brilliance of his fourth, in 1894, after he had been sold to New York along with Duke Farrell for $7,500 and two marginal players. Pitching in new surroundings, Meekin won 36 games against only 10 losses, leading the league with a .783 percentage and tying for the lead in wins. Meekin's 3.70 ERA was second in the league. He was also second in hits per inning, third in strikeouts and innings pitched, and fourth in games. But despite his brilliance and despite the presence of Amos Rusie, the league's other 36-game winner, the Giants managed only a second-place finish, 3 games behind Baltimore.

Although Meekin never duplicated his marvelous 1894 season, he did put together three straight solid seasons for the Giants. His won-lost records in 1895, 1896 and 1897 respectively were 16-11, 26-14 and 20-11, with ERAs of 5.30, 3.82 and 3.76. However, only in the latter year did the Giants challenge for the pennant, finishing in third place, 9½ games behind first-place Boston. Meekin slipped to 16-18 in 1898, although his 3.77 ERA suggests bad luck as much as loss of form.

Meekin started slowly in 1899, as did the Giants. This was the year in which the syndicate plan of "pooling" teams and players reached its controversial peak. In August, with the Giants mired in the second division, unpopular Giants owner Andrew Freedman sold Meekin's contract to Boston, where Freedman had established what David Voigt calls a "community of interest." Although technically not part of the pool system, this move nonetheless outraged both Giant partisans and league observers and came to epitomize the cynical and manipulative ownership of the late 1890s.

Meekin's acquisition by Boston was of little help to the Beaneaters in their pursuit of Brooklyn. Meekin had a mediocre 7-6 record and Boston finished a distant 8 games back. Meekin finished his career in 1900, pitching 2 games for the Pirates and losing them both. Meekin ended with 156 wins, 134 losses and a 4.07 ERA. Always plagued by control problems, even in his best seasons, Meekin walked more than 100 batters six times and ended his career with more walks than strikeouts.

Meekin was a good hitter. He hit 3 triples in a game at Cleveland on July 4, 1894. On the 28th of that month, he saved himself a defeat by hitting a home run in the bottom of the 12th as the Giants won 11-10 in 13 innings, and he hit a 2-run homer in the bottom of the 9th to win a game from Pittsburgh, 6-5, on September 6 of that season.

He died in New Albany on December 14, 1944.

— Jim Sumner

			G	R	H	BA	SA	POS	E	FA	GP	W-L	R	H
1887	Scranton	PaStAs						p			7	4-3	46	85
	Scranton	IL	14	9	14	.259		p	4	.917	12	4-7	101	216
1888	Hutchinson	WL												
1889	St. Paul	WA	28	14	24	.245		p	9	.845	25		184	234
1890	St. Paul	WA	70	39	54	.224		p-1b	25	.928	49	11-34	306	407
1891	St. Paul	WA	13	5	11	.234		p	5	.853	13	4-8	96	146
	Louisville	AA	33	14	21	.216	.309	p	1	.976	29	10-17	159	227
1892	Louv-Wash	NL	34	14	11	.105	.171	p			33	10-20	199	280
1893	Washington	NL	33	15	29	.257	.398	p	7	.903	31	10-16	203	289
1894	New York	NL	52	26	49	.282	.466	p	4	.949	52	33-9	237	404
1895	New York	NL	31	16	28	.292	.427	p			29	16-12	170	296
1896	New York	NL	43	27	43	.299	.451	p	8	.908	42	26-13	201	378
1897	New York	NL	42	22	39	.281	.324	p	11	.864	37	20-11	183	328
1898	New York	NL	38	16	28	.217	.271	p			38	16-18	180	329
1899	NY-Boston	NL	31	11	20	.200	.310	p	5	.853	31	12-17	154	280
1900	Pittsburgh	NL	2	0	0	.000	.000	p	2	.000	2	0-2	21	20

LEVI SAMUEL MEYERLE

Born: July 1845 (49?), Philadelphia, Pa.
Died: November 4, 1921, Philadelphia, Pa.
BR TR 6-1, 177

When "Long Levi" Meyerle died of heart trouble in his native Philadelphia, not one of the city's newspapers published anything about it on the sports page. He had, as Lee Allen once noted "simply been swallowed up by the city, and his name meant nothing" to the current generation.

Exactly 50 years earlier, however, the scene was strikingly different. The Philadelphia Athletics, in the National Association's initial season, were champions of the baseball world. They had beaten the White Stockings in the decisive game of the season, 4-1, a game played on the neutral Union Grounds in Brooklyn on October 30. (The White Stockings had been homeless since the Chicago fire three weeks earlier.) Philadelphia celebrated the capture of the "whip pennant," and the exploits of their starting third baseman, for it had been a typical Meyerle performance: 3 hits, 1 error.

In that banner year of 1871, "Long Levi" batted .492, at once winning pro baseball's first batting title and posting the highest mark in major league history. Following that season, he fell back to mere excellence, averaging .353 against baseball's best in five NA campaigns. He was, quite simply, an extraordinary hitter.

He was also a mediocre fielder, making errors — lots of errors. On May 16, 1874, playing for the White Stockings against the A's (his only NA season away from Philadelphia), Meyerle made 6 errors at third base. Some angrily charged that he assisted his old friends. But, as one commentator later observed, "Levi could field this way most any time he got a bit rattled." He was tall, and lacked quickness, a lethal combination on the playing fields of the day. (Remember how "Pebbly Jack" Glasscock got his name, landscaping at shortstop?) Moreover, Meyerle's frequent changes of defensive position could not have added to his confidence (any more than they improved Cap Anson's rough field-ing during the NA years).

Levi Meyerle may have been the original "good hit, no field" player. In 1867, during the baseball boom which followed the Civil War, he was elected pitcher for the Geary baseball club of Philadelphia. By 1869, he was "first substitute" for the A's, appearing as catcher, pitcher, third baseman and rightfielder in 34 of 49 games. The following season, for $1,500, he joined the original pro Chicago White Stockings as third baseman and pitcher. By 1871, he had already built a reputation as one of the best batters in the country, and returned to Philadelphia to enjoy his finest season and to live with his parents, Jacob and Margaret Meyerle.

In his hometown uniform, Meyerle was in the A's lineup for the first game in NL history, April 22, 1876. (As second baseman he got 1 hit — and made no errors!) That season, for a 14-45 team, he batted .340 (only 2 strikeouts), but fielded .790. In December, the A's and New York Mutuals were expelled for failing to play out their schedules. For 1877, Meyerle began with the A's as they entered the irregularly scheduled, 13-team League Alliance, but was picked up by the woeful Cincinnati Reds as a shortstop/second baseman soon after. There, in 27 games, he batted .327 before severely spraining his ankle. Meyerle's brief NL career was over (.326) and he never again was quite the same player.

For the next several seasons, Meyerle continued his career, but in a path which took him away from Philadelphia to stops in Springfield, Mass., Washington, D.C., and Rochester, N.Y. No longer able to move so well, he increasingly played first base. In the off-season, he lived with his parents, working as a lather, plasterer and carpenter. By 1880 this routine had become less rewarding and when his Rochester team folded before the season's end, "Long Levi" went home to stay.

There was one act left in his career. In 1884, manager Fergy Malone of the Philadelphia Keystones (UA) asked Levi to sign on as first sacker. Malone had been his teammate a dozen years before, as catcher on the 1871 A's champions. Meyerle tried his best for his old friend, but after three games gave up the chase. It was time to marry, which he did (Anna died in 1905 — there were no children), and to enjoy memories of glory days with oldtimers like West Fisler. He continued to work at the construction trades in a growing Philadelphia, until the onset of his chronic heart trouble. In death, he was buried next to Anna in Oakland Cemetery.

Was Levi Meyerle one of pro baseball's first Jewish players? Surviving relatives say no. Was he the tallest player of his era? Nat Hicks, Everett Mills and Al Spalding may have been taller. Was his "good hit, no field" tag deserved? At least halfway so. Alfred H. Spink: "A big, stout fellow was Levi Meyerle, the third baseman of the Athletics of Philadelphia in 1871, when they were the champions. Meyerle was a very fair fielder, but his best asset was his ability to hit the ball hard."

— James D. Smith, III

			G	R	H	BA	SA	POS	E	FA	GP	W-L	R	H
1867	Geary of Phila		25	110	-		(43 outs)							
1869	Athletic		34	-	128	-	(205TB)							
1870	Chicago		23	-	42	-	(71TB)	3b-p						
1871	Athletic	NA	26	45	64	.496	.705	3b	44	.654	1	0-0	1	1
1872	Athletic	NA	27	31	48	.329	.479	rf	13	.809				
1873	Philadelphia	NA	48	53	83	.350	.485	3b	56	.774				
1874	Chicago	NA	53	66	102	.402	.484	2-s-3	86	.727				
1875	Philadelphia	NA	68	55	95	.320	.428	2-3-1	61	.866				
1876	Athletic	NL	55	46	87	.340	.449	3b	54	.790	2	0-2	23	27
1877	Athletic	(Ind)						3b						
	Cincinnati	NL	27	11	35	.327	.430	ss-2b	24	.855				
1878	Springfield	IA	14	6	17	.283	.300	ss-2b	11	.862				
1879	National	NA	42		-	.300		1b	-	.950				
1880	Balt-Roch	NA	18	19	17	.212	.238	3b-1b	16	.879				
1884	Keystone	UA	3	0	1	.091	.182	1b-of	4	.789				

JOHN FRANCIS MORRILL
(Honest John)

Born: February 19, 1855, Boston, Mass.
Died: April 2, 1932, Boston, Mass.
BR TR 5-10 ½, 155

For a city that prides itself on its baseball heritage, Boston has produced precious few major league stars. One of the best of this exclusive fraternity was Boston's first home-grown hero, John Morrill.

After starring with the amateur Stars and Lowells, Morrill earned a five-year contract with Boston's fledgling National League entry in 1876 when he outperformed the veteran catchers while playing for the Picked Nine in the annual Fast Day Game.

Morrill was not a heavy hitter (.260 lifetime), but his versatility (he played every position) and glovework made him a fixture. He led NL first basemen in fielding in 1883 and 1887 and was the top third baseman in 1879.

Morrill replaced George Wright as Boston captain in 1879 and succeeded Harry Wright as manager in 1882. He relinquished the captaincy to Jack Burdock at the start of the 1883 campaign while remaining road manager, but took over again in July with the team in second place and led the club on a 33-11 spree that earned him his only pennant. His career-high .319 average sparked the comeback.

Morrill's reaction earned him his nickname, Honest John. "Good pitching and catching, and lucky hitting won for us," he said. "When the season started, I thought we would finish fourth or fifth."

His 13-season honeymoon in Boston ended in 1889 when he refused to serve as captain of the Picked Nine for the Fast Day Game (King Kelly captained Boston) and was sold to Washington the next day. The fans accorded Morrill "the greatest ovation (five minutes in duration) ever given to a ballplayer in this country" when he returned to Boston at the Washington helm on June 13, 1889, but a broken finger limited his playing ability and Morrill was released in July.

He played 2 games for Boston's Brotherhood team in 1890, and stayed around the game for years, as a writer and umpire. He opened a baseball supply house in 1890, but soon joined former teammate George Wright's sporting goods firm, Wright and Ditson, as general manager, a position he held for 39 years.

— Bob Richardson

			G	R	H	BA	SA	POS	E	FA	GP	W-L	R	H
1875	Lowell of Boston		47		60	.287			63					
1876	Boston	NL	66	38	73	.263	.295	2b-c	86	.822				
1877	Boston	NL	61	47	73	.302	.331	3-1-o	37	.884				
1878	Boston	NL	60	26	56	.240	.270	1b	28	.957				
1879	Boston	NL	84	56	98	.282	.362	3b-1b	34	.936				
1880	Boston	NL	86	51	81	.237	.348	1b-3b	38	.937	3	0-0	4	9
1881	Boston	NL	81	47	90	.289	.379	1b	25	.969	2	0-0	3	9
1882	Boston	NL	83	73	101	.289	.424	1b	28	.964	1	0-0	0	3
1883	Boston	NL	97	83	129	.319	.525	1b	21	.974	2	1-0	3	15
1884	Boston	NL	111	80	114	.260	.356	1b-2b	37	.966	7	0-1	30	34
1885	Boston	NL	111	74	89	.226	.343	1b-2b	41	.964				
1886	Boston	NL	117	86	106	.247	.381	s-1-2	65	.929	1	0-0	1	5
1887	Boston	NL	124	79	175	.331	.475	1b	18	.985				
1888	Boston	NL	135	60	96	.197	.278	1b	31	.979				
1889	Washington	NL	44	20	27	.185	.260	1b	8	.979				
1890	Boston	PL	2	1	1	.143	.143	1b-ss	1	.947				

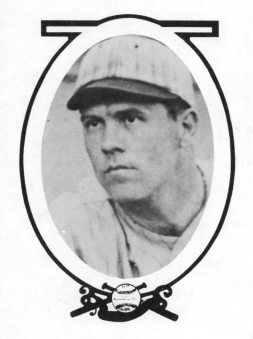

EDWARD MORRIS
(Cannonball)

Born: September 29, 1862, Brooklyn, N.Y.
Died: April 12, 1937, Pittsburgh, Pa.
BR TL 156

Ed Morris was an outstanding left-handed pitcher for Pittsburgh in the mid-1880s, but poor habits limited his professional career to eight seasons.

He was born in Brooklyn in 1862, where his father was a prominent ballplayer. The family moved west, and young Ned developed his skills on the lots of San Francisco. He was an all-around star in California, and in June 1883, he accepted an offer from the Active club of Reading, Pennsylvania, to come east to play professionally in the Interstate Association. He played center field when not pitching and usually occupied the leadoff spot in the batting order for the Actives.

In 1884 he moved up into the major leagues with the Columbus club in the American Association and was an immediate success. Morris won 34 games and lost 13 to pace Columbus to a second-place finish. On May 29, 1884, Ed pitched a no-hitter against the Alleghenies, 1 base on balls marring an otherwise perfect game. After the season ended, the Columbus club disbanded, and Morris and the rest of the players were sold to Pittsburgh.

Ed quickly established himself as a star in Pittsburgh, and he adopted the area as his home, although he continued to return to Cal-

ifornia for winter ball during his playing career. In 1885 he compiled a 39-24 record and was the only Allegheny pitcher to win more than 7 games. With an improved team in 1886, Morris established the all-time Pittsburgh records for wins (41) and shutouts (12). This earned him a $2,500 contract for 1887.

Ed's forte was his fastball, but he also had a good curve and an effective change of pace. He was a fierce competitor who was at his best in close games, as his 45-25 lifetime record in 1-run decisions attests. His fiery temperament led to occasional outbursts at poor play by his teammates, however, and he was never the most popular of players.

In 1887, Morris received a rude setback to his career from the new rules that restricted the pitcher to just one forward step in his delivery. Since Morris was of the hop-skip-and-jump school of pitching, he was unable to adjust readily and suffered a sore arm in the early going. When he refused at the last minute to pitch a game in early May, he was suspended. When he got back into action he was ineffective and finished the season with a lackluster 14-22 record. He was also in trouble with Pittsburgh manager Horace Phillips for his drinking and, like many of his teammates, was often fined for his carousing.

During the winter of 1887-88, however, Morris joined the YMCA, reformed his habits and worked on mastering the new pitching re-

strictions. As a result, the club returned his fines from 1887, and Ed responded with a strong season in 1888. He was once again the team's leading pitcher, compiling a 29-24 record. His best stretch came from September 8 through 15, when he hurled 4 consecutive shutouts, winning 2-0 twice and 1-0 twice. The streak was ended by the champion Giants on September 17, when Morris pitched a 3-hitter but lost to Mickey Welch, 1-0.

A billiards enthusiast, Morris operated a pool hall with teammate Willie Kuehne in Pittsburgh. During the winter of 1888-89, they were hauled into court on charges of running a gambling establishment, but the case was dropped when a key witness failed to appear.

Back on the field, Morris' fortunes declined rapidly. In 1889 he started out with a sore arm and later suffered a muscle pull in the stomach. He wound up with only 6 wins. In 1890 he joined the Pittsburgh Brotherhood team but pitched sparingly. At one point he was released for excessive drinking but was later reinstated. After an 8-7 season, Morris called it quits.

He opened a saloon in Allegheny City (now part of Pittsburgh) and later served as a deputy warden at the Western Pennsylvania Penitentiary and as a county employee. He remained a baseball fan and was frequently seen at Pirate games until his death in 1937.

— Robert L. Tiemann

			G	R	H	BA	SA	POS	E	FA	GP	W-L	R	H
1880	S.F.National	Pac						ss						
1881	Mystic	Cal												
1882	S.F.National	Cal												
	Philadelphia		14		-	.090		c	-	.893				
1883	Reading	InstAs	46	44	60	.300		p-of	18	.859	25	16-6	102	181
1884	Columbus	AA	57	19	37	.181	.279	p-of	23	.823#	52	34-13	173	335
1885	Pittsburgh	AA	64	19	44	.187	.226	p	20	.854	63	39-24	244	459
1886	Pittsburgh	AA	64	26	39	.174	.250	P	10	.917	64	41-20	250	455
1887	Pittsburgh	NL	38	15	30	.229	.267	p	5	.919	38	14-22	216	446
1888	Pittsburgh	NL	55	12	19	.101	.122	p	8	.940	55	29-23	217	470
1889	Pittsburgh	NL	21	2	7	.097	.111	p	2	.953	21	6-13	105	196
1890	Pittsburgh	PL	18	7	9	.146	.146	p	5	.919	18	8-7	102	178
1892	Memphis	SL	14	1	7	.200		p-of	1	.962	12	3-5	48	81

TONY MULLANE

Born: January 30, 1859, Cork, Ireland
Died: April 25, 1944, Chicago, Ill.
BB TR 5-10 ½, 165

Despite Tony Mullane's dandified appearance, which resulted in his being dubbed "The Count," he was an enormously talented and strong-willed player. He won 285 games as a pitcher, even though he missed one full and one partial season due to contract disputes.

Born in 1859 at Cork, Ireland, Mullane moved to Erie, Pennsylvania as a youngster. In 1876 he signed his first profesional contract with the Geneva, Ohio, team for a dollar a day plus room and board. Subsequently he played for the Akron, Ohio, team before joining the Detroit Nationals in August 1881, to begin a 14-year major league career.

Mullane aggressively sought the ballclub willing to pay him the highest salary, and he was with four different teams in his first four years. With Detroit he refused to merely "try out," and held out for a regular contract instead. After being released, he signed with Louisville in the AA in 1882 and then St. Louis in 1883 (for $1,400). In 1884 he jumped to the Union Association only to jump back to the AA Toledo club for a $2,500 contract before the season even began. After the season, with Toledo's franchise folding, the St. Louis Browns purchased his release and reached agreement on a $3,500 contract. But when the obligatory ten-day waiting period expired, Mullane signed with Cincinnati for $5,000 instead. The Browns' outraged owner, Chris Von der Ahe, was able to have Mullane suspended for the season, and Tony was forced to return the $1,000 the Reds had advanced him. Mullane settled down with Cincinnati for seven full seasons, although he jumped the club in the latter part of 1892 when his salary was slashed $700 in mid-season. On June 18, 1893, he was traded to Baltimore, and on July 15, 1894, the Orioles sent him to Cleveland, where he finished the year.

In each of Mullane's first five full seasons in the majors, he won 30 or more games. As often as not during this period, he pitched for infe-

rior teams. His batterymate on one of those teams, the 1884 Toledos, was Moses Fleetwood Walker, major league baseball's first black player. The team also included Walker's brother Wesley, a utility player. In his years with Cincinnati, Tony was usually the mainstay of what became a fine pitching staff.

Mullane was one of baseball's first "showmen." His handsome dark features and beautifully waxed mustache made him look like a nobleman, hence "The Count." He generally attracted a contingent of female fans to the games that he pitched. Sometimes he pitched with either arm, even switching arms when pitching to the same batter.

However, Mullane was as talented as showy. He had an extremely strong and durable right arm, pitching more than 400 innings six different times and never experiencing serious arm trouble. He was primarily a fastball pitcher, but he also threw an effective drop ball and was adept at making hitters chase bad pitches. He had a pronounced penchant for hitting batsmen and was one of the prime reasons that the AA first instituted the rule giving the batter first base when hit by a pitch (1884).

Mullane was a competent batsman as well, and a fine defensive outfielder who could also play any infield position. He performed several iron-man pitching feats. On September 20, 1888, he pitched both games of a doubleheader and won, 1-0 and 2-1. On June 30, 1892, he pitched a 20-inning, 7-7 tie against Chicago and Ad Gumbert. On September 11, 1882, he pitched a 2-0 no-hitter against Cincinnati, walking 3.

After departing the majors, Mullane spent a few years in the minors, primarily with the St. Paul club in the Western League. After finishing his playing career, he became a minor league umpire, but made an unexpected comeback. In 1902 Mullane was umpiring in the Pacific Northwest League until mid-season, when he became an active player for Spokane. He appeared in more than 20 games and was 3-0 as a hurler. That was his last appearance in organized baseball. After leaving the game, Mullane became a Chicago policeman, and pitched in Chicago semi-pro leagues for some years. He died in Chicago in 1944 at the age of 85.

— Dennis Goldstein, L. Robert Davids,
and Lefty Blasco

			G	R	H	BA	SA	POS	E	FA	GP	W-L	R	H
1880	Akron							p						
1881	Akron							p						
	Detroit	NL	5	0	5	.263	.263	p	2	.917	5	1-4	42	56
1882	Louisville	AA	77	46	77	.255	.305	p-1-o	24	.940	55	30-24	213	418
1883	St. Louis	AA	83	38	70	.228	.303	p-of	21	.897	53	35-15	230	372
1884	Toledo	AA	95	49	98	.276	.372	p-of	32	.909	68	36-26	273	485
1885	Cincinnati	AA						(suspended - did not play)						
1886	Cincinnati	AA	91	59	73	.225	.293	p-of	27	.885	63	31-27	300	500
1887	Cincinnati	AA	56	35	60	.279	.377	p-of	7	.942	48	31-17	238	550
1888	Cincinnati	AA	51	27	44	.251	.337	p	13	.888	44	26-16	179	341
1889	Cincinnati	AA	63	53	59	.301	.423	p-3-o	22	.878	33	11-9	140	218
1890	Cincinnati	NL	81	41	79	.276	.364	o-p-3	37	.861	25	12-10	94	175
1891	Cincinnati	NL	64	16	31	.148	.172	p-of	10	.930	51	24-26	259	390
1892	Cincinnati	NL	39	14	20	.169	.212	p	6	.950	37	21-14	133	222
	Butte	MonSt												
1893	Cinc-Balt	NL	54	26	41	.247	.289	p	5	.964	49	18-22	258	407
1894	Balt-Clev	NL	25	3	23	.343	.403	p			25	8-11	140	201
1895	St. Paul	WL	95	75	114	.320		1b-p	15	.975#	31	18-9	189	275
1896	St. Paul	WL	69	53	83	.353		p-1b			49	27-18	256	420
1897	St. Paul	WL	53	31	41	.264	.314	p-1-3	15	.918	29	15-11	162	249
1898	St.Paul-Detr	WL	16	5	13	.236	.255	p-2-3	4	.925	7	3-2	39	52
1899	Toronto	EL	4	4	3	.231	.286	p-of	0	1.00	3	2-1	23	34
1902	Spokane	PacNW	20	9	26	.307	.387	3-2-o	6	.887#	3	3-0		

JAMES J. MUTRIE
(Truthful Jim)

Born: June 13, 1851, Chelsea, Mass.
Died: January 24, 1938, New York, N.Y.

Jim Mutrie's lifetime won-lost average of .611 as a major league manager has been exceeded only by Joe McCarthy's .614. And, like McCarthy, Mutrie never appeared as a player in a major league game.

He joined the Androscoggin club of Lewiston, Maine, in 1875 after several years on an amateur club in his native Chelsea, Massachusetts.

The following two years, he played short-stop for Fall River, Massachusetts, also acting as team captain the first year and as manager the next.

In the summer of 1880, only a few weeks after the collapse of a franchise he had organized and managed in Brockton, Mass., Mutrie arrived in New York. With the financial backing of local businessman John B. Day and the aid of the Manhattan Polo Club, Mutrie secured a lease of the Polo Grounds, in upper Manhattan. Players were chiefly recruited from the lately dissolved Rochester franchise.

That team, known as the Metropolitans, was successful from the moment of its September 15 debut and its home opener at the Polo Grounds 14 days later. During the three years of its existence, the Metropolitans played a total of 344 games against both amateur and professional opposition. The result was 201 won, 136 lost and 7 tied.

On October 24, 1882, New York was admitted to membership in the American Association and on December 6, 1882, into the National League, replacing Troy.

John B. Day controlled both teams, while Mutrie took over the managerial helm of the AA entry, which retained the "Metropolitan" name.

After a fourth-place finish in 1883, the Metropolitans gave New Yorkers their first pennant the following year. In August of that year, when it appeared likely that the Mets

and Providence would win the AA and NL flags, Mutrie challenged Providence manager Frank Bancroft to a championship series between their teams. The result was baseball's first World Series, won by Providence.

In April 1885, Day decided to transfer Metropolitan stars Tim Keefe and Dude Esterbrook to his National League entry. Mutrie took both players to Bermuda, to avert efforts by other Association clubs to acquire them during the critical moment of transfer. The ploy was not appreciated in the Association, which passed a motion barring Mutrie from further employment in the league. Although it was rescinded at the end of the 1885 season, the resolution proved academic as Mutrie took over the managerial reins of New York's NL club for that year.

A few days before the opening of the 1885 season, during an exhibition game, Mutrie exhorted his team with the words "come on, you giants," creating a name in sports that has endured for a century.

As manager, other than fixing the lineup for each game, Mutrie generally delegated to team captains such as John Ward and Buck Ewing the responsibility for determining game strategy. This resulted in underrating by some writers of Mutrie's role in the success of the Giants.

And success they had. After a spectacular .759 average in 1885 — the greatest ever accomplished by a non-pennant-winner — and

.630 and .553 marks in 1886 and 1887, the Giants won both pennants and World Series in 1888 and 1889.

The championship 1889 team lost 13 men to the Players' League in 1890, and the team dipped below .500, at 63-68.

At the end of the 1890 campaign, the New York teams of the Players' League and National League consolidated, leaving Day with only a minority voice in the Giant management.

On November 7, 1891, the new Executive Committee made its first move toward taking over total control of the Giants. It voted 2 to 1, overriding Day's vote, to release Jim Mutrie.

Most of Mutrie's later years were spent in poverty, to be finally relieved in the mid-1920s by a pension established by Charles Stoneham and John McGraw. Cancer claimed him at the age of 86.

His role as the father of professional baseball in New York City and creator of the World Series has earned Mutrie a permanent place in baseball history. His energy and creativity have long been noted, but his contemporaries also remembered his geniality and kindness. A few weeks before Mutrie's release, Jim O'Rourke noted that "every player on the team had a deep affection for him and it was always a pleasure to do what he wanted."

— John J. O'Malley

			G	R	H	BA	SA	POS	E	FA	GP	W-L	R	H
1876	Fall River		27		-	.250		ss						
1877	Fall River		86	56	65	.186	.203	ss	49	.898				
1878	Hartford	IA	3	0	2	.167	.167	ss	3	.786				
	New Bedford		101	45	77	.186		ss-p	52	.888				
1879	Worc-NewBdfd	NA						ss-1b						
1880	Brockton													
	Metropolitan		1	0	1	.200		p	0	1.00	1			

JAMES EDWARD O'NEILL
(Tip)

Born: May 25, 1858, Woodstock, Ont., Can.
Died: December 31, 1915, Montreal, Que., Can.
BR TR 6-0 ½, 167

"Tip" O'Neill was one of the most famous sluggers of his time, although he became an outfielder only after a promising pitching career went bad. His stature as the third man in the batting order of the champion St. Louis Browns and his gentlemanly bearing made him one of the most popular players of his era.

Born to second-generation Irish-Canadian parents, he began playing as a teen-ager with amateur clubs in Woodstock and Harrison, Ontario. In 1880 he pitched Woodstock to the Canadian national championship. The following year he joined the Hiawatha Grays, a professional barnstorming team operating from Detroit. In 1882 he joined the Metropolitans of New York, the country's top independent team.

In 1883 the Mets' ownership acquired franchises in both the American Association and the National League, and O'Neill was assigned to the Nationals, for which he had a disappointing season. At the end of the year he was formally released to the AA Mets, but the deal was voided by association secretary Jimmy Williams. Tip then signed with the St. Louis Browns, which, not coincidentally, had just engaged Williams as their manager.

Tip was the St. Louis Opening Day pitcher in 1884, but his control was poor, and his arm was often sore. Luckily he had begun to display some batting prowess and he was converted into an outfielder in the second half of the season.

In early 1885 he emerged as the batting terror of the Association and was carrying a batting average of .372 when he hurt his right leg badly in a basepath collision on June 13. The injury sidelined him until September, and even then he needed a pinch-runner whenever he batted.

He was healthy all year in 1886 and again among the AA batting leaders. He also had developed into a good leftfielder, able to save a game with a great catch or a strong throw. He showed good speed on the bases, but his poor sliding made him one of the poorer runners on the team. In the 1886 World Series he went 8-for-20, poling 2 home runs in one of the games.

In 1887 the rules were changed, allowing 5 balls for a walk and 4 strikes for an out (instead of the old 6-and-3). And a new scoring rule gave credit for a "hit" when a batter reached base on balls. The results were a large increase in scoring and an even greater jump in batting averages. O'Neill led the way, his batting average hovering around .500 all year. He finished at .492 and became the only man in major league history to lead his league in doubles, triples and homers in the same season. Against last-place Cleveland Tip went 60 for 92 (.652) including 10 walks. But he hit only .200 in the World Series against Detroit, although he did start 3 double plays from the outfield.

A righthander, O'Neill generally pulled the ball to left, but he had power to all fields. And he did his incredible slugging using one of the tiniest bats in history. He was idolized in St. Louis, and adoring boys vied for the privilege of carrying his bag from the boarding house to the ballpark.

Brooklyn tried hard to buy his contract in 1888, and former teammate Doc Bushong even wrote Tip a letter hinting that if he "played for his release" from the Browns, Brooklyn would give him a big contract. But Tip remained loyal and won another batting title, even though his average dropped 160 points. He again had a disappointing World Series (.237), but he did hit an extra-inning home run and a bases-loaded homer.

After another strong season in 1889, O'Neill followed Browns' captain Charlie Comiskey to the Chicago Players League team in 1890. He returned with Commy to the Browns in 1891 and then jumped with him to Cincinnati in 1892. Batting only .250, he was benched in August of the year for misplaying a fly ball and then sat out the final six weeks due to illness.

After his playing days, O'Neill moved with his mother and two of his brothers to Montreal. He made brief comeback attempts in the minor leagues, served as president of Montreal's Eastern League team and umpired in the Eastern League, 1910-1912. A lifelong bachelor, he operated a saloon and restaurant with his brothers. On the last day of 1915 he died of a heart attack on a Montreal street corner.

— Robert L. Tiemann and William E. Akin

			G	R	H	BA	SA	POS	E	FA	GP	W-L	R	H
1882	Metropolitan		40	34	42	.249		p	12	.905	35		159	266
1883	New York	NL	23	7	15	.179	.214	p-of	8	.869	19	5-12	129	182
1884	St. Louis	AA	78	49	82	.276	.424	of-p	25	.816	17	11-4	90	125
1885	St. Louis	AA	52	44	72	.350	.466	of	12	.881				
1886	St. Louis	AA	138	106	195	.339	.457	of	23	.927				
1887	St. Louis	AA	124	166	277	.492	.728	of	30	.896				
1888	St. Louis	AA	130	106	176	.332	.443	of	17	.934				
1889	St. Louis	AA	134	125	180	.337	.478	of	19	.936				
1890	Chicago	PL	137	113	173	.302	.405	of	17	.935				
1891	St. Louis	AA	129	112	167	.321	.447	of	14	.935				
1892	Cincinnati	NL	109	63	105	.250	.329	of	17	.922				

DAVID L. ORR

Born: September 29, 1859, New York, N.Y.
Died: June 3, 1915, Brooklyn, N.Y.
BR TR 5-10, 240

Only four 19th century batters retired with a lifetime slugging percentage over .500. Brouthers, Delahanty, and Thompson are in the Hall of Fame. David Orr is not. He is not excluded because of his .342 lifetime average (never posting a season mark below .300). Nor is he harmed by being the first player to collect 300 total bases in a single season (1886). At various times he led his circuit in hits, triples, home runs and batting average, as well as putouts, assists and fielding average at first base.

Why then is "Big Dave" not better recognized? There are two reasons. First, Orr played most of his career on the New York American Association club, overshadowed (after '84) by the exploits of colorful manager Jim Mutrie, then by the NL Giants and their Hall-of-Fame slugger Roger Connor. More decisively, at the top of his game, Orr's career was ended in 1890 by the effects of a crippling stroke (a stroke some laid to Dave's overweight condition). After only eight seasons, he was finished.

The son of immigrant parents, Dave began his baseball career in New York playing on independent teams like the "Alaskas" of Brooklyn. In 1883, following his father's death, he joined the Metropolitan Reserves of Newark (later Hartford, Conn.) That season he was recruited as a fill-in for one NL contest, then was shifted to owner John B. Day's "other" team, the Metropolitans.

In 1884, teamed with Tim Keefe, Orr's league-leading batting (.354, 162 hits) paced the Mets to an Association championship and the first World Series ever. Though the Series was lost to Providence and its ace Hoss Radbourn, the man with "the frame of a giant and the face of a boy" became a popular player in the city. By December 16, he was also a hero: in the face of a massive train wreck near Poughkeepsie, passenger Orr used his immense strength to free a trapped child and carry him to safety.

Orr's physique was both a blessing and a curse. In late October 1887, he was able to defend a Mrs. Heinzel of East 112th St., New York City, from a would-be assailant by pitching the churl down the stairs. The bad news, however, was that this time the hero lost his balance and fell down the stairs himself, breaking his elbow, fracturing his hand and spraining his ankle. This capped off an eventful season, in which Orr had earlier suffered a lame hand, a burst blood vessel and, in a foul-fly chase collision with rookie catcher Pete Sommer, two lost teeth and assorted bruises.

The press was not always charitable to Orr, as in this 1885 note: "The fat ballplayer from New York showed considerable animation in St. Louis today. Orr made a three-base hit, a homer for anyone else. Then he had to sit down on the bag, panting with exhaustion. A man who can't run three bases without being tired should get off the ball field . . . (The Mets) are nice fellows and good ballplayers when not too fat to play." The final score that day, by the way, was Mets 9, Browns 7. No doubt Orr contributed to his own injury-proneness by remaining so heavy. But, at his best, how he could hit!

In that first 300-TB season (1886), playing his home games on Staten Island's new (and fenceless) St. George Grounds, (and doubtless watching the Statue of Liberty be riveted together beyond the grandstand during lulls

in the action) Orr led the league with 7 home runs and 31 triples (second most ever.) It's hard to escape the image of a ball being cannonaded past outfielders who were playing as deep as they could possibly wish.

Unfortunately, after that banner 1884 season, the Mets slid consistently downhill. In '85, they lost Mutrie, Keefe and Esterbrook to the Giants. In '86, Orr batted .338 on a team that hit .224. In '87, plagued by the aforementioned injuries, he batted .368, stole 17 bases, and served as interim manager (3-5). At season's end, Brooklyn's Charles Byrne purchased the team, and it was dissolved. After a single season with the Bridegrooms, Orr was sold to the new Columbus AA team and, in 1890, joined the leap to the Players' League.

In that final season, Orr was managed by Monte Ward, as the Brooklyn team was known as "Ward's Wonders." Home again, and matched against baseball's best, Big Dave batted .373 and drove in 124 runs, becoming the league's runnerup in both categories. He played in pain, having had two ribs broken by a pitched ball in a July 12 game against Boston.

It was later in the season, however, that tragedy struck. During an October exhibition game in Renova, Pa., Orr was stricken with a paralysis which affected his whole left side. Throughout the winter, he was described as "very cheerful," and hoped that therapy in

(continued on page 144)

			G	R	H	BA	SA	POS	E	FA	GP	W-L	R	H
1883	New York	NL	1	0	0	.000	.000	of	0	1.00				
	Metropolitan	AA	13	6	15	.306	.633	1b	8	.949				
1884	Metropolitan	AA	110	82	162	.352	.537	1b	32	.977				
1885	Metropolitan	AA	107	76	162	.366	.558	1b	30	.974	3	0-0	12	11
1886	Metropolitan	AA	136	93	196	.346	.537	1b	27	.982				
1887	Metropolitan	AA	85	63	147	.404	.544	1b	26	.970				
1888	Brooklyn	AA	99	57	120	.305	.388	1b	22	.979				
1889	Columbus	AA	134	70	182	.325	.441	1b	20	.985				
1890	Brooklyn	PL	107	98	180	.388	.574	1b	19	.982				

RICHARD J. PEARCE
(Dickey)

Born: February 29, 1836, Brooklyn, New York
Died: September 18, 1908, Onset, Massachusetts
BR TR 5-3 ½, 161

As early as 1855, Dickey Pearce was the first man to play shortstop as we know it today. He joined the Atlantics of Brooklyn in 1855 and, still a novice, began playing for following year. The Atlantics placed him at shortstop, reasoning this fat, undersized, stubby-legged fellow could do the least harm at the unimportant position. Shortstops then seldom moved far from their accustomed spot between second and third. But Dicky soon revolutionized the position, roaming into the near outfield to grab fly balls, flowing logically where each defensive situation dictated, shifting in/out/right/left according to his acquired knowledge of each batter's tendencies, and making the long throw to first unhurriedly and accurately.

Pearce was the leadoff batter for the Athletics throughout much of the 1860s, when the club was the most dominant in the game. Besides shortstop, Dickey played many important games at catcher, which was then considered the most important defensive position. Pearce was Brooklyn's shortstop in the famous Fashion Course New York-Brooklyn all-star games in 1858, and he was behind the plate handling Jim Creighton's pitching in a similar all-star game played in Hoboken in 1861.

He starred for the Atlantics until they disbanded after the 1870 season, except for two months he spent with the Excelsiors of Brooklyn in 1866. Next Pearce played short for the Mutuals of New York (NA, 1871-72), the reactivated Atlantics (NA, 1873-74), the St. Louis Browns (NA, 1875, NL, 1876), and in 1877, performed for the Rhode Islands of Providence but returned to the Browns late in the season. Afterward he played with local St. Louis clubs and elsewhere in the minor leagues, finishing his long career in the Northwestern League during 1884, first as player-manager at Quincy, Illinois, and then,

after an injury, as an umpire. He had umpired in the NL briefly in 1878 and 1882. Subsequently he stayed in close touch with baseball from his Brooklyn residence. In 1890 he was groundskeeper for the New York (PL) club at what later became known as the Polo Grounds.

His pudgy, ungainly physique ruled out good running speed but he compensated with extremely able judgment, anticipation, competitiveness, unflappable coolness and mastery of the playing rules. Critics like Henry Chadwick, Sam Crane, William Rankin and A.H. Spink marveled at his efficiency, headwork and innovative genius. Presumably a right-handed batter and fielder, he was a contact hitter, not a slugger. He developed place-hitting to a fine art before "Hit-'em-where-they-ain't" Willie Keeler was born there in Brooklyn. Some claimed Pearce in-

vented the bunt but all agreed he did discover the fair-foul hit and used it to better effect than anyone except Ross Barnes until rule changes in 1877 eliminated it.

The meager statistics of his time obscure Pearce's greatness. Besides his importance as a pioneer in developing better techniques, strategies and mechanics of play, he was generally regarded for 20 years as the best all-round offensive and defensive shortstop in baseball, except during George Wright's very top seasons. After discovering how to overcome his physical limitations, he determined how to best utilize his skills, and did so. Above all, he understood fully the mental aspects of the game and how to employ them to win.

— Frank V. Phelps

			G	R	H	BA	SA	POS	E	FA	GP	W-L	R	H
1856-58	Atlantic of Bkn		-					ss						
1859	Atlantic		-	(3.5 r/g)		(1.8 o/g)								
1860	Atlantic		16	37	-	(46 outs)		ss-c						
1861	Atlantic		10	37	-	(27 outs)		c-ss						
1862	Atlantic		-	(2.1 r/g)		(2.2 o/g)								
1863	Atlantic		11	30	-	(32 outs)								
1864	Atlantic		20	94	-	(62 outs)		c						
1865	Atlantic		17	64	-	(55 outs)								
1866	Atlantic		12	41	-	(39 outs)		ss-rf						
1867	Atlantic		23	83	-	(70 outs)		ss						
1868	Atlantic		48	206	185	(143)	(222TB)	ss-rf						
1869	Atlantic		47	-	175		(236TB)	c-ss						
1870	Atlantic		19	-	85		(100TB)	ss						
1871	Mutual	NA	33	31	44	.270	.301	ss	39	.786				
1872	Mutual	NA	44	32	40	.193	.227	ss	31	.849				
1873	Atlantic	NA	55	42	71	.273	.300	ss	72	.788				
1874	Atlantic	NA	56	48	75	.294	.298	ss	49	.845				
1875	St. Louis	NA	70	51	77	.247	.285	ss	73	.817				
1876	St. Louis	NL	25	12	21	.206	.216	ss	14	.896				
1877	Rhode Island	LgAl	68		-	.233		ss	-	.879				
	St. Louis	NL	8	1	5	.172	.172	ss	3	.927				

NATHANIEL FREDERICK PFEFFER
(Fred)

Born: March 17, 1860, Louisville, Ky.
Died: April 10, 1932, Chicago, Ill.
BR TR 5-10½, 168

The second baseman in the White Stockings' "Stonewall Infield" was Fred Pfeffer. Playing without a glove, he was the perennial fielding leader at the position. A German speaker, he was a favorite of that ethnic community in Chicago.

Pfeffer started playing for the Eclipse club in his hometown of Louisville in 1879. He came to the majors in 1882 as a shortstop for the Troy team and, after it folded, was signed by Anson for the following year. He became a leader in the Brotherhood Movement and hence defected in 1890, taking most of the Chicago players with him and even bringing in Charlie Comiskey as manager of the rebel team. Chicago's Cap Anson took him back in 1891, but he was traded to Louisville for Jimmy Canavan in 1892. He managed the Louisville team for about two-thirds of that season and then stayed with them through 1895. After a brief stint with the Giants in 1896, he returned to Chicago, his career ending with his release in June 1897. Subsequently, he coached at the University of Wisconsin, played semipro ball and managed Decatur of the Three-I League in 1902. He later owned a

bar behind the McVickers Theater in Chicago but was forced out of business by Prohibition. In his last years he was in charge of press boxes at the race tracks. He died of heart disease at 72.

Pfeffer wasn't a top-notch hitter, but he had fairly good "peripherals." His lifetime BA of .255 was about eight points under the league average, and when he hit .308 in 1894 the league average was .309. He had some power, hitting 95 career home runs. Aided by the friendly dimensions of Lake Front Park, Pfeffer hit 25 in 1884 to finish second to Ned Williamson (Chicago had four men with more than 20; the next highest was Brouthers of Buffalo with 14). Three years later, in the slightly larger West Side Park, Pfeffer hit 16. A sample of his ability as a money player was the home run he hit against New York to virtually clinch the pennant in 1885. Cap Anson must have had some regard for Pfeffer's hitting, as Fred batted fifth behind Anson for five years, 1885-1889. In the 1885 World Series he hit .407. He batted cleanup in the 1886 Series, hitting .273, and he homered in both Series.

He was one of the fastest players of his time; he won a contest against five other players before the 1885 World Series, circling the bases in 15¾ seconds. For the years for which we have statistics he averaged about 40 stolen bases a season. But what primarily distinguishes Fred Pfeffer is his fielding, as he could be regarded as the Bill Mazeroski of his era. Between 1884 and 1891 (counting the year in the Players' League) Pfeffer led in putouts eight straight years, in assists four times, in double plays six times, and in total chances per game seven times. He made a lot of errors, but that can be attributed to aggressiveness, which was penalized more in those days. He held the NL record in putouts for 28 years and in assists briefly. He shattered the double play mark with 85 in 1884, but his chief competitor, Bid McPhee, had 90 in the American Association two years later, broke the NL record with 86 in 1892, and then topped 100 in 1893. Pfeffer still tops all second basemen in career total chances per game (6.9) and is second to McPhee in putouts per game.

— William McMahon

			G	R	H	BA	SA	POS	E	FA	GP	W-L	R	H
1881	Eclipse		47	-	71	.330		2b	-	.862				
1882	Troy	NL	85	26	72	.218	.273	ss	73	.857				
1883	Chicago	NL	96	41	87	.235	.340	2b-ss	86	.877				
1884	Chicago	NL	112	105	135	.289	.514	2b	88	.903	1	0-0	2	3
1885	Chicago	NL	112	90	113	.241	.324	2b	86	.893	5	2-1	15	26
1886	Chicago	NL	119	88	125	.264	.386	2b	73	.903				
1887	Chicago	NL	123	95	167	.326	.476	2b	72	.917				
1888	Chicago	NL	135	90	129	.250	.373	2b	65	.931				
1889	Chicago	NL	134	85	128	.241	.309	2b	56	.943				
1890	Chicago	PL	124	86	133	.267	.365	2b	76	.916				
1891	Chicago	NL	137	92	123	.245	.346	2b	62	.935				
1892	Louisville	NL	124	79	122	.262	.350	2b	52	.929	1	0-0	2	4
1893	Louisville	NL	125	85	129	.254	.376	2b	45	.944				
1894	Louisville	NL	104	66	125	.298	.433	2b-ss	49	.928	1	0-0	6	8
1895	Louisville	NL	11	8	13	.289	.311	s-2-1	14	.839				
1896	NY-Chicago	NL	99	46	90	.240	.336	2b	33	.944				
1897	Chicago	NL	32	10	26	.230	.239	2b	21	.888				

LIPMAN EMANUEL PIKE
(Lip, The Iron Batter)

Born: May 25, 1845, New York, N.Y.
Died: October 10, 1893, Brooklyn, N.Y.
BL TL 5-8, 158

Such things can never be said with certainty, but it is generally agreed by historians of the game that Lip Pike was the first Jewish ballplayer. Assuming this to be true, then it also can be said he was baseball's first Jewish manager.

Pike started to play ball with junior clubs in Brooklyn and soon progressed to the strongest nines of the late 1860s. He played his first game with the Atlantics of Brooklyn (not yet up to their postwar strength and reputation) on July 14, 1865. Pike, who despite his lefthandedness, played much of his career as an infielder, joined the Athletics of Philadelphia in 1866. After one season, he signed on with Boss Tweed's New York Mutuals, for whom he played in 1867 and 1868. In 1869 and 1870 he played for the Atlantics of Brooklyn,

by then considered along with the Cincinnati Red Stockings the premier clubs in the land. Pike was at second base on June 14, 1870, when the Atlantics defeated the Red Stockings, 8-7, in 11 innings, in what many consider the greatest game of the pre-league years. The Red Stockings had not lost a game in a season and a half.

Starting out as manager of the Haymakers of Troy in 1871, Pike played all five years of the National Association's existence. In later seasons he was with Baltimore, Hartford (manager, '74) and St. Louis. He played for St. Louis in 1876, the NL's inaugural season. He later played with Cincinnati, Providence and Worcester. He played one final game with the New York Metropolitans (AA) in 1887 when he was 42. He was an NL manager for Cincinnati

in 1877. He quit the post after the team won just 3 of 14 games, but remained on to play second base.

Pike batted .304 in a short major league career of just 163 games. His NA statistics are more imposing: .321 in 260 games. According to a sketch in the *New York Clipper* (1881), "Pike ranked high as a batsman, being, like all lefthanded men, a very hard hitter. And he has accomplished many brilliant feats as fielder, being a sure catch, a remarkably fast runner, and singularly graceful in all his movements."

Pike had a brother, Jay, who played in one game for Hartford (NL) in 1877.

Lip died in Brooklyn in 1893 at the age of 48.
— Joseph M. Overfield

			G	R	H	BA	SA	POS	E	FA	GP	W-L	R	H
1866	Athletic		16	100		(49 outs)		3b						
1867	Mutual		29	78		(78 outs)		3b						
1868	Mutual		25	60	82	(83 outs)		lf						
1869	Atlantic		48	-	175	(325TB)		2b						
1870	Atlantic		21	-	84	(153TB)		2b						
1871	Troy	NA	28	42	49	.380	.659	o-2-1	20	.855				
1872	Baltimore	NA	55	67	83	.295	.438	o-2-3	48	.779				
1873	Baltimore	NA	56	71	89	.309	.455	rf	16	.795				
1874	Hartford	NA	52	58	81	.340	.471	o-s-2	55	.804				
1875	St. Louis	NA	70	61	107	.343	.481	cf-2	26	.865				
1876	St. Louis	NL	63	55	91	.323	.472	cf	11	.905				
1877	Cincinnati	NL	58	45	78	.298	.420	of-2	52	.806				
1878	Cinc-Prov	NL	36	32	52	.311	.365	of-2	16	.807				
1879	Sprgf-Hylk-Alby	NA	53	-		.356		of						
1880	Albany	NA												
	Union of Bkn Metropolitan		12	11	13	.241		cf	1	.941				
1881	Atlantic Worcester	NL	5	1	2	.111	.111	2b	7	.611				
1887	Metropolitan	AA	1	0	0	.000	.000	cf	0	1.00				

JOSEPH QUEST

Born: November, 1851, New Castle, Pa.
BR TR 5-6, 160

Joseph Quest never compiled a remarkable record during his 10-year major league career, which began in 1871 with the Cleveland Forest Cities of the NA and ended in 1886 with Philadelphia (AA). Still, he is responsible for one memorable thing: Quest has been credited with coining the phrase "Charley horse" used to describe a severe muscle cramp.

In 1882, while Quest was playing second base with Cap Anson's Chicago National League club, he and a dozen other Chicago players visited a South Side Chicago racetrack where a horse named Charley would be running. The players had been tipped that the horse was a sure winner.

All the players with the exception of Quest felt comfortable with the tip and bet on the horse. As the horses were preparing to start, Quest received a steady chaffing from the other players for his reluctance to place a bet.

The horses got away with Charley leading the pack. He continued increasing his lead until the back stretch where he was 12 lengths in front. But in the last turn, Charley stumbled and went lame in his hind right leg. As the rest of the horses quickly passed Charley, Quest yelled to the others, "Look at your old Charley horse now!"

The following day, the Chicagos were playing New York in Chicago. While Quest was coaching third base, he sent a signal to George Gore, the club's center fielder who was on first, to steal second. About halfway to second, Gore went down just as the horse did the day before. As Quest ran toward Gore, he yelled to the others who'd been to the track: "There's your old Charley horse — he'd have made it all right if it hadn't been for that old Charley horse."

Gore was out, but the term lived on.

Quest, a right-handed batsman, compiled a .217 average during his major league career. A noted fielder, Quest led National League second basemen in 1878 in fielding average with a .925 mark and in assists with 331.

Quest also put time in at shortstop, third base and the outfield during his career. After playing with the Cleveland Forest Cities, he next played with the the National League's Indianapolis club in 1878, then with Chicago from 1879 until 1882 followed by Detroit (NL), St. Louis (AA), Pittsburgh (AA), Detroit again and finally the Athletics (AA).

While Quest's play was not very noteworthy, he did manage to play for some great teams. Chicago won the NL championship from 1880 through 1882 compiling a .728 winning percentage during those years. He was benched for a time in 1882 but was restored to the lineup in September and his fielding helped spark the Whites to 15 victories in the final 16 games as the team overtook Providence for the pennant.

Quest umpired in the National League during 1887, although he apparently did not receive much respect for his arbitrating from both fans and players alike. That June he had to be escorted from a game at New York after he called the Giants' Monte Ward out at the plate with what would have been the game-tying run. Some fans continued after Quest when he left the park and even stoned his carriage.

After leaving baseball, Quest worked as a bookkeeper. While employed by the City Clerk of Chicago (his old manager Adrian Anson) in 1907, Quest was implicated in an embezzlement scandal. He dropped out of sight, and the date and place of his death are unknown.

— Richard A. Puff and Robert L. Tiemann

			G	R	H	BA	SA	POS	E	FA	GP	W-L	R	H
1871	ForCtyClev	NA	3	1	3	.250	.333	ss-2b	5	.615				
1875	Meadville		9	18	15	.333		3b						
1876	Allegheny							2b						
1877	Indianapolis	LgAl	121	106	168	.300		2b	89	.887				
1878	Indianapolis	NL	62	45	57	.205	.230	2b	60	.876				
1879	Chicago	NL	83	38	69	.207	.260	2b	48	.925				
1880	Chicago	NL	82	37	71	.237	.283	2b	58	.895				
1881	Chicago	NL	78	35	72	.246	.273	2b	37	.929				
1882	Chicago	NL	42	23	32	.201	.252	2b	33	.879				
1883	Detroit	NL	37	22	32	.234	.321	2b	26	.897				
	St. Louis	AA	19	12	20	.256	.321	2b	12	.891				
1884	St.Louis-Pitt	AA	93	48	73	.207	.269	2b	62	.896				
1885	Detroit	NL	55	24	39	.195	.235	2b-ss	37	.885				
1886	Athletic	AA	42	14	30	.203	.250	ss	29	.876				
1887	Eau Claire	NWL	55	46	93	.378		2b	36	.931				
1888	Lowell	NEng	40	22	39	.232		2b	21	.917				

THOMAS A. RAMSEY
(Toad)

Born: August 8, 1864, Indianapolis, In.
Died: March 27, 1906, Indianapolis, In.
BR TL

Thomas "Toad" Ramsey, a lefthanded pitcher in the American Association, is best known for one of the most dramatic single-season turnarounds in big league history, and for being baseball's first knuckleball pitcher, a delivery that never tired his arm. But habitual drunkenness ruined his career.

Ramsey was acquired from Chattanooga by the Louisville Colonels in 1885, He pitched briefly for the Colonels, compiling a 3-6 record, albeit with an impressive 1.94 ERA. The next two years he was the workhorse of the Colonels' staff. In 1886, pitching 50 feet from the plate, Ramsey pitched an impressive 589 innings, a total that led both the Association and the rival National League. Ramsey won 38 games with 27 losses for the Colonels, who finished four games below .500. Ramsey was among the league leaders with a 2.45 ERA, 499 strikeouts and 66 complete games. Hitters were completely baffled by his "drop curve," as his famous pitch was then called. He

struckout seventeen batters, pitched a one-hitter in a thirteen-inning game and had another seventeen strike-outs in nine innings.

Ramsey basically duplicated this season in 1887. Pitching 65 games and 561 innings, he won 37 and lost 27 with a 3.43 ERA. He led the league with 355 strikeouts. On June 20, 1887, he performed the remarkable feat of striking out seventeen batters despite the four-strike rule in effect that year. The Colonels finished a solid fourth in 1887, winning 76 and losing 60. The next year, however, the Colonels collapsed along with their star pitcher. Demoralized by incompetent and stingy ownership, the Colonels finished the 1888 season 48-87, a dismal 44 games out of first. The hapless Ramsey won only 8 of 38 decisions, despite a highly respectable 3.42 ERA, a little over the league average of 3.06 for that year, and 228 strikeouts. Thus in one short season Ramsey went from 10 games over .500 to a staggering 22 games under.

Louisville hit rock bottom in 1889, winning only 27 games against 111 losses. Ramsey had a record of 1-16 with a 5.59 ERA. However, he did not finish the season with the Colonels. Involved in a tight pennant race with Brooklyn, the powerful St. Louis Browns acquired Ramsey in July. But captain Charlie Comiskey gave him little work. Ramsey won 3 and lost 1 as the Browns finished a close second. Ramsey finished his career with St. Louis in the chaotic 1890 season. He went 24-17 before being released in September because of his personal habits.

Ramsey had one of the more remarkable up-and-down careers of the 19th century. His final career totals were 114 wins, 124 losses, and a 3.29 earned run average. Ramsey died in Indianapolis on March 27, 1906, at the age of 41.

— Jim Sumner and Robert L. Tiemann

			G	R	H	BA	SA	POS	E	FA	GP	W-L	R	H
1885	Chattanooga	SL	42	10	17	.118		p	10	.978	41	17-23	177	222
	Louisville	AA	9	2	4	.129	.129	p	4	.946	9	3-6	38	44
1886	Louisville	AA	67	29	58	.241	.282	p	23	.817	67	38-27	297	447
1887	Louisville	AA	65	19	62	.254	.270	p	31	.754	65	38-27	351	711
1888	Louisville	AA	42	12	17	.120	.162	p	18	.783	40	8-30	279	362
1889	Louisvll-StL	AA	23	5	20	.260	.286	p	13	.787	23	4-17	197	219
1890	St. Louis	AA	44	17	33	.228	.283	p	14	.806	44	25-17	219	325
1891	Denver	WA	1					p			1	0-1	6	10
1894	Savannah	SL	16	7	9	.237	.263	p			16	8-6		

ALFRED JAMES REACH

Born: May 25, 1840, London, England
Died: January 14, 1928, Atlantic City, N.J.
BL TL 5-6, 155

Al Reach's playing career was confined to the pre-professional era and to the NA years (1871-1875). While he was considered one of the best players of his time, his contributions to baseball as an executive and as an innovative purveyor of sporting equipment were of much greater importance.

Reach's life story was quintessential Horatio Alger. Born in England, he was brought to America as an infant. As a poor boy in Brooklyn, he earned his first pennies peddling newspapers and later worked as an iron molder. When he died, he was a captain of industry, reputedly worth millions.

Early in life, Reach was attracted to the game of baseball. Despite his small stature, he soon became skilled enough to join the well-known Eckford club of Brooklyn. It was while playing for the Eckfords that he received an offer of $25 in "expense money" to join the Athletics of Philadelphia. Some sources say he was the first paid player; others say the honor belongs to James Creighton. Was it Reach or Creighton? No matter, the seeds that would grow into full-fledged professionalism had been planted.

Reach played with the Athletics in all five of their Association years, ending his active diamond career with the birth of the NL in 1876. In 1871 Reach was chosen by the *New York Clipper* as second baseman on baseball's first all-star team. In the five seasons (he managed in 1874 and 1875), he batted a modest .252.

His playing days over, Reach opened a sporting goods emporium in Philadelphia, and later formed the A.J. Reach Company to manufacture equipment. One of his later partners was Benjamin F. Shibe, who was to develop the cork-center ball and to devise many of the techniques used to mass-produce baseballs. Meanwhile Albert G. Spalding, who already had his own sporting goods company, had acquired a substantial interest in the Reach firm. In 1892 Spalding combined his own company with Reach's and others into A.G. Spalding and Bros. The consolidated companies continued to operate more or less independently under their old names, ostensibly competing against each other. For years, Spalding published the National League Guide, while Reach published

the American League Guide. Spalding balls were used in the National League, while Reach balls were official in the American. What was not known by the general public was that both balls were made in the same plant in Philadelphia.

Deeply involved though he was in business, Reach was also an active part of the baseball establishment. He and Col. John I. Rogers gained control of the Philadelphia franchise when it returned to the NL in 1883. In 1895, after their old wooden ballpark had gone up in flames, the Phillies completed the first steel stadium on the Huntingdon Avenue site.

Reach sold his interest in the Phillies in 1903 to devote his full time to business matters. He kept in close contact with the game, however, and was a member of the Spalding-dominated committee that determined in 1907 that baseball had been invented at Cooperstown in 1839 by Abner Doubleday.

An ardent golfer, Reach played until he was well into his 80s. He died at the age of 87 on January 14, 1928.

— Joseph M. Overfield

			G	R	H	BA	SA	POS	E	FA	GP	W-L	R	H
1861	Eckford		9	20		(25 outs)		rf						
1862	Eckford													
1863	Eckford		8	16		(27 outs)								
1864	Eckford		4	11		(9 outs)		1b						
1865	Athletic		15	57		(44 outs)		2b						
1866	Athletic		23	134		(61 outs)		2b						
1867	Athletic		45	270		(112 outs)		2b						
1868	Athletic		42	216		(121 outs)		2b						
1869	Athletic		46	-	242	(419 TB)		2b						
1870	Athletic		37	-	75	(113 TB)		2b						
1871	Athletic	NA	26	38	41	.353	.416	2b	68	.844				
1872	Athletic	NA	24	21	23	.195	.195	rf-1b	5	.945				
1873	Athletic	NA	16	13	16	.219	.315	2b-of	6	.910				
1874	Athletic	NA	14	8	7	.127	.164	rf	8	.784				
1875	Athletic	NA	3	4	4	.286	.357	rf-2b	3	.571				
1877	Athletic	NA	94	85	139			rf						

ABRAM HARDING RICHARDSON
(Hardie)

Born: April 21, 1855, Clarksboro, N.J.
Died: January 14, 1931, Utica, New York
BR TR 5-9 ½, 170

When Hardie Richardson died in Utica, New York, in 1931, one obituary described him as "the Babe Ruth of the last century." In 14 major league seasons, he batted .299 and hit 303 doubles, 124 triples and 73 home runs — most impressive statistics, but not quite up to those of his longtime Buffalo teammate, Dan Brouthers, who batted .343 with 461 doubles, 206 triples and 106 home runs and was the true "Babe Ruth of the last century."

Richardson began to play ball with amateur nines in the Philadelphia area and became a professional with a semipro club there in 1876. In 1877 he took his first full-fledged professional assignment with the Binghamton Crickets of the International Association, baseball's pioneer minor league. The next year he moved to Utica in the same league, winning the *New York Clipper* award as the best fielding centerfielder. In 1879 he joined Buffalo, then making its NL debut. He played all seven of the Queen City's National

League seasons and while there became a member of the famed "Big Four," along with Dan Brouthers, Jack Rowe and Jim White.

Near the end of the 1885 season, the financially strapped Buffalo club sold all of its players to Detroit for $7,000 in one of baseball's first mass player deals. Actually, the Wolverines were interested only in the "Big Four." Richardson enjoyed three strong seasons with Detroit, batting .351, .328 and .289, and was a strong factor in the 1887 pennant-winning year.

After the 1888 season, Richardson was sold to Boston, where in three years he had the distinction of playing with Boston clubs in three different leagues in successive seasons: the NL in '89, PL in '90 and AA in '91. His '90 season was the biggest of his career. He batted .326, with 26 doubles, 14 triples and 11 home runs, along with an astronomical 143 RBIs. Richardson closed out his major league career with the New York Giants in 1892.

Richardson was almost as well known for his versatility as for his hitting. Second base was his favorite position, but at various times he played all nine positions, including six games as a catcher and five as a pitcher. While not an outstanding base stealer, he was fast enough to bat in the leadoff spot regularly, although he also hit cleanup a good deal.

Off the field, Richardson was a crackerjack shot, especially in on-the-wing shooting, and left open at all times a $1,000 challenge to anyone who thought he could outshoot him. The challenge was never taken up.

When his playing days were over, he operated a hotel in Utica. Later he moved to nearby Ilion, where he was employed in the Remington Typewriter Works. He was 75 when he died.

— Joseph M. Overfield

			G	R	H	BA	SA	POS	E	FA	GP	W-L	R	H
1876	Binghamton		31	25	40			3-c-o	33	.794				
1877	Binghamton		84		-	.274		of	-	.856				
1878	Utica	IA	40	30	59	.324	.423	o-2-c	14	.966				
1879	Buffalo	NL	79	54	95	.283	.396	3b	44	.843				
1880	Buffalo	NL	83	48	89	.259	.359	3b	47	.848				
1881	Buffalo	NL	83	62	100	.291	.422	of	21	.914				
1882	Buffalo	NL	83	61	96	.271	.387	2b	63	.898				
1883	Buffalo	NL	92	73	124	.311	.439	2b	68	.903				
1884	Buffalo	NL	102	85	132	.301	.444	2b-of	53	.901				
1885	Buffalo	NL	96	90	136	.319	.458	2b-of	49	.904	1	0-0	2	5
1886	Detroit	NL	125	125	189	.351	.504	of-2b	31	.923	4	2-0	6	11
1887	Detroit	NL	120	130	208	.363	.503	2b-of	35	.940				
1888	Detroit	NL	58	60	77	.289	.440	2b	29	.925				
1889	Boston	NL	132	122	163	.304	.438	2b-of	51	.926				
1890	Boston	PL	130	125	184	.332	.516	of	11	.965				
1891	Boston	AA	74	45	71	.255	.399	of-3b	8	.957				
1892	Wash-NY	NL	74	38	59	.207	.305	2-o-1	17	.928				

J. LEE RICHMOND

Born: May 5, 1857, Sheffield, Ohio
Died: September 30, 1929, Toledo, Ohio
TL 5-10, 142

J. Lee Richmond burst upon the baseball world in 1879. He led his Brown University nine to the college championship and pitched a no-hitter in his professional debut. Pitching alternately as an amateur and as a professional, his composite record for the season included 47 wins and a batting average over .350.

Richmond's first baseball experience was pitching at Oberlin College from 1873 to 1876. He enrolled at Brown in 1876 and immediately began playing the outfield for Brown's fall season. He continued the next two seasons pitching and playing the outfield for Brown, at the same time playing on a part-time basis for the Rhode Islands of Providence.

Richmond labored in Brown's gymnasium the winter of 1878-79 developing a set of curved deliveries. His curves broke up and down rather than in and out, and proved to be devastating.

He was engaged by Frank Bancroft to pitch an exhibition game for Worcester against the Chicago White Stockings on June 2. He responded with a no-hitter and was promptly signed. (A week later he nailed down the college championship for Brown.) His pitching was so effective that the Worcester team, struggling before he joined it, was considered to be one of baseball's finer teams by season's end. He threw a second no-hitter later in the season. His contributions turned the Worcester franchise around to the point that it would join the National League in 1880. Richmond was paid a record $2,400 for his services that year.

Richmond used baseball to finance his education. He earned bachelor's, master's and medical degrees while still in the game. For seven years it was baseball in the summer and school in the winter for him. He "retired" in 1883 to practice medicine in Ohio. He later gave up medicine for a career in education that spanned 40 years.

Richmond's statistical record doesn't indicate his level of contribution to the game. He had a large hand in changing pitching strategies. He was the major leagues' first star left-handed pitcher. He employed a change of pace and a sharply breaking curve. He studied hitters and kept a book on them. He was known for cunning, deception and strategy.

Richmond accounted for many baseball "firsts" during his short career, most notably pitching baseball's first perfect game. Playing concurrently as an amateur and a professional, he was the reason for the first rules barring professionals from participating with amateurs. He struck out a record five consecutive batters in his major league debut. He gave up the first National League grand slam home run. When his team was the first to hit three home runs in an inning and four in a game, Richmond was one of the sluggers. He was the first pitcher to win 20 games for a last-place team. He was one of the first collegians to play in the majors and the first medical doctor to do so.

His portside delivery led to the first platooning and brought switch-hitting into vogue. He was the first to relieve and to be relieved for an opposite-side hurler. His successes set off a search for left-handed pitching talent that continues to this day. How many times have you heard, "If we only had a lefty"?

— John Richmond Husman

			G	R	H	BA	SA	POS	E	FA	GP	W-L	R	H
1879	Brown University		10	25	15	.278	.536	p	2	.965	10	7-2	35	61
	Worcester	NA	29	37	45	.366	.569	p	24	.911	29	18-10	104	165
	Boston	NL	1	0	2	.333	.333	p	0	1.00	1	1-0	6	4
1880	Worcester	NL	77	44	70	.227	.278	p-of	23	.827#	74	31-32	287	541
1881	Worcester	NL	61	31	63	.250	.278	p-of	8	.937#	53	25-26	304	547
1882	Worcester	NL	55	50	64	.281	.430	p-of	21	.851	48	14-33	334	525
1883	Providence	NL	49	41	55	.284	.402	of-p	25	.748	12	3-7	52	122
1886	Cincinnati	AA	8	3	8	.286	.286	of-p	5	.583	3	0-2	22	23

WILLIAM H. ROBINSON
(Yank)

Born: September 19, 1859, Philadelphia, Pa.
Died: August 25, 1894, St. Louis, Mo.
BL TR 5-6 ½, 170

Agile, versatile, and quick witted, William "Yank" Robinson scrambled out of the sandlots to a 10-year professional career, but was dead before he was 35. Although he played every position except center field, Robinson was best-known as the walk-wheedling, hard-running ambidextrous second baseman of the St. Louis Browns of the American Association, for which he played in four World Series.

A poor youth from Philadelphia, Billy left home at a young age and went to Boston, where he eventually became a sought-after ballplayer. He was 23 years old and playing for Natick in August 1882, when the Detroit Wolverines found themselves in Boston without a serviceable shortstop. Robinson made good in a one-game tryout and stayed with the Detroits through the end of the season. In 1883 he was shortstop and captain for Saginaw. The team finished a close second in the Northwestern League race, although Robinson hit only .215 and fielded only .814. The following season he played for the Baltimore Unions, supplementing his infield duties with work at both pitcher and catcher.

Chris Von der Ahe of the St. Louis Browns was impressed by this versatility, and Robinson was signed to a $2,100 contract for 1885. Von der Ahe wanted to use him as a catcher, but Yank made it clear that he would go behind the plate only in emergencies. He was the team's nominal substitute in 1885, but his versatility helped the Browns overcome some key injuries and still win the pennant. Yank filled in for left fielder Tip O'Neill for nearly three months and played second, third and catcher because of injuries to others. He even held down first base one game when he himself was hobbled by a sprained ankle. In the post-season series versus Chicago, Robbie

played three games as catcher and the other four as right fielder.

The Browns thereupon sold Sam Barkley and installed Robinson as starting second baseman in 1886. Short, somewhat stocky and without outstanding athletic ability, Robinson excelled at second base because of his agility and quickness. He was especially good at racing into the outfield for short pop-ups, and his contortions while turning double plays delighted the fans. He didn't use a glove and was less than outstanding on ground balls. But he showed good range in knocking them down and could make quick, accurate throws to the bases. When necessity dictated, he could even make good throws to second or third base using his left hand. He batted lefthanded but was a weak, opposite-field slasher with little power. He could bunt, and the keystone of his offensive game was drawing bases on balls. Once he got on he was a quick and daring runner.

A smart player, Robbie became one of Captain Comiskey's chief lieutenants. And his sociable disposition put him in the role of pacifier when his teammates squabbled. Yank lifted many a beer with the boys, and he

was often in trouble with the ownership because of his lax habits. After a celebrated shouting match with owner Von der Ahe on May 2, 1889, Robinson jumped the team, complaining that the owner had fined him "enough in aggregate to build a stone front house." The rest of the Browns nearly staged a sympathy strike before the $25 fine was rescinded.

In 1890 Robinson jumped to Pittsburgh (PL), where he continued to be fined for drunkenness. In 1891 he was with Kelly's Killers in Cincinnati (AA) until that club folded in August. Robbie caught on with Washington in May 1892, when the Senators were desperate for a third baseman. But Yank's skills and health had slipped badly.

A report that he was dying of "quick consumption" appeared in Sporting Life in March 1893, although the once robust Robinson tried to deny that his condition was really serious. Although he had once been reputed to be rather rich, his health ate away at his bank account as well as at his body, and he was dependent upon the charity of friends by the time he passed away in August 1894.

— Robert L. Tiemann

			G	R	H	BA	SA	POS	E	FA	GP	W-L	R	H
1882	Detroit	NL	11	1	7	.179	.205	ss	8	.805	1	0-0		
1883	Saginaw	NWL	64	54	53	.220	.332	ss	45	.814				
1884	Baltimore	UA	102	101	111	.267	.359	3-s-c	82	.868	11	3-3	42	96
1885	St. Louis	AA	78	63	74	.259	.343	of-2	32	.878				
1886	St. Louis	AA	133	89	134	.279	.390	2b	67	.897	1	0-1	11	10
1887	St. Louis	AA	125	102	223	.427	.510	2b	79	.897	1	0-0	2	6
1888	St. Louis	AA	134	111	106	.231	.314	2b-ss	79	.883				
1889	St. Louis	AA	132	99	95	.210	.289	2b	80	.889				
1890	Pittsburgh	PL	98	57	72	.239	.276	2b	67	.883				
1891	Cincinti-StL	AA	98	48	61	.177	.235	2b	78	.867				
1892	Washington	NL	67	26	39	.179	.225	3b	34	.852				

M. MORTIMER ROGERS

Born: Brooklyn, N.Y.
Died: May 13, 1881, New York, N.Y.

Mort Rogers and the game of baseball were first wed in Brooklyn. His name first turns up in 1863, the year of the founding of the Resolute Base Ball Club of Brooklyn, one of the finest teams in New York City at the time. The Resolutes played Excelsiors, the Atlantics, Eckfords and other "big time" clubs in annual season series.

Rogers was not only the team's leader, pitcher and representative in all inter-club organizational meetings, but he was looked to as an authority in national baseball decisions. He was a thinking man's athlete, a rare breed in early sporting circles. Mort's brother, Albert N. Rogers, was the Resolute scorer and bookkeeper, as well as secretary for the National Association of Base Ball Players in 1864-1867. Mort served the organization as first vice president in 1866 and treasurer from 1867 to 1869.

Rogers led the Resolutes on tours, mostly along the Eastern Seaboard. These jaunts took the players to Washington, Baltimore, Philadelphia and Boston, where they met challengers from the three Beantown power-houses, the Tri-Mountains, the Harvards and the Lowells. On these visits Mort became a favorite of the Lowell of Boston team. He no doubt received some inducement to play for the Massachusetts club, for he moved to Boston to join them in 1866. It was in a match with the Granite B.B.C. of Holliston, Mass., on September 29 that Rogers first appeared in a Lowell uniform.

Mortimer's arrival in Boston brought new respectability to the game there. He was a nationally prominent figure who had taken a major role in fashioning America's first country-wide association, which brought all teams under the same rules.

A star on the field and off, he continued as a player into the early 1870s. Though famous as a pitcher for the Resolutes, he switched to the outfield in Boston. But already the cogs of Rogers' business mind were turning. He saw a market for thorough and intelligent baseball news, and he decided to supply it.

In 1869 he started the *New England Chronicle*, a weekly paper devoted to information about the pastime in all its complexities, from all over the nation. It was published in Boston and circulated as far as Philadelphia. But the difficulties in establishing and managing a distribution network, keeping books and making shipments as far as 500 miles away, all with horses, wagons and the railway, were too much to handle. This highly ambitious project came to an end in the midst of the 1870 season, after little more than a year's run.

Mort was not done, however. In 1871 he produced a series of scorecards for sale at the ball park in Boston, where the Red Stockings always drew big crowds. These cards featured a photo of a prominent player from Boston or an opponent; a number of these handsome products still exist. After the issuance of these pieces in 1872 no more has been found on baseball's first entrepreneur. He played a key role in the development of the game, but lived before accurate records of careers were recorded.

— Mark Rucker

		G	R	Outs	H	TB
1861	Resolute of Brooklyn	-(2#6 runs/game)				
1862	Resolute of Brooklyn					
1863	Resolute of Brooklyn	7	14	21		
1864	Resolute of Brooklyn	16	39	40		
1865	Resolute of Brooklyn	5	18	13		
1866	Resolute of Brooklyn					
1867	Lowell of Boston	6	32	14		
1868	Lowell of Boston	11	47	32	39	51
1869	Lowell of Boston	23	-		67	119

JOHN CHARLES ROWE

Born: December 18, 1856, Harrisburg, Pa.
Died: April 25, 1911, St. Louis, Mo.
BL TR 5-8, 170

In addition to being a top-notch catcher and shortstop and a feared hitter (.286 lifetime in the majors), Jack Rowe was the Joe Sewell of his day. In 12 major league seasons, he fanned only 177 times. (Sewell struck out 114 times in 14 seasons.) According to the Macmillan *Encyclopedia*, Rowe, in 1882, did not strike out a single time in 75 games and 308 at bats.

Rowe began organized play in 1876 with an amateur nine in Jacksonville, Illinois, as a catcher, became a semipro with the Peoria Reds in 1877 and a full-fledged professional with Rockford, Illinois, in 1879. When that club folded late in the year, he joined the Buffalo National League club in time to get into eight games. He went on to play six solid seasons with the Bisons before being sold to Detroit. While with Buffalo, Rowe, along with Dan Brouthers, Hardy Richardson and Deacon White, became known as the "Big Four." It was these four players that Detroit wanted

when it purchased the Buffalo club for $7,000 in August of 1885. Rowe and his compatriots played well for the Wolverines and led them to a pennant in 1887.

After the 1888 campaign, Rowe and Deacon White bought the Buffalo International League franchise, fully expecting to co-manage and play for their own team. It was not to be. Detroit had sold their contracts to Pittsburgh and owner Bill Nimick of the latter club refused to release them. Further, he threatened to have the Buffalo club blacklisted if Rowe and White tried to play. Midway through the 1889 season, Rowe and White capitulated and reported to Pittsburgh. But with the formation of the Players' league in 1890, Rowe and White jumped their Pittsburgh contracts to become part-owners of the Buffalo club in the new league.

The next year Rowe moved to the minors, joining his brother, Dave, at Lincoln, Nebraska (Western Association) in 1891, then return-

ing to Buffalo (Eastern) in 1892 and 1893. In 1896 his pal, Jim Franklin, owner of the Buffalo club, persuaded him to take over as manager. In three seasons as Buffalo skipper, he developed such players as Claude Richey, Chick Stahl and catcher Harry Smith. His all-redheaded outfield on the 1897 club of Billy Clymer, Larry Gilboy and R.C. Grey was later immortalized in a famous baseball story, The Redheaded Outfield, written by Zane Grey, a former professional ballplayer himself and R.C. Grey's older brother. In the story, manager Rowe became manager Delaney.

Once his baseball days were over, Rowe became quite a public figure in his adopted home town of Buffalo. His downtown cigar store was a popular gathering place for sporting figures of the city. About 1910, with his health failing, he moved to a daughter's home in St. Louis, where he died in 1911.

— Joseph M. Overfield

			G	R	H	BA	SA	POS	E	FA	GP	W-L	R	H
1877	Milwaukee		12	7	5	.111	-	c	17	.734				
1878	Peoria		24		-	.230		c	-	.897				
1879	Rockford	NWL	22	22	33	.324	.451	c-o-2	7	.933				
	Buffalo	NL	8	8	12	.353	.382	c-of						
1880	Buffalo	NL	79	43	82	.252	.328	c-of	43	.883				
1881	Buffalo	NL	64	30	82	.333	.467	c-s-3	25	.900#				
1882	Buffalo	NL	75	43	82	.266	.360	c-ss	26	.933				
1883	Buffalo	NL	87	65	104	.278	.372	c-o-s	60	.859				
1884	Buffalo	NL	93	85	126	.315	.450	c-of	36	.931				
1885	Buffalo	NL	98	62	122	.290	.406	s-c-o	67	.867				
1886	Detroit	NL	111	97	142	.303	.421	ss	54	.880				
1887	Detroit	NL	124	135	210	.365	.483	ss	51	.907				
1888	Detroit	NL	105	62	125	.277	.373	ss	72	.861				
1889	Pittsburgh	NL	75	57	82	.259	.334	ss	39	.896				
1890	Buffalo	PL	125	77	125	.248	.317	ss	67	.901				
1891	Lincoln	WA	93	68	106	.283	.390	ss	31	.901				
1892	Buffalo	EL	18	17	20	.299	.358	2b-ss	10	.857				
1893	Buffalo	EL	110	113	158	.340	.445	2b	48	.930				

JAMES E. RYAN

Born: February 11, 1863, Clinton, Mass.
Died: October 29, 1923, Chicago, Ill.
BR TL 5-9, 162

To many fans Jimmy Ryan isn't as well known as the Chicago stars of the early 1880s. He was just starting his career with the last of the championship White Stocking teams. But he had a longer and more productive major league career than any of them except Anson, playing for 18 years and amassing such totals as 2,012 games, 8,177 at-bats, 1,643 runs, 2,531 hits, 451 doubles, 157 triples and at least 408 stolen bases. Ryan was not one of Anson's favorites; Cap wrote of him that he couldn't cover much ground in the outfield, and lacked hustle.

After playing at Holy Cross, Ryan got his professional start with Bridgeport of the Eastern League in 1885 and was acquired by Chicago at the end of the season. He didn't get into the World Series that year, but in 1886 as the semi-regular right fielder he played in all the Series games, even going in to pitch when Ned Williamson was knocked out in Game 5. He hit .238 in the Series, with 1 double, and handled 19 of 20 chances. In 1888 Ryan led the league in hits (182), doubles (33), home runs (16) and slugging (.515).

He jumped to the PL in 1890 but returned to the White Stockings the following year, holding down centerfield until the advent of Bill Lange, when he was moved to right. Anson alleged that Ryan conspired with club president James A. Hart to undermine his authority and ultimately remove him as manager. The other side of the dispute is that Anson was a sanctimonious, stubborn man, and a change was necessary for the team to progress. But Ryan wasn't very well liked and once even beat up a sportswriter.

Ryan stayed with Chicago through 1900, and after a year with St. Paul of the Western League he was picked up by the Washington Senators and spent his last two years as a

player in the AL. He managed Colorado Springs of the Western League in 1904 and later played for a semipro team in the Rogers Park area of Chicago. He was a deputy sheriff when he died at 60.

In evaluating Ryan as a player one should not consider the "peak value" but the total career. Apart from 1888, in any given year there might be several others who had better seasons. Yet Ryan's offensive statistics are well above average, e.g., a BA of about 33 points above the league. He scored more than 100 runs eight times. Defensively, he led the league in assists and in double plays once each, and in total chances per game twice (this includes his last year, 1903, when, at age

40, he led the AL.) But if one is to stake a claim to the Hall of Fame for Jimmy, it is the longevity figures that must be taken in account. When he retired after 1903, he ranked third in career games played and times at bat, fourth in doubles and home runs, fourth or fifth in runs scored (allowing for divergent figures in different sources), fifth in hits, 12th or 13th in triples, and 12th to 14th in bases on balls. Despite being primarily a leadoff hitter, Ryan even ranked 11th in RBIs. As for defense, among outfielders he is 3rd in all-time assists (1st for his era) and and 9th in double plays (4th for his time). The cumulative stats are impressive.

— William McMahon

Year	Team	League	G	R	H	BA	SA	POS	E	FA	GP	W-L	R	H
1884	Lynn	MassSt						of						
1885	Bridgeport	SoNEng						of						
	Bridgeport	EL	29	18	26	.217	.283	of	6	.889				
	Chicago	NL	3	2	6	.462	.538	ss-of	8	.680				
1886	Chicago	NL	84	58	100	.306	.434	of	23	.828	5	0-0	14	19
1887	Chicago	NL	126	117	198	.356	.466	of	33	.857	8	2-1	48	53
1888	Chicago	NL	129	115	182	.332	.519	of	35	.878	8	4-0	32	47
1889	Chicago	NL	135	140	187	.325	.498	of-ss	57	.880				
1890	Chicago	PL	118	101	164	.330	.463	of	29	.864				
1891	Chicago	NL	118	109	145	.289	.435	of	23	.920	2	0-0	10	11
1892	Chicago	NL	128	105	148	.293	.438	of	25	.916				
1893	Chicago	NL	83	82	102	.299	.428	of-ss	25	.895	1	0-0	2	3
1894	Chicago	NL	108	133	173	.360	.484	of	26	.904				
1895	Chicago	NL	108	83	143	.323	.454	of	17	.911				
1896	Chicago	NL	128	83	153	.312	.427	of	20	.921				
1897	Chicago	NL	136	104	160	.309	.463	of	14	.945				
1898	Chicago	NL	144	122	185	.323	.446	of	25	.921				
1899	Chicago	NL	125	91	158	.301	.394	of	13	.956				
1900	Chicago	NL	105	66	115	.277	.393	of	18	.913				
1901	St. Paul	WL	108	77	143	.323	.413	of						
1902	Washington	AL	120	92	155	.320	.448	of	16	.949				
1903	Washington	AL	114	42	109	.249	.373	of	6	.980				
1904	Col. Spgs	WL	125	94	151	.296		of	13	.951				

ALBERT KARL SELBACH
(Kip)

Born: March 24, 1872, Columbus, Ohio
Died: February 17, 1956, Columbus, Ohio
BR TR 5-9, 190

He was born March 24, 1872, in Columbus, Ohio, and lived there all of his 83 years. At age 18 Selbach captained a local nine that toured Ohio. He impressed Gus Schmelz, manager of the Columbus AA team. Schmelz wanted to sign the youngster but his old-world German parents refused until Kip was of age. So when he turned 21 in 1893, Gus snagged him to catch for his Chattanooga club. Selbach hit only .250 but when Schmelz returned to the National League to manage Washington he brought Kip along.

Deacon McGuire was Washington's catcher, so Selbach became a leftfielder. Despite his stout build, he covered a lot of outfield ground, often leading all outfielders in putouts. *Sporting Life* labeled him a "crack outfielder." He was a fine batter, too, knocking .300 all five years in Washington. Kip usually hit first or second to take advantage of his speed and batting eye. The other Schmelz recruits were less successful; the team finished dismally — 11th, 10th, 9th, 6th and 11th — during Selbach's day.

In 1899 Kip shifted to Cincinnati. On a better team, he took some flak. "Selbach's strongest point is making his toilet while standing at the plate," wrote Ren Mulford. *Sporting Life* later complained that he dallied too long: "he hitches his trousers, kneels and dusts off, pulls his cap . . ." He chewed gum and stuck the wad on the bottom of his cap while he batted. Cincinnati owner John T. Brush was part-owner of the Giants and transferred many players to Andy Freedman's club, including Kip.

Kip hit .337 in 1900 but fell off to .289 the next. On June 9, against Cincinnati, he got 6 hits in 7 trips. George Van Haltren and Charley Hickman added 5 each to set a single-game record for one outfield. However, New York was a last-place team and *Sporting Life* reported "Al Selbach wants to get away from New York . . . [he is] . . . under the ban of the bleacherites." Both Boston teams wanted him

but John McGraw slipped in first, and for $4,000 a year, Kip jumped to Baltimore and the new AL. "New York has lost the two best men on the team in [George] Davis and Selbach," wrote Tim Murnane.

McGraw led an in-house rebellion in Baltimore, selling out to Brush and Freedman. They swooped in to gather the talent, but Selbach and Jimmy Willliams refused to leave. Kip had a two-year pact and no interest in going back to New York. He became the team captain, and hit .320, but Baltimore limped in last and the franchise was dissolved. Selbach was awarded to Washington, where he hit only .252 and was again the target of fan abuse on a last-place team.

For years he toured in the off season as captain of a bowling team and in 1903 he and Herm Collin won the ABC doubles title with a three-game score of 1,227. "When the old tin can is pulled on him for good," he will give Columbus the best bowling alley they ever had, said *Sporting Life*. In 1908 he was on the champion Columbus team.

Yet in baseball he was on another last place team and in June Ban Johnson suspended him for indifferent play after he made three errors in one inning. Shortly thereafter he was swapped to Boston for Tip O'Neill. He plugged the leftfield hole created by the trade of Pat Dougherty and when the team sagged he took over the leadoff spot. He was on a winner. Well past his prime, Kip contributed timely hits and some solid fielding. *The Washington Post* asked how many fans would prefer to have Tip or Kip.

When choosing his career highlight Kip picked a play he made on the last day of the season. "Two men were out and a man on third for New York," he wrote Ellery Clark in 1954. "Elberfield came to bat and hit a hard line hit over the shortstop. I came in fast from left and caught it knee-high to end the game . . . this made us win the American League Championship."

Two years later, hitting .211 on yet another last-place team, Kip was sold to Providence. He finished up with five years in the Tri-State League with Harrisburg before going back home to open his bowling alley.

— Rich Eldred

			G	R	H	BA	SA	POS	E	FA	GP	W-L	R	H
1893	Chattanooga	SL	75#	55	66	.247	.356	of-c	15	.924				
1894	Washington	NL	97	70	115	.309	.505	of-ss	38	.875				
1895	Washington	NL	129	116	168	.324	.488	of	29	.914				
1896	Washington	NL	127	100	151	.310	.421	of	18	.946				
1897	Washington	NL	126	114	154	.317	.472	of	15	.955				
1898	Washington	NL	132	88	156	.303	.417	of	21	.941				
1899	Cincinnati	NL	140	104	154	.296	.407	of	19	.953				
1900	New York	NL	141	98	176	.337	.461	of	18	.951				
1901	New York	NL	125	89	145	.289	.376	of	14	.942				
1902	Baltimore	AL	128	86	161	.320	.427	of	19	.941				
1903	Washington	AL	140	68	134	.251	.356	of	12	.956				
1904	Wash-Boston	AL	146	65	146	.264	.356	of	16	.950				
1905	Boston	AL	124	54	103	.246	.342	of	15	.928				
1906	Boston	AL	60	15	48	.211	.268	of	4	.966				
	Providence	EL	74	28	69	.258	.328	of	7	.956				
1907	Harrisburg	TriSt	128	56	131	.282	.400	of	12	.949				
1908	Harrisburg	TriSt	85	35	90	.294	.395	of	1	.993				
1910	Harrisburg	TriSt	77	43	75	.277	.339	of	4	.969				

FRANK GIBSON
SELEE

Born: October 26, 1859, Amherst, New Hampshire
Died: July 5, 1909, Denver, Co.

Add the Chicago Cubs' pennants in 1906, 1907, 1908 and 1910 to Frank Selee's record and his place among baseball's best known managers would be secure. After all, Selee did assemble the nucleus of the Cubs' dynasty before tuberculosis forced him to surrender the reins to Frank Chance midway through the 1905 season.

Even without help from the Cubs, Selee's five pennants in 15 seasons rank him among baseball's top 10 managers and his .598 career won-lost percentage is exceeded only by contemporary Jim Mutrie and Hall of Famers Charles Comiskey and Joe McCarthy.

Selee's managerial philosophy ("If I make things pleasant for the players, they reciprocate") might not be applicable today, but it worked like a charm in the 1890s. Pennant-winners at Oshkosh (Northwest League, 1887) and Omaha (Western Association, 1889) earned Selee an opportunity in the majors. The Boston team he inherited in 1890 was depleted by the Brotherhood, but Selee recruited some of the Western Association's top players, including Hall-of-Fame pitcher Kid

Nichols, and brought them home a respectable fifth. When the defectors returned in 1891, Selee had his first National League pennant winner. Strengthened by additions from the defunct American Association, Boston repeated in 1892 and made it three in a row in 1893. After three seasons of decline, Selee had Boston back on top in 1897 and 1898 with a largely rebuilt lineup. Defectors to the American League in 1901 foiled Selee's second rebuilding job in Boston, but he took over the Cubs in 1902 and turned a sixth-place club into a first-division outfit before illness cut short his career.

According to second baseman Bobby Lowe, who played on all five Boston pennant winners, the secret to Selee's success was that "he was a good judge of players." He proved that in both Boston and Chicago as he scoured the minor leagues not for stars, but for players who filled the gaps in his lineup. And he wasn't afraid to experiment, converting catchers Fred Tenney and Frank Chance into two of the best first basemen ever.

Lowe also noted that Selee was "wonderful

with young players," a useful trait in building a team without the benefit of large capital outlays, a tactic Boston abandoned after being disappointed with the celebrated purchases of King Kelly and John Clarkson.

"He didn't bother with a lot of signals," said Lowe, "but let his players figure out their own plays. He didn't blame them if they took a chance that failed."

It was that spirit of cooperation that kept Boston competitive with the fiery Baltimore Orioles in the '90s. Like the Orioles, Selee "believed in place-hitting, sacrifice-hitting and stealing," according to Lowe, but Selee's standards of conduct were different. "I want them (his players) to be temperate and live properly. I do not believe that men who are engaged in such exhilarating exercise should be kept in strait jackets, but I expect them to be in condition to play." And he added, "I do not want a man who cannot appreciate such treatment."

Apparently, Frank Selee found quite a few players who appreciated his loose rein.

— Bob Richardson

			G	R	H	BA	SA	POS	E	FA	GP	W-L	R	H
1884	Lawrence	MassSt	1					cf						

ELMER SMITH

Born: March 23, 1868, Pittsburgh, Pa.
Died: November 3, 1945, Pittsburgh, Pa.
BL TL 5-11, 178

Elmer Smith was a 30-game winner at 19, was released with a dead arm at age 21, and came back to spend 10 years in the majors as a hard-hitting outfielder. In all, he spent 14 years in the majors, and his professional career lasted from 1886 through 1906.

Born and raised in Allegheny, Pennsylvania, now part of the city of Pittsburgh, Elmer developed into a left-handed pitcher with good size and lots of speed. In 1886, at 18, he signed with Nashville in the Southern League. He soon moved up to Cincinnati, but missed most of the season with a sore arm. Elmer was a respectable 4-4 as a rookie and was invited back for 1887. Smith had some trouble breaking into the Reds' three-man rotation, but once he got his chance, he showed outstanding stuff. He won 13 of 14 decisions in one stretch (losing a 2-1 game because of his own double error) and finished with 33 wins in all.

Young Elmer rested on his laurels during the off-season. Then he tried to show his famous fastball too soon in spring training and developed a sore shoulder. He was only 5-9 through the Fourth of July, but then rounded into shape and finished the 1888 season with a 22-17 record.

The sore shoulder reappeared in 1889, and Smith pitched less and less as the season progressed. Finally he was released in October. In 1890 he signed with Kansas City in the Western Association. His arm showed signs of revival, thanks to the massages given to him by some local firemen. But the team didn't have a catcher to hold his speed. And, more importantly, Smith was beginning to make a name for himself as a hitter. After batting .331 and .308 in two years in Kansas City, Elmer was sought after by several National League clubs. He signed with his hometown Pirates for 1892. Although he pitched occasionally that year (7-6 record, with a one-hit shutout), his main job was as starting left fielder. In 1893 he had his biggest year

with the bat, posting career highs in hits, triples and home runs (and runs batted in, according to retroactive studies).

Elmer was a fast runner and good base stealer, so he was used in the leadoff spot a fair amount. His ability to pull the ball as a left-handed hitter also led to his use in the No. 2 spot sometimes. But he spent more of his career batting fourth or fifth because of his extra-base power. He swung one of the heaviest bats in history, up to 54 ounces. He didn't hit the ball as far as some, but his running speed allowed him to challenge outfielders for extra bases.

Although he was a little rough when he first moved to the outfield, he developed into a pretty good flyhawk. He covered plenty of ground and still possessed a strong throwing arm. Teamed with Jake Stenzel and Patsy Donovan, he helped give the Pirates one of the best outfields in the league.

He lived his whole life in urban Allegheny City and worked in the iron and steel mills in the winters. But he loved animals, and his home was always surrounded by chickens, ducks, and lots and lots of dogs.

Smith enjoyed six productive years with Pittsburgh before being sent to Cincinnati with Pink Hawley in a two-for-four trade. Elmer hit .342 as the Reds made a bid for the pennant. In 1889, his average slipped below .300, and Elmer missed the last month of the season to be with his wife, who was dying of tuberculosis.

Smith was sold to New York in June 1900, then was released by the Giants at the end of the season. He signed with Pittsburgh in 1901 but came up with a broken finger and was shipped to Boston. After a couple of months with the Beaneaters, Elmer slipped to the minors.

— Robert L. Tiemann

			G	R	H	BA	SA	POS	E	FA	GP	W-L	R	H
1886	Nashville	SL	10	7	13	.351	.405	p	4	.846	10	4-4	45	88
	Cincinnati	AA	10	7	9	.281	.375	p	3	.750	10	4-5	62	65
1887	Cincinnati	AA	52	26	57	.288	.384	p	13	.851	52	34-17	242	551
1888	Cincinnati	AA	40	14	29	.220	.256	p	11	.867	40	22-17	161	309
1889	Cincinnati	AA	29	12	23	.277	.410	p	5	.881	29	9-12	169	253
1890	Kansas City	WA	112	128	150	.331	.512	of-p	24	.895	36	23-9	114	205
1891	Kansas City	WA	121	115	150	.314	.479	of	28	.895	10	1-4	76	83
1892	Pittsburgh	NL	138	86	140	.274	.384	of	31	.885	17	6-7	120	140
1893	Pittsburgh	NL	128	119	183	.366	.554	of	24	.923				
1894	Pittsburgh	NL	125	129	175	.352	.537	of	20	.935	1	0-0	2	6
1895	Pittsburgh	NL	124	109	146	.297	.390	of	32	.894				
1896	Pittsburgh	NL	122	121	175	.362	.500	of	18	.946				
1897	Pittsburgh	NL	123	101	145	.310	.463	of	28	.904				
1898	Cincinnati	NL	123	79	166	.342	.432	of	18	.942	1	0-0	2	2
1899	Cincinnati	NL	87	64	101	.295	.377	of	16	.922				
1900	Cinc-New York	NL	114	61	112	.265	.369	of	10	.943				
1901	Pitts-Boston	NL	20	5	10	.164	.230	of	4	.846				
1902	Kansas City	AA	111	69	127	.308	.437	of	19	.926				
1903	Minneapolis	AA	75	55	97	.323	.420	of	5	.956				
1904	Kansas City	AA	12	6	13	.295	.318	of	1	.955				
	Ilion	NYSt	110	56	125	.326		1b	25	.970				
1905	Scranton	NYSt	114	52	138	.329		of	5	.961				
1906	Binghamton	NYSt	119	43	124	.313		of	9	.966				

LOUIS FRANCIS SOCKALEXIS
(Chief)

Born: October 24, 1871, Old Town, Maine
Died: December 24, 1913, Burlington, Maine
BL TR 5-11, 185

If, as Robert Smith described him in *Baseball*, Lou Sockalexis was the "Gentle Indian," he also was a baseball player with enormous talent. Some have actually argued that he was the greatest player who ever lived. Hughie Jennings, one of the game's legendary managers, was less extreme when he stated that Sockalexis *should* have been the greatest player of all time.

Whether the "greatest player who ever lived" or simply a "player with enormous talent," the descriptions seem excessively generous for a man with just 367 major league at-bats and 115 hits (3 homers and a lifetime batting average of .313).

Clearly this is a story of what might have been . . . Louis Francis Sockalexis, resident of Old Town, Maine, Penobscot Indian, basket weaver, canoeist, woodsman. There was an intellectual side that won him a prep school scholarship at nearby Houlton Academy. Further, there was a physical and athletic side, and playing baseball became a passion. Lou's father was disappointed as his son became more and more engrossed in the "sport of the white man."

But there was no holding this great athlete back. On to Holy Cross to become a baseball star. On to Notre Dame, where his mentor had found a new job. On to the Polo Grounds with the Notre Dame team in 1896 for a well publicized exhibition match with the New York Giants. The first pitch from Amos Rusie was hit by Sockalexis into deep center field for a home run.

The Cleveland Spiders moved fast and signed him to a major league contract. This young Indian, who seemed to have come from nowhere, apparently could run faster, throw farther and hit better than anyone. There is some doubt whether the wild war whoops that greeted Sockalexis everywhere he played were supportive or derisive, but his fame spread quickly. His noble appearance and friendly ways did make him personally popular. His exceptional baseball skills were admired by all. Many began to call the Cleveland team "the Indians." Later, of course, the name became official.

The first half of that first season, 1897, was phenomenal. Sockalexis, "Chief of Sockem," was hitting .413 by late July, and the future

couldn't have appeared brighter. However, alcohol did him in. Whether to avoid ridicule, or to have fun with his new friends, he turned to drink in increasing amounts. By the end of the season he had fallen to pieces and could no longer perform on the field. His '97 batting average ended at a respectable .338, but that did not reveal the truth.

Two more seasons of comeback attempt after comeback attempt resulted in 89 more major league at-bats and very few hits. A broken ankle hampered his running ability, but it was alcohol that ended the promise. Sockalexis drifted down through the minors (Hartford and Lowell) to various semipro teams, then to street-begging and hobo jungles, and finally back to the reservation, where his spent body gave up at the age of 42.

Belatedly, in 1934, Maine honored him with a dignified ceremony and appropriate memorial at his grave site. Today we can remember Louis Francis Sockalexis as one who might have been the greatest of all.

— Dan Hotaling

			G	R	H	BA	SA	POS	E	FA	GP	W-L	R	H
1895	Lewiston	NEng	1	1	1	.250	.500	of	0	1.00				
1896	Holy Cross	College	26	38		.444		of	8	.888				
1897	Cleveland	NL	66	43	93	.331	.452	of	16	.887				
1898	Cleveland	NL	21	11	15	.224	.254	of	1	.967				
1899	Cleveland	NL	7	0	6	.273	.318	of	2	.883				
	Hartford	EL	24	8	18	.198	.231	of	5	.918				
	Wtrbry-Brstl	Conn	61	35	85	.320	.421	of						
1902	Lowell	NEng	105	50	117	.288	.377	of	29	.800				

JOSEPH START
(Old Reliable)

Born: October 14, 1842, New York, N.Y.
Died: March 27, 1927, Providence, R.I.
BL TL 5-9, 165

Joe Start, whose 28-year playing career spanned baseball's most formative years, established the model for play at first base. He is credited with being the first at his position to play off the bag, and was known for his ability to field balls hit to him. But it was his exceptional skill at catching thrown balls (in a day when fielders played barehanded) that — together with his personal integrity — earned him the nickname "Old Reliable" before he had reached age 30.

Start played his first dozen years of organized ball in Brooklyn. After two years with the Enterprise Club, he joined the Atlantics in 1861 at age 18. In his decade with the Atlantics he helped lead them to "national" championships with undefeated seasons in 1864 and 1865. In 1870 he hit a crucial 11th-inning triple in the Atlantic victory over the great Cincinnati Red Stockings that ended Cincinnati's season and a half of undefeated play. About 1867 Start turned professional, as baseball's leading clubs gradually turned away from their roots in strict amateurism toward the fully professional game.

In 1871, when the Atlantics reverted for a year to amateur status, Start joined the New York Mutuals of the new National Association, and remained with them through 1876. When the Mutuals were expelled from the NL for failing to play the required number of games, Start signed with Hartford for a year, then with Chicago and, in 1879, with the Providence Grays, who that year won the NL pennant. He remained with Providence seven seasons until its demise, in 1884 captaining the team to a second pennant, and to victory over the New York Metropolitans in baseball's first "World Series." He ended his career in baseball at age 43, with Washington in 1886.

Though not one of baseball's great bats-

men, Start hit well above average. In professional league play he batted more than .300 six times, in four seasons finishing among the NL's top half dozen hitters. His finest year at the bat was 1878, when he hit .351 for Chicago and led the league in hits.

Fielding statistics can be variously interpreted, but Start's stats there appear to support the judgment of his contemporaries that he was one of his era's finest first basemen. In his 10 full NL seasons, for example, he finished first or second in putouts six times. Five times he was first or second among first base-

men in fielding average, and five times in chances per game. His average of nearly 10.9 putouts per game in National League play — although not listed in the Encyclopedia because he played fewer than 1,000 NL games — is higher than that of the recognized all-time leading first baseman, as is also his average of nearly 11.5 chances per game.

When Start retired from playing ball, he settled in Rhode Island, where he operated a country hotel in Lakewood, a few miles south of Providence.

— Frederick Ivor-Campbell

			G	R	H	BA	SA	POS	E	FA	GP	W-L	R	H
1860	Enterprise							1b						
1861	Enterprise		7	29		(12 outs)		1b						
1862	Atlantic													
1863	Atlantic		9	23		(26 outs)								
1864	Atlantic		18	82		(47 outs)		1b						
1865	Atlantic		18	82		(39 outs)		1b						
1866	Atlantic		16	69		(37 outs)		1b						
1867	Atlantic		19	83		(40 outs)		1b						
1868	Atlantic		53	236	233	(125")	(283TB)	1b						
1869	Atlantic		46	-	203		(341TB)	1b						
1870	Atlantic		51	-	161		(269TB)	1b						
1871	Mutual	NA	33	35	58	.360	.422	1b	29	.921				
1872	Mutual	NA	55	61	74	.264	.282	1b	25	.954				
1873	Mutual	NA	53	42	67	.266	.341	1b	18	.960				
1874	Mutual	NA	63	67	94	.306	.384	1b	29	.952				
1875	Mutual	NA	68	56	87	.282	.375	1b	36	.948				
1876	Mutual	NL	56	40	73	.277	.299	1b	21	.964				
1877	Hartford	NL	60	55	90	.332	.399	1b	27	.964				
1878	Chicago	NL	61	58	100	.351	.439	1b	33	.957				
1879	Providence	NL	66	70	101	.319	.483	1b	22	.973				
1880	Providence	NL	82	53	96	.278	.354	1b	29	.971				
1881	Providence	NL	79	56	114	.328	.397	1b	33	.963				
1882	Providence	NL	82	58	117	.329	.404	1b	25	.974				
1883	Providence	NL	87	63	105	.284	.373	1b	42	.959				
1884	Providence	NL	93	80	105	.276	.344	1b	20	.980				
1885	Providence	NL	101	47	103	.275	.326	1b	31	.972				
1886	Washington	NL	31	10	27	.221	.254	1b	10	.973				

JOHN ELMER STIVETTS
(Happy Jack)

Born: March 31, 1868, Ashland, Pa.
Died: April 18, 1930, Ashland, Pa.
BR TR 6-2, 185

An outstanding pitcher and a heavy hitter, Jack Stivetts won more than 200 games while compiling a lifetime batting average near .300. Once in 1892 he hit a extra-inning home run to win a game one day and then pitched a no-hit shutout the next day.

John Elmer Stivetts was born in the town of Ashland in the heart of the anthracite coal region of eastern Pennsylvania in 1868. Growing to a big 6-foot 2-inch height, he began his professional baseball career as a pitcher with his hometown team in the Central Pennsylvania League in 1888. Later that year he moved up to Allentown in the Central League. In 1889 he was with York in the Middle States League, where he was sensational. He won 15 of 18 games and in his last 9 games allowed only 1 earned run before his contract was purchased by the St. Louis Browns in late June.

He had plenty of speed, but his wildness kept him on the bench much of the summer as the Browns battled Brooklyn for the American Association pennant. When St. Louis fell back in the race in September, captain Charlie Comiskey put Stivetts into the rotation, and Jack won seven games in a row to aid a late charge toward the league lead. Stivetts lost a critical game on the last day of the season, but he had established himself as a big league pitcher.

In 1890 he also established himself as a big league hitter, besides becoming the workhorse of the St. Louis staff. On June 10 he won a game for himself, 9-8, with two home runs, one of them coming with the bases loaded in the ninth inning. He had another fine all-around year in 1891, winning 33 games and batting .305. But he also had some run-ins with owner Chris Von der Ahe, and with a month to go in the season he signed with Boston in the rival National League for 1892.

With the Beaneaters in '92, Stivetts enjoyed a spectacular season, winning 35 games and batting about .300. On August 5, while filling in in left field, he broke up a scoreless pitchers' duel with a 12th-inning home run. Against the same Brooklyn club the next day he pitched an 11-0 no-hitter and pounded out a double and a triple himself. On Labor Day he pitched both the morning and afternoon games against Louisville, winning 2-1 in 11 innings and 5-2 in 9 innings. On the final day of the season he tossed a 5-inning no-hitter against Washington. In the split-season championship series, Stivetts battled to a 0-0 tie in 11 innings against Cleveland's Cy Young in the opener and then went on to win his other two starts as Boston won the series in five straight decisions.

Despite his size and strength, Jack had a tendency to tire in the late going and give up lots of 9th-inning runs. And he was prone to streaks as a pitcher. The extreme example was 1894, when he lost 8 games in a row only to turn right around and win his next 11 decisions. Overall, he remained an effective

pitcher through 1896, and manager Frank Selee often called upon him to fill in in the outfield because of his big bat and his fielding ability. He was nicknamed "Happy Jack" because of his personality, although he had a well-publicized altercation with Tommy McCarthy in a Louisville hotel in 1895. Jack liked to drink, which occasionally got him into trouble, as did his habit of extending his midseason visits back to his hometown.

Stivetts strained a ligament in his forearm at the outset of 1897. By the time he recovered, he had lost his spot in the pitching rotation. He made some contributions as a substitute, both pitching and batting, but Boston finally traded him to St. Louis in August 1898. Jack refused to report and sat out the remainder of the season. He was transferred to Cleveland in 1899, but he did little, and his big salary was cut in June.

He retired from the game and returned to Ashland, where he worked as a carpenter for many years. He died there of a heart attack in 1930.

— Robert L. Tiemann

			G	R	H	BA	SA	POS	E	FA	GP	W-L	R	H
1888	Ashland	CenPa						p						
	Allentown	Cent						p			7	2-5	35	51
1889	York	MidSt						p			18	15-3		
	St. Louis	AA	27	12	18	.228	.304	p	5	.909	26	11-7	90	153
1890	St. Louis	AA	67	36	65	.288	.500	p-of	17	.901	54	27-20	248	399
1891	St. Louis	AA	85	45	92	.305	.421	p-of	17	.906	64	33-22	197	357
1892	Boston	NL	70	40	72	.301	.410	p-of	14	.926	53	35-16	221	349
1893	Boston	NL	49	32	51	.297	.448	p-of	8	.917	39	20-12	196	315
1894	Boston	NL	68	56	82	.336	.545	p-of	12	.891	45	22-15	289	429
1895	Boston	NL	46	20	32	.210	.296	p	3	.961	38	17-17	213	341
1896	Boston	NL	67	44	78	.353	.471	p-of	15	.911	42	22-14	223	353
1897	Boston	NL	61	43	76	.388	.571	of-p	6	.937	18	11-4	74	147
1898	Boston	NL	41	16	28	.252	.333	of-lb	8	.931	2	0-1	12	17
1899	Cleveland	NL	18	8	7	.171	.195	of-p	2	.935	7	0-4	44	48

HARRY DUFFIELD STOVEY

Born: December 20, 1856, Philadelphia, Pa.
Died: September 20, 1937, New Bedford, Mass.
BR TR 5-11 ½, 180

Harry Stovey was baseball's premier power hitter during the 1880s, but he was a complete ballplayer. Beginning as a pitcher, he showed some early success, but spent most of his major league career in the outfield and at first base. He was a hard hitter, clever baserunner, and excellent fielder, noted for his sure hands, strong and accurate arm and vast range. The SABR 19th Century Committee voted him the player of his era most deserving of Hall-of-Fame recognition who has not yet received it.

Born Harry Stow, he changed his name to prevent his mother from learning that he was playing ball. He began his amateur career as pitcher for the Defiance Club of his native Philadelphia in 1877.

He made his professional debut with the Philadelphia Athletics September 4, 1877, besting Chicago 6-5. He completed that season with several more solid pitching performances for the A's.

In 1878 Stovey was signed by Frank Bancroft of New Bedford of the International Association. He played first base and outfield and did some pitching for two seasons there. On October 15, 1879, in a game against Fall River, he had 7 hits: a home run, a triple, 3 doubles and a pair of singles.

He followed Bancroft to Worcester, and began his 14-year major league career there in 1880. He split his time between first base and the outfield and played the entire, albeit short, history of the Worcester franchise. As a rookie he showed his budding power by leading the NL in triples and home runs.

Stovey moved to Philadelphia of the rival AA in 1883 for the beginning of a seven-year stint there. He signaled his arrival and the success to come by again leading his league in home runs, winning the "Gold Glove" at first base, and helping his team to the pennant.

At Philadelphia, he blossomed into one of the game's finest hitters. His greatest hitting season came in 1884. He led the AA in hits, doubles, home runs, runs scored, batting average (.404), slugging average (.648), and total bases. Although RBI figures are not available, this was a Triple Crown-class year. His slugging average of .648 was baseball's first over .600 and some 58 points higher than had ever been achieved before. He had 3 triples in one game on August 18, 1884, 2 in one inning. Throughout his time at Philadelphia, he continued to excel in the field and as a baserunner.

Stovey went to Boston for the PL's sole season, and helped his club to the pennant. He finished second in the league home run chase, and led in steals with 97.

He moved back to the NL in 1891 and rounded out his career with three seasons split among Boston, Baltimore and Brooklyn. In 1891 his Boston club won the pennant. That year he set a less-than-honorable record, striking out five times in one game. He led the league that season with 69 whiffs.

During his major league career he played for six teams in three leagues, and was on a pennant-winner in each league. His impressive hitting statistics include league-leading efforts in batting average, hits (twice), doubles, triples (four times), home runs (six times), runs scored (four times), and slugging (three times). He also led in steals one year, and is credited with being the first player to wear sliding pads. He made 5 hits in a game five times. He was the leading home run hitter for the decade of the 1880s with 90. He was the first player to lead two leagues in home runs, and narrowly missed a third. The first man to hit 20 triples in a season, his 25 in 1885 still ranks 14th on the all-time list. During his career, he scored an amazing 1,494 runs in 1,488 games, which rates third on the all-time list for runs scored per game.

After baseball, Harry Stovey returned to New Bedford, Massachusetts, where he became a policeman. He died there in 1937.

— John Richmond Husman

			G	R	H	BA	SA	POS	E	FA	GP	W-L	R	H
1877	Athletic		24	28	34	—	—	p	—	—				
1878	New Bedford		81	52	90	.257		1b	48	.948				
1879	New Bedford	NA	47		-	.287		1b						
1880	Worcester	NL	83	76	94	.265	.454	of-1b	35	.938	2	0-0	3	8
1881	Worcester	NL	75	57	92	.270	.402	of-1b	32	.950				
1882	Worcester	NL	94	90	104	.289	.422	of-1b	45	.928				
1883	Athletic	AA	94	110	148	.352	.565	1b	27	.963	1	0-0	3	5
1884	Athletic	AA	106	126	179	.404	.648	1b	32	.972				
1885	Athletic	AA	112	130	164	.342	.525	1b-of	42	.958				
1886	Athletic	AA	123	115	154	.317	.467	1b-of	39	.954	1	0-0	3	2
1887	Athletic	AA	124	124	219	.402	.527	of-1b	35	.949				
1888	Athletic	AA	130	128	171	.318	.481	of-1b	10	.957				
1889	Athletic	AA	138	154	180	.330	.553	of	32	.911				
1890	Boston	PL	118	140	148	.308	.481	of	13	.942				
1891	Boston	NL	134	118	152	.279	.499	of	23	.910				
1892	Bos-Baltimore	NL	112	79	101	.235	.371	of	24	.923				
1893	Balt-Brooklyn	NL	56	47	49	.244	.363	of	16	.893				

THEODORE P. SULLIVAN

Born: County Clare, Ireland, 1851 (?)
Died: July 5, 1929, Washington, D.C.

Theodore P. Sullivan, or more usually "T.P." or "Ted" Sullivan, was a player, manager, owner, league organizer and promoter from the late 1870s until well into the 20th century.

Probably born in Ireland about 1851, his family immigrated to the United States in 1860. He spent much of his childhood in Milwaukee and then attended St. Louis University and St. Mary's College of Kansas.

When he was a senior at St. Mary's he played on the college baseball team with freshman Charles Comiskey. After college, Sullivan was a railroad news agent in Dubuque, Iowa. In 1878 he organized an independent team he called the Dubuque Rabbits and signed Comiskey to his first professional contract. In 1879, Sullivan organized the Northwestern League, considered by some historians as the first minor league, to provide steady opposition for his club. Sullivan's Dubuque club had Comiskey and several stars back and added future Hall of Famer Charles Radbourne to pitch. The Dubuque club crushed all opposition and the league folded in July. It was in Dubuque that Sullivan taught Comiskey to play off the bag and stretch for throws to first base. This style of first base play helped Comiskey gain great fame and success.

In 1883 Sullivan joined the St. Louis Browns of the American Association as manager and assistant to eccentric owner Chris Von der Ahe. The stay was successful (53-26) but tumultuous and brief. It was here that Sullivan coined the word "fan," a fact certified by the *Oxford English Dictionary*. Sullivan thought the baseball fanatics who bothered him constantly with opinions and suggestions on baseball matters deserved a name of their own, thus "fans."

In 1884 Sullivan played a key role in acquiring players for the Union Association and managed the St. Louis entry to 20 consecutive wins to start the season. Later that season he managed and was financially involved in the Kansas City club.

In later years Sullivan organized, promoted and placed teams in a score of leagues. He is known to have played key roles in the organization of the first Western League, several Eastern and Southern Leagues and several revivals of the Texas League.

Sullivan seems to have profited adequately from his baseball ventures. He claimed, for instance, in August 1892 to have cleared $8,000 already that season in a year when many were claiming major losses.

Sullivan was a master at locating young talent, and parlayed that ability plus an uncommon flair for innovation and promotion into a 40-year career in professional baseball. Among the ideas Sullivan synthesized, if not originated, was Ladies Day in order to increase "respectable" attendance at games. Sullivan was also involved in at least one early attempt to play baseball at night under electric lights. At least one of Sullivan's ideas, however, went unappreciated. *Sporting Life* called Sullivan "a queer genius" for advocating sending only 8 men to the plate and not letting pitchers bat because they are a lot of whippoorwill swingers.

Sullivan was involved in several efforts to promote baseball in Europe. He also attempted to import professional English football to the United States in 1894 but the operation was unsuccessful.

Sullivan worked a number of years for the Chicago White Sox, owned by his old discovery Charles Comiskey. Sullivan was managing director of Comiskey's White Sox-Giants World Tour of 1913-14.

Sullivan wrote a book about that tour called *History of World's Tour* (1914). Other literary works based on Sullivan's many years in baseball included *Humorous Stories* (1903) and several plays.

Sullivan died in Washington, D.C., in July 1929.

— Harold Dellinger

		G	R	H	BA	SA	POS	E	FA	GP	W-L	R	H
1884	Kansas City UA	4	2	4	.333	.333	o-s-p	5	.545	1	0-1	17	15

In several other seasons, Sullivan played a few games for the team he managed.

WILLIAM ASHLEY SUNDAY
(Billy)

Born: November 18, 1862, Ames, Iowa
Died: November 6, 1935, Chicago, Ill.
BL TR 5-10, 160

During his eight-year tenure in the NL, Billy Sunday became widely known as a fair batter (.248 in 499 games), a first-rate outfielder and the fastest man on spikes. In five seasons with Chicago he played on two pennant winners, and performed capably in playoffs against the AA St. Louis Browns (1885 and 1886). Yet "the famous sprinter with the sabbatical name" remains best known for his post-playing career. For, having had a Christian conversion experience in 1887, he went on to become one of the most noted evangelists in American history.

Billy was the last of three sons born to William and Mary Jane Sunday. His father, a Union soldier in the Civil War, was killed only weeks after Billy's birth. The impoverished widow sent her sons to homes for soldiers' orphans in Glenwood, then in Davenport, Iowa. Leaving in his mid-teens, Sunday worked in Nevada, Iowa, first in a hotel, then doing farm labor. Meanwhile he attended the local high school, working as a janitor. His subsequent move to Marshalltown (Ia.) brought not only a furniture store job but a place on the local ball team — where he caught the attention of fellow Iowan (and Chicago player-manager) Cap Anson. By 1883, Sunday was a baby-faced rookie in the White Stockings outfield.

How good was Billy Sunday as a ballplayer? The best assessment came from Al Spalding: "People love to see him run." In no season with Chicago did his weak bat appear in more than 50 games, but blinding speed made him an important weapon. In 1887, *Boston Herald* readers placed him behind King Kelly and Monte Ward as the League's best baserunners. Sunday could reputedly round the bases in 14 seconds flat. A match race with the vaunted Arlie Latham attracted national attention. Sunday won. Fans remembered him winning a game by stealing second, third and home on successive pitches. But only after leaving Chicago did Sunday become an everyday player, stealing 71 bases for Pittsburgh ('88) and a career-high 84 with Pittsburgh and Philadelphia in his final season, 1890.

Moreover, Sunday worked hard on his defensive game. With discipline, his speed became a marvelous asset. He had fielded a primitive .663 in 1884, but four seasons later it was .939 as he led his peers in putouts and total chances per game. In 1890 he paced the league's outfielders in double plays. His play in the field was magnetic.

It was during the 1887 season, however, that the course of his life was changed. On a Sunday afternoon he sat, "tanked up," with friends at the corner of State and Madison streets in Chicago. Across the street a gospel troupe appeared, playing instruments and singing hymns Sunday remembered from his childhood. Beginning to sob, Sunday arose and followed them to the Pacific Garden Mission, addressing his pals, "Goodbye boys, I'm through. I'm going to Jesus Christ. We've come to a parting of the ways."

Although he continued to play ball through 1890, he refused Sunday games, shunned drinking, smoking, cards and the theater, and passed his free time giving inspirational talks at local YMCA chapters. In 1888 he married Helen (Nell) Thompson, a solid Presbyterian woman of Chicago, and she bore him four children. Finally, in the spring of 1891, aged 28, Billy Sunday announced his retirement from baseball to enter full-time Christian work.

He began at the Chicago "Y," but then worked as advance agent and occasional preacher for a traveling ministry. By early 1896, Billy Sunday was on his own. He moved from Midwest small towns to large cities within a decade, in meetings held in specially-built tabernacles, holding up to 15,000. Sunday's peak of popularity came in the decade 1910-1920 (notably in New York City, 1917), as he revisited the great NL cities.

On April 17, 1911, in Toledo, he preached the funeral service for 31-year-old hurler Addie Joss, who had died of tubercular meningitis. The famed evangelist never lost his interest in baseball, even though he remained strongly opposed to playing ball on the Sabbath. He made a great hit as guest umpire at semipro games in various cities where he was preaching.

In his preaching, as befit his background, Billy Sunday was athletic and dramatic, earthy and colorful. Sermons were filled with baseball language: the "fastball at the devil," the sinners "dying on second or third base," the "rally" for Christ and country. Some accused Sunday of being intolerant, some of being too theatrical, some materialistic (although his crusades raised a fortune for charities). But he was always uniquely himself. And in the end, his potent message rang more decisively across America than any ball he struck on the diamond.

— James D. Smith, III
and L. Robert Davids

			G	R	H	BA	SA	POS		E	FA	GP	W-L	R	H
1883	Chicago	NL	14	6	13	.241	.315	of		5	.706				
1884	Chicago	NL	43	25	39	.222	.324	of		27	.662				
1885	Chicago	NL	46	36	44	.256	.343	of		11	.825				
1886	Chicago	NL	28	16	25	.243	.291	of		5	.914				
1887	Chicago	NL	50	41	79	.359	.455	of		25	.766				
1888	Pittsburgh	NL	120	69	119	.236	.275	of		21	.939				
1889	Pittsburgh	NL	81	62	77	.240	.321	of		10	.946				
1890	Pitts-Phil	NL	117	84	127	.265	.309	of		29	.908	1	0-0	2	2

EZRA BALLOU SUTTON

Born: September 17, 1850, Palmyra, N.Y.
Died: June 20, 1907, Braintree, Mass.
BR TR 5-8 ½, 153

Ezra Ballou Sutton was perhaps the best third baseman who played in the 19th century. He played all five years of the National Association and then for another 13 years in the National League (1876-1888), compiling a lifetime .296 batting average including a .327 average during his NA days.

Sutton was born in Palmyra, N.Y., on September 17, 1850. He played with amateur clubs in nearby Rochester before joining the Forest City club of Cleveland in 1870. The Cleveland nine was a charter member of the NA, and Sutton happened to be the first player to homer in a championship game. Later in the same game (May 8, 1871) he also hit the second home run in NA history. In late July and early August, he had a string of three consecutive games in which he hit two triples each.

In 1873, he joined the Athletics where he continued his reputation as an outstanding right-handed hitter with a strong throwing arm, which was termed "remarkable for its swiftness and accuracy," by the *New York Clipper*. The *Clipper* also called Sutton "one of the best baserunners" in the game (twice he scored more than 100 runs in a season). *Sporting Life* noted him as being "a grand and scientific batsman, and especially apt in judging and catching foul flies."

His throwing abilities not only earned him respect in America, but also in England. During a visit there with the Athletic and Boston clubs in 1874, Sutton placed second in a throwing contest by tossing a ball 366 feet.

An injury to his right arm in 1876 forced Sutton to play a majority of his games at first base with the Athletics. Throughout his career, Sutton filled in occasionally at shortstop, second base, first base and the outfield. On June 14, 1876, Sutton placed his name in the record book when he and teammate George Hall became the first players to hit three triples in one NL game.

Sutton's injury improved in 1877, which saw him move on to the Boston Red Stockings (NL) where he played out his major league career. During his time in Boston, Sutton tied for the league lead in hits in 1884 with 162 and led the league that season in fielding percentage for third basemen with a .908 mark. He also paced all third basemen in double plays in 1885 with 13. Additionally, Sutton placed third in runs batted in in 1877 with 39 and in batting average (.346) in 1884.

While good fortune showered Sutton during his playing career, it did not follow him in his life after leaving the diamond. A sawmill business he retired to in Palmyra failed. His wife died January 11, 1906, six weeks after a lamp explosion in their home set her dress afire causing her severe burns.

Sutton died on June 20, 1907 in Braintree, Massachusetts, after suffering from paralysis of his limbs since 1890.

— Richard A. Puff

			G	R	H	BA	SA	POS	E	FA	GP	W-L	R	H
1870	ForCtyCleveland							3b						
1871	ForCtyClev	NA	29	35	45	.352	.547	3b	27	.779				
1872	ForCtyClev	NA	21	30	30	.288	.375	3b	27	.748				
1873	Athletic	NA	51	51	81	.335	.421	3b-ss	57	.790				
1874	Athletic	NA	55	54	72	.295	.352	3b-ss	49	.813				
1875	Athletic	NA	75	83	116	.324	.399	3b	78	.799				
1876	Athletic	NL	54	45	70	.297	.419	1-2-3	59	.882				
1877	Boston	NL	58	43	74	.292	.379	ss-3b	34	.872				
1878	Boston	NL	60	31	54	.226	.301	3b	25	.888				
1879	Boston	NL	84	54	84	.249	.311	ss-3b	47	.864				
1880	Boston	NL	76	41	72	.250	.295	ss-3b	35	.893				
1881	Boston	NL	83	43	97	.291	.348	3b	38	.877				
1882	Boston	NL	81	44	80	.251	.301	3b	41	.856				
1883	Boston	NL	94	101	134	.324	.478	3b	41	.872				
1884	Boston	NL	110	102	162	.346	.455	3b	31	.908				
1885	Boston	NL	110	78	143	.313	.420	3b-ss	53	.878				
1886	Boston	NL	116	83	138	.277	.357	o-s-3	53	.873				
1887	Boston	NL	77	58	112	.330	.451	s-o-2	58	.877				
1888	Boston	NL	28	16	24	.218	.291	3b	13	.859				
	Rochester	IA	50	34	61	.289	.390	3b	22	.894				
1889	Milwaukee	WA	87	88	105	.307		2b-3b	30	.920				

CHARLES J. SWEENEY

Born: April 13, 1863, San Francisco, Ca.
Died: April 4, 1902, San Francisco, Ca.
BR TR 160

On June 7, 1884, 21-year-old Charlie Sweeney reached the high point of his one brilliant season when he struck out 19 Boston batsmen, pitching Providence to a 2-1 win and an edge over Boston for first place in the National League. His strikeout total established a major league record for a single game that lasted until 1986.

Sweeney began playing ball in his native San Francisco, but first gained attention as a pitcher in Eureka, Nevada, in 1882. He went east that same year and played one game in the outfield for Providence. The next season he became a big-league pitcher. Although Sweeney's won-lost record with Providence in 1883 was only 7-7, Frank Bancroft, the club's new manager, decided to alternate him in the box in 1884 with Providence ace Charlie Radbourn. Reports of Sweeney's dominance pitching winter ball in California confirmed Bancroft in his decision.

After a strong preseason in 1884, Sweeney matched Radbourn's record for the first few weeks of the regular season before dropping out of the two-man rotation with a sore arm.

He recovered by mid-July, but then his drinking and hot temper brought him down.

On July 22 he reported for practice late and hung over, then walked off the field during the game in a dispute with manager Bancroft. Under the rules of the day, Providence had to complete the game with only eight men, and lost what had earlier seemed a sure victory. That evening Sweeney was expelled from the club and from the National League.

He signed immediately with St. Louis, in the outlaw Union Association. There, he was deprived by UA rules of the overhand pitching that had made him so overpowering in the NL and his earned run average slipped a bit, from 1.55 to 1.83. But he won 24 games in his half season with St. Louis, losing only 7, for an overall season record of 41-15. His pitching helped both Providence and St. Louis win their league championships.

When St. Louis was admitted to the NL in 1885 after the demise of the Union Association, Sweeney's eligibility to play in the league was restored. His arm, however, had not recovered from the strain of pitching 60

games the previous year. He pitched in fewer than half the 71 games he played in 1885 (the rest of the time he played outfield), winning only 11. The next year he pitched only 11 games, winning 5.

Although Sweeney rested his sore elbow by not pitching in California that winter, his arm did not recover. Signed by Cleveland (AA) for 1887, he ended his major league career primarily as an infielder. He lost the only three games he pitched, and was vilified in the press for his public drunkenness and for assaulting another player.

Sweeney returned home to California, where he pitched occasionally, but his drinking and temper continued to plague him. In 1894 he shot and killed an abusive acquaintance in a San Francisco barroom. He pleaded self-defense, but was convicted of manslaughter and sentenced to 10 years imprisonment. Although he was released before the completion of his term, he had contracted tuberculosis. He died a few days short of his thirty-ninth birthday.

— Frederick Ivor-Campbell

			G	R	H	BA	SA	POS	E	FA	GP	W-L	R	H
1881	S.F.Athletics	Cal						p						
1882	Providence	NL	1	0	0	.000	.000	of	1	.500				
1883	S.F.Niantic	Cal												
	Providence	NL	22	9	19	.218	.241	p-of	13	.847	20	7-7	92	142
1884	Providence	NL	41	24	50	.298	.369	p-of	6	.930	27	17-8	70	153
	St. Louis	UA	45	31	54	.316	.439	p-of	8	.934	33	24-7	91	207
1885	St. Louis	NL	73	28	56	.207	.237	of-p	27	.846	35	11-21	167	276
1886	St. Louis	NL	17	4	16	.250	.281	p-o-s	11	.766	11	5-6	72	108
	Syracuse	IL	3								2	0-2	21	20
	S.F.Haverly	Cal												
1887	Cleveland	AA	36	22	30	.226	.316	1b-of	16	.916	3	0-3	36	42
	SFHav-A&GStk	Cal	35	37	40	.249	.259	3b-of	34	.754				
1888	A&G Stockton	Cal	67	51	76	.272		ss-1b	51	.883				
1889	Stckn-SF	Cal	88	57	95	.274		2b-1b	46	.930				
1890	SF-Oakl	Cal	57	44	61	.235	.299	1b	21	.951				
1892	Oakland	Cal	9	4	7	.189	.216	1b	2	.981				

OLIVER WENDELL TEBEAU
(Patsy)

Born: December 5, 1864, St. Louis, Mo.
Died: May 15, 1918, St. Louis, Mo.
BR TR 5-8, 163

Player-manager for the strong Cleveland Spider teams of the 1890s was Patsy Tebeau. His obituary notes that he "was generally known as a guardian of the initial cushion," although he played almost as much at third base. He was especially known as a fighter and inspirational leader. His brother, George "White Wings" Tebeau, also played in the majors and was with Pat in Cleveland in 1894-95. The Cleveland *Plain Dealer* obituary gives Tebeau's name as Oliver Patrick and hence conflicts with the Macmillan *Encyclopedia* on this.

Tebeau first appeared in the majors as a reserve for the Chicago White Stockings in 1887. He hit only .162, however, and went down to the minors. Cleveland bought him from Omaha for 1889. He originally was a third baseman, switching to first in 1893. He joined the rebel Cleveland (PL) in 1890, finishing the season as its manager. He returned to the Spiders the following year, and after being injured early in the season, took over the helm in July when Bob Leadley was fired. The Spiders, who had such notables as Cupid Childs, Ed McKean, Jesse Burkett and pitchers Cy Young, Nig Cuppy and John Clarkson,

soon became contenders under Tebeau's leadership.

In 1892 a championship series between the split-season winners was played. Cleveland faced Boston (which had the best record overall), and after the opener ended in an 11-inning scoreless tie, the Beaneaters swept all five of the remaining games. After finishing third in 1893 and sixth in 1894, the second-place Spiders were in the Temple Cup series in 1895 against the notorious Baltimore Orioles. Led by Cy Young's three victories, the Spiders won the cup, four games to one.

In 1896 Tebeau was fined for assaulting an umpire but took the case to court and won on the ground that he was denied due process. Cleveland again finished second, but was swept four straight by Baltimore in the Series. Tebeau had winning seasons the next two years. He then moved to St. Louis in 1899, when the Robison brothers bought that team and took all their good players with them. Tebeau stayed with the St. Louis team that year and most of the next, retiring from baseball to go into the saloon business. On May 15, 1918, he was found dead by suicide in his saloon, a revolver tied to his right wrist. The

body was returned to Cleveland for burial.

As a player, Tebeau must be regarded as mediocre. His lifetime BA of .280 is only about three points above the league average. He had little extra-base power (his slugging average was only .343). He led the league in some defensive categories as a third baseman in 1890 and as a first baseman in 1896-98, but there is nothing exceptional there. His main claim to fame is as a manager, and in that capacity he was one of the best of his day. His teams had a .560 won-lost average, and he had losing seasons only in his first and last years in the National League. After the great Baltimore Orioles and Boston Beaneaters, his Spiders were as good as anyone in the league. Indicative of Tebeau's managerial attitude is the quotation, "Show me a team of fighters, and I'll show you a team that has a chance." His teams paralleled the Orioles for aggressiveness (or nastiness, if you wish). He was a fighter of the McGraw-Durocher-Stanky mold, an indefatigable umpire-baiter, and an on-the-field brawler who would probably make Billy Martin look tame.

— William McMahon

			G	R	H	BA	SA	POS	E	FA	GP	W-L	R	H
1886	St. Joseph	WL	-	81	85	.294		2b	57	.875				
1887	Denver	WL	95	112	205	.424	.552	3b	47	.884				
	Chicago	NL	20	8	15	.208	.236	3b	10	.868				
1888	Mpls-Omaha	WA	89	46	86	.259	.428	3b	41	.895				
1889	Cleveland	NL	136	72	147	.282	.390	3b	54	.897				
1890	Cleveland	PL	110	86	135	.300	.418	3b	66	.872				
1891	Cleveland	NL	61	38	68	.261	.329	3b	33	.884				
1892	Cleveland	NL	86	47	83	.244	.318	3b	25	.911				
1893	Cleveland	NL	116	90	160	.329	.440	1b-3b	41	.953				
1894	Cleveland	NL	125	82	158	.302	.390	1b	26	.977				
1895	Cleveland	NL	63	50	84	.318	.405	1b-2b	8	.987				
1896	Cleveland	NL	132	56	146	.269	.343	1b	21	.985	1	0-0	0	1
1897	Cleveland	NL	109	62	110	.267	.347	1b-2b	9	.991				
1898	Cleveland	NL	131	53	123	.258	.304	1b-2b	26	.979				
1899	St. Louis	NL	77	27	69	.246	.313	1b-ss	22	.971				
1900	St. Louis	NL	1	0	0	.000	.000	ss	3	.700				

FRED TENNEY

Born: November 26, 1871, Georgetown, Mass.
Died: July 3, 1952, Boston, Mass.
BL TL 5-9, 155

Fred Tenney came perilously close to being the first of a long line of highly-touted college stars who flopped in the majors.

Although he batted .327 during his first three seasons after moving directly from Brown University to the majors in 1894, Tenney couldn't find a position. A left-handed catcher, he "proved a serious frost as a backstop," so he was shifted to the outfield, but "was nothing much as a gardener," according to A.H. Spink.

Early in 1897 (Tenney's fourth season), Boston manager Frank Selee had a flash. He replaced slow-footed veteran Tom Tucker at first base with Tenney, completing what may have been the best fielding infield of the 19th century (Tenney, second baseman Bobby Lowe, third baseman Jimmy Collins and shortstop Herman Long).

Tenney quickly became the "wonder and admiration of the league," stretching for throws and ranging farther from the bag than

any first baseman had before. "Tenney's actions are catlike," reported the Chicago *News.* "It is worth the price of admission to watch him play the bag." Tenney's specialty was the 3-6-3 double play, a trick he first turned June 14, 1897, against Cincinnati.

Tenney batted .325 and .334 respectively as Boston cruised to NL titles in 1897 and 1898. He hit .347 the following season, but his hitting declined with Boston's fortunes and the introduction of the foul strike rule as the new century dawned. Still, Tenney remained a fixture in Boston, outlasting all his championship teammates and serving as manager from 1905 through 1907. His baserunning ability and bat control made him a perfect second-place hitter.

The teams he managed were bad, finishing seventh, eighth and seventh, but the Boston owners promised Tenney a bonus if they made money and he obliged, reportedly scrambling into the stands to rescue base-

balls. After failing to put together a group to buy the Boston franchise in 1906, Tenney brokered the sale in 1907 and wound up with a share of the team himself. However, his relationship with the new principal owners, the Dovey brothers, deteriorated and he was fired as manager after the 1907 season. In December he was traded to the New York Giants.

After two injury-plagued seasons in New York (his absence from the lineup set up Fred Merkle's date with immortality), he played for Lowell of the New England League before taking the reins of the Boston Nationals again in 1911. After another eighth-place finish, Tenney retired to the shoe business. He managed Newark (International) in 1916, then entered the insurance business, where he prospered until his death in 1952.

— Bob Richardson

			G	R	H	BA	SA	POS	E	FA	GP	W-L	R	H
1892	Binghamton	EL	1	0	1	.250	.250	of	1	1.00				
1894	Boston	NL	27	23	34	.395	.570	c-of	11	.885				
1895	Boston	NL	49	35	47	.272	.353	of-c	7	.950				
	New Bedford	NEng	1	1	3	.750	1.00	of	0					
1896	Springfield	EL	13	9	22	.373	.492	1b-of	7	.937				
	Boston	NL	88	64	117	.336	.411	of-c	16	.932				
1897	Boston	NL	132	125	180	.318	.376	1b	16	.988				
1898	Boston	NL	117	107	163	.335	.409	1b	21	.982				
1899	Boston	NL	150	115	209	.347	.439	1b	38	.976				
1900	Boston	NL	112	77	122	.279	.339	1b	19	.983				
1901	Boston	NL	115	66	127	.282	.322	1b	28	.976				
1902	Boston	NL	134	88	154	.315	.376	1b	22	.984				
1903	Boston	NL	122	79	140	.313	.396	1b	33	.974				
1904	Boston	NL	147	76	144	.270	.341	1b	23	.986				
1905	Boston	NL	149	84	158	.288	.332	1b	32	.982	1	0-0	1	5
1906	Boston	NL	143	61	154	.283	.340	1b	28	.983				
1907	Boston	NL	150	83	151	.273	.334	1b	19	.989				
1908	New York	NL	156	101	149	.256	.304	1b	18	.990				
1909	New York	NL	101	43	88	.235	.291	1b	16	.986				
1910	Lowell	NEng	96	48	91	.268	.324	1b	11	.989				
1911	Boston	NL	102	52	97	.263	.328	1b	15	.985				
1916	Newark	IL	16	0	7	.318	.318	1b	0	1.00				

MICHAEL JOSEPH TIERNAN
(Silent Mike)

Born: January 21, 1867, Trenton, N.J.
Died: November 9, 1918, New York, N.Y.
BL TL 5-11, 165

On May 12, 1890, the New York Giants, with Amos Rusie pitching, and the Boston team with Kid Nichols on the mound, were hooked up in a scoreless stalemate in a game that went into extra innings. With 24 zeroes on the scoreboard and one out in the top of the 13th frame, Silent Mike Tiernan strode to the plate and knocked a long home run to win the drawn-out battle between the NL teams.

Such dramatic exploits were numerous during the career of Tiernan, an outfielder and slugger of great stature in baseball before the turn of the century.

On June 15, 1887, Tiernan scored 6 runs in a game between New York and Philadelphia in the Giants' home park. This feat has been equaled several times in NL history but never surpassed. To accomplish this, Silent Mike had 2 triples, 3 singles and 1 base on balls. The final score was New York 29, Philadelphia 1.

A reporter at the game wrote that "Harry Wright, the Philadelphia manager, was frantic. He watched the defeat of his pupils with feelings of disgust and when the last man was out, he breathed a long sigh, placed his spectacles in a case, walked to the elevated station with a measured tread, hid in a remote corner of the forward car and communed with himself all the way downtown."

Tiernan was born in Trenton, New Jersey, across the street from Trenton State Prison. He played on the Athletic Juniors team as a youth. He also was a gifted ice skater and trackman, running the 100 yard dash in 9.9 seconds.

He was called Silent Mike because he disliked publicity and always maintained silence and reserve on the field even when he disagreed with the umpire.

Tiernan began his baseball career as a pitcher at age 17 with the Williamsport (Pa.) town team in 1884. In one exhibition game against the Providence NL club, he whiffed 15, earning the praises of Providence manager Frank Bancroft. Later in the season, he pitched a shocking win over the Philadelphia NL team. Acquired by the New York Giants before the 1887 season, Tiernan refused to sign because he preferred the outfield to the mound and New York wanted to engage his services as a pitcher. The Giants finally relented and sent Tiernan to the outfield, and he was a fixture there for more than a dozen years.

In his initial season with the Giants, at age 20, Mike batted a sparkling .340 and quickly gained respect for his excellent fielding and baserunning.

His best year with the bat was in 1896, when he hit at a .361 clip. In 1889, he was the NL league leader in runs scored with 146 and in 1891 led the league in home runs with 17, an impressive number in the days when the ball was dead as a doornail. In 1890 and again in 1891, Mike topped the league in slugging percentage. During his career, he amassed 449 stolen bases, including 56 in 1890 and 54 in 1891.

After retiring from baseball, Tiernan owned a cafe in New York City. He died on November 9, 1918 at age 51, a victim of tuberculosis.

His obituary in *The New York Times* noted: "In the early days of the Giants, the name Mike Tiernan was on the lips of every baseball fan and to this day old timers talk about the long drives he hit in Harlem."

— Randy Linthurst

			G	R	H	BA	SA	POS	E	FA	GP	W-L	R	H
1884	Chambersburg	Keyst												
1885	Trenton	EL	89	53	84	.238	.319	p-of	22	.893	42	17-18	233	234
1886	Jersey City	EL	85	85	123	.332	.491	of-p	16	.900	14	6-4	65	116
1887	New York	NL	103	81	149	.340	.479	of	25	.865	5	1-2	24	40
1888	New York	NL	113	75	130	.293	.411	of	8	.960				
1889	New York	NL	122	146	167	.335	.489	of	23	.896				
1890	New York	NL	133	132	168	.304	.495	of	26	.896				
1891	New York	NL	134	111	166	.306	.500	of	18	.897				
1892	New York	NL	116	80	134	.297	.404	of	18	.905				
1893	New York	NL	125	114	158	.309	.481	of	15	.927				
1894	New York	NL	112	87	121	.282	.429	of	13	.933				
1895	New York	NL	120	128	168	.353	.527	of	12	.940				
1896	New York	NL	133	132	190	.361	.504	of	8	.964				
1897	New York	NL	129	123	177	.331	.453	of	12	.942				
1898	New York	NL	103	89	118	.286	.408	of	2	.986				
1899	New York	NL	36	17	35	.250	.307	of	3	.939				
1900	Derby	ConnSt	18	9	17	.243	.314	of	7	.800				

THOMAS JOSEPH TUCKER
(Tommy)

Born: October 28, 1863, Holyoke, Mass.
Died: October 22, 1935, Montague, Mass.
BB TR 5-11, 165

Tommy Tucker was a fancy-fielding first baseman who hit for average but not with much power in a 13-year major league career (1887-1899).

Tucker started his career down the road from his hometown, with Springfield in the Massachusetts State Association in 1884. The league disbanded on August 23, and no records are available. In 1885 and 1886 he played at Newark in the Eastern League, batting .222 and .265 while fielding .969 and .963. In 1887 he began a 13-year stay in the major leagues, after which he had three more minor league campaigns, first with Springfield of the Eastern League in 1900, then two years in the Connecticut League with New London and Meriden, where he was the manager in 1902, finishing in a tie for sixth place.

Though he never batted better than .279 in the minor leagues, Tucker was a fairly good hitter in the major leagues. He batted over .300 four times, with a high of .372 in 1889 with Baltimore (AA). He also hit .330 in 1894, .304 in

1896 with Boston (NL) and .333 in 93 games for Washington and four with Boston in 1897.

By far his best year with the bat was 1889. He led in batting with .372 and in hits with 196, was third in slugging at .484, and fourth in total bases with 255.

Basically a singles hitter who was adept at being hit by pitches, Tucker batted first or second in the order during his early years. His aggressive baserunning led to numerous altercations with opponents, and his kicking aggravated many an umpire. Although generally popular with the fans because of his humorous fulminations on the coaching lines, Tommy suffered a broken cheekbone on July 17, 1894, when he was assaulted by spectators in Philadelphia. Extra police kept order at the park the next day, but Tucker was again assaulted on the ride back to the hotel.

During the decade of the 1890s, his defensive performance stacked up this way, as compared to Hall-of-Fame first baseman Jake Beckley: Tucker led in games played, 1,281 to

1,263 for Beckley; in putouts, 12,534 to 12,384. His 598 assists were second only to Beckley's 746. He had 278 errors, 10 more than Jake, and 13,410 total chances, 12 more than Beckley. Tucker's fielding average was .979, about mid-point with others of his era.

Tucker was versatile enough to play 20 games in the outfield and even pitched a couple of times with no record. He was noted for his speed, ranking high on the all-time list of base stealers from his period, with 352 thefts in his career. His best year was his rookie season with Baltimore, when he pilfered 85.

He led the American Association in batting in 1889 with a .372 average — highest ever for a switch hitter. He went 6 for 6 (5 singles and a double) off Ehret and Rhines of Cincinnati on July 15, 1897. He scored more than 100 runs five different years. He led the league in being hit by pitches five times, and accumulated at least 270 for his career.

— Al Glynn and L. Robert Davids

			G	R	H	BA	SA	POS	E	FA	GP	W-L	R	H
1884	Springfield	Conn						1b						
1885	Newark	EL	22	7	18	.222	.284	1b	6	.969				
1886	Newark	EL	94	60	103	.281	.357	1b	29	.981				
1887	Baltimore	AA	136	114	174	.315	.408	1b	35	.976				
1888	Baltimore	AA	136	74	152	.291	.404	1b	36	.975	1	0-0	1	4
1889	Baltimore	AA	134	101	198	.375	.487	1b	41	.967				
1890	Boston	NL	132	104	159	.295	.362	1b	29	.979				
1891	Boston	NL	140	103	149	.273	.330	1b	34	.975	1	0-0	2	3
1892	Boston	NL	149	85	153	.282	.341	1b	40	.974				
1893	Boston	NL	121	83	138	.284	.362	1b	27	.979				
1894	Boston	NL	123	112	165	.330	.420	1b	19	.984				
1895	Boston	NL	125	87	115	.249	.335	1b	28	.978				
1896	Boston	NL	122	74	144	.304	.395	1b	20	.985				
1897	Bos-Wash	NL	97	52	122	.333	.456	1b	17	.967				
1898	Bkn-St.Louis	NL	145	53	139	.260	.318	1b	30	.982				
1899	Cleveland	NL	127	40	110	.241	.296	1b	30	.977				
1900	Springfield	EL	126	59	133	.279		1b	33	.976				
1901	New London	ConnSt	63	35	63	.253		1b						
1902	Meriden	ConnSt	102	48	106	.258	.290	1b	18	.985				

JAMES ALEXANDER TYNG

Born: March 27, 1856, Philadelphia, Pa.
Died: October 30, 1931, New York, N.Y.
BR TR 5-9, 155

Jim Tyng may have been the best player ever to wear a Harvard uniform, but his place in baseball history is simply as a footnote. He wore the first catcher's mask.

Tyng's major league career consisted of three games with Boston in 1879 and one with Philadelphia in 1888, all of them as a pitcher. He starred at third base and centerfield on a Harvard team that was strong enough to beat Boston's major leaguers twice during his career (1873-1879). He moved behind the plate in 1877 because he was the only one who could handle the delivery of Crimson ace Harold Ernst. "Tyng was the best all-around natural ballplayer of my time, but he had been hit by foul tips and had become more or less timid," recalled Harvard captain Fred Thayer, who devised the mask, which Tyng first wore against the Live Oaks of Lynn on April 11, 1877.

After graduating from Harvard Law School and passing the bar in 1879, Tyng remained in the Boston area, playing for the amateur Boston Beacons. Late that summer Boston ace Tommy Bond was injured and his backup, Curry Foley, was ineffective. Boston manager Harry Wright needed a pitcher for a showdown series with archrival Providence with the National League pennant at stake. He called on Tyng, who, although wild at first, pitched a 5-hitter to defeat the Grays 7-3 on September 23. Tyng started again the next day, but rain halted play after three innings. Wright went to the well again the following day, but Tyng "was batted right, left and square between the eyes," yielding 18 hits as Providence romped 15-4. The Grays beat Tyng again the next day, 7-6, to clinch the pennant.

Four straight days of pitching against the best team in baseball apparently killed Tyng's appetite for professional baseball. He moved to New York, concentrated on his career and played amateur baseball until old friend Wright lured him back to the NL in 1888. Shunning an offer from the Athletics for "social reasons," Tyng accepted the job of director of athletic sports for the Phillies' ballpark rather than signing a conventional player's contract. Despite the fanfare, Tyng made only a single relief appearance before returning to the amateur ranks, where he continued to play well into the 1890s. Then he switched sports, winning the Metro New York Senior golf championship in 1915 and playing an active role in revising the rules of that game.

— Bob Richardson

			G	R	H	BA	SA	POS	E	FA	GP	W-L	R	H
1873	Harvard Univ.													
1874	Harvard Univ.							3b						
1875	Harvard Univ.													
1876	Harvard Univ.							of-c						
1877	Harvard Univ.							c						
1878	Harvard Univ.		25	27	36	.300		c	19	.926				
1879	Harvard Univ.		17	-	18	.254	.338	c		.891				
	Boston	NL	3	2	5	.357	.429	p			3	1-2	25	35
1888	Philadelphia	NL	1	0	0	.000	.000	p	0	1.00	1	0-0	4	8

GEORGE EDWARD MARTIN
VAN HALTREN
(Rip)

Born: March 30, 1866, St. Louis, Mo.
Died: September 29, 1945, Oakland, Ca.
BL TL 5-11, 170

A few weeks before his 20th birthday, George Van Haltren pitched his first "official" game, a nonleague contest for the Greenhood and Morans of Oakland against the Californias of San Francisco. He scattered 5 hits and struck out 7 in a 5-4 loss.

Sixteen months later, Cap Anson introduced him to 8,000 Chicago fans before his first major league start. And he struck out the leadoff batter, Boston lefthander Joe Hornung.

"Rip" would spend 16 more seasons in the majors, three of the first four in the box (67 starts, 65 complete games; 40 wins, 30 losses; 4.05 ERA). When not pitching, he roamed the outfield, so it is hitting and baserunning that account for his career of 1,984 games, 8,021 at-bats and a lifetime average of .316.

Born in St. Louis in 1866, he grew up in Oakland, California, and was ending his teens just as baseball in the San Francisco Bay area was moving from amateur to professional.

Van Haltren came to the notice of Eastern managers in the winter of 1886-87 while pitching for the locals against a postseason touring team that called itself "Louisville" but included utility players from other clubs.

Pittsburgh signed him in February 1887 at $1,400 for the coming season, but when his mother became seriously ill, he was permitted to report later.

Meanwhile he was traded to Chicago for another pitcher, Jim McCormick, Anson's No. 2 starter. Van Haltren continued to pitch for the Greenhood and Morans, helping to keep them at the top of the California League throughout April and May.

Apparently Rip did not want to leave Oakland and regretted signing. He was even under pressure not to desert his teammates and their winning ways. Spalding, needing his new lefthander, issued statements about blacklisting Van Haltren if he broke his contract and "debarring" teams and players who

would play with or against him in the future.

The situation finally resolved itself, unhappily, when Mrs. Van Haltren died in late May. By June 20 George was on the train east, meeting his new team on the 26th and making his debut the next day.

Although that first big league game started grandly, Rip walked 16 batters and Chicago lost 17-11, with Anson lodging a formal protest over an interference decision and ball-and-strike calls.

But Van Haltren ended the season with an 11-7 record and a 3.86 ERA, completing all 18 starts. He appeared as a pitcher in two other games (one save) and in the outfield for 25 more. However, his season batting average

was a skimpy .203.

He returned to California, rejoining the Greenhood and Morans for the final two months of the season. But he couldn't keep them from finishing last in the four-team league.

The following season was probably Van Haltren's best as a pitcher. Despite a 13-13 record, his ERA fell to 3.52. He gave up but 60 walks in 245 innings, struck out 139 and had 4 shutouts. Even his batting average improved (.286), which undoubtedly explains why he didn't pitch in 1889. That year he played in 134 games, scored 126 runs, drove in 81 and batted .309.

(continued on page 144)

			G	R	H	BA	SA	POS	E	FA	GP	W-L	R	H
1886	Oakland G&M	CalSt												
	Oakland G&M	Cal												
1887	S.F. Haverly	Cal	15	26	32	.478	.687	p	6	.930	15		70	94
	Chicago	NL	45	30	51	.272	.342	of-p	8	.901	20	11-7	102	243
1888	Chicago	NL	81	46	90	.283	.409	of-p	17	.904	30	13-11	160	263
1889	Chicago	NL	134	126	168	.309	.433	of	28	.898				
	Oakland	Cal	10	9	11	.244		of-p						
1890	Brooklyn	PL	92	86	130	.346	.449	of-p	21	.914	28	15-10	190	272
1891	Baltimore	AA	139	136	180	.318	.443	of-ss	39	.876	6	0-1	30	34
1892	Balt-Pitts	NL	148	116	179	.296	.402	of	54	.859	4	0-0	8	28
	Oakl-SanJose	Cal	11	10	8	.178	.311	of-p	3	.893	4	2-0	18	29
1893	Pittsburgh	NL	124	129	179	.338	.423	of	38	.869				
1894	New York	NL	139	110	177	.333	.440	of	33	.911				
1895	New York	NL	131	112	175	.338	.484	of	32	.899	1	0-0	12	13
1896	New York	NL	133	138	199	.353	.488	of	18	.942	2	1-0	2	5
1897	New York	NL	129	117	186	.330	.417	of	21	.934				
1898	New York	NL	156	129	204	.312	.413	of	25	.927				
1899	New York	NL	151	117	182	.301	.356	of	18	.949				
1900	New York	NL	141	114	180	.315	.398	of	23	.939	1	0-0	0	1
1901	New York	NL	135	82	182	.335	.405	of	18	.941	1	0-0	10	12
1902	New York	NL	24	14	23	.261	.318	of	5	.912				
1903	New York	NL	84	42	72	.257	.286	of	6	.959				
1904	Seattle	PCL	221	159	253	.269	.340	of	31	.947				
1905	Oakland	PCL	220	-	220	.256	.307	of	26	.950				
1906	Oakland	PCL	152	101	151	.217	.267	of						
1907	Oakland	PCL	193	101	193	.269	.305	of	21	.955				
1908	Oakland	PCL	186	80	171	.242	.283	of	14	.969				
1909	Oakland	PCL	55	14	24	.219		of	4	.962				

CHRISTIAN FREDERICK WILHELM VON DER AHE

Born: November 7, 1851, Halle, Germany
Died: June 7, 1913, St. Louis, Mo.

Chris Von der Ahe's roller-coaster career as a baseball team owner spanned the last two decades of the 19th century. During it he resurrected big league baseball in St. Louis, molded the St. Louis Browns into an American Association powerhouse, then allowed the team to disintegrate after it joined the National League.

Popular histories exaggerate his German accent and often remember him only as a buffoon. Yet he was a crafty entrepreneur, often warmhearted to foe as well as friend, and a man who truly loved baseball.

Chris Von der Ahe was born in Germany in 1851 and came to America at age 16. Shortly afterward he settled in St. Louis, whose inhabitants thirsted as much for baseball as for their beer. Beer helped launch Chris into a grocery-saloon business, which he eventually moved to a corner lot a block down from a baseball field called the Grand Avenue Park, home of an NL team in 1876-77.

After listening to a former outfielder eager to again play professionally, Von der Ahe rebuilt the park in 1881, then bought enough stock to become "boss president" of the newly formed Sportsman's Park and Club Association. He also enrolled the group's Brown Stockings in the new American Association. All this led the city's sporting press to hail him as a savior.

Free-spending Chris backed talent scouts who attracted ballplayers good enough to turn the Browns into Association champs from 1885 through 1888. Chris liberally rewarded his players and boasted that he paid them the highest salaries in the game. He frequently took back small portions of those earnings in the form of fines, usually for what he perceived as a lack of discipline or unprofessional behavior. (He once fined third baseman Arlie Latham for "singing and otherwise acting up" during a contest.)

Yet Von der Ahe often fiercely supported his players. Manager Charlie Comiskey once thought it was too dark to continue a game past the seventh inning, so Von der Ahe put lighted candles in front of the bench to egg on the ump.

Von der Ahe prided himself on being a sportsman who wanted fair play from both his team and its opponents. But he was a businessman first. When police said a new Missouri law prohibited baseball on Sunday, the best drawing day, Chris allowed himself to be arrested at the park after he'd defied authorities and had his team play anyway. He won the court case, to the rejoicing of Browns fans who included the police chief. Von der Ahe sold five of the team's stars to other AA clubs after 1887 because he knew his team's unchallenged success threatened both home attendance and the Association's balance. Those teams improved — and the Browns won another pennant in 1888.

Von der Ahe's shoot-from-the-hip style in fining his players created dissension and cost him a fifth straight pennant. It also drove his best players to other clubs and when they became free agents the Association died in 1891. Von der Ahe took the Browns to the National League, but since he sold his good players to make ends meet, the team never contended. This and his adding shoot-the-chutes and night horse racing to the ballpark caused the press that had lionized him to now call him the "Tricky Teuton." Von der Ahe's wife divorced him after accusing him of adultery, his son virtually disowned him, and the trust company that held title to the team's heavily mortgaged property ousted him in a highly publicized court fight in 1898-99.

His return to the saloon business wasn't successful. But baseball didn't forget Von der Ahe. In 1908 the Browns and Cardinals played an exhibition game for his benefit, and former colleagues and competitors from the '80s and '90s contributed to the pot. When Von der Ahe died in 1913, his pallbearers included several players from the first Browns team in the Association.

— Jim Rygelski

MOSES FLEETWOOD WALKER

Born: October 7, 1856, Mt. Pleasant, Ohio
Died: May 11, 1924, Cleveland, Ohio
BR TR

Moses Fleetwood Walker, gentleman, scholar and barehanded catcher, was the first Negro major leaguer, playing for Toledo of the American Association in 1884. Like Jackie Robinson, whose major league debut occurred 63 years later, Walker was a well-educated man who adroitly handled the pressures of being a pioneer.

Raised in Steubenville, Ohio, Walker attended Oberlin College and the University of Michigan, playing baseball for both though receiving a degree from neither. His career in organized baseball began in Toledo of the Northwestern League in 1883. The following year he made the jump to the major leagues when Toledo joined the AA.

In 1884 he shared the catching duties with Jim "Deacon" McGuire, who went on to play in the major leagues for 26 seasons. Such an opportunity would not be available to Walker, who watched the color line being drawn in the 1880s. An ominous sign of the future was his relationship with the team's star pitcher, Tony Mullane, who later recalled that Walker "was the best catcher I ever worked with, but I disliked a Negro and whenever I had to pitch to him I used to pitch anything I wanted without looking at his signals." White player opposition to Negroes would ultimately foreclose racial toleration in baseball, but in

1884, "Fleet," as he was called, was warmly received by Toledo fans and the sporting press. Despite facing hostility in a few southern towns, he was popular in other league cities.

After spending 1885 and 1886 in Cleveland (Western League) and Waterbury, Connecticut (Eastern League), Walker signed on with Newark, in the prestigious International League, in 1887. There he teamed up with George Stovey to form the first all-Negro battery in organized baseball. The IL 1887 season proved to be the high-water mark for blacks in 19th century organized baseball, as seven Negroes played for six teams, with varying degrees of success . . . and tribulation. The greatest indignity Walker and Stovey suffered occurred on July 14, when Cap Anson was able to prohibit them from playing in an exhibition game against Chicago. On that same day, the league directors ordered that black players would be forbidden in the future, citing opposition by white players. Subsequently, the league modified this ruling, but the writing was on the wall for Negro players. Walker played two more seasons in the league, both with Syracuse. In 1889 Syracuse won the championship, with Walker being the only Negro in the league. After a brief attempt to catch on with Terre Haute

(Western Interstate League) in 1890, Walker retired from baseball at the age of 33.

Although not an outstanding hitter, Walker was regarded as a dependable catcher with a strong arm. He also had good speed and was an aggressive baserunner. He was a popular player who was vigorously defended by fans and the press when he was subjected to racial epithets. Tall, lean, and handsome, he was admired for his deportment wherever he played. After his playing days were over, he became an articulate advocate of black emigration to Africa as the best response to increasing racial intolerance in America. He outlined his views in *Our Home Colony*, a book he wrote in 1908, and *The Equator*, a newspaper he published in Steubenville. He also owned a theater-opera house in Cadiz, Ohio, and applied for several patents in the nascent motion picture industry.

Despite his gloomy forecast for the future of his race in America, Walker was warmly remembered in Steubenville for his friendly, gracious manner. In about 1922 Walker retired to Cleveland, where he died in 1924. He is buried in a family plot in Union Cemetery in Steubenville.

— Jerry Malloy

			G	R	H	BA	SA	POS		E	FA	GP	W-L	R	H
1883	Toledo	NWL	60	45	59	.251	.353	c		78	.783				
1884	Toledo	AA	42	23	40	.263	.316	c		37	.887				
1885	Cleveland	WL	18	11	19	.279	.441	c							
	Waterbury	EL	10	5	6	.154	.154	c		4	.960				
	Waterbury	SoNEng						c-of							
1886	Waterbury	EL	47	23	37	.218		c-o-1		37	.895#				
1887	Newark	IL	69	44	67	.264	.315	c		31	.945				
1888	Syracuse	IA	77#	38	48	.170		c		45	.919				
1889	Syracuse	IA	50	29	37	.216	.234	c		29	.865				

CURT WELCH

Born: February 11, 1862, East Liverpool, Ohio
Died: August 29, 1896, East Liverpool, Ohio
BR TR 5-10, 175

A natural athlete but an uncouth and uneducated man, Curt Welch drank himself out of the major leagues by age 31 and into the grave by age 34. In the heyday of his career, however, he was perhaps the finest fielding centerfielder of the 19th century. A smart hitter and talented baserunner as well, Welch achieved his greatest fame playing for the champion St. Louis Browns of the mid-1880s.

Welch was the man who scored the winning run in the decisive game of the 1886 World Series. This has come down in legend as "Curt Welch's $15,000 Slide," although there is no contemporary evidence to suggest that Welch actually slid across the plate.

Born poor in the pottery town of East Liverpool, Ohio, Welch's athletic ability saved him from a life as a plate-maker. His professional career began when he signed with the Toledo Club in the Northwestern League in June 1883. Curt was 21 at the time. The following season, Toledo moved into the American Association with Welch as the regular centerfielder. Although he generally hit in the middle of the batting order with Toledo, his 1884 average was just .224.

When the season ended the club folded, and Welch was among the players signed by Chris Von der Ahe of the St. Louis Browns. An aggressive player and an enthusiastic umpire-baiter, Curt fit very well into captain Charlie Comiskey's team. He was among the many Browns to use the controversial headfirst slide, and his running speed allowed him to steal many a base.

But it was his spectacular flycatching ability that set Curt Welch apart. Fast and surehanded, he led all AA outfielders in putouts each of his three seasons with St. Louis. It was said he could judge the distance that a fly ball would travel by the sound of the crack of the bat. As soon as a long drive was hit, he was off and running. Never looking back, he invariably ran to the spot where the ball came down. This talent allowed him to play a very shallow centerfield (even by the standards of the day), and he was adept at making headlong, diving catches of sinking line drives. He also possessed a fine throwing arm. Welch was generally acknowledged as the best defensive outfielder of his time, with the possible exceptions of Pop Corkhill and Jim Fogerty.

On offense, he was a team-oriented player so his statistics do not reflect his overall contribution. He was an outstanding base stealer and one of the earliest sacrifice-bunt specialists. He was also especially good at getting hit by pitches. In that famous World Series finale, he got himself nicked by a pitch, but Chicago captain Anson convinced the umpire that he had gotten hit intentionally, so Welch had to bat again. Curt then lined a clean single to center. After an error and a bunt, Welch scored on a very wild pitch, trotting across the plate with no play being made on him, and the Browns collected the $14,000 gate receipts in the winner-take-all Series.

But his conduct off the field was unsavory, and when Von der Ahe broke up his team after the 1887 World Series, Welch was sent to the Athletics for catcher Jocko Milligan and $3,000. He had three fairly good seasons in Philadelphia, even being appointed captain in 1890. But when the club went bankrupt late in 1890, Welch was sold to Baltimore along with Wilbert Robinson and Sadie McMahon.

Welch lasted with Baltimore until mid-1892, but his talents were already noticeably eroded. Released to Cincinnati, he was suspended for "boozing" by his old manager Comiskey in August. Opening Day in 1893 found Curt playing left field for Louisville, but he was soon released. He caught on with Syracuse, where he played until 1895, finishing up with Hazleton in the Pennsylvania State League.

Out of baseball in 1896, he died August 29 in East Liverpool, reportedly "a wreck from drink."

— Robert L. Tiemann

			G	R	H	BA	SA	POS	E	FA	GP	W-L	R	H
1883	Toledo	NWL	50	59	59	.294	.383	of	8	.901				
1884	Toledo	AA	109	61	96	.234	.317	of	29	.888				
1885	St. Louis	AA	112	84	115	.266	.359	of	11	.959				
1886	St. Louis	AA	138	114	158	.285	.399	of	14	.959				
1887	St. Louis	AA	131	98	173	.307	.405	of	25	.936				
1888	Athletic	AA	136	125	160	.291	.365	of	10	.968				
1889	Athletic	AA	125	131	140	.273	.379	of	29	.920				
1890	Athletic-Balt	AA	122	116	115	.248	.332	of	17	.943	1	0-0	6	6
1891	Baltimore	AA	132	122	138	.268	.368	of-2b	26	.940				
1892	Balt-Cinc	NL	88	56	76	.230	.281	of	19	.911				
1893	Louisville	NL	14	5	8	.170	.191	of	3	.906				
	E. Liverpool	OhMich	2	2	4	.364	.364	p			2			
1894	Syracuse	EL	111	117	137	.308	.378	of	10	.963				
1895	Syracuse	EL	89	87	81	.229	.249	of	20	.900				
	Hazleton	PaSt												

PERCIVAL WHERRIT WERDEN
(Perry)

Born: July 21, 1865, St. Louis, Mo.
Died: January 9, 1934, Minneapolis, Minn.
BR TR 6-2, 220

Perry Werden was one of the colorful performers in baseball in the 1890s, particularly in the minors, where he was the first great slugger. In 1882 he began playing with the Libertys, a fast semipro team in St. Louis, which he served primarily as a pitcher. In 1884 he signed with the St. Louis entry in the major league Union Association. Perry ran up a 12-1 W-L record for the club, which completely dominated the league. The fans lost interest and the ill-fated league folded.

Werden then moved on to Lincoln and later Topeka in the Western League, Des Moines in the Northwestern League, Troy in the International Association, and Memphis and New Orleans in the Southern League. First base was his primary position, although he still pitched occasionally. He was big and powerful for a player of his era, 6 feet 2 and weighing 220 pounds, and ran the bases well. He hit the long ball, but this was reflected more in triples than in home runs because of the way most of the parks were built. In 1888, for example, when he was with New Orleans, he led the league with 5 home runs. He also led with 65 stolen bases.

Werden led the International Association with a .394 batting average in 1889. The next year he was with Toledo in the major league AA and led the circuit with 20 triples. In 1891 he hit 18 for Baltimore. When the Association folded he moved on to St. Louis in the NL where in 1893 he hit 33 triples (one source credits him with 29). It was the highest figure in baseball up to that point.

Werden made the switch to Minneapolis in the Western League in 1894, and while this was a step down in classification, it was a step up in popularity for the big, blustery first baseman. The Millers' home grounds at Athletic Park were enclosed with fairly short right and left field fences. That was the deadball era, but it was made to order for a big guy like Werden. He hit 43 home runs that season, far more than the organized baseball record

up to that time. He also batted .417. The next year at Minneapolis he averaged two hits a game and topped the league with a .428 average. He hit 45 home runs, 7 triples and 39 doubles on a very heavy-hitting team. In one game in 1895, he hit four homers and a single in five trips.

Some revisions were made to Athletic Park the next season, but Werden again led the Western League in home runs with 18, plus 18 triples and 42 doubles. He went to NL Louisville in 1897 and batted .302. But manager Fred Clarke felt his boisterous behavior, which appealed to most fans, was not quite right for the team, and Werden was welcomed back to Minneapolis the next season. Unfortunately, he broke a leg in an exhibition

game and missed the entire season.

Although Werden batted .346 when he returned in 1899, he suffered from minor injuries and at age 35 was not in the best shape. His weight was up to 230 and he didn't run the bases with the dash he used to display. Instead of "Peach-Pie Perry," fans now called him "Moose." Still, when Minneapolis became part of the newly named American League in 1900, Werden led the circuit in home runs and doubles. It was not a major league that season, but included numerous high caliber players who the year before had played in the 12-team NL, since reduced to eight teams.

Werden remained active for several more *(continued on page 144)*

			G	R	H	BA	SA	POS	E	FA	GP	W-L	R	H
1884	St. Louis	UA	18	7	18	.237	.263	p-of	16	.853	16	12-1	58	113
1885	Memphis	SL	28	24	30	.254	.356	1b	14	.941				
1886	Lincoln	WL	68	67	83	.317	.546	1b	39	.930				
1887	Topeka	WL	78	102	149	.396	.582	of-1b	23	.914				
	Des Moines	NWL	14	11	21	.368	.544	1b-of	-					
1888	New Orleans	SL	56	38	61	.277	.418	o-1-2	28	.909				
	New Orleans	Tx-Sou	3	1	4	.333	.333	1b						
	Troy	IA	46	21	33	.185	.242	2b-of						
	Washington	NL	3	0	3	.300	.300	of	1	.857				
1889	Toledo	IA	109	107	167	.394	.535	1b	32	.969				
1890	Toledo	AA	128	113	147	.295	.456	1b	35	.972				
1891	Baltimore	AA	139	102	160	.290	.424	1b	30	.980				
1892	St. Louis	NL	149	73	154	.258	.355	1b	28	.982				
1893	St. Louis	NL	125	73	138	.276	.448	1b	40	.969				
1894	Minneapolis	WL	114	140	216	.417	.761	1b	33	.973				
1895	Minneapolis	WL	123	179	241	.428	.762	1b	24	.981				
1896	Minneapolis	WL	140	145	217	.377	.607	1b	31	.979				
1897	Louisville	NL	131	76	153	.302	.429	1b	23	.985				
1898	Minneapolis	WL						(did not play - broken leg)						
1899	Minneapolis	WL	111	70	150	.346	.452	1b	28	.975				
1900	Minneapolis	AL	127	64	161	.315	.468	1b	26	.983				
1901	StPaul-DesMns	WL	121	61	150	.322	.444	1b						
1902	Minneapolis	AA	138	64	156	.293	.375	1b	38	.975				
1903	Memphis	SL	125	60	145	.297	.414	1b	28	.978				
1904	Fargo	Nrthrn	51	32	58	.306	.434	1b	17	.972				
1905	Hattiesburg	CotSt	37	14	43	.328	.374	1b	9	.979				
1906	Vicksburg	CotSt	49	14	39	.220	.288	1b	11	.978	2	0-0	10	13
1908	Indianapolis	AA	2	1	1	.500	.500	Ph						

GUS WEYHING

Born: September 29, 1866, Louisville, Ky.
Died: September 3, 1955, Louisville, Ky.
BR TR 5-10, 145

The name Weyhing first appeared on a team sponsored by the M.J. Latterle company of Louisville in 1884. It would keep turning up for years to come.

Gus Weyhing entered organized ball the next season with Richmond in the Virginia League, winning 19 games and losing 3. This fine record led him to Charleston of the fast Southern League. That spring the Philadelphia Nationals trained in Charleston and played several preseason games against the locals. Gus's initial game against major league competition was lost 8-4. A writer covering the game commented "Weyhing pitched excellently, barring some wildness." This would characterize much of his pitching.

As the championship season went on, the Philadelphia Athletics of the AA and others tried to buy Charleston's star pitcher. All offers were refused. To make staying in the minors more attractive, Charleston raised his salary to $75 a month. But in July he pitched his last game for Charleston. Weyhing left the team saying unconvincingly that he had a sore arm.

During the winter of 1887 Gus signed with the Philadelphia Nationals. Although he made a good impression in the spring, the Nationals decided they were carrying too many men. The rival Athletics were allowed to purchase Weyhing's contract.

His first major league start, on May 2, 1887, was a 17-6 win over Brooklyn. After a few more such solid performances the Nationals management was being criticized for releasing Weyhing.

During his first three seasons he won 26, 29 and 28, pitching more than 400 innings all three seasons. Feats like this earned him the nickname Rubber-Winged Gus. On July 31, 1888, Weyhing pitched a no-hitter, allowing only two Kansas City Cowboys to reach first base. Both were caught stealing, so Gus faced the minimum number of batters.

In 1890 Weyhing joined Brooklyn (PL). He won 30 games for the first time. The team finished second, highest of any he played for. After the league folded, he was back in the Athletics' lineup, winning 31 games, even though he didn't pitch from August 16 through 27.

When the AA folded after 1891, Weyhing went to the Philadelphia Nationals, which had regretted releasing him six years earlier. From 1892-1894, Gus won 71 games and lost 51 with the Phillies.

After two games in 1895 Weyhing was released. He pitched one game for Pittsburgh, then finished the year with Louisville, where he had a 7-19 record for a team that won only 35 games. After five starts in 1896 he was released by Louisville, and pitched for Dallas of the Texas League in 1897. Weyhing returned to the majors the next season with

Washington. He was solid but the team was unspectacular, and he was 32-49 over the 1898 and '99 seasons. Four brief stops in 1900 and 1901 concluded his big league career, and he pitched in the minors through 1903.

Gus returned to his hometown, Louisville, to operate a cigar store and tavern. In 1910 he tried managing Tulsa of the Western Association, but was fired after the opening game. He then pitched 3 games for Galveston in the Texas League before finishing the season as an umpire.

As part of their fiftieth anniversary, the Boston Red Sox honored old timers at several of their games. Gus Weyhing was one of them. But since then people seem to have lost track of a pitcher who won 264 major league games.

— Jack Little and L. Robert Davids

			G	R	H	BA	SA	POS	E	FA	GP	W-L	R	H
1886	Charleston	SL	33	11	17	.148	.165	p	14	.899	32	13-18	144	229
1887	Athletic	AA	57	19	47	.229	.268	p	24	.815	55	26-28	336	465
1888	Athletic	AA	48	19	40	.219	.355	p	17	.871	47	28-18	193	314
1889	Athletic	AA	54	16	26	.135	.146	p	8	.912	54	30-21	268	382
1890	Brooklyn	PL	49	23	31	.185	.250	p	12	.848	49	30-16	246	419
1891	Athletic	AA	54	11	22	.111	.146	p	8	.926	52	31-20	234	428
1892	Philadelphia	NL	66	14	29	.136	.159	p-o	22	.807	59	32-21	212	411
1893	Philadelphia	NL	43	14	22	.150	.170	p	5	.947	42	23-16	236	399
1894	Philadelphia	NL	38	9	20	.168	.218	p	-	.845	38	16-14	212	365
	Athletic	PaSt	1					p			1	1-0	3	6
1895	Phi-Pit-Louv	NL	31	11	21	.216	.289	p			31	8-21	232	318
1896	Louisville	NL	5	2	2	.133	.133	p	0	1.00	5	2-3	46	62
	Rochester	EL	12	6	8	.205	.205	p			12	5-6	75	137
1897	Dallas	Tx	35#	12	33	.256		p	12	.875	45	21-23	241	441
1898	Washington	NL	46	12	25	.177	.199	p	-	.858	45	15-26	229	428
1899	Washington	NL	43	13	26	.206	.246	p	-	.791	43	17-23	227	414
1900	St.L-Bkn	NL	15	3	6	.154	.154	p	4	.851	15	6-6	75	126
1901	Grand Rapids	WA		-	12	.181	.227	p	3	.948	20	14-6	-	160
	Cleveland	AL	2	0	0	.000	.000	p	0	1.00	2	0-0	11	20
	Cincinnati	NL	1	0	0	.000	.000	p	0	1.00	1	0-1	9	11
1902	Kansas City	AA	9	0	4	.182	.182	p			7	3-4	55	77
	Memphis	SL	24#	2	5	.208		p	7	.860	29	11-14	-	237
1903	Atlnta-LtRck	SL	28#	5	14	.158		p	7	.867	35	18-15	-	280
1910	Tulsa	WA	1					2b						
	Galveston	Tx	3		0	.000	.000	p	0	1.00	3	0-2	9	-

JAMES LAURIE WHITE
(Deacon)

Born: December 7, 1847, Caton, New York
Died: July 7, 1939, Aurora, Illinois
BL TR 5-11, 175

In 1890 Henry Chadwick, faithful chronicler of the game's early years, wrote of Deacon White: "What we most admired about White was his quiet, effective way. Kicking is unknown to him. And there is one thing in which White stands preeminent, and that is the integrity of his character. Not even a whisper of suspicion has ever been heard about Jim White. Herein lies as much of his value to his team as his great skills."

When White died in 1939 at the age of 91, *The Sporting News* obituary said the end had been hastened by disappointment at his not being named to the Hall of Fame along with such contemporaries as Spalding, Ewing, Radbourne, Comiskey and Cummings. He had not even been invited to baseball's centennial celebration at Cooperstown on June 12, 1939.

How good was White? Judging from what was written about him when he played, it would be safe to say that the Hall of Famers above named were his peers but not his betters. He played 15 years in the majors and batted .303 overall. This does not include five NA years, where he batted .315, .336, .382, .321 and .355. In the 1870s he was the predominant catcher in the game. Indicative of his versatility and all-around skill was the success he later attained at third base and in the outfield.

One of professional baseball's true pioneers, starting his pro career in Cleveland in 1869, he played in every one of the NA's five seasons. He played in the NL from its founding through the 1889 season. He was a member of both of the famed "Big Fours," with Spalding, McVey and Barnes at Boston, and with Brouthers, Richardson and Rowe at Buffalo. He fought for players' rights and in 1889 he and Jack Rowe threatened to take the "reserve clause" to the courts after they had purchased the Buffalo International League

club, but could not play for it because they were reserved by Pittsburgh, which would not release them. White and Rowe eventually reported to Pittsburgh, finished the 1889 season and then became part owners of the Buffalo Brotherhood nine. A skillful and innovative player, White was said to be the first to move up under the batter. White and Al Spalding also developed a "quick pitch" technique that fooled many an unwary batter. While with Buffalo in 1884, he and Jim O'Rourke designed a rubber chest and abdomen protector, forerunner of the modern catcher's chest protector. A year later, he and the rest of the "Big Four" were sold to Detroit for $7,000 in one of baseball's first mass player deals.

White started 1891 as captain and manager of the Elmira team (N.Y.-Penn. League) but was fired July 6. He returned to Buffalo, working for his brother Will as a lens grinder and later opening a livery stable. About 1910 he moved to Aurora, Illinois, to be with his daughter. He died there at the age of 91, having lived and seen more baseball than any other man extant. Though overlooked by Cooperstown, he was not forgotten in his adopted home, Buffalo. In 1986 he was inducted into the Buffalo Baseball Hall of Fame, with his niece, Orpha White Meyer, on hand to accept the plaque.

— Joseph M. Overfield

			G	R	H	BA	SA	POS	E	FA	GP	W-L	R	H
1868	ForestCtyClev		23	73										
1869	ForestCtyClev							c-p						
1870	ForestCtyClev		36	-	108		(184TB)	c						
1871	ForestCtyClev	NA	29	40	47	.326	.444	c	38	.813				
1872	ForestCtyClev	NA	21	21	37	.356	.413	c-2-o	14	.883				
1873	Boston	NA	60	78	122	.394	.497	c-of	31	.901				
1874	Boston	NA	70	75	106	.302	.382	c-of	70	.818				
1875	Boston	NA	80	77	136	.365	.432	c-of	109	.807				
1876	Chicago	NL	66	66	104	.343	.419	c	69	.842	1	0-0	0	1
1877	Boston	NL	59	51	103	.387	.545	1-o-c	28	.935				
1878	Cincinnati	NL	61	41	81	.314	.337	c-of	41	.895				
1879	Cincinnati	NL	78	58	110	.310	.398	c-of	55	.879				
1880	Cincinnati	NL	35	21	42	.330	.423	of	16	.738				
1881	Buffalo	NL	78	58	99	.310	.398	1-2-o	63	.875				
1882	Buffalo	NL	83	51	95	.282	.353	3b-c	55	.854				
1883	Buffalo	NL	94	62	114	.292	.353	3b-c	66	.837				
1884	Buffalo	NL	110	82	147	.325	.442	3b	66	.825				
1885	Buffalo	NL	98	54	118	.292	.329	3b	40	.888				
1886	Detroit	NL	124	65	142	.289	.348	3b	68	.847				
1887	Detroit	NL	111	71	162	.342	.435	3b	64	.848				
1888	Detroit	NL	125	75	157	.298	.380	3b	65	.857				
1889	Pittsburgh	NL	55	35	57	.253	.311	3b	24	.872				
1890	Buffalo	PL	122	63	116	.264	.308	3b-1b	44	.952	1	0-0	12	18
1891	Elmira	NYPa	10	7	8	.229	.229	c-3b	3	.976				

SOLOMON WHITE
(Sol)

Born: June 12, 1868, Bellaire, Ohio
Died: 1955, New York, N.Y.
BR TR 5-9, 170

Sol White's distinguished career in the early days of black baseball spanned almost 40 years. Between 1887, when he played for the Pittsburgh Keystones of the ill-fated Colored League, and 1926, when he managed the Newark Browns, White played with and/or managed many of the brightest stars of the invisible world of Negro baseball, including Bud Fowler, Frank Grant, George Stovey, Grant Johnson, Bill Monroe, Rube Foster, Pete Hill, Bruce Petway, Spottswood Poles, and John Henry Lloyd.

Since White began his professional career just as the color line was being drawn on the field, his playing career in organized baseball was limited to 152 games and 641 at bats, scattered over five seasons (1887, 1889-91, and 1895). But records kept during his brief career in organized ball reveal that the 5-9, 170-pound infielder was a sterling hitter. He never hit below .333 in any season, and his career batting average was a robust .360.

During the 1890s he played for many of the greatest all-Negro teams in the country. Although he played one season each with the Page Fence Giants of Adrian, Michigan, and the Columbia Giants of Chicago, White spent most of his career with outstanding teams in the East, such as the Gorhams of New York, the Cuban Giants and the Cuban X-Giants.

After the turn of the century, White's career as a player-manager blossomed when he settled down with the Philadelphia Giants from 1902-1909. He was also co-founder of the team, along with sportswriter H. Walter Schlichter. During his tenure, the Philadelphia Giants were one of the dominant teams in the nation, attracting many of the greatest Negro ballplayers in the land. In 1905, when they won 134 games and lost only 21, their challengers for the post-season series to determine the champions of "colored" baseball did not even bother to show up. The following season, when they went 108-31, their offer to play the winner of the Cubs-White Sox World Series went unanswered.

White remained active in Negro baseball for many years after the Philadelphia Giants folded in 1910, achieving the status of venerable sage and commentator. Yet as successful as he was as a player, manager and organizer, Sol White's greatest contribution to 19th-century baseball was literary. In 1907 he published *Sol White's Official Base Ball Guide: History of Colored Base Ball*. White's writing ability may have been developed while he attended Wilberforce University during the off-seasons between 1886 and 1890. Or perhaps the book was ghostwritten by his business partner, Schlichter. In any case, the 128-page booklet is an invaluable source for

researchers investigating 19th-century black baseball. In it, White wrote, "I have endeavored to follow the mutations of colored base ball as accurately as possible, from the organization of the first colored professional team in 1885, to the present." Although often sketchy, and with a predominant focus on the East Coast, *Sol White's Guide* is a fascinating pastiche of history, lore, instruction and even poetry, enriched with 57 pages of photographs of teams, players, managers and owners.

He acknowledged that "the field for the colored professional is limited . . . Consequently he loses interest. He knows that, so far shall I go, and no farther . . ." Yet he was optimistic that "in the near future" the color line would be removed, so Negro players should sharpen their skills in order to be prepared when the great opportunity arrived to "walk hand-in-hand with the opposite race" in baseball. He remained hopeful that "some day the bar will drop and some good man will be chosen from out of the colored profession that will be a credit to all, and pave the way for others to follow." Sol White had to wait 39 years for that "good man," Jackie Robinson, to breach the color line.

White easily lived long enough to see that day. He died in New York City in 1955 at the age of 87.

— Jerry Malloy

			G	R	H	BA	SA	POS	E	FA	GP	W-L	R	H
1887	Pittsburgh	NatCol	7	5	12	.308	.385	2b						
	Wheeling	Ohio	52	54	84	.370	.502	3b	48	.775				
1889	Trenton	MidSt	31	20	35	.333	.400	2b-p	-	-				
1890	York	EIntst	54	78	84	.356	.483	2b	28	.921				
1891	Ansonia	ConnSt	4#	3	6	.375	.625	2b						
1895	Fort Wayne	WIntst	10	15	20	.385	.577	2b						
	Page Fence		12#	15	21	.404	.577	2b						

WILLIAM HENRY WHITE

Born: October 11, 1854, Caton, N.Y.
Died: August 30, 1911, Port Carling, Ont., Can.
BB TR 5-9 ½, 175

1. Will White was the first major leaguer to wear glasses. 2. He and his older brother, Jim, made up baseball's first brother battery (Cincinnati Nationals, 1878-1880). 3. He quit as Cincinnati manager in 1884 when the team's record was 44-27, saying he had neither the temperament nor the personality to manage.

All true, and enough to make Will White at least a footnote to baseball history.

Actually, he deserves to be remembered for more compelling reasons. In a 10-year major league career, foreshortened by arm trouble, he won 229 games and lost 166 (.580). This record becomes even more impressive considering he compiled all but 3 wins and 5 defeats in seven seasons. When his arm was fit, he never spared it. With Cincinnati (NL) from 1878 to 1880, his log shows 30-21, 43-31 and 18-42, as he worked 468, 680 and 517 innings, respectively, and completed 185 of 189 starts. His 75 games started and finished in '79 is a record that has stood for a century and will never be broken. After his 42 losses

in 1880, he was shipped to Detroit but, troubled by a sore arm, he pitched in only two games. He returned to Cincinnati and spent the summer of 1881 pitching with local semi-pro teams. In 1882 he was signed by the Cincinnati club in the new American Association, where he began another incredible streak. From 1882 through 1885 his record was 40-12, 43-22, 34-18 and 18-15. In this span he pitched 480, 577, 456 and 293 innings and completed 204 games in 205 starts, a phenomenal performance even in those no-relief-pitcher days. It was not that he was left in to take his beatings, since his career ERA is 2.28, 10th on the all-time list.

After the 1885 season, his arm had nothing left. He pitched a few games in 1886 (1-2), but his career was over except for one last fling with his brother's 1889 Buffalo (International) club, for which he was 6-13.

When his playing days were over, White studied ophthalmics at Corning, New York, then settled in Buffalo, where he founded the

Buffalo Optical Company, still a thriving business. A deeply religious man, he was the founder and main benefactor of the Christ Mission in Buffalo. On August 30, 1911 (Macmillan says August 31), at his summer home at Port Carling, Ontario, he was teaching a young niece to swim, even though he could not swim himself. While in the water, he suffered a heart attack and drowned. He was 56 years old. In his will he left 10 percent of his $21,000 estate to Christ Mission and directed the ultimate beneficiary, his daughter, Katherine Shull, to do the same with her share.

Few pitchers in the game's history accomplished so much in a short career as White did. Others who come to mind are Sandy Koufax, Dizzy Dean and Addie Joss. These three are honored at Cooperstown. As for Will White, he is remembered most because he was the first major leaguer to wear glasses.

— Joseph M. Overfield

			G	R	H	BA	SA	POS	E	FA	GP	W-L	R	H
1875	Lynn							p						
1876	Binghamton		62	45	46			p	76	.588				
1877	Boston	NL	3	4	3	.200	.200	p	1	.875	3	1-2	15	27
1878	Cincinnati	NL	52	15	28	.142	.157	p	15	.873	52	30-21	257	477
1879	Cincinnati	NL	76	28	40	.136	.156	p	26	.834	76	43-31	351	676
1880	Cincinnati	NL	62	16	35	.169	.213	p	10	.895	62	18-42	320	550
1881	Detroit	NL	2	0	0	.000	.000	p			2	0-2	18	24
	Cincinnati							p						
1882	Cincinnati	AA	54	28	55	.266	.285	p	9	.965	54	40-12	161	411
1883	Cincinnati	AA	65	38	55	.230	.272	p	24	.855	65	43-22	263	473
1884	Cincinnati	AA	52	28	35	.190	.234	p	19	.824	52	34-18	233	479
1885	Cincinnati	AA	34	9	20	.169	.212	p	6	.882	34	19-15	166	295
1886	Cincinnati	AA	3	1	1	.111	.111	p	2	.714	3	1-2	23	28
1889	Buffalo	IA	20	6	10	.147	.206	p	6	.903	18	6-12	99	160

JAMES EVANS WHITNEY
(Grasshopper Jim)

Born: November 10, 1857, Conklin, New York
Died: May 21, 1891, Binghamton, New York
BL TR 6-1, 172

James "Grasshopper Jim" Whitney was one of the premier right-handed pitchers of the 1880s and a ten-year veteran of the early major leagues.

Whitney grew up in Binghamton, New York, where he and his brother, Charlie, began playing baseball early. Both turned professional in the mid-1870s, playing for some of the better independent clubs of the day. When on the same team the Whitney brothers occasionally formed one of the more unusual brother batteries as each pitched to and caught the other.

James Whitney first rose to prominence with the Crickets of Binghamton in 1878. He was also with the celebrated Omaha Pacifics in 1879 and the Knickerbockers of San Francisco in 1880.

In 1881 he joined the Boston Nationals and was an instant success with 57 complete games pitched and a 31-33 record. He pitched for Boston through 1885; his best season was 1883, when he led his team to the National League championship with a 37-21 record, 58 complete games, 345 strikeouts (including 16 in one game) and only 35 bases on balls in 514

innings. His best pitch was a rifle-shot fastball which, coupled with wonderful control, was very effective at the short pitching distances of the 1880s.

After his Boston days Whitney had less successful stints with Kansas City (NL), Washington (NL), Indianapolis (NL) and Philadelphia (AA) before he retired during the 1890 season. The Macmillan *Encyclopedia* calculates his pitching record at 192-207, which included five seasons of 24 or more wins (two of 31 or more) plus seven seasons of 21 or more losses (including three of 30 or more). Whitney compiled during his career what seems to be the second best (to Tommy Bond) strikeouts-to-walks ratio of all time: 1,571 to 411.

Whitney was also a quality major league batter and often played the outfield or first base when not pitching. He hit .261 with 18 home runs in his career. During 1883 he batted third and leadoff before settling into the cleanup spot during Boston's pennant drive. He set National League records on June 9, 1883, when he scored 6 runs and batted 8 times in a single game. Both records still

stand although they have been tied several times.

Whitney, although an unusually good baseball player and a decent man, was a man of peculiar looks and often irritating personality, if contemporary accounts are to be believed. He was tall and thin (about 6 feet 1, 172 pounds) and was described "as having a head about the size of a wart with a forehead slanting at about an angle of 45 (degrees). . . . He is the best batter among the pitchers and the worst kicker." Also, Whitney "worries an umpire from the commencement of a game to the end, never for an instant stopping his kicking and demanding everything within a foot of the plate. When at bat he is the same." Whitney even had an unusual gait that accounted for his nickname, "Grasshopper Jim."

James Whitney feared consumption all his brief life and began showing signs of it during his brief 1890 season. He retired from baseball and then died in May 1891 at Binghamton, New York.

— Harold Dellinger

			G	R	H	BA	SA	POS	E	FA	GP	W-L	R	H
1878	Binghamton	IA	2			.143	.143	of	-	.500				
	Oswego													
1879	Omaha	NWL	18	10	26	.347	.427	p-1-c	-		10	4-6	48	69
1880	Knickerbocker	Cal						p						
1881	Boston	NL	75	37	72	.255	.337	p-of	28	.808#	66	31-33	290	548
1882	Boston	NL	61	49	81	.323	.510	p-of	20	.882	49	24-22	233	404
1883	Boston	NL	96	78	116	.282	.432	p-of	25	.870	62	38-22	264	492
1884	Boston	NL	66	41	70	.259	.393	p-o-l	10	.956	38	22-14	132	272
1885	Boston	NL	72	35	68	.234	.290	p-of	26	.894	51	18-32	286	503
1886	Kansas City	NL	67	25	59	.239	.340	p-of	18	.898	46	12-32	322	484
1887	Washington	NL	54	29	71	.324	.447	p-of	12	.902	47	24-21	258	490
1888	Washington	NL	42	13	24	.170	.191	p	11	.882	39	18-21	181	317
1889	Indianapolis	NL	10	6	12	.375	.563	p-of	0	1.00	9	2-7	73	106
	Buffalo	IA	29	12	20	.210		p	6	.920	24	13-11	128	244
1890	Athletic	AA	7	3	5	.238	.238	p	1	.909	6	2-2	27	61

EDWARD NAGLE WILLIAMSON
(Ned)

Born: October 24, 1857, Philadelphia, Pa.
Died: March 3, 1894, Willow Springs, Ark.
BR TR 5-11, 170

Ned Williamson was a husky infielder for the great Chicago NL teams of the 1880s. He excelled in all-around play and many contemporary baseball writers and players ranked him the best in the game at either third base or shortstop. His longtime manager, Cap Anson, went so far as to call him, "In my opinion, the best all-around ballplayer the country ever saw."

Williamson was born in Philadelphia in 1857 and he advanced through the local amateur ranks to the well-regarded Neshannocks of New Castle, where he was a teammate of catcher Charlie Bennett. Williamson's professional career began in 1877 as a shortstop with the Allegheny club in the inaugural season of the International Association, the first minor league. Ned was 19 at the time. The following season, 1878, he began his major league career with the Indianapolis team in the National League.

Except for that first year with Indianapolis and his last year in 1890 with Chicago (PL), Williamson played for the Cap Anson men in Chicago (NL). He was part of the famous "Stonewall Infield" formed with Anson, Fred Pfeffer and Tommy Burns. Williamson was the third baseman through 1885, then switched positions with Burns and became the shortstop in 1886. This team, which also included the famous outfield of Mike Kelly, George Gore and Abner Dalrymple, won pennants in 1880, 1881, 1882, 1885 and 1886. It was the National League's first dynasty in baseball's first "Golden Age."

Williamson was well-read, observant and articulate, as were a sizeable number of his contemporaries on the field. He was good-natured and kind-hearted and consequently very popular among fellow players and the fans throughout the land. He enjoyed high living and was an avid cardplayer and gambler.

For an infielder in the 1880s, Williamson was large, almost six feet tall, with a playing weight of around 175 pounds, although he ballooned to "aldermanic proportions" in his last years. In spite of his size, he was quick on his feet and covered a lot of ground. He was famous for his strong, accurate throws and set a record for long-distance throwing. In four different seasons he led the League's third basemen in fielding.

Williamson also excelled in offensive skills. He was a speedy runner and an excellent slider, using the "Kelly Spread" much like the modern hook slide. He was a hard, heavy right-handed hitter although he did not hit for a high average. When Chicago's Lake Front Park was renovated in 1883 to reduce the distance to the rightfield fence to under 200 feet, Williamson showed quite a knack for poking the ball over the short barrier. In 1883, when the ground rules made such a hit worth two bases, he led the league in doubles. In 1884, the ground rules allowed a home run, and Williamson hit 27 (25 at home) to set the major league record that lasted until Babe Ruth broke it 35 years later. Ned was also good at waiting for good balls to hit, ranking among the leaders in bases on balls in several seasons.

In March 1889, he suffered an injury in Paris, France, while on Spalding's "Around the World" baseball tour. He tore up his knee on a sharp stone while sliding on the sand and gravel playing surface. This injury cut short his brilliant career.

After retiring, he opened a Chicago saloon in partnership with Jimmy Wood, the old ballplayer. But Williamson's health deteriorated rapidly, and he died of dropsy of the stomach in 1894 at age 36.

— Dennis Goldstein

			G	R	H	BA	SA	POS	E	FA	GP	W-L	R	H
1876	Neshannock		36	43	49			3b-c	48					
	Allegheny							3b						
1877	Allegheny	IA	19	15	14	.173	.210	3-2-c						
1878	Indianapolis	NL	63	31	58	.232	.300	3b	36	.850				
1879	Chicago	NL	80	66	94	.294	.447	3b	41	.871				
1880	Chicago	NL	75	65	78	.251	.328	3b-c	27	.893#				
1881	Chicago	NL	82	56	92	.268	.350	3b	31	.909	3	1-1	8	14
1882	Chicago	NL	83	66	98	.282	.414	3b	43	.881	1	0-0	8	9
1883	Chicago	NL	98	83	111	.276	.435	3b	87	.807	1	0-0	1	1
1884	Chicago	NL	107	84	116	.278	.554	3b	70	.859	2	0-0	5	8
1885	Chicago	NL	113	87	97	.238	.337	3b	45	.894	2	0-0	0	2
1886	Chicago	NL	121	69	93	.216	.330	ss	78	.867	2	0-0	2	2
1887	Chicago	NL	127	77	190	.371	.512	ss	61	.890	1	0-0	2	2
1888	Chicago	NL	132	75	113	.250	.387	ss	62	.889				
1889	Chicago	NL	47	16	41	.237	.295	ss	43	.844				
1890	Chicago	PL	73	32	53	.204	.281	3b-ss	46	.809				

WILLIAM VAN WINKLE WOLF
(Chicken)

Born: May 12, 1863, Louisville, Ky.
Died: May 16, 1903, Louisville, Ky.
BR TR 5-9, 190

When American Association players of the 19th century are mentioned, the typical names are Pete Browning, Harry Stovey, Tony Mullane and Tip O'Neill. However, the player who spent all 10 years in the league (1882-1891) and led in most batting categories was William (Chicken) Wolf. He played the most games (1,195), collected the most hits (1,438), most doubles (214), triples (109), and total bases (1,921). (Stovey led in home runs and runs scored and Browning and Dave Orr had the highest Association batting average.)

Wolf learned to play on the local grounds. Browning and the Reccius twins were contemporary Louisville acquaintances on and off the diamond. When Louisville entered the newly organized AA in 1882, Wolf, just 19, was recruited to play right field. He led league outfielders in assists that first year while Browning led in hitting. It was Browning who christened Wolf with the nickname "Chicken," after the youngster disobeyed manager John Dyler's orders and gorged himself on a pregame meal of stewed chicken, and then proceeded to make several errors in the game.

In fact, making errors was much more Browning's forte. He could carry the team with his hitting, but Wolf had his hands full playing next to him in the outfield. Browning led the league in errors with totals as high as 44 and 46. Yet Wolf was a fine fielding rightfielder; in 1882, he led the American Association in outfield assists with 21 and the following year he participated in the most double plays for an outfielder when he doubled up six runners. Wolf was primarily a rightfielder, although he played all nine positions at Louisville. He also was the most stable and durable player on the team, playing the full schedule of games five seasons, 1883-1885, 1887 and 1890. He did not hit with power but was a fast base runner.

Wolf was one of the participants in an unusual and amusing incident in a game against Cincinnati at Eclipse Park August 22, 1886. In the 11th inning of a 3-3 game, Chicken hit a long drive to center. Ab Powell, the Redlegs centerfielder, ran for the ball and so did a stray dog. Powell got there first but the deprived canine grabbed him by the leg and would not let go. Under the circumstances, Powell was not able to throw. The fans thought it was hilarious and Wolf, seeing Powell's preoccupation, circled the bases with a game-winning home run. It was his second homer of the game, a rare occurrence since he hit only 17 in his career.

While Wolf had an outstanding career with the Louisville club, *Sporting Life* in 1896 credited him with being the lowest paid professional baseball player in history. When Wolf signed his first contract with Louisville in 1882, he was paid a mere $9 per week.

Louisville did not have a very good team through most of Wolf's career. Managers would come and go, and even Wolf had a stint at the helm during the abysmal 1889 season when the club finished with a 27-111 record. However, the club had a quick turnaround in 1890, thanks largely to Wolf's greatest season. He topped the league in batting average with a .363 mark and also led in hits and total bases. He was no longer in the shadow of Browning, who had gone on to the Players' League. With the departure went the not-too-pleasing name of Chicken. Most acquaintances by that time were calling him Jim or Jimmy, the derivation of which is not known.

Louisville won the 1890 AA pennant by a comfortable margin and went on to play Brooklyn in the World Series. Wolf was also the star of the Series, which ended in a tie after seven games (three wins each plus a tie). He led the regulars in batting with a .360 average, collecting 14 total bases and driving in 8 runs.

After the AA shut down, Wolf played briefly with the NL St. Louis team in 1892 before calling it quits. His career batting average was .290.

Back in Louisville, Jimmy Wolf joined the city fire department in June 1894. Several years later he was the engine driver when the horse-drawn vehicle was involved in a serious accident. He was thrown from his seat, hitting his head on the cobblestone street and was then dragged by the horses. The head injury caused him to become mentally unbalanced and he was institutionalized for much of the remainder of his short life. The man who played next to him in the field, Pete Browning, spent time in the Lakeland Insane Asylum with Wolf. And two years after Wolf died on May 16, 1903, Browning was buried in the same cemetery.

— L. Robert Davids and Richard A. Puff

			G	R	H	BA	SA	POS	E	FA	GP	W-L	R	H
1881	Eclipse		28	-	26	.220		of	-	.850				
1882	Louisville	AA	78	46	94	.294	.378	of-ss	19	.885	1	0-0	11	11
1883	Louisville	AA	98	59	105	.269	.367	of-c	40	.890				
1884	Louisville	AA	112	79	151	.303	.417	of	30	.892				
1885	Louisville	AA	113	93	141	.288	.411	of	22	.905	1	0-0	1	1
1886	Louisville	AA	130	93	148	.272	.363	of	15	.940	1	0-0	8	7
1887	Louisville	AA	137	103	194	.324	.419	of	17	.930				
1888	Louisville	AA	128	80	159	.298	.386	of-ss	46	.874				
1889	Louisville	AA	130	74	159	.291	.377	o-1-2	36	.927				
1890	Louisville	AA	134	98	200	.367	.483	of	12	.940				
1891	Louisville	AA	134	67	136	.253	.320	of	14	.933				
1892	Syracuse	EL	27	16	24	.209	.243	of	6	.895				
	St. Louis	NL	3	1	2	.143	.143	of	0	1.00				
1893	Buffalo	EL	114	94	161	.343	.455	of	12	.948				

GEORGE A. WOOD
(Dandy)

Born: November 9, 1858, Boston, Mass.
Died: April 4, 1924, Harrisburg, Pa.
BL TR 5-10½, 175

George A. "Dandy" Wood was a power hitting outfielder in the NL and AA for 13 years from 1880 until 1892. A left-handed hitter, Wood won the NL home run crown in 1882 when he unloaded 7 home runs.

Wood was born in Boston on November 9, 1858. His first professional team was the Lynn Live Oaks in 1878 in the International Association. Later that season he played with Worcester and Baltimore. The following year he played with Manchester before returning to Worcester.

The Worcester club joined the NL in 1880, and Wood's major league career started off slowly with just a .245 average that season. His batting picked up in succeeding seasons as he banged out triples at an average of more than 10 per season while compiling a lifetime .273 batting average. In 1882 and 1886, he placed second in the league in three-baggers. He also scored often, three times

scoring more than 100 runs a season. He hit the first official home run at the park that became Baker Bowl, clearing the rightfield wall his first at-bat on Opening Day, 1887.

Wood later would play with Detroit (NL) from 1881 through 1885, the Philadelphia Phillies from 1886 through the latter part of the 1889 season when he joined the Baltimore AA club. He also played with the Philadelphia clubs in both the Players' League and the American Association and for Baltimore and Cincinnati in the NL.

In the winter of 1888-1889, Wood was a member of the first professional baseball team to tour the world. He was selected to be a part of an All-America team which toured the world playing 46 games against Al Spalding's Chicago club.

Wood was a noted outfielder with a rifle arm. In 1879, it was reported that he threw a baseball 366 feet. Twice he led his league's

outfielders in double plays while also leading in assists and putouts.

The right-handed throwing Wood also showed his arm's strength from the pitcher's box as he was called on to appear as a pitcher in five games during his career.

In Wood's next-to-last season he served as player-manager for the Athletics (AA) squad for most of the 1891 season. The team compiled a 67-55 record under his leadership.

Wood also served as an umpire in the New England League.

Prior to his death on April 4, 1924 in Harrisburg, Pa., Wood served as marshal of the Pennsylvania state Public Service Commission, a post he was appointed to by Pennsylvania Governor John M. Tener, who had pitched for the Chicago team on the 1889 World Tour.

— Richard A. Puff

			G	R	H	BA	SA	POS	E	FA	GP	W-L	R	H
1878	Worcester	IA	27		-	.327		of	7	.845				
1879	Manch-Worc	NA	52		-	.368		of	-	.844				
1880	Worcester	NL	81	37	80	.245	.324	of	17	.887				
1881	Detroit	NL	80	54	100	.297	.424	of	24	.862				
1882	Detroit	NL	84	69	101	.269	.421	of	23	.884				
1883	Detroit	NL	99	81	133	.302	.444	of	34	.876	1	0-0	7	8
1884	Detroit	NL	114	79	119	.252	.378	of	25	.895				
1885	Detroit	NL	82	62	105	.290	.425	of-3b	23	.878	1	0-0	8	5
1886	Philadelphia	NL	106	81	123	.273	.407	of	17	.904				
1887	Philadelphia	NL	113	118	182	.343	.518	of	24	.873				
1888	Philadelphia	NL	106	67	99	.229	.356	of	20	.905	2	0-0	3	3
1889	Philadelphia	NL	97	77	106	.251	.336	of	16	.915	1	0-0	2	2
	Baltimore	AA	3	2	2	.200	.200	of	0	1.00				
1890	Philadelphia	PL	132	115	161	.304	.404	of	24	.942				
1891	Athletic	AA	132	105	163	.309	.413	of	16	.939				
1892	Balt-Cinc	NL	51	19	38	.208	.279	of	12	.872				
1893	Wilkes-Barre	EL	38	34	54	.318	.447	of	6	.894				
1894	Allentown	PaSt	79	89	89	.250	.396	of-2b	-					

THOMAS J. YORK

Born: July 13, 1851, Brooklyn, N.Y.
Died: February 17, 1936, New York, N.Y.
BL 5-9, 165

Thomas J. York was as highly respected off the field as he was for his skills as an outfielder and batsman.

A profile of him in the *New York Clipper* in the early 1880s said the lefty swinging York had "the reputation of being a hard-working and reliable player and his affable and courteous demeanor has won him a popularity surpassed by no other of the professional fraternity. As an outfielder," the article continued, "he ranks among the very best, being extremely quick in his movements, able to judge a fly-catch with almost unerring certainty, and possessing the necessary qualification of being a good thrower . . . we may add that in the most trying moments of a contest he is the same cool, good-natured and courteous gentleman as he is off the ballfield."

After appearing with amateur nines in the late 1860s in New York City, York joined the Troy Haymakers of the NA for the 1871 season. He later would play with the Lord Baltimores,

Philadelphias and Hartfords from 1872 through 1875 in the Association.

In 1876, York moved on to the new National League where he starred for Hartford, Providence and Cleveland until 1883. When his contract was sold to Baltimore (AA) for $500, York considered retirement. However, he signed after receiving a bonus — the scorecard concession at Oriole Park. He retired after the 1885 season.

York served as captain of the Providence Grays in 1881 and 1882 with fair success. He took over a sub-.500, fifth-place team in early August and led it to a second-place finish. In 1882, he had the team in first when he turned over the captaincy on June 17 to George Wright, who had finally come to terms with Providence management after a two-year dispute.

He tried umpiring in the NL in 1886 but quit in July, saying, "I would rather live on a dollar a day than stand the blackguarding which every umpire is subject to."

York banged out 1,091 hits during his 13-year career for a lifetime batting average of .270. During his career, he led the NL in several categories — triples (10) and total bases (125) in 1878, bases on balls (37) in 1883, and fielding percentage for leftfielders (.934) in 1880. He also had placed in the top three in these categories in addition to doubles and slugging percentage at other times in his career.

When York died in New York on February 17, 1936, plans were underway to honor him along with George Wright, Deacon White and Tommy Bond at that season's All-Star Game in Boston as the last players still alive who had played in the National League's inaugural season of 1876.

For several seasons, including the year before he died, York served as a guard in the press box at Yankee Stadium, a position given to him by Yankee owner Colonel Jacob Ruppert.

— Richard A. Puff

			G	R	H	BA	SA	POS	E	FA	GP	W-L	R	H
1870	Eckford-Troy							of						
1871	Troy	NA	29	37	36	.247	.404	of	10	.868				
1872	Baltimore	NA	50	64	63	.258	.336	of	15	.904				
1873	Baltimore	NA	57	70	83	.297	.355	of	18	.910				
1874	Baltimore	NA	50	36	58	.259	.321	of	19	.894				
1875	Hartford	NA	86	68	112	.297	.363	of	29	.871				
1876	Hartford	NL	67	47	68	.259	.369	of	18	.899				
1877	Hartford	NL	56	43	67	.283	.422	of	21	.865				
1878	Providence	NL	62	56	83	.309	.465	of	15	.873				
1879	Providence	NL	81	69	106	.310	.421	of	14	.898				
1880	Providence	NL	53	21	43	.212	.276	of	7	.934				
1881	Providence	NL	85	57	96	.304	.427	of	29	.859				
1882	Providence	NL	81	48	86	.268	.389	of	24	.876				
1883	Cleveland	NL	100	56	99	.260	.378	of	30	.864				
1884	Baltimore	AA	84	64	72	.228	.318	of	22	.832				
1885	Baltimore	AA	22	6	23	.271	.365	of	4	.919				

PETE BROWNING
(continued from page 19)

for the next decade. In June 1905, it all fell apart. Years of drinking as hard as he hit (he frequently boasted while playing: "I can't hit the ball until I hit the bottle!") and a crudely treated mastoid infection had resulted in irreversible brain damage. Following several months of erratic behavior, he was mistakenly judged to be insane and committed to the Central Kentucky Lunatic Asylum outside Louisville. Released shortly thereafter, he spent the last months of his life in and out of old City (now University) Hospital, where he died at age 44 on September 10, 1905.

Illiterate ("Oh, yeah? What league was he in?" he reportedly asked a writer who had just told him President Garfield had died from an assassin's bullet), deaf, a defensive liability and eccentric as well as being a chronic alcoholic, Browning was perfect game for the lively press of his day, who gave him his moniker because of his frequent battles with them, the bottle and flyballs. Indeed, his eccentricities alone, his refusal to slide, his one-legged defensive posture, naming and then "retiring" his bats after they had reached their "quota" of hits, and increasing the "power" of his eyes by staring directly into the sun ensured the creation of a legend.

— Philip Von Borries

COUNT CAMPAU
(continued from page 24)

league player of the century by most experts on 19th century minor league baseball although the Count played 490 more games during the 1800s and accumulated an additional 379 runs, 347 hits, 35 doubles, 79 triples, and 303 stolen bases than did Werden.

Among Campau's other career highlights are hitting 3 homers on June 7, 1887. The crowd was so moved that they showered the field with more than $60 in coins. On May 10, 1898, he went 4 for 5 for Minneapolis with 4 runs, a steal, 2 homers and a double. He finished the season that year for Kansas City, after being picked up and dropped by Comiskey for St. Paul in between. He caught the final out of the season, in right field, for K.C., as they won the pennant. In 1904, at the age 41, he still played some center field for Binghamton, one of three cities where he spent five seasons. He played parts of seven seasons in the Western League, six in the International/Eastern League and five in both the New York State League and the Southern Association.

Campau's playing career ended with the Binghamton Bingos in July of 1905. As a tribute to his popularity, he was given an elk's head ring by his teammates. He then tried his hand at umpiring. During July 1906, he was signed by the Eastern League. After being dropped by them, he moved to the Southern League. He resigned on August 23 after hav-

ing to be rescued from an angry mob in Shreveport.

The Count compiled some large numbers in a long career spent in the high minors. He ranks third in stolen bases with 692. He is 18th on the career list for most extra base hits compiled by Bob Davids.

— Cappy Gagnon

JACK GLASSCOCK
(continued from page 51)

1890 National League batting title.

After a poor year with the Giants in 1891, Jack played with St. Louis in 1892 and early 1893. He was traded to Pittsburgh on June 30, 1893 and helped lead a late, unsuccessful pennant drive by the Pirates. But his skills were fading and he was released late in the 1894 season. His arm went bad the next spring and he was released by Louisville in May and by Washington in July. He finished the 1895 season with Wheeling in the Interstate League. In 1896 he signed on with Charlie Comiskey's St. Paul Saints. Playing first base, Glasscock batted a resounding .431 that year with 263 hits to lead the Western League in both statistics. In one game on July 5, he went 8-for-9 with 7 runs scored in a 41-8 shellacking of Minneapolis. Jack lasted with St. Paul through 1898 and then managed in Fort Wayne and Sioux City during the next two seasons.

He retired in 1901 and returned to Wheeling to ply his trade of carpentry. He remained an interested follower of baseball until his death in 1947.

— Robert L. Tiemann

GEORGE HALL
(continued from page 56)

There was one more player suspended: antagonistic co-conspirator Bill Craver. In December, the League affirmed these suspensions, as did all clubs of the newly-formed "League Alliance." Having batted .323 while appearing in all his club's games, Hall was banished for life. St. Louis had already signed him and Devlin to 1878 contracts. It didn't matter.

Following the scandal, Hall began, by choice, to fade into obscurity. Unlike Devlin and Craver, his (fruitless) appeal for reinstatement in December 1878 was not made in person — only by mail. Rumors of continued play in New Jersey are inconclusive. What appears certain is that, at age 28, George Hall moved back to Brooklyn (near his brother Jim, an NA player from 1872-1875) and labored quietly for a few years as an engraver. In later life he served as a clerk in an art museum. When death came, due to heart trouble, he was buried at Evergreen Cemetery, Brooklyn, near his wife, Ida Aurelia (who had died in 1912). Most remember him less for his skill than for his shame.

— James D. Smith III

NED HANLON
(continued from page 57)

Wilbert Robinson and then Hugh Jennings to manage the team, Hanlon often favored the interests of the minor league club over those of the Brooklyn club. This led to more conflicts with Ebbets, who finally gained a controlling interest in Brooklyn in 1905. Hanlon was forced to sign a contract for the first time in years, and his salary was slashed from $12,000 to $6,500. Worse still, Ebbets interfered with personnel decisions, and the Superbas finished in last place. Although not officially fired, Hanlon quit Brooklyn to accept an offer to manage in Cincinnati in 1906. After two unsuccessful seasons with the Reds, however, he was fired.

Hanlon remained as president of the Baltimore club until November 1909, when he sold it to manager Jack Dunn, whom he had hired in 1907. At the time, it was estimated that Hanlon's personal worth was half a million dollars, mostly in real estate in Pittsburgh, Brooklyn and Baltimore. He remained active in the Baltimore community and interested in baseball, holding a position with the Baltimore Federal League club for a time in 1914 and later serving as president of the Baltimore City Park Board. He died in that city in 1937.

— Robert L. Tiemann

ARLIE LATHAM
(continued from page 76)

the oldest major leaguer, at 49, to steal a base. He coached three seasons and the Giants of 1911 stole a record 347 bases on their way to the pennant.

After World War I, Latham lived for 17 years in England, where he was Administrator (Commissioner) of baseball. While there he mingled with royalty, becoming a close friend of the Prince of Wales.

Latham spent the last 16 years of his long life in America working for the New York major league clubs. He ended his baseball career as custodian of the New York Yankees press box in 1952. He was 92 years old.

Arlie Latham bested the .300 mark three times in his 17 major league seasons. He led the league in at bats, steals and runs scored one time each. He stole more than 100 bases twice and had 679 steals throughout his career. Defensively, Latham was the league leader at third base in double plays, assists, errors, and total chances several times each. He remains in the record books as a career standout at his position, ranking eighth in assists, 12th in put outs, and sixth in total chances. Additionally, he ranks seventh on the all-time list in runs scored per game.

— John Richmond Husman

BOBBY MATHEWS
(continued from page 83)

utive seasons, and, seconded by old NA pitching rival George Washington Bradley (dueling mustaches), led the A's to their only AA championship. The homecoming of the Athletics to Philadelphia on October 12 was a spectacle in itself. Crowds estimated at more than half a million lined the Broad Street parade route for festivities culminating in a grand banquet at which medals were presented to each of the champions. Mathews, who had long ago found Baltimore "a little slow," matched the Philadelphians toast-for-toast.

During his 5 seasons with the Athletics, offering "strategic pitching" at its best, Mathews was 106-61. By 1886, however, his arm was giving him problems and by the following summer it was definitely useless. At age 36, with "small stature, careless habits and not too robust constitution," he began looking for the second career he never found. Over the years he had done some umpiring, and appears to have filled that role in the AA during the 1888 and 1891 seasons, punctuated by service in the Players' League. Owing in part to his age, however, he took a great deal of abuse and never settled into that vocation or any of the odd jobs in which he later labored. He had saved little from the glory days.

The end was not long in coming. By the mid-'90s, Mathews was suffering from paresis. Eventually his mind failed, and incurable and harmless, he was moved from the Maryland University Hospital to Spring Grove Asylum and finally to his parents' home in Baltimore, where he died. Mathews never married.

— James D. Smith, III

DAVID ORR
(continued from page 100)

Hot Springs, Ark., would allow him to return in 1891. It was not to be, however, as at age 31, he began a new chapter in life.

"No occupation following injury while playing ball," wrote a nephew for the Hall of Fame biographical questionnaire. This, however, does not tell the story of Dave Orr's courage. Using what strength and dexterity he had, he labored as a stonecutter and, later as a stagehand in the New York theater.

The "gentle giant" never gave up, nor did his interest in baseball wane. When Ebbets

Field was being built, Orr was named caretaker. Later, when the Brooklyn Feds opened at Washington Park in 1914, he was put in charge of the press box. The following summer, he was taken by heart disease, and buried with his wife Emily Ann in Woodlawn Cemetery, Bronx. There were no children.

"Old time fans will best remember Orr for his batting. Cap Anson at his best had nothing on Orr," claimed *The Sporting News*. However, any examination of his record must put Dave Orr in the company of his century's greatest sluggers, throughout a career that was all too brief. "Like Roger Connor and Dan Brouthers, he was a giant with the stick."

— James D. Smith, III

GEORGE VAN HALTREN
(continued from page 129)

Over the next four years he was on three teams in three leagues, the result, of course, of the "players' revolt" of 1890. But his performance did not suffer. He pitched, played the outfield and occasionally each of the infield spots.

For Brooklyn (PL) he won 15 and lost 10 with a 4.28 ERA, and batted .335 in 92 games. At Baltimore the next year he appeared in 139 games, only 6 as a pitcher. His batting average slipped to a still-respectable .318 and he captained the team.

Manager for 11 games at the beginning of the 1892 season, he played 135 games but batted only .302, which no doubt contributed to his being traded to Pittsburgh near the end of the season for Joe Kelley.

In Pittsburgh in 1893 he hit .338, his best average so far. The next year he was sold to the Giants and reunited with his player-manager of the Brooklyn Brotherhood team, Monte Ward.

New York was Van Haltren's last stop in the majors. Here he had his best season, reaching a batting peak of .351 in 1896.

For eight consecutive years with New York he played nearly every game and never hit below .300. He led the league in at-bats in 1898 (654), and shared the lead in stolen bases in 1900 with 45. (He averaged 39 steals a season during his 14 full seasons.)

On May 22, 1902, in Pittsburgh, he broke his ankle sliding (safely) into second in the sixth inning, and was out for the rest of the season.

Coming back in 1903, he played in only 84 games, batting .257, the lowest since his rookie year. In 1904 John McGraw let him go to

Seattle in the Pacific Coast League as player-manager. The next year Oakland lured him "home," where he continued in both positions into the 1909 season, when he was let go, probably because of conflicts with a "co-manager" and the front office.

Van Haltren spent a few more years umpiring in the area and occasionally scouted for Pittsburgh. Most of his time, however, was spent in the construction industry as a lather. But he showed up frequently for PCL old-timer games until his death at 79 in 1945.

— Frances J. Pendleton

PERRY WERDEN
(continued from page 133)

years, playing with St. Paul and Des Moines in 1901, Minneapolis again in 1902, Memphis in 1903, Fargo in 1904, and then Hattiesburg and Vicksburg in the Cotton States League in 1905-06. He sometimes served as player-manager and was still a gate attraction, but he was in his early 40s and his active days were about over.

He worked as an AA umpire in 1907 and coached for the Indianapolis club in 1908. He appeared as a pinch hitter twice. The Indianapolis *Star* reported on September 2 that the Toledo crowd cheered wildly when Werden "stung the ball between the center and left fielders." In the same game the umpire chased him off the coaching lines because he "was getting too personal with his jokes." Werden, who had used all the tricks in the trade as an umpire baiter, was chief of umpires in the Northern League in 1913-14. He served in a similar capacity in the Dakota League in 1920-22.

At other times between 1908 and 1920 Werden was managing and touring with his Werden's All-Stars, a colorful collection of stars who played against black and other professional teams in the Midwest. Big in stature and personality, he collected a crowd whenever he played, managed, coached, officiated or just attended a game of baseball. He died of a heart attack in Minneapolis on January 9, 1934, at the age of 68. He had lived there for much of the time since his great hitting exploits for the Millers in 1894-96. His season high of 45 home runs was the best in baseball until broken by Babe Ruth with the Yankees in 1920. His career high of 195 home runs was the best until passed by Bunny Brief in 1922.

— L. Robert Davids